D1590624

ECUMENICAL TERMINOLOGY

TERMINOLOGIE OECUMÉNIQUE

ÖKUMENISCHE TERMINOLOGIE

TERMINOLOGÍA ECUMÉNICA

WORLD COUNCIL OF CHURCHES, GENEVA
1975

ISBN: 2-8254-0501-9
Cover design: N. Witte-Brooymans

T A B L E   O F   C O N T E N T S

T A B L E   D E S   M A T I E R E S

viii

x

PREFACE

Before the IVth Assembly in Uppsala in 1968,
the World Council of Churches produced a small
ecumenical glossary in its three working languages, English, French and German. The present
edition of that handbook is published prior to
the Vth Assembly in Nairobi. It has been completely revised by the Language Service of the
World Council of Churches and expanded to con-
tain equivalents in Spanish as well as in the
other three languages. The contents reflect the
increasing scope and diversity of the work going
on within the ecumenical movement.

The book is in two parts. The first includes a
chronological table of major ecumenical events
from 1910 to 1975 together with a list of world
and regional assemblies and conferences and
their themes. This is followed by information
about the World Council of Churches, its Member
Churches, Associated Churches and Councils, its
structures and certain studies since these are
frequently mentioned in ecumenical documents
and meetings and consistency is essential in the
translation of official titles.

The second section deals specifically with terminology. It gives a representative, though by
no means exhaustive, selection of current ecumenical vocabulary chosen on the basis of material translated by the Language Service and in

AVANT-PROPOS

Avant sa Quatrième Assemblée (Upsal 1968), le
Conseil oecuménique des Eglises a publié un
glossaire oecuménique en trois langues (anglais, français, allemand). Le présent volume,
qui paraît à la veille de la Cinquième Assemblée (Nairobi 1975), est une édition entièrement revue et augmentée de ce glossaire.
Rédigée en quatre langues (anglais, français,
allemand, espagnol), elle reflète la grande
diversité des activités entreprises dans le
cadre du mouvement oecuménique.

Cette nouvelle édition comprend deux parties.
La première contient une table chronologique
des événements oecuméniques de 1910 à 1975,
les thèmes des grandes assemblées et conférences mondiales et régionales de cette période,
et un certain nombre d'informations relatives
au Conseil oecuménique, que le lecteur trouvera
utile d'avoir à sa disposition dans un seul
et même volume: un organigramme du Conseil,
suivi d'un tableau de ses secrétariats et programmes, la liste des Eglises membres et des
Eglises et conseils associés, et les études
dont les titres apparaissent fréquemment dans
les textes oecuméniques.

La deuxième partie de l'ouvrage, intitulée
"Terminologie", offre en éventail représentatif, mais nullement exhaustif, des termes uti-

VORBEMERKUNG

Vor der IV. Vollversammlung im Jahre 1968 in Uppsala gab der Ökumenische Rat eine"Ökumenische Terminologie" in drei Sprachen (Englisch, Französisch, Deutsch) heraus. Das vorliegende Handbuch, das unmittelbar vor der V. Vollversammlung (Nairobi 1975) erscheint, ist eine vollständig überarbeitete und erweiterte Ausgabe dieser Terminologie, nunmehr in vier Sprachen (Englisch, Französisch, Deutsch und Spanisch).Das Handbuch gliedert sich in einen chronologischen und informativen sowie in einen terminologischen Teil und spiegelt die vielfältigen Aktivitäten der ökumenischen Bewegung wider.

Der erste Teil des Buches enthält eine ökumenische Zeittafel (1910 - 1975), die Themen der Konferenzen und Vollversammlungen auf regionaler und weltweiter Ebene, die in diesem Zeitraum stattgefunden haben, und eine Reihe von Informationen über den Ökumenischen Rat der Kirchen, die erstmalig in dieser Form in einem Band zusammengetragen wurden: eine schematische Darstellung der Struktur des Rates, eine Liste der Sekretariate und Programme, eine Liste der Mitgliedskirchen und angeschlossenen Kirchen und Räte sowie die Titel der in ökumenischen Dokumenten am häufigsten erwähnten ÖRK-Studien.

Die zweite Hälfte des Buches bietet eine repräsentative, wenn auch keineswegs erschöpfende Auswahl

PREFACIO

En 1968, antes de la celebración de la Cuarta Asamblea en Upsala, el Consejo Mundial de Iglesias publicó un glosario ecuménico en tres idiomas (inglés, francés, alemán). Esta nueva edición que se publica en vísperas de la Quinta Asamblea en Nairobi, es una versión revisada, corregida y ampliada de ese primer glosario. Contiene equivalentes en cuatro idiomas (inglés, francés, alemán, español) y refleja la gran diversidad de los temas que se tratan en el movimiento ecuménico.

Esta edición comprende dos partes. En la primera figuran un índice cronológico de los acontecimientos ecuménicos de 1910 a 1975, los temas de las grandes asambleas y conferencias mundiales y regionales durante este período, y un cierto número de informaciones sobre el Consejo Mundial, que los usuarios podrán disponer en un sólo volumen: un organigrama del Consejo, un cuadro de sus secretarías y programas, una lista de las iglesias miembros y de las iglesias y consejos asociados, así como los estudios cuyos títulos aparecen con frecuencia en los textos ecuménicos.

En la segunda parte, bajo el título "Terminología", figura una selección representativa pero no exhaustiva del vocabulario ecuménico corriente, extraído de textos traducidos por

consultation with the responsible departments. The terms given cover the main fields dealt with in World Council programmes and studies, specialized vocabulary relating to them, and certain words and phrases which are difficult to translate. Since the procedure adopted involved working from English into the other languages and seldom the reverse, it has obviously not been possible to give so many alternative translations for English. Except in the case of titles and specialized vocabulary, the equivalents offered are suggested possible translations and should not be taken as the only way to render a particular word or phrase. While some terminological reference point is essential in the interests of consistency and clarity in a movement which contains such diversity, the handbook is not intended to dictate or standardize the language used. Its purpose is to help translators, interpreters, participants at ecumenical meetings and all those in church or ecumenical organizations who are responsible for drafting or preparing documents and dealing with correspondence.

It is hoped that in fulfilling this purpose it will make a small contribution to furthering ecumenical understanding and dialogue.

Language Service, WCC

lisés dans les différents domaines d'étude et d'activité du Conseil oecuménique. C'est en collaboration avec les divers secrétariats responsables que ces termes ont été choisis sur la base des documents traduits par le Service linguistique. Il s'agit à la fois de termes techniques ayant trait aux domaines d'intérêt du Conseil, de notions clés propres au langage et à la recherche oecuméniques, d'expressions et de concepts plus généraux présentant des difficultés de traduction, et d'un certain nombre de titres officiels fréquemment utilisés dans les textes. Exception faite des ces titres et des termes techniques, il va de soi que les équivalents proposés dans les différentes langues sont avant tout des suggestions. Signalons enfin que dans la plupart des cas, l'anglais a été la langue de départ, ce qui explique que celui-ci ne propose souvent qu'un seul terme là où les autres langues offrent plusieurs solutions.

Cet ouvrage vise essentiellement à une plus grande clarté dans les échanges, et l'on se gardera d'y voir une volonté d'uniformisation de la langue. Il a été conçu pour faciliter le travail des traducteurs, interprètes et collaborateurs de toute organisation ecclésiastique, et favoriser par là même la rencontre et le dialogue oecuméniques.

Service linguistique, COE

aus der heute in der ökumenischen Bewegung ge-
bräuchlichen Terminologie. Die Auswahl der Begriffe erfolgte in enger Zusammenarbeit mit den zu-
ständigen Abteilungen des Rates auf der Grundlage
von Texten, die dem ÖRK-Sprachendienst zur Übersetzung vorgelegen haben. Bei den aufgeführten
Begriffen handelt es sich um Fachtermini und
Schlüsselbegriffe aus den Arbeitsgebieten des Rates; ausserdem wurden verschiedene allgemeine Begriffe und eine Reihe von offiziellen Titeln mit-
aufgenommen, deren Übersetzung häufig Schwierigkeiten bereitet. Die angebotenen Äquivalente sind
lediglich als Übersetzungsvorschläge gedacht.
Hinzugefügt sei noch, dass das Englische weit-
gehend als Ausgangssprache diente und daher häufig
eine geringere Anzahl von Alternativen bietet als
die anderen drei Sprachen.

Das vorliegende Handbuch will in keiner Weise
die sprachliche Kommunikation uniformieren; vielmehr soll es im Interesse einer besseren Verständi-
gung den Mitarbeitern in der ökumenischen Bewegung, einschliesslich der Dolmetscher und Über-
setzer, terminologische Orientierungshilfen bieten
und damit einen Beitrag leisten zur Intensivierung
der Begegnung und des Dialogs.

ÖRK-Sprachendienst

el Servicio Lingüístico del Consejo Mundial
de Iglesias y en colaboración con diversas
secretarías responsables. Esta segunda
sección comprende términos técnicos relativos
a los campos principales de los programas y
estudios del Consejo Mundial, algunas nociones
claves, proprias del lenguaje y pensamiento
ecuménicos, una serie de expresiones o de conceptos más generales que ofrecen dificultades
de traducción, y un cierto número de títulos
oficiales, utilizados a menudo en los textos.
Con excepción de los títulos y de los términos técnicos, se sobreentiende que los equivalentes propuestos son tan sólo sugerencias.
Se hace notar además que en la mayoría de los
casos se hizo el trabajo a partir del inglés,
lo que explica que mientras en este idioma
se propone un solo término, en los otros idiomas se ofrecen varias soluciones.

El objetivo de esta obra es lograr una mayor
claridad en los intercambios y no un intento
de uniformar el idioma. Esta recopilación fue
hecha para facilitar el trabajo de traductores,
intérpretes y colaboradores de cualquier organización eclesiástica, favoreciendo así el
encuentro y el diálogo ecuménicos.

Por último, llamamos la atención a los usuarios
sobre el hecho de que esta obra tiene segura-
mente errores y omisiones y agradaceremos pro-
fundamente las observaciones que deseen hacer.

Servicio Lingüístico, CMI

I

CHRONOLOGICAL TABLE OF ECUMENICAL EVENTS

1910:

World Missionary Council, Edinburgh, Scotland

1910:

Beginnings of the Faith and Order Movement. At its meeting in Cincinnatti, the General Assembly of the Protestant Episcopal Church in the USA (Anglican) (PECUSA) constituted a committee for the promotion of a World Conference on Faith and Order.

1921:

Foundation of the International Missionary Council (ICM), Lake Mohonk, N.Y., USA

1923:

2nd Meeting of the International Missionary Council, Oxford, England

1924:

Foundation of the Near East Christian Council (NECC), Mount Olives, Jerusalem

I

TABLE CHRONOLOGIQUE DES EVENEMENTS OECUMENIQUES

Conférence mondiale des missions, Edimbourg, Ecosse

Debut du mouvement de Foi et constitution. L'Assemblée générale de l'Eglise protestante épiscopale aux Etats-Unis, réunie à Cincinnatti, établit un comité en vue de préparer une Conférence mondiale de Foi et constitution.

Fondation du Conseil international des missions (CIM), Lake Mohonk, N.Y., Etats-Unis

2e Conférence du Conseil international des missions, Oxford, Angleterre

Fondation du Conseil chrétien du Proche-Orient (NECC), Mont des oliviers, Jérusalem

I

ÖKUMENISCHE ZEITTAFEL

1910:

Weltmissionskonferenz, Edinburgh,
Schottland

1910:

Anfänge der Bewegung für Glauben und Kirchenverfassung. Die Generalversammlung der Bischöf-
lichen Protestantischen Kirche der Vereinigten
Staaten in Cincinnatti setzt einen Ausschuss
zur Vorbereitung einer Weltkonferenz für
Glauben und Kirchenverfassung ein.

1921:

Gründung des Internationalen Missionsrates
(IMR), Lake Mohonk, N.Y., USA

1923:

2. Tagung des Internationalen Missionsrates,
Oxford, England

1924:

Gründung des Nahöstlichen Christenrates
(NECC), Ölberg, Jerusalem

I

INDICE CRONOLOGICO DE LOS ACONTECIMIENTOS ECUMENICOS

Conferencia Mundial de las Misiones,
Edimburgo, Escocia

Iniciación del Movimento de Fe y Constitución.
La Asamblea General de la Iglesia Protestante
Episcopal en los Estados Unidos, reunida en
Cincinnatti, constituyó un comité para preparar
una Conferencia Mundial de Fe y Constitución.

Fundación del Consejo Misionero Internacional,
(CMI), Lake Mohonk, N.Y., Estados Unidos

2a. Conferencia del Consejo Misionero Internacional, Oxford, Inglaterra

Fundación del Consejo Cristiano del Cercano
Oriente (NECC), Monte de los Olivos, Jerusalén

1925:

Universal Christian Conference on Life and Work, Stockholm, Sweden	Conférence mondiale du Christianisme pratique, Stockholm, Suède

1927:

1st World Conference on Faith and Order, Lausanne, Switzerland	1ère Conférence mondiale de Foi et constitution, Lausanne, Suisse

1928:

3rd Meeting of the International Missionary Council, Jerusalem	3e Conférence du Conseil international des missions, Jérusalem

1930:

Formation of the World Council for Life and Work (to replace the Continuation Committee of the Stockholm Conference)	Création du Conseil mondial du Christianisme pratique (remplaçant le comité de continuation de la Conférence de Stockholm)

1937:

2nd World Conference on Life and Work, Oxford, England	2e Conférence mondiale du Christianisme pratique, Oxford, Angleterre

1937:

2nd World Conference on Faith and Order, Edinburgh, Scotland	2e Conférence mondiale de Foi et constitution, Edimbourg, Ecosse

1925:

Weltkonferenz für Praktisches Christentum,
Stockholm, Schweden

Conferencia Cristiana Universal sobre
Vida y Acción, Estocolmo, Suecia

1927:

1. Weltkonferenz für Glauben und Kirchenverfassung, Lausanne, Schweiz

1a. Conferencia Mundial de Fe y Constitución,
Lausana, Suiza

1928:

3. Tagung des Internationalen Missionsrates, Jerusalem

3a. Conferencia del Consejo Misionero
Internacional, Jerusalén

1930:

Bildung des Ökumenischen Rates für Praktisches Christentum (anstelle des Fort-
setzungsausschusses der Weltkonferenz von
Stockholm)

Creación del Consejo Mundial de Vida y
Acción (en substitución del Comité Continu-
ación de la Conferencia de Estocolmo)

1937:

2. Weltkonferenz für Praktisches Christentum, Oxford, England

2a. Conferencia Mundial de Vida y Acción,
Oxford Inglaterra

1937:

2. Weltkonferenz für Glauben und Kirchenverfassung, Edinburgh, Schottland

2a. Conferencia Mundial de Fe y Constitución,
Edimburgo, Escocia

1938:

4th Meeting of the International Missionary Council, Tamberam, Madras, India	4e Conférence du Conseil international des missions, Tambaram, Madras, Inde

1938

World Council of Churches "in process of formation", Utrecht, Netherlands	Conseil oecuménique des Eglises "en formation", Utrecht, Pays-Bas

1939:

1st World Conference of Christian Youth, Amsterdam, Netherlands	1ère Conférence mondiale de la jeunesse chrétienne, Amsterdam, Pays-Bas

1947:

1st Assembly of the Lutheran World Federation, Lund, Sweden	1ère Assemblée de la Fédération luthérienne mondiale, Lund, Suède

1947:

5th Meeting of the International Missionary Council, Whitby, Toronto, Canada	5e Conférence du Conseil international des missions, Whitby, Toronto, Canada

1947:

2nd World Conference of Christian Youth, Oslo, Norway	2e Conférence mondiale de la jeunesse chrétienne, Oslo, Norvège

1938:

4. Tagung des Internationalen Missionsrates, Tambaram, Madras, Indien

4a. Conferencia del Consejo Misionero Internacional, Tambaram, Madrás, India

1938:

Ökumenischer Rat der Kirchen "im Aufbau begriffen", Utrecht, Niederlande

Consejo Mundial de Iglesias "en proceso de formación", Utrecht, Países Bajos

1939:

1. Christliche Weltjugendkonferenz, Amsterdam, Niederlande

1a. Conferencia Mundial de Juventud Cristiana, Amsterdam, Países Bajos

1947:

1. Vollversammlung des Lutherischen Weltbundes, Lund, Schweden

1a. Asamblea de la Federación Luterana Mundial, Lund, Suecia

1947:

5. Tagung des Internationalen Missionsrates, Whitby, Toronto, Kanada

5a. Conferencia del Consejo Misionero Internacional, Whitby, Toronto, Canadá

1947:

2. Christliche Weltjugendkonferenz, Oslo, Norwegen

2a. Conferencia Mundial de Juventud Cristiana, Oslo, Noruega

7

1948:

1st Assembly of the World Council of Churches (WCC), Amsterdam, Netherlands

1ère Assemblée du Conseil oecuménique des Eglises (COE), Amsterdam, Pays-Bas

1948:

1st Meeting of the Central Committee of the WCC, Amsterdam, Netherlands

1ère session du Comité central du COE, Amsterdam, Pays-Bas

1949:

Joint IMC/WCC Conference, preparation for the East Asia Christian Conference, Bangkok, Thailand

Conférence mixte CIM/COE, projet de formation de la Conférence chrétienne d'Asie orientale, Bangkok, Thaïlande

1949:

2nd Meeting of the Central Committee of the WCC, Chichester, England

2e session du Comité central du COE, Chichester, Angleterre

1950:

3rd Meeting of the Central Committee of the WCC, Toronto, Canada

3e session du Comité central du COE, Toronto, Canada

1950:

The World Sunday School Association becomes the World Council of Christian Education and Sunday School Association (WCCESSA). 1st Assembly of the WCCESSA, Toronto, Canada

L'Assemblée mondiale des écoles du dimanche devient le Conseil mondial de l'éducation chrétienne et association des écoles du dimanche (CMECAED) - 1ère Assemblée du CMECAED, Toronto, Canada

1948:

1. Vollversammlung des Ökumenischen Rates
der Kirchen (ÖRK), Amsterdam, Niederlande

1a. Asamblea del Consejo Mundial de
Iglesias (CMI), Amsterdam, Países Bajos

1948:

1. Tagung des Zentralausschusses des
ÖRK, Amsterdam, Niederlande

1a Reunión del Comité Central del CMI,
Amsterdam, Países Bajos

1949:

Gemeinsame IMR/ÖRK - Konferenz, Vorbereitung der Ostasiatischen Christlichen
Konferenz, Bangkok, Thailand

Conferencia Conjunta Consejo Misionaro In-
ternacional/Consejo Mundial de Iglesias,
proyecto de formación de la Conferencia
Christiana de Asia Oriental, Bangkok,
Tailandia

1949:

2. Tagung des Zentralausschusses des
ÖRK, Chichester, England

2a. Reunión del Comité Central del CMI,
Chichester, Inglaterra

1950:

3. Tagung des Zentralausschusses des
ÖRK, Toronto, Kanada

3a Reunión del Comité Central del CMI,
Toronto, Canadá

1950:

Der Weltsonntagschul-Verband wird der
Weltrat für christliche Erziehung und
Sonntagsschulvereinigung (WCCESSA). Voll-
versammlung des WCCESSA, Toronto, Kanada

La Asamblea Mundial de Escuelas Dominicales
se transforma en el Consejo Mundial de
Educación Cristiana y Asociación de Escuelas
Dominicales (CMECAED). 1a. Asamblea del CMECAED,
Toronto, Canadá

9

1951:

4th Meeting of the Central Committee of the
WCC, Rolle, Switzerland

4e session du Comité central du COE,
Rolle, Suisse

1952:

6th Meeting of the International Missionary
Council, Willingen, Federal Republic of
Germany

6e Conférence du Conseil international
des missions, Willingen, République fédérale d'Allemagne

1952:

2nd Assembly of the Lutheran World
Federation, Hanover, Federal Republic of
Germany

2e Assemblée de la Fédération luthérienne
mondiale, Hanovre, République fédérale
d'Allemagne

1952:

3rd World Conference on Faith and Order,
Lund, Sweden

3e Conférence mondiale de Foi et constitution,
Lund, Suède

1952/53:

5th Meeting of the Central Committee of
the WCC, Lucknow, India

5e session du Comité central du COE,
Lucknow, Inde

1954:

17th General Council of the Alliance of
the Reformed Churches throughout the
World holding the Presbyterian Order

17e Assemblée générale de l'Alliance réformée
mondiale, Princeton, Etats-Unis

1951:

4. Tagung des Zentralausschusses des
ORK, Rolle, Schweiz

4a. Reunión del Comité Central del CMI,
Rolle, Suiza

1952:

6. Tagung des Internationalen Missionsrates, Willingen, Bundesrepublik Deutschland

6a. Conferencia del Consejo Misionero
Internacional, Willingen, República
Federal de Alemania

1952:

2. Vollversammlung des Lutherischen Weltbundes, Hannover, Bundesrepublik Deutschland

2a. Asamblea de la Federación Luterana
Mundial, Hanover, República Federal de
Alemania

1952:

3. Weltkonferenz für Glauben und Kirchenverfassung, Lund, Schweden

3a. Conferencia Mundial de Fe y Constitución, Lund, Suecia

1952/53:

5. Tagung des Zentralausschusses des
ORK, Lucknow, Indien

5a. Reunión del Comité Central del CMI,
Lucknow, India

1954:

17. Generalversammlung des Reformierten
Weltbundes, Princeton, USA

17a. Asamblea General de la Alianza
Reformada Mundial, Princeton, Estados
Unidos

11

(also known as the World Presbyterian
Alliance and the World Alliance of Reformed
Churches) Princeton, USA

1954:

6th Meeting of the Central Committee of
the WCC, Evanston, Ill., USA

6e session du Comité central du COE,
Evanston, Ill., Etats-Unis

1954:

2nd Assembly of the World Council of
Churches, Evanston, Ill., USA

2e Assemblée du Conseil oecuménique des
Eglises, Evanston, Ill., Etats-Unis

1954:

7th Meeting of the Central Committee of
the WCC, Evanston, Ill., USA

7e session du Comité central du COE,
Evanston, Ill., Etats-Unis

1955:

8th Meeting of the Central Committee of
the WCC, Davos, Switzerland

8e session du Comité central du COE,
Davos, Suisse

1956:

9th Meeting of the Central Committee of
the WCC, Galyatetö, Hungary

9e session du Comité central du COE,
Galyatetö, Hongrie

1954:

6. Tagung des Zentralausschusses des ÖRK, Evanston, Ill., USA

6a. Reunión del Comité Central del CMI, Evanston, Ill., Estados Unidos

1954:

2. Vollversammlung des Ökumenischen Rates der Kirchen, Evanston, Ill., USA

2a. Asamblea del Consejo Mundial de Iglesias, Evanston, Ill., Estados Unidos

1954:

7. Tagung des Zentralausschusses des ÖRK, Evanston, Ill., USA

7a. Reunión del Comité Central del CMI, Evanston, Ill., Estados Unidos

1955:

8. Tagung des Zentralausschusses des ÖRK, Davos, Schweiz

8a. Reunión del Comité Central del CMI, Davos, Suiza

1956:

9. Tagung des Zentralausschusses des ÖRK, Galyatetö, Ungarn

9a. Reunión del Comité Central del CMI, Galyatetö, Hungría

1957:

10th Meeting of the Central Committee
of the WCC, New Haven, Conn., USA

10e session du Comité central du COE,
New Haven, Conn., Etats-Unis

1957:

Foundation of the East Asia Christian
Conference (EACC), Prapat, Sumatra,
Indonesia

Fondation de la Conférence chrétienne
d'Asie orientale (CCAO), Prapat,
Sumatra, Indonésie

1957:

Preparatory Conference for the Conference
of European Churches, Liselund, Denmark

Conférence préparatoire de la Conférence
des Eglises européennes, Liselund,
Danemark

1957:

3rd Assembly of the Lutheran World
Federation, Minneapolis, USA

3e Assemblée de la Fédération luthérienne
mondiale, Minneapolis, Etats-Unis

1958:

Assembly of the International Missionary
Council, Accra, Ghana

Assemblée du Conseil international des
missions, Accra, Ghana

1958:

Establishment of the Theological Education
Fund, Ghana

Création du Fonds pour l'enseignement
théologique, Ghana

1957:

10. Tagung des Zentralausschusses des
ÖRK, New Haven, Conn., USA

10a. Reunión del Comité Central del CMI,
New Haven, Conn., Estados Unidos

1957:

Gründung der Ostasiatischen Christlichen
Konferenz, Prapat, Sumatra
Indonesien

Fundación de la Conferencia Cristiana de
Asia Oriental (CCAO), Prapat, Sumatra,
Indonesia

1957:

Vorbereitende Tagung für die Konferenz
Europäischer Kirchen, Liselund, Dänemark

Conferencia Preparatoria de la Conferencia
de Iglesias Europeas, Liselund, Dinamarca

1957:

3. Vollversammlung des Lutherischen Weltbundes, Minneapolis, USA

3a. Asamblea de la Federación Luterana
Mundial, Mineápolis, Estados Unidos

1958:

Vollversammlung des Internationalen
Missionsrates, Accra, Ghana

Asamblea del Consejo Misionero Internacional, Accra, Ghana

1958:

Errichtung des Theologischen Ausbildungsfonds, Ghana

Creación del Fondo de Educación Teológica,
Ghana

15

1958:

Meeting of African Churches, Ibadan, Nigeria
(proposal to found an All Africa Conference
of Churches)

Réunion des Eglises d'Afrique, Ibadan,
Nigéria (proposition de fonder une
Conférence des Eglises de toute l'Afrique)

1958:

11th Meeting of the Central Committee of
the WCC, Nyborg, Denmark

11e session du Comité central du COE,
Nyborg, Danemark

1959:

1st Assembly of the Conference of European
Churches (Nyborg I), Nyborg, Denmark

1ère Assemblée de la Conférence des Eglises
européennes (Nyborg I), Nyborg, Danemark

1959:

1st Assembly of the East Asia Christian
Conference, Kuala Lumpur, Malayan
Federation

1ère Assemblée de la Conférence chrétienne
d'Asie orientale, Kuala Lumpur, Fédération
de Malaisie

1959:

18th General Council of the World Alliance
of Reformed Churches, Sao Paulo, Brazil

18e Assemblée générale de l'Alliance réformée mondiale, Sao Paulo, Brésil

1959:

12th Meeting of the Central Committee of
the WCC, Rhodes, Greece

12e session du Comité central du COE,
Rhodes, Grèce

1958:

Tagung Afrikanischer Kirchen, Ibadan, Nigeria
(Vorschlag zur Gründung einer Gesamtafrikanischen Kirchenkonferenz)

Reunión de las Iglesias de Africa, Ibadan,
Nigeria (propuesta de creación de una Conferencia de Iglesias de toda el Africa)

1958:

11. Tagung des Zentralausschusses des
ÖRK, Nyborg, Dänemark

11a. Reunión del Comité Central del CMI,
Nyborg, Dinamarca

1959:

1. Vollversammlung der Konferenz Europäischer Kirchen (Nyborg I), Nyborg, Dänemark

1a. Asamblea de la Conferencia de Iglesias
Europeas (Nyborg I), Nyborg, Dinamarca

1959:

1. Vollversammlung der Ostasiatischen
Christlichen Konferenz, Kuala Lumpur,
Malaiischer Bund

1a. Asamblea de la Conferencia Cristiana
de Asia Oriental, Kuala Lumpur,
Federación de Malasia

1959:

18. Generalversammlung des Reformierten
Weltbundes, Sao Paulo, Brasilien

18a. Asamblea General de la Alianza Reformada
Mundial, San Pablo, Brasil

1959:

12. Tagung des Zentralausschusses des
ÖRK, Rhodos, Griechenland

12a. Reunión del Comité Central del CMI,
Rodas, Grecia

17

1960:

13th Meeting of the Central Committee of
the WCC, St. Andrews, Scotland

13e session du Comité central du COE,
St. Andrews, Ecosse

1960:

Meeting of the Commission on Faith and Order, St. Andrews, Scotland

Session de la Commission de foi et
constitution, St. Andrews, Ecosse

1960:

European Youth Assembly, Lausanne,
Switzerland

Conférence européenne de la jeunesse,
Lausanne, Suisse

1960:

2nd Assembly of the Conference of European Churches (Nyborg II), Nyborg, Denmark

2e Assemblée de la Conférence des Eglises
européennes (Nyborg II), Nyborg, Danemark

1960:

Meeting of the Churches in the Pacific which
launched the Continuation Committee of the
Pacific Conference of Churches, Malua, Samoa

Réunion des Eglises du Pacifique, création du
Comité de continuation de la Conférence des
Eglises du Pacifique, Malua, Samoa

1961:

Assembly of the International Missionary
Council, New-Delhi, India

Assemblée du Conseil international des
missions, Nouvelle-Delhi, Inde

1960:	
13. Tagung des Zentralausschusses des ÖRK, St. Andrews, Schottland	13a. Reunión del Comité Central del CMI, St. Andrews, Escocia
1960:	
Tagung der Kommission für Glauben und Kirchenverfassung, St. Andrews, Schottland	Reunión de la Comisión de Fe y Constitución, St. Andrews, Escocia
1960:	
Europäische Jugendkonferenz, Lausanne, Schweiz	Conferencia Europea de Juventud Lausana, Suiza
1960:	
2. Vollversammlung der Konferenz Europäischer Kirchen (Nyborg II), Nyborg, Dänemark	2a. Asamblea de la Conferencia de Iglesias Europeas (Nyborg II), Nyborg, Dinamarca
1960:	
Tagung der Kirchen im Pazifik, Gründung des Fortsetzungsausschusses der Konferenz der Kirchen im Pazifik, Malua, Samoa	Reunión de las Iglesias del Pacífico, creación de la Conferencia de Iglesias del Pacífico, Malua, Samoa
1961:	
Vollversammlung des Internationalen Missionsrates, Neu-Delhi, Indien	Asamblea del Consejo Misionero Internacional, Nueva Delhi, India

1961:

14th Meeting of the Central Committee of
the WCC, New Delhi, India

14e session du Comité central du COE,
Nouvelle-Delhi, Inde

1961:

3rd Assembly of the World Council of Churches,
New-Delhi, India (integration of the WCC and
IMC)

3e Assemblée du Conseil oecuménique des
Eglises, Nouvelle-Delhi, Inde (intégration
du CIM au COE)

1961:

15th Meeting of the Central Committee of
the WCC, New-Delhi, India

15e session du Comité central du COE,
Nouvelle-Delhi, Inde

1961:

1st Meeting of the Commission on World Mission
and Evangelism, New-Delhi, India

1ère session de la Commission des missions
et de l'évangelisation, Nouvelle-Delhi, Inde

1962:

2nd Assembly of the World Council of Christian
Education and Sunday School Association,
Belfast, Ireland

2ème Assemblée du Conseil mondial de
l'éducation chrétienne et association des
écoles du dimanche , Belfast, Irlande

1962:

16th Meeting of the Central Committee of the
WCC, Paris, France

16e session du Comité central du COE,
Paris, France

1961:

14. Tagung des Zentralausschusses des
ORK, Neu-Delhi, Indien

14a.Reunión del Comité Central del CMI,
Nueva Delhi, India

1961:

3. Vollversammlung des Ökumenischen Rates
der Kirchen, Neu-Delhi, Indien (Zusammen-
schluss des ÖRK und des IMR)

3a. Asamblea del Consejo Mundial de Iglesias,
Nueva Delhi, India (Integración del Consejo
Misionero Internacional al Consejo Mundial
de Iglesias)

1961:

15. Tagung des Zentralausschusses des
ÖRK, Neu-Delhi, Indien

15a.Reunión del Comité Central del CMI,
Nueva Delhi, India

1961:

1. Tagung der Kommission für Weltmission
und Evangelisation, Neu-Delhi, Indien

1a.Reunión de la Comisión de Misión
Mundial y Evangelización, Nueva Delhi, India

1962:

2. Vollversammlung des Weltrates für
 hristliche Erziehung und Sonntagsschulvereinigung, Belfast, Irland

2a. Asamblea del Consejo Mundial de Educación
Cristiana y Asociación de Escuelas Dominicales
Belfast, Irlanda

1962:

16. Tagung des Zentralausschusses des
ÖRK, Paris, Frankreich

16a.Reunión del Comité Central del CMI,
París, Francia

1962:

3rd Assembly of the Conference of European Churches (Nyborg III), Nyborg, Denmark

3e Assemblée de la Conférence des Eglises européennes (Nyborg III), Nyborg, Danemark

1962:

All Africa Christian Youth Assembly, Nairobi, Kenya

Assemblée de la jeunesse chrétienne de toute l'Afrique, Nairobi, Kenya

1963:

Foundation of the All Africa Conference of Churches, Kampala, Uganda

Fondation de la Conférence des Eglises de toute L'Afrique, Kampala, Ouganda

1963:

4th World Conference on Faith and Order, Montreal, Canada

4e Conférence mondiale de Foi et constitution, Montréal, Canada

1963:

4th Assembly of the Lutheran World Federation, Helsinki, Finland

4e Assemblée de la Fédération luthérienne mondiale, Helsinki, Finlande

1963:

17th Meeting of the Central Committee of the WCC, Rochester, N.Y., USA

17e session du Comité central du COE, Rochester, N.Y., Etats-Unis

1962:

3. Vollversammlung der Konferenz Europäischer Kirchen (Nyborg III), Nyborg, Dänemark

3a. Asamblea de la Conferencia de Iglesias Europeas (Nyborg III), Nyborg, Dinamarca

1962:

Gesamtafrikanische Christliche Jugendversammlung, Nairobi, Kenia

Asamblea de la Juventud Cristiana de toda el Africa, Nairobi, Kenia

1963:

Gründung der Gesamtafrikanischen Kirchenkonferenz, Kampala, Uganda

Fundación de la Conferencia de Iglesias de toda el Africa, Kampala, Uganda

1963:

4. Weltkonferenz für Glauben und Kirchenverfassung, Montreal, Canada

4a. Conferencia Mundial de Fe y Constitución, Montreal, Canadá

1963:

4. Vollversammlung des Lutherischen Weltbundes, Helsinki, Finnland

4a. Asamblea de la Federación Luterana Mundial, Helsinki, Finlandia

1963:

17. Tagung des Zentralausschusses des ÖRK, Rochester, N.Y., USA

17a. Reunión del Comité Central del CMI, Rochester, N.Y., Estados Unidos

1963:

2nd Meeting of the Commission on World Mission and Evangelism, Mexico City, Mexico	2e session de la Commission des missions et de l'évangélisation, Mexico City, Mexique

1964:

2nd Assembly of the East Asia Christian Conference, Bangkok, Thailand	2e Assemblée de la Conférence chrétienne d'Asie orientale, Bangkok, Thaïlande

1964:

19th General Council of the World Alliance of Reformed Churches, Frankfurt on Main, Federal Republic of Germany	19e Assemblée générale de l'Alliance réformée mondiale, Francfort-sur-le-Main, République fédérale d'Allemagne

1964:

Meeting of the Commission on Faith and Order, Aarhus, Denmark	Session de la Commission de foi et constitution, Aarhus, Danemark

1964:

4th Assembly of the Conference of European Churches (Nyborg IV), m.v."Bornholm"	4e Assemblée de la Conférence des Eglises européennes (Nyborg IV), M.S. "Bornholm"

1965:

18th Meeting of the Central Committee of the WCC, Enugu, Nigeria	18e session du Comité central du COE, Enugu, Nigéria

1963:

2. Tagung der Kommission für Weltmission und Evangelisation, Mexico City, Mexiko	2a.Reunión de la Comisión de Misión Mundial y Evangelización, México, México

1964:

2. Vollversammlung der Ostasiatischen Christlichen Konferenz, Bangkok, Thailand

2a. Asamblea de la Conferencia Cristiana de Asia Oriental, Bangkok, Tailandia

1964:

19. Generalversammlung des Reformierten Weltbundes, Frankfurt am Main, Bundesrepublik Deutschland

19a. Asamblea General de la Alianza Reformada Mundial, Francfort del Main, República Federal de Alemania

1964:

Tagung der Kommission für Glauben und Kirchenverfassung, Aarhus, Dänemark

Reunión de la Comisión de Fe y Constitución, Aarhus, Dinamarca

1964:

4. Vollversammlung der Konferenz Europäischer Kirchen (Nyborg IV), M.S. "Bornholm"

4a. Asamblea de la Conferencia de Iglesias Europeas (Nyborg IV), M.S. "Bornholm"

1965:

18. Tagung des Zentralausschusses des ORK, Enugu, Nigeria

18a.Reunión del Comité Central del CMI, Enugu, Nigeria

1966:

19th Meeting of the Central Committee of the
WCC, Geneva, Switzerland

19e session du Comité central du COE,
Genève, Suisse

1966:

1st Assembly of the Pacific Conference of
Churches, Lifou, Loyalty Islands

1ère Assemblée de la Conférence des Eglises
du Pacifique, Lifou, Iles Loyauté

1966:

World Consultation on Inter-Church Aid,
Swanwick, England

Colloque mondial pour l'Entraide des
Eglises, Swanwick, Angleterre

1966:

World Conference on Church and Society,
Geneva, Switzerland

Conférence mondiale d'Eglise et société,
Genève, Suisse

1967:

Meeting of the Commission on Faith and
Order, Bristol, England

Session de la Commission de foi et constitution, Bristol, Angleterre

1967:

20th Meeting of the Central Committee of
the WCC, Heraklion, Crete, Greece

20e session du Comité central du COE,
Héraclion, Crète, Grèce

1966:

19. Tagung des Zentralausschusses des ÖRK, Genf, Schweiz	19a.Reunión del Comité Central del CMI, Ginebra, Suiza

1966:

1. Vollversammlung der Konferenz der Kirchen im Pazifik, Lifou, Loyalty-Inseln	1a. Asamblea de la Conferencia de Iglesias del Pacífico, Lifou, Islas Lealtad

1966:

Weltkonsultation für Zwischenkirchliche Hilfe, Swanwick, England	Consulta Mundial sobre Ayuda Intereclesiástica Swanwick, Inglaterra

1966:

Weltkonferenz für Kirche und Gesellschaft, Genf, Schweiz	Conferencia Mundial de Iglesia y Sociedad, Ginebra, Suiza

1967:

Tagung der Kommission für Glauben und Kirchenverfassung, Bristol, England	Reunión de la Comisión de Fe y Constitución, Bristol, Inglaterra

1967:

20. Tagung des Zentralausschusses des ÖRK, Heraklion, Kreta, Griechenland	20a. Reunión del Comité del CMI, Heraklion, Creta, Grecia

1967:

5th Assembly of the Conference of European Churches (Nyborg V), Pörtschach,Austria

5e Assemblée de la Conférence des Eglises européennes (Nyborg V), Pörtschach, Autriche

1967:

The World Council of Christian Education and Sunday School Association becomes the World Council of Christian Education (WCCE) - World Assembly of the WCCE, Nairobi Kenya

Le Conseil mondial de l'éducation chrétienne et association des écoles du dimanche devient le Conseil mondial de l'éducation chrétienne (CMEC) - Assemblée mondiale du CMEC, Nairobi, Kenya

1968:

3rd Assembly of the East Asia Christian Conference, Bangkok, Thailand

3e Assemblée de la Conférence chrétienne d'Asie orientale, Bangkok, Thaïlande

1968:

21st Meeting of the Central Committee of the WCC, Uppsala, Sweden

21e session du Comité central du COE, Upsal, Suède

1968:

4th Assembly of the World Council of Churches, Uppsala, Sweden

4e Assemblée du Conseil oecuménique des Eglises, Upsal, Suède

1968:

22nd Meeting of the Central Committee of the WCC, Uppsala, Sweden

22e session du Comité central du COE, Upsal, Suède

1967:

5. Vollversammlung der Konferenz Europäischer Kirchen (Nyborg V), Pörtschach,
Österreich

5a. Asamblea de la Conferencia de Iglesias
Europeas (Nyborg V), Pörtschach, Austria

1967:

Der Weltrat für christliche Erziehung und
Sonntagsschulvereinigung wird der Weltrat
für christliche Erziehung (WCCE) - Vollversammlung des WCCE, Nairobi, Kenia

El Consejo Mundial de Educación Cristiana
y Asociación de Escuelas Dominicales se
transforma en el Consejo Mundial de Educación Cristiana (CMEC) - Asamblea Mundial del
CMEC, Nairobi, Kenya

1968:

3. Vollversammlung der Ostasiatischen
Christlichen Konferenz, Bangkok, Thailand

3a. Asamblea de la Conferencia Cristiana de
Asia Oriental, Bangkok, Tailandia

1968:

21. Tagung des Zentralausschusses des
ÖRK, Uppsala, Schweden

21a. Reunión del Comité Central del CMI,
Upsala, Suecia

1968:

4. Vollversammlung des Ökumenischen Rates
der Kirchen, Uppsala, Schweden

4a. Asamblea del Consejo Mundial de Iglesias,
Upsala, Suecia

1968:

22. Tagung des Zentralausschusses des
ÖRK, Uppsala, Schweden

22a. Reunión del Comité Central del CMI,
Upsala, Suecia

1969:

International Consultation on Racism, World
Council of Churches, London, England

Colloque international sur le racisme,Conseil
oecuménique des Eglises, Londres, Angleterre

1969:

23rd Meeting of the Central Committee of
the WCC, Canterbury, England

23e session du Comité central du COE,
Cantorbéry, Angleterre

1969:

2nd Assembly of the All Africa Conference of
Churches, Abidjan, Ivory Coast

2e Assemblée de la Conférence des Eglises
de toute l'Afrique, Abidjan, Côte d'Ivoire

1970:

Ecumenical Consultation on Ecumenical
Assistance for Development Projects, WCC/
SODEPAX, Montreux, Switzerland

Conférence mondiale sur l'aide oecuménique
aux projets de développement, COE/SODEPAX,
Montreux, Suisse

1970:

5th Assembly of the Lutheran World
Federation, Evian, France

5e Assemblée de la Fédération luthérienne
mondiale, Evian, France

1970:

20th General Council of the World Alliance
of the Reformed Churches (WARC) = Uniting
General Council of the WARC and the International Congregational Council, Nairobi,
Kenya

20e Assemblée générale de l'Alliance réformée mondiale (ARM) = Assemblée générale constitutive de l'ARM et du Conseil congrégationaliste international, Nairobi, Kenya

1969:

Internationale Studientagung über Rassismus, Ökumenischer Rat der Kirchen, London, England	Consulta Internacional sobre Racismo, Consejo Mundial de Iglesias, Londres, Inglaterra

1969:

23. Tagung des Zentralausschusses des ÖKR, Canterbury, England	23a.Reunión del Comité Central del CMI, Canterbury, Inglaterra

1969:

2. Vollversammlung der Gesamtafrikanischen Kirchenkonferenz, Abidjan, Elfenbeinküste	2a. Asamblea de la Conferencia de Iglesias de toda el Africa, Abidjan, Costa de Marfil

1970:

Weltkonferenz über ökumenische Unterstützung für Entwicklungsprojekte, ÖRK/SODEPAX, Montreux, Schweiz	Consulta Mundial sobre Ayuda Ecuménica a los Proyectos de Desarrollo, CMI/SODEPAX, Montreux, Suiza

1970:

5. Vollversammlung des Lutherischen Weltbundes, Evian, Frankreich	5a. Asamblea de la Federación Luterana Mundial, Evian, Francia

1970:

20. Generalversammlung des Reformierten Weltbundes (RWB) = Vereinigende Generalversammlung des RWB und des Internationalen Kongretionalistenrates, Nairobi, Kenia	20a. Asamblea General de la Alianza Reformada Mundial (ARM) = Asamblea General Constitutiva de la ARM y del Consejo Congregacionalista Internacional, Nairobi, Kenia

1971:

24th Meeting of the Central Committee of
the WCC, Addis Ababa, Ethiopia

24e session du Comité central du COE,
Addis-Abéba, Ethiopie

1971:

5th Assembly of the Conference of European
Churches, (Nyborg VI), Nyborg, Denmark

6e Assemblée de la Conférence des Eglises
européennes (Nyborg VI), Nyborg, Danemark

1971:

2nd Assembly of the Pacific Conference of
Churches, Davuilevu, Fiji

2e Assemblée de la Conférence des Eglises
du Pacifique, Davuilevu, Fidji

1971:

World Assembly of the World Council of
Christian Education, Lima, Peru

Assemblée du Conseil mondial de l'éducation
chrétienne, Lima, Pérou

1971:

Meeting of the Commission of Faith and
Order, Louvain, Belgium

Session de la Commission de foi et constitution, Louvain, Belgique

1972:

Integration of the WCCE with the WCC

Intégration du CMEC au COE

1971:

24. Tagung des Zentralausschusses des
ÖRK, Addis Abeba, Äthiopien

24a.Reunión del Comité Central del CMI,
Addis Abeba, Etiopía

1971:

6. Vollversammlung der Konferenz Europäischer Kirchen (Nyborg VI), Nyborg, Dänemark

6a. Asamblea de la Conferencia de Iglesias
Europeas, Nyborg, Dinamarca

1971:

2. Vollversammlung der Konferenz der Kirchen
im Pazifik, Davuilevu, Fidschiinseln

2a. Asamblea de la Conferencia de Iglesias
del Pacífico, Davuilevu, Fiji

1971:

Vollversammlung des Weltrates für christliche Erziehung, Lima, Peru

Asamblea del Consejo Mundial de Educación
Cristiana, Lima, Perú

1971:

Tagung der Kommission für Glauben und Kirchenverfassung, Löwen, Belgien

Reunión de la Comisión de Fe y Constitución,
Lovaina, Bélgica

1972:

Integration des WCCE und des ÖRK

Integración del CMEC al CMI

1972:

25th Meeting of the Central Committee of the WCC, Utrecht, The Netherlands

25e session du Comité central du COE, Utrecht, Pays-Bas

1972/73:

World Conference and Assembly of the Commission on World Mission and Evangelism, Bangkok, Thailand

Conférence mondiale et Assemblée de la Commission de mission et d'évangélisation, Bangkok, Thaïlande

1973:

5th Assembly of the East Asia Christian Conference, Singapore

5e Assemblée de la Conférence chrétienne d'Asie orientale, Singapour

1973:

Reorganization of the EACC as: Christian Conference of Asia

Réorganisation de la CCAO et changement de nom: Conférence chrétienne d'Asie

1973:

26th Meeting of the Central Committee of the WCC, Geneva, Switzerland

26e session du Comité central du COE, Genève, Suisse

1973:

Foundation of the Caribbean Conference of Churches, Kingston, Jamaica

Fondation de la Conférence des Eglises des Caraïbes, Kingston, Jamaïque

1972:

25. Tagung des Zentralausschusses des
OKR, Utrecht, Niederlande

25a.Reunión   del Comité Central del CMI,
Utrecht, Países Bajos

1972/73:

Weltkonferenz und Vollversammlung der Kommission für Weltmission und Evangelisation,
Bangkok, Thailand

Conferencia Mundial y Asamblea de la
Comisión de Misión Mundial y Evangelización, Bangkok, Tailandia

1973:

5. Vollversammlung der Ostasiatischen
Christlichen Konferenz, Singapur

5a. Asamblea de la Conferencia Cristiana
de Asia Oriental, Singapur

1973:

Neustrukturierung der Ostasiatischen Christlichen Konferenz und Umbenennung in Asiatische Christliche Konferenz

Reorganización   de la CCAO y cambio de
nombre: Conferencia Cristiana de Asia

1973:

26. Tagung des Zentralausschusses des
ÖRK, Genf, Schweiz

26a.Reunión del Comité Central del CMI,
Ginebra, Suiza

1973:

Gründung der Karibischen Konferenz der
Kirchen, Kingston, Jamaika

Fundación de la Conferencia de Iglesias
del Caribe, Kingston, Jamaica

1974:

3rd Assembly of the All Africa Conference
of Churches, Lusaka, Zambia

3e Assemblée de la Conférence des Eglises
de toute l'Afrique, Lusaka, Zambie

1974:

Reorganization of the NECC: foundation
of the Middle East Council of Churches,
Nicosia, Cyprus

Réorganisation du NECC: fondation du Conseil des Eglises du Moyen-Orient, Nicosie,
Chypre

1974:

27th Meeting of the Central Committee of
the WCC, West Berlin

27e session du Comité central du COE, Berlin-
Ouest

1974:

7th Assembly of the Conference of European
Churches, (Nyborg VII), Engelberg, Switzerland

7e Assemblée de la Conférence des Eglises
européennes, (Nyborg VII), Engelberg,
Suisse

1975:

5th Assembly of the World Council of
Churches, Nairobi, Kenya

5e Assemblée du Conseil oecuménique
Eglises, Nairobi, Kenya

1974:

3. Vollversammlung der Gesamtafrikanischen
Kirchenkonferenz, Lusaka, Sambia

3a. Asamblea de la Conferencia de Iglesias
de toda el Africa, Lusaka, Zambia

1974:

Neustrukturierung des NECC: Gründung des
Rates der Kirchen im Mittleren Osten,
Nicosia, Zypern

Reorganización del NECC: Fundación del
Consejo de Iglesias del Oriente Medio,
Nicosia, Chipre

1974:

27. Tagung des Zentralausschusses des
ÖRK, Berlin (West)

27a. Reunión del Comité Central del CMI,
Berlín Occidental

1974:

7. Vollversammlung der Konferenz Europäischer Kirchen (Nyborg VII), Engelberg,
Schweiz

7a. Asamblea de la Conferencia de Iglesias
Europeas (Nyborg VII), Engelberg, Suiza

1975:

5. Vollversammlung des Ökumenischen Rates
der Kirchen, Nairobi, Kenia

5a. Asamblea del Consejo Mundial de
Iglesias, Nairobi, Kenia

II	II
A. ASSEMBLIES:	A. ASSEMBLEES:
1. WORLD ASSEMBLIES	1. ASSEMBLEES MONDIALES
<u>WORLD COUNCIL OF CHURCHES</u>	<u>CONSEIL OECUMENIQUE DES EGLISES</u>

<u>Amsterdam 1948</u>	
First Assembly of the WCC, Amsterdam 1948	Première Assemblée du COE, Amsterdam 1948
Main Theme: Man's Disorder and God's Design	Thème principal: Désordre de l'homme et dessein de Dieu
Section I The Universal Church in God's Design	Section I L'Eglise universelle dans le dessein de Dieu
Section II The Church's Witness to God's Design	Section II Le dessein de Dieu et le témoignage de l'Eglise
Section III The Church and the Disorder of Society	Section III L'Eglise et le désordre de la société
Section IV The Church and the International Disorder	Section IV L'Eglise et le désordre international
The original Basis: The World Council of Churches is a Fellowship of churches which accept our Lord Jesus Christ as God and Saviour	Ancienne Base: Le Conseil oecuménique des Eglises est une association fraternelle d'Eglises qui acceptent notre Seigneur Jésus-Christ comme Dieu et Sauveur.
<u>Evanston 1954</u>:	
Second Assembly of the WCC, Evanston 1954	Deuxième Assemblée du COE, Evanston 1954

A. VOLLVERSAMMLUNGEN:

1. VOLLVERSAMMLUNGEN AUF WELTWEITER EBENE:

ÖKUMENISCHER RAT DER KIRCHEN

Amsterdam 1948

Erste Vollversammlung des ÖRK, Amsterdam 1948

Hauptthema:
Die Unordnung der Welt und Gottes Heilsplan

Sektion I   Die Kirche in Gottes Heils-
              plan

Sektion II   Die Kirche bezeugt Gottes Heils-
              plan

Sektion III   Die Kirche und die Auflösung
              der gesellschaftlichen Ordnung

Sektion IV   Die Kirche und die internatio-
              nale Unordnung

Die alte Basis:
Der Ökumenische Rat der Kirchen ist eine Gemeinschaft von Kirchen, die unseren Herrn
Jesus Christus als Gott und Heiland aner-
kennen.

Evanston 1954

Zweite Vollversammlung des ÖRK, Evanston 1954

A. ASAMBLEAS:

1. ASAMBLEAS MUNDIALES:

CONSEJO MUNDIAL DE IGLESIAS

Primera Asamblea del CMI, Amsterdam 1948

Tema central:
Eldesorden del hombre y el designio de Dios

Sección I   La Iglesia Universal en el
              designio de Dios

Sección II   El designio de Dios y el
              testimonio de la Iglesia

Sección III   La Iglesia y el desorden de la
              sociedad

Sección IV   La Iglesia y el desorden inter-
              nacional

Base original:
El Consejo Mundial de Iglesias es una comunidad
de Iglesias que aceptan a nuestro Señor
Jesucristo como Dios y Salvador.

Segunda Asamblea del CMI, Evanston 1954

Main Theme:
Christ, the Hope of the World

Section I	Faith and Order:Our Oneness in Christ and our Disunity as Churches
Section II	Evangelism: The Mission of the Church to those Outside Her Life
Section III	Social Questions: The Responsible Society in a World Perspective
Section IV	International Affairs: Christians in the Struggle for World Community
Section V	Intergroup Relations: The Churches amid Racial and Ethnic Tensions
Section VI	The Laity: The Christian in his Vocation

Thème principal:
Le Christ, seul espoir du monde

Section I	Foi et constitution: notre unité en Christ et notre désunion en tant qu' Eglises
Section II	Evangélisation: la mission de l'Eglise auprès de ceux de dehors
Section III	Questions sociales: la société et ses responsabilités sur le plan mondial
Section IV	Affaires internationales: les chrétiens à la recherche de la communauté mondiale
Section V	Relations entre groupes humains: l'Eglise au milieu des tensions raciales et ethniques
Section VI	Les laïcs: le chrétien dans sa vie professionnelle

New-Delhi 1961

Third Assembly of the WCC, New-Delhi 1961

General Theme:
Jesus Christ, the Light of the World

Troisième Assemblée du COE, Nouvelle-Delhi 1961

Thème général:
Jésus-Christ, lumière du monde

Hauptthema:
Christus - die Hoffnung für die Welt

| Sektion I | Glauben und Kirchenverfassung - Unser Einssein in Christus und unsere Uneinigkeit als Kirchen |

Sektion II   Missionarische Verkündigung - Die Verpflichtung der Kirche gegenüber den ihr Fernstehenden

Sektion III   Soziale Fragen - Verantwortliche Gesellschaft in weltweiter Sicht

Sektion IV   Internationale Angelegenheiten- Christen im Ringen um die rechte Ordnung der Welt

Sektion V   Gemeinschaftsprobleme - Die Kirche inmitten rassischer und völkischer Spannungen

Sektion VI   Die Laienfrage - Der Christ in seinem Beruf

Tema central:
Cristo, la Esperanza del mundo

Sección I   Fe y Constitución: Nuestra unidad en Cristo, nuestra desunión como Iglesias

Sección II   Evangelización: La misión de la Iglesia hacia los de afuera

Sección III   Cuestiones sociales: La sociedad responsable en une perspectiva mundial

Sección IV   Asuntos internacionales: Los cristianos en la lucha por una comunidad mundial

Sección V   Relaciones entre grupos humanos: La Iglesia en medio de las tensiones raciales y étnicas

Sección VI   Los laicos: El cristiano en el ejercicio de su vocación

Neu-Delhi 1961

Dritte Vollversammlung des ÖRK, Neu-Delhi 1961

Tercera Asamblea del CMI, Nueva Delhi 1961

Generalthema:
Jesus Christus, das Licht der Welt

Tema general:
Jesucristo, la Luz del mundo

Section on	Witness	Section	témoignage
Section on	Service	Section	service
Section on	Unity	Section	unité

The New Basis:
The World Council of Churches is a fellowship of churches which confess the Lord
Jesus Christ as God and Saviour according
to the Scriptures and therefore seek to
fulfil together their common calling to
the glory of the one God, Father, Son and
Holy Spirit.

Nouvelle Base:
Le Conseil oecuménique des Eglises est une
association fraternelle d'Eglises qui con-
fessent le Seigneur Jésus-Christ comme Dieu
et Sauveur selon les Ecritures et s'efforcent
de répondre ensemble à leur commune vocation,
pour la gloire du seul Dieu, Père, Fils et
Saint-Esprit.

Uppsala 1968

Fourth Assembly of the WCC, Uppsala 1968

Quatrième Assemblée du COE, Upsal, 1968

Main Theme:
Behold, I Make All Things New

Thème principal:
Voici, je fais toutes choses nouvelles

Section I	The Holy Spirit and the Catholicity of the Church	Section I	L'Esprit Saint et la catholicité de l'Eglise
Section II	Renewal in Mission	Section II	Renouveau de la mission
Section III	World Economic and Social Development	Section III	Le développement économique et social
Section IV	Towards Justice and Peace in International Affaires	Section IV	Vers la justice et la paix dans les affaires internationales

Sektion	Zeugnis		Sección	Testimonio
Sektion	Dienst		Sección	Servicio
Sektion	Einheit		Sección	Unidad

Die neue Basis:
Der Ökumenische Rat der Kirchen ist eine
Gemeinschaft von Kirchen, die den Herrn
Jesus Christus gemäss der Heiligen Schrift
als Gott und Heiland bekennen und darum ge-
meinsam zu erfüllen trachten, wozu sie berufen sind, zur Ehre Gottes, des Vaters und
des Sohnes und des Heiligen Geistes.

. Nueva Base:
El Consejo Mundial de Iglesias es una comunidad de Iglesias que confiesan al Señor
Jesucristo como Dios y Salvador según el
testimonio de las Escritura y que procuran
responder juntas a su vocación común, para
gloria del único Dios, Padre, Hijo y
Espíritu Santo.

Uppsala 1968

Vierte Vollversammlung des ÖRK, Uppsala 1968

Cuarta Asamblea del CMI, Upsala 1968

Hauptthema:
Siehe, ich mache alles neu

Tema central:
He aquí, yo hago nuevas todas las cosas

Sektion I	Der Heilige Geist und die die Katholizität der Kirche		Sección I	El Espíritu Santo y la catolicidad de la Iglesia
Sektion II	Erneuerung in der Mission		Sección II	Renovación en la misión
Sektion III	Wirtschafliche und soziale Weltentwicklung		Sección III	El desarrollo económico y social
Sektion IV	Auf dem Wege zu Gerechtigkeit und Frieden in internationalen Anglegenheiten		Sección IV	Hacia la justicia y la paz en los asuntos internacionales

43

Section V	Worship	Section V	Le culte
Section VI	Towards new Styles of Living	Section VI	Vers de nouveaux styles de vie

Sektion V	Gottesdienst	Sessión V	El culto
Sektion VI	Auf der Suche nach neuen Lebensstilen	Sessión VI	Hacia nuevos estilos de vida

LUTHERAN WORLD FEDERATION

Lund 1947

First Assembly of the Lutheran World
Federation, Lund 1947

Theme:
The Lutheran Church in the World Today

Hanover 1952

Second Assembly of the Lutheran World
Federation, Hanover 1952

Theme:
The Living Word in a Responsible Church

Minneapolis 1957

Third Assembly of the Lutheran World
Federation, Minneapolis, Minn. 1957

Theme:
Christ Frees and Unites

Helsinki 1963

Fourth Assembly of the Lutheran World
Federation, Helsinki 1963

Theme:
Christ Today

FEDERATION LUTHERIENNE MONDIALE

Première Assemblée de la Fédération
luthérienne mondiale, Lund 1947

Thème:
L'Eglise luthérienne dans le monde
d'aujourd'hui

Deuxième Assemblée de la Fédération
luthérienne mondiale, Hanovre 1952

Thème:
La parole vivante dans une Eglise
responsable

Troisième Assemblée de la Fédération
luthérienne mondiale, Minneapolis, Minn.
1957
Thème:
Le Christ libère et unit

Quatrième Assemblée de la Fédération
luthérienne mondiale, Helsinki 1963

Thème:
 Christ aujourd'hui

LUTHERISCHER WELTBUND

Lund 1947

Erste Vollversammlung des Lutherischen
Weltbundes, Lund 1947

Hauptthema:
Die Lutherische Kirche in der Welt von heute

Hannover 1952

Zweite Vollversammlung des Lutherischen
Weltbundes, Hannover 1952

Hauptthema:
Das lebendige Wort in einer verantwortlichen
Kirche

Minneapolis 1957

Dritte Vollversammlung des Lutherischen
Weltbundes, Minneapolis, Minn. 1957

Hauptthema:
Christus befreit und eint

Helsinki 1963

Vierte Vollversammlung des Lutherischen
Weltbundes, Helsinki 1963

Hauptthema:
Christus Heute

FEDERACION LUTERANA MUNDIAL

Primera Asamblea de la Federación
Luterana Mundial, Lund 1947

Tema:
La Iglesia Luterana en el mundo de hoy

Segunda Asamblea de la Federación
Luterana Mundial, Hanover 1952

Tema:
La Palabra Viviente en una iglesia
responsable

Tercera Asamblea de la Federación
Luterana Mundial, Minneapolis, Minn. 1957

Tema:
Cristo libera y une

Cuarta Asamblea de la Federación
Luterana Mundial, Helsinki 1963

Tema:
Cristo hoy

Evian 1970

Fifth Assembly of the Lutheran World
Federation, Evian 1970

Theme:
Sent into the World

Cinquième Assemblée de la Fédération
luthérienne mondiale, Evian 1970

Thème:
Envoyés dans le monde

Evian 1970

Fünfte Vollversammlung des Lutherischen
Weltbundes, Evian 1970

Hauptthema:
Gesandt in die Welt

Quinta Asamblea de la Federación
Luterana Mundial, Evian 1970

Tema:
Enviados al mundo

WORLD ALLIANCE OF REFORMED CHURCHES

Princeton 1954

17th General Council of the Alliance of the
Reformed Churches Throughout the World Holding
the Presbyterian Order (also known as the
World Presbyterian Alliance and the World
Alliance of Reformed Churches), Princeton
1954

Main Theme:
The Witness of the Reformed Churches in
the World Today

Sao Paulo 1959

18th General Council of the World Alliance
of Reformed Churches, Sao Paulo 1959

Main theme:
The Servant Lord and His Servant People

Frankfurt on Main 1954

19th General Council of the World Alliance
of Reformed Churches, Frankfurt on Main 1964

Main Theme:
Come, Creator Spirit!

Nairobi 1970

20th General Council of the World Alliance

ALLIANCE REFORMEE MONDIALE

17e Assemblée générale de l'Alliance
réformée mondiale, Princeton 1954

Thème général:
Le témoignage des Eglises réformées dans
le monde d'aujourd'hui

18e Assemblée générale de l'Alliance
réformée mondiale, Sao Paulo 1959

Thème général:
Disciples d'un Seigneur qui sert

19e Assemblée générale de l'Alliance
réformée mondiale, Francfort-sur-le-Main
1964
Thème général:
Viens, Esprit créateur!

20e Assemblée générale de l'Alliance

REFORMIERTER WELTBUND

Princeton 1954

17. Generalversammlung des Reformierten
Weltbundes, Princeton 1954

Hauptthema:
Das Zeugnis der Reformierten Kirchen in
der Welt von heute

Sao Paulo 1959

18. Generalversammlung des Reformierten
Weltbundes, Sao Paulo 1959

Hauptthema:
Der Herr - ein Knecht, wir seine Knechte

Frankurt am Main 1964

19. Generalversammlung des Reformierten
Weltbundes, Frankfurt am Main 1964

Hauptthema:
Komm, Schöpfer Geist!

Nairobi 1970

20. Generalversammlung des Reformierten

ALIANZA REFORMADA MUNDIAL

17a. Asamblea General de la Alianza
Reformada Mundial, Princeton 1954

Tema central:
El testimonio de las Iglesias Reformadas
en el mundo de hoy

18a. Asamblea General de la Alianza
Reformada Mundial, San Pablo 1959

Tema central:
Servidores de un Señor que es siervo

19a. Asamblea General de la Alianza
Reformada Mundial, Francfort del Main 1964

Tema central:
Ven, Espíritu creador!

20a. Asamblea General de la Alianza

51

of Reformed Churches (WARC) = Uniting
General Council of the WARC and the
International Congregational Council,
Nairobi 1970

Main Theme:
God Reconciles and Makes Free

réformée mondiale (ARM) = Assemblée
générale constitutive de l'ARM et du
Conseil congrégationaliste international,
Nairobi 1970

Thème général:
Dieu réconcilie et libère

Weltbundes (RWB) = Vereinigende Generalversammlung des RWB und des Internationalen
Kongregationalistenrates, Nairobi 1970

Hauptthema:
Gott versöhnt und macht frei

Reformada Mundial (ARM) = Asamblea
General Constitutiva de la ARM y del
Consejo Congregacionalista Internacional,
Nairobi 1970

Tema central:
Dios reconcilia y libera

2. REGIONAL ASSEMBLIES

ALL AFRICA CONFERENCE OF CHURCHES

1963:

1st Assembly, Kampala, Uganda

Theme:
Freedom and Unity in Christ

1969:

2nd Assembly, Abidjan, Ivory Coast

Theme:
With Christ at Work in Africa Today

1974:

3rd Assembly, Lusaka, Zambia

Theme:
Living no more for Ourselves, but for Christ

2. ASSEMBLEES REGIONALES

CONFERENCE DES EGLISES DE TOUTE L'AFRIQUE

1ère Assemblée, Kampala, Ouganda

Thème:
Liberté et unité en Christ

2e Assemblée, Abidjan, Côte-d'Ivoire

Thème:
Avec Christ à l'oeuvre en Afrique aujourd'hui

3e Assemblée, Lusaka, Zambie

Thème:
Ne plus vivre pour nous-mêmes, mais pour Christ

2. REGIONALE VOLLVERSAMMLUNGEN

GESAMTAFRIKANISCHE KIRCHENKONFERENZ

1963:

1. Vollversammlung, Kampala, Uganda

Thema:
Freiheit und Einheit in Christus

1969:

2. Vollversammlung, Abidjan, Elfenbeinküste

Thema:
Wirken mit Christus in Afrika heute

1974:

3. Vollversammlung, Lusaka, Sambia

Thema:
Nicht mehr für uns selbst, sondern für
Christus leben

2. ASAMBLEAS REGIONALES

CONFERENCIA DE LAS IGLESIAS DE TODA EL AFRICA

1a. Asamblea, Kampala, Uganda

Tema:
Libertad y unidad en cristo

2a. Asamblea, Abidjan, Costa de Marfil

Tema:
Trabajando con Cristo en Africa hoy

3a. Asamblea, Lusaka, Zambia

Tema:
No vivir más para nosotros mismos, sino
para Cristo

CARIBBEAN CONFERENCE OF CHURCHES

1973:

Inaugural Assembly, Kingston, Jamaica

Theme:
The Right Hand of God

CONFERENCE DES EGLISES DES CARAÏBES

1ère Assemblée, Kingston, Jamaïque

Thème:
La main droite de Dieu

KARIBISCHE KONFERENZ DER KIRCHEN

1973:

Eröffnungsversammlung, Kingston, Jamaika

Thema:
Die rechte Hand Gottes

CONFERENCIA DE LAS IGLESIAS DEL CARIBE

1a. Asamblea, Kingston, Jamaica

Tema:
La mano derecha de Dios

SELECT BIBLIOGRAPHY

BIBLIOGRAPHIE SOMMAIRE

AUSGEWÄHLTE BIBLIOGRAPHIE

SINTESIS BIBLIOGRAFICA

CONFERENCE OF EUROPEAN CHURCHES	CONFERENCE DES EGLISES EUROPEENNES
1959 Nyborg I	
European Christianity in Today's Secularised World	La chrétienté européenne dans le monde sécularisé d'aujourd'hui
1960 Nyborg II	
The Service of the Church in a Changing World	Le service de l'Eglise dans un monde en transformation
1962 Nyborg III	
The Church in Europe and the Crisis of Modern Man	L'Eglise en Europe et la crise de l'homme contemporain
1964 Nyborg IV	
Living Together as Continents and Generations	Vivre ensemble, comme continents et générations
1967 Nyborg V	
To Serve and Reconcile: The Task of the European Churches Today	Servir et réconcilier: la tâche des Eglises européennes aujourd'hui
1971 Nyborg VI	
Servants of God, Servants of Men	Serviteurs de Dieu, serviteurs des hommes

KONFERENZ EUROPÄISCHER KIRCHEN

CONFERENCIA DE LAS IGLESIAS EUROPEAS

1959 Nyborg I

Die europäische Christenheit in der heutigen säkularisierten Welt

La cristiandad europea en el mundo secularizado de hoy

1960 Nyborg II

Der Dienst der Kirche in einer sich verändernden Welt

El servicio de la Iglesia en un mundo en proceso de cambio

1962 Nyborg III

Die Kirche in Europa und die Krise des modernen Menschen

La Iglesia en Europa y la crisis del hombre contemporáneo

1964 Nyborg IV

Zusammen leben als Kontinente und Generationen

Vivir juntos como continentes y generaciones

1967 Nyborg V

Dienen und Versöhnen - Die Aufgabe der europäischen Kirchen heute

Servir y reconciliar: la tarea actual Iglesias Europea

1971 Nyborg VI

Diener Gottes, Diener der Menschen

Siervos de Dios, siervos de los hombres

59

1974 Nyborg VII

Act on the Message (Jas.1,22)
Unity in Christ and Peace in the World:
Christian Hope and the Promise of the Gospel

Pratiquez la parole (Ja. 1,22)-
unité en Christ et paix sur la terre:
espérance chrétienne et promesse évangélique

1974 Nyborg VII

Seid Täter des Wortes (Jak. 1, 22)
Einheit in Christus und Frieden für die Welt -
Hoffnung der Christenheit und Verheissung des
Evangeliums

Hacedores de la palabra (Sant.1, 22) -
Unidad en Cristo y paz sobre la tierra:
Esperanza cristiana y promesa evangélica

61

EAST ASIA CHRISTIAN CONFERENCE [1]	CONFERENCE CHRETIENNE D'ASIE ORIENTALE [1]
1957:	
Constituting Assembly, Prapat, Sumatra Indonesia	Assemblée constituante, Prapat, Sumatra, Indonésie
Theme: The Common Evangelistic Task of the Churches in East Asia	Thème: La tâche évangélique commune des Eglises en Asie orientale
1959:	
1st. Assembly, Kuala Lumpur, Malayan Federation	1ère Assemblée, Kuala Lumpur, Fédération de Malaisie
Theme: Witnesses Together	Thème: Témoigner ensemble
1964:	
2nd Assembly, Bangkok, Thailand	2e Assemblée, Bangkok, Thaïlande
Theme: The Christian Community within the Human Community	Thème: La communauté chrétienne dans la communauté humaine
1968:	
4rd Assembly, Bangkok, Thailand	4e Assemblée, Bangkok, Thaïlande
Theme: In Christ all Things hold together	Thème: Toutes choses subsistent en Christ

1) See also page 33 under 1973

1) Voir aussi page 33 sous 1973

1) See also page 33 under 1973
1) Voir aussi page 33 sous 1973

<u>OSTASIATISCHE CHRISTLICHE KONFERENZ</u> [1]	<u>CONFERENCIA CRISTIANA DE ASIA ORIENTAL</u> [1]
1957:	
Gründungsversammlung, Prapat, Sumatra, Indonesien	Asamblea constitutiva, Prapat, Sumatra, Indonesia
Thema: Verkündigung als gemeinsame Aufgabe der Kirchen in Ostasien	Tema: La tarea evangelizadora común de las iglesias en Asia Oriental
1959:	
1. Vollversammlung, Kuala Lumpur, Malaiischer Bund	1a. Asamblea, Kuala Lumpur, Federación de Malasia
Thema: Gemeinsam Zeugnis ablegen	Tema: Dar testimonio juntos
1964:	
2. Vollversammlung, Bangkok, Thailand	2a. Asamblea, Bangkok, Tailandia
Thema: Christliche Gemeinschaft in der menschlichen Gemeinschaft	Tema: La comunidad cristiana en la comunidad humana
1968: 4. Vollversammlung, Bangkok, Thailand	4a. Asamblea, Bangkok, Tailandia
Thema: In Christus hat alles Bestand	Tema: Por Cristo todas las cosas subsisten

---

1) s. auch Seite 34 unter 1973   1) Véase también pag. 34 , 1973

1973:

5th Assembly, Singapore

Theme:
Christian Action in the Asian Struggle

5e Assemblée, Singapour

Thème:
L'action des chrétiens dans la lutte
asiatique

1973:

5. Vollversammlung, Singapur

Thema:
Christliches Handeln in Asiens Kampf

5a. Asamblea, Singapur

Tema:
La acción de los cristianos en la lucha
asiática

PACIFIC CONFERENCE OF CHURCHES	CONFERENCE DES EGLISES DU PACIFIQUE

1966:

Inaugural Assembly, Lifou, Loyalty Islands

Theme:
Go Ye ...

1971:

2nd Assembly, Davuilevu, Fiji

Theme:
God's Purpose for His People

1ère Assemblée, Lifou, îles Loyauté

Thème:
Allez dans le monde

2e Assemblée, Davuilevu, îles Fidji

Thème:
Le dessein de Dieu pour son peuple

PAZIFISCHE KONFERENZ DER KIRCHEN

1966:

Eröffnungsversammlung, Lifou, Loyalty-Inseln

Thema:
Gehet hin

1971:

2. Vollversammlung, Davuilevu, Fidschi-
inseln
Thema:
Gottes Heilsplan für sein Volk

CONFERENCIA DE LAS IGLESIAS DEL PACIFICO

1a. Asamblea, Lifou, Islas Lealtad

Tema:
Id por el mundo

2a. Asamblea, Davuilevu, Fiji

Tema:
El designio de Dios para su pueblo

B. WORLD CONFERENCES			B. CONFERENCES MONDIALES	

FAITH AND ORDER

FOI ET CONSTITUTION

Lausanne 1927

First World Conference on Faith and Order

Première Conférence mondiale de Foi et constitution

Section I	The Call to Unity	Section I	L'appel à l'unité
Section II	The Church's Message to the World: The Gospel	Section II	Le message de l'Eglise au monde: l'Evangile
Section III	The Nature of the Church	Section III	La nature de l'Eglise
Section IV	The Church's Common Confession of Faith	Section IV	La confession de foi commune de l'Eglise
Section V	The Church's Ministry	Section V	Le ministère de l'Eglise
Section VI	The Sacraments	Section VI	Les sacrements
Section VII	The Unity of Christendom and the Relation Thereto of Existing Churches	Section VII	L'unité de la chrétienté et les Eglises actuelles

Edinburgh 1937

Second World Conference on Faith and Order

Deuxième Conférence mondiale de Foi et constitution

Section I	The Grace of our Lord Jesus Christ	Section I	La grâce de notre Seigneur Jésus-Christ

B. WELTKONFERENZEN

GLAUBEN UND KIRCHENVERFASSUNG

Lausanne 1927:

Erste Weltkonferenz für Glauben und Kirchenverfassung

Sektion I	Der Ruf zur Einheit
Sektion II	Die Botschaft der Kirche an die Welt
Sektion III	Das Wesen der Kirche
Sektion IV	Das gemeinsame Glaubensbe-kenntnis der Kirche
Sektion V	Das geistliche Amt der Kirche
Sektion VI	Die Sakramente
Sektion VII	Die Einheit der Christenheit und das Verhältnis der bestehenden Kirchen zu ihr

Edingburgh 1937

Zweite Weltkonferenz für Glauben und Kirchenverfassung

Sektion I	Die Gnade unseres Herrn Jesus Christus

B. CONFERENCIAS MUNDIALES

FE Y CONSTITUCION

Primera Conferencia Mundial de Fe y
Constitución

Sección I	El llamado a la unidad
Sección II	El mensaje de la Iglesia al mundo: el Evangelio
Sección III	La naturaleza de la Iglesia
Sección IV	La confesión de fe común de la Iglesia
Sección V	El ministerio de la Iglesia
Sección VI	Los sacramentos
Sección VII	La unidad de la cristiandad y las iglesias actuales

Segunda Conferencia Mundial de Fe y
Consitución

Sección I	La Gracia de Nuestro Señor Jesucristo

| Section II | The Church of Christ and the Word of God | Section II | L'Eglise du Christ et la Parole de Dieu |

Section II — The Church of Christ and the Word of God — Section II — L'Eglise du Christ et la Parole de Dieu

Section III — The Church of Christ: Ministry and Sacraments — Section III — L'Eglise du Christ: ministère et sacrements

Section IV — The Church's Unity in Life and Worship — Section IV — L'unité de l'Eglise dans la vie et le culte

Lund 1952

Third World Conference on Faith and Order

Troisième Conférence mondiale de Foi et constitution

Section I — Christ and His Church — Section I — Jésus-Christ et son Eglise

Section II — Continuity and Unity — Section II — Continuité et unité

Section III — Ways of Worship — Section III — Formes de culte

Section IV — Intercommunion — Section IV — Intercommunion

Theological Commissions:

Commissions théologiques:

Theological Commission on Worship

Commission théologique sur le culte

Theological Commission on Tradition and Traditions

Commission théologique sur la Tradition et les traditions

Theological Commission on Christ and the Church

Commission théologique sur Christ et l'Eglise

Study Commission on Institutionalism

Commission d'étude sur l'institutionnalisme

Sektion II	Die Kirche Christi und das Wort Gottes		Sección II	La Iglesia de Cristo y la Palabra de Dios
Sektion III	Die Kirche Christi – Das geistliche Amt und die Sakramente		Sección III	La Iglesia de Cristo: ministerio y sacramentos
Sektion IV	Die Einheit der Kirche in Leben und Gottesdienst		Sección IV	La unidad de la Iglesia en la vida y el culto

Lund 1952

Dritte Weltkonferenz für Glauben und Kirchenverfassung

Tercera Conferencia Mundial de Fe y Constitución

Sektion I	Christus und Seine Kirche		Sección I	Jesucristo y su Iglesia
Sektion II	Kontinuität und Einheit		Sección II	Continuidad y unidad
Sektion III	Formen des Gottesdienstes		Sección III	Formas de culto
Sektion IV	Interkommunion		Sección IV	Intercomunión

Theologische Kommissionen:

Comisiones teológicas:

Theologische Kommission über den Gottesdienst

Comisión teológica sobre culto

Theologische Kommission über Tradition und Traditionen

Comisión teológica sobre Tradición y tradiciones

Theologische Kommission über Christus und die Kirche

Comisión teológica sobre Cristo y la Iglesia

Studienkommission für Institutionalismus

Comisión de estudio sobre institucionalismo

Montreal 1963

Fourth World Conference on Faith and Order

Section I	The Church in the Purpose of God
Section II	Scripture, Tradition and Traditions
Section III	The Redemptive Work of Christ and the Ministry of the Church
Section IV	Worship and the Oneness of Christ's Church
Section V	"All in each place": The Process of Growing Together

Quatrième Conférence mondiale de Foi et constitution

Section I	L'Eglise dans le dessein de Dieu
Section II	L'Ecriture, la Tradition et les traditions
Section III	L'oeuvre rédemptrice du Christ et le ministère de l'Eglise
Section IV	Le culte et l'unité de l'Eglise du Christ
Section V	"Tous en un même lieu": notre cheminement commun

Aarhus 1964

Meeting of the Commission of Faith and Order

Committee I	Creation, New Creation and the Unity of the Church
Committee II	Christ, the Holy Spirit and the Ministry
Committee III	The Eucharist, a Sacrament of Unity

Session de la Commission de foi et constitution

Comité I	Création, nouvelle création et unité de l'Eglise
Comité II	Christ, le Saint-Esprit et le ministère
Comité III	L'eucharistie, sacrement d'unité

Montreal 1963

Vierte Weltkonferenz für Glauben und Kirchenverfassung		Cuarta Conferencia Mundial de Fe y Constitución	
Sektion I	Die Kirche in Gottes Plan	Sección I	La Iglesia en el designio de Dios
Sektion II	Schrift, Tradition und Traditionen	Sección II	Ecritura, Tradición y tradiciones
Sektion III	Das Erlösungswerk Christi und das Amt seiner Kirche	Sección III	Obra redentora de Cristo y ministerio de la Iglesia
Sektion IV	Der Gottesdienst und das Einssein der Kirche Christi	Sección IV	Culto y unidad de la Iglesia de Cristo
Sektion V	"Alle an jedem Ort" - Der Vorgang des Zusammenwachsens	Sección V	"Todos en todo lugar": haciendo el camino juntos

Aarhus 1964

Tagung der Kommission für Glauben und Kirchenverfassung		Reunión de la Comisión de Fe y Constitución	
Ausschuss I	Schöpfung, neue Schöpfung und die Einheit der Kirche	Comité I	Creación, nueva creación y unidad de la Iglesia
Ausschuss II	Christus, der Heilige Geist und das Amt	Comité II	Cristo, el Espíritu Santo y el ministerio
Ausschuss III	Die Eucharistie - Sakrament der Einheit	Comité III	La eucaristía , sacramento de unidad

73

Committee IV Spirit, Order and Organization	Comité IV L'Esprit, la constitution et l'organisation

Bristol 1967

Meeting of the Commission on Faith and Order	Session de la Commission de foi et constitution
Section I Creation, New Creation and the Unity of the Church	Section I Création, nouvelle création et l'unité de l'Eglise
Section II The Eucharist, a Sacrament of Unity	Section II L'eucharistie, sacrement d'unité
Section III Ministry, Church Union Negotiations, Ecumenical Commitment and Christian Education	Section III Le ministère, les négociations d'union entre Eglises, l'engagement oecuménique et l'éducation chrétienne
Section IV Tradition and Traditions	Section IV La Tradition et les traditions
Section V General Faith and Order Problems	Section V Des problèmes généraux de Foi et constitution

Louvain 1971

Meeting of the Commission on Faith and Order	Session de la Commission de foi et constitution
Theme: The Unity of the Church and the Unity of Mankind	Thème: L'unité de l'Eglise et l'unité de l'humanité
Section I The Unity of the Church and the Struggle for Justice in Society	Section I L'unité de l'Eglise et la lutte pour la justice sociale

Ausschuss IV Geist, Ordnung und Organisation	Comité IV El Espíritu, la constitución y la organización

Bristol 1967

Tagung der Kommission für Glauben und Kirchenverfassung

Sektion I	Schöpfung, neue Schöpfung und die Einheit der Kirche	Sección I	Creación, nueva creación y unidad de la Iglesia
Sektion II	Die Eucharistie - Sakrament der Einheit	Sección II	La eucaristía, sacramento de unidad
Sektion III	Das Amt, Kirchenunionsverhandlungen, Ökumenisches Engagement und Christliche Erziehung	Sección III	Ministerio, negaciaciones para la unión de las Iglesias, compromiso ecuménico y educación cristiana
Sektion IV	Tradition und Traditionen	Sección IV	Tradición y tradiciones
Sektion V	Allgemeine Probleme von Glauben und Kirchenverfassung	Sección V	Problemas generales de Fe y Constitución

Reunión de la Comisión de Fe y Constitución

Louvain 1971

Tagung der Kommission für Glauben und Kirchenverfassung

Reunión de la Comisión de Fe y Constitución

Thema:
Die Einheit der Kirche und die Einheit der Menschheit

Tema:
La unidad de la Iglesia y la unidad de la humanidad

Sektion I	Die Einheit der Kirche und der Kampf um Gerechtigkeit in der Gesellschaft	Sección I	La unidad de la Iglesia y la lucha en favor de la justicia en la sociedad

75

Section II	The Unity of the Church and the Encounter with Living Faiths	Section II	L'unité de l'Eglise et la rencontre avec les croyances de notre temps
Section III	The Unity of the Church and the Struggle against Racism	Section III	L'unité de l'Eglise et la lutte contre le racisme
Section IV	The Unity of the Church and the Handicapped in Society	Section IV	L'unité de l'Eglise et les handicapés dans la société
Section V	The Unity of the Church and Differences in Culture	Section V	L'unité de l'Eglise et les différences de culture

Sektion II	Die Einheit der Kirche und die Begegnung mit den Religionen unserer Zeit	Sección II	La unidad de la Iglesia y el encuentro con las religiones de nuestro tiempo
Sektion III	Die Einheit der Kirche und der Kampf gegen den Rassismus	Sección III	La unidad de la Iglesia y la lucha contra el racismo
Sektion IV	Die Einheit der Kirche und die Behinderten in der Gesellschaft	Sección IV	La unidad de la Iglesia y los físicamente disminuídos en la sociedad
Sektion V	Die Einheit der Kirche und kulturelle Unterschiede	Sección V	La unidad de la Iglesia y las diferencias culturales

CHURCH AND SOCIETY	EGLISE ET SOCIETE
Geneva 1966	
World Conference on Church and Society	Conférence mondiale d'Eglise et société
Theme: Christians in the Technical and Social Revolutions of our Time	Thème: Engagement chrétien dans la révolution technique et sociale
Section I Economic Development in a World Perspective	Section I Le développement économique et social dans une perspective mondiale
Section II The Nature and Function of the State in a Revolutionary Age	Section II Rôle de l'Etat à une époque révolutionnaire
Section III Structures of International Cooperation: Living Together in Peace in a Pluralistic World Society	Section III Pluralisme et collaboration internationale: à la recherche de nouvelles formules
Section IV Man and Community in Changing Societies	Section IV Effets des bouleversements sociaux actuels sur l'individu et le groupe
Working Group A Potentialities of the Contemporary Technological and Scientific Revolution	Groupe de travail A Les promesses de la révolution technique et scientifique contemporaine
Working Group B Theological Issues in Social Ethics	Groupe de travail B Problèmes théologiques d'éthique sociale
Working Group C The Church's Action in Society	Groupe de travail C Action de l'Eglise dans la société

KIRCHE UND GESELLSCHAFT	**IGLESIA Y SOCIEDAD**

KIRCHE UND GESELLSCHAFT

Geneva 1966

Weltkonferenz für Kirche und Gesellschaft

Thema:
Christliche Antwort auf die technische
und gesellschaftliche Revolution unserer
Zeit

Sektion I — Wirtschaftliche Entwicklung in weltweiter Sicht

Sektion II — Wesen und Auftrag des Staates
in einer Zeit des Umbruchs

Sektion III — Strukturen internationaler
Zusammenarbeit - Friedliches
Zusammenleben in einer plura-
listischen Weltgemeinschaft

Sektion IV — Mensch und Gemeinschaft in
sich wandelnden Gesellschafts-
formen

Arbeitsgruppe A — Möglichkeiten in der ge-
genwärtigen technischen
und wissenschaftlichen Revolution

Arbeitsgruppe B — Theologische Probleme in
der Sozialethik

Arbeitsgruppe C — Das Wirken der Kirche in
der Gesellschaft

IGLESIA Y SOCIEDAD

Conferencia Mundial de Iglesia y Sociedad

Tema:
El compromiso cristiano en la revolución
técnica y social de nuestro tiempo

Sección I — El desarrollo económico y
social en una perspectiva
mundial

Sección II — Carácter y papel del Estado en una
época revolucionaria

Sección III — Estructuras de la cooperación
internacional: convivir en
paz en una sociedad mundial
pluralista

Sección IV — El hombre y la communidad en
sociedades en proceso de
cambio

Grupo de trabajo A — Posibilidades de la
revolución técnica y
científica contem-
poránea

Grupo de trabajo B — Problemas teológicos
de ética social

Grupo de trabajo C — Acción de la Iglesia
en la sociedad

WCC/SODEPAX		COE/SODEPAX	

WCC/SODEPAX

Montreux 1970

Ecumenical Conference, WCC/SODEPAX

Theme:
Ecumenical Assistance to Development
Projects

Working Group I	The Debate about Development
Working Group II	Policy and Procedures for Church Support to Development
Working Group III	Structure and Organization of Ecumenical Assistance to Development Projects
Working Group IV	Technical Assistance for Church-Sponsored Development
Working Group V	The Mobilization of Funds

COE/SODEPAX

Conférence mondiale, COE/SODEPAX

Thème:
L'aide oecuménique aux projets de
développement

Groupe de travail I	La discussion sur le développement
Groupe de travail II	Orientation et méthodes de l'aide des Eglises aux projets de développement
Groupe de travail III	Structure et organisation de l'aide oecuménique aux programmes et projets de développement
Groupe de travail IV	Assistance technique aux projets de développement parrainés par les Eglises
Groupe de travail V	La mobilisation des fonds

ÖRK/ SODEPAX

Montreux 1970

Weltkonferenz, ÖRK/SODEPAX

Thema:
Ökumenische Unterstützung für
Entwicklungsprojekte

Arbeitsgruppe I   Die Entwicklungsdis-
                   kussion

Arbeitsgruppe II   Konzeption und Metho-
                   den kirchlicher Projekt-
                   hilfe

Arbeitsgruppe III Struktur und Organisa-
                   tion der ökumenischen
                   Programme und Projekt-
                   hilfe

Arbeitsgruppe IV   Technische Hilfe für
                   Entwicklungsprojekte der
                   Kirche

Arbeitsgruppe V   Kapitalbeschaffung

CMI/SODEPAX

Conferencia Mundial, CMI/SODEPAX

Tema:
La ayuda ecuménica a los proyectos de
desarrollo

Grupo de trabajo I   El debate sobre el
                      desarrollo

Grupo de trabajo II   Política y métodos
                      de la ayuda de las
                      iglesias a los pro-
                      yectos de desarrollo

Grupo de trabajo III Estructura y organi-
                      zación de la ayuda
                      ecuménica a los pro-
                      gramas y proyectos de
                      desarrollo

Grupo de trabajo IV   Asistencia técnica a
                      los proyectos de
                      desarrollo auspicia-
                      dos por las iglesias

Grupo de trabajo V   Mobilización de
                      fondos

81

WORLD MISSION AND EVANGELISM	MISSION ET EVANGELISATION

Bangkok 1972/73

World Conference of the Commission on
World Mission and Evangelism

Conférence mondiale de la Commission de
mission et d'évangélisation

Theme:
Salvation Today

Thème:
Le salut aujourd'hui

Section I	Culture and Identity	Section I	Culture et idendité
Section II	Salvation and Social Justice	Section II	Salut et justice sociale
Section III	Churches Renewed in Mission	Section III	Le renouveau des Eglises par l'engagement missionnaire

WELTMISSION UND EVANGELISATION

Bangkok 1972/73

Weltkonferenz der Kommission für Weltmission und Evangelisation

Thema:
Das Heil der Welt heute

Sektion I   Kultur und Identität

Sektion II   Heil und soziale Gerechtig-
                 keit

Sektion III   Erneuerung der Kirchen in
                 der Mission

MISION MUNDIAL Y EVANGELIZATION

Conferencia Mundial de la Comisión
de Misión Mundial y Evangelización

Tema:
La Salvación hoy

Sección I   Cultura e identidad

Sección II   Salvación y justicia
                 social

Sección III   La renovación de las
                 iglesias a través de la
                 tarea de la misión

III

III

ECUMENCIAL CENTRE

CENTRE OECUMENIQUE

ORGANIZATIONS AND CHURCH REPRESENTATIONS
LOCATED WITHIN THE ECUMENICAL CENTRE

ORGANISATIONS ET REPRESENTATIONS ECCLE-
SIASTIQUES AYANT LEUR SIEGE AU CENTRE
OECUMENIQUE

World Council of Churches (WCC)

Conseil oecuménique des Eglises (COE)

Lutheran World Federation (LWF)

Fédération luthérienne mondiale (FLM)

World Alliance of Reformed Churches (WARC)

Alliance réformée mondiale (ARM)

World Methodist Council

Conseil méthodiste mondial

Conference of European Churches (CEC)

Conférence des Eglises européennes (KEK)

United Presbyterian Church in the United
States of America (UPCUSA, UPUSA)

Eglise presbytérienne unie aux Etats-Unis
d'Amérique (UPUCSA, UPUSA)

United Church of Christ, United States
of America (UCC, USA)

Eglise unie du Christ, Etats-Unis
d'Amérique (UCC, USA)

Brethren Service

Brethren Service

Churches' Committee on Migrant Workers
(CETMI)

Comité des Eglises auprès des travailleurs
migrants (CETMI)

International Christian Youth Exchange
(ICYE)

Echange international chrétien de
jeunesse (ICYE)

III

ÖKUMENISCHES ZENTRUM

ORGANISATIONEN UND KIRCHENVERTRETUNGEN
MIT SITZ IM ÖKUMENISCHEN ZENTRUM

Ökumenischer Rat der Kirchen (ÖRK)

Lutherischer Weltbund (LWB)

Reformierter Weltbund (RWB)

Weltrat Methodistischer Kirchen

Konferenz Europäischer Kirchen (KEK)

Vereinigte Presbyterianische Kirche in
den Vereinigten Staaten von Amerika
(UPUCSA, UPUSA)

Vereinigte Kirche Christi, Vereinigte
Staaten von Amerika (UCC, USA)

Brethren Service

Ausschuss der Kirchen für Fragen ausländischer Arbeitnehmer (CETMI)

Internationaler Christlicher Jugend-
austausch (ICJA)

III

CENTRO ECUMENICO

ORGANIZACIONES Y REPRESENTACIONES ECLE-
SIASTICAS QUE TIENEN SU SIEDE EN EL
CENTRO ECUMENICO

Consejo Mundial de Iglesias (CMI)

Federación Luterana Mundial (FLM)

Alianza Reformada Mundial (ARM)

Consejo Metodista Mundial

Conferencia de las Iglesias Europeas (KEK)

Iglesia Presbiteriana Unida en los Estados
Unidos de América (UPCUSA, UPUSA)

Iglesia Unida de Cristo, Estados Unidos de
América (UCC,USA)

Brethren Service

Comité de las Iglesias para los Trabajadores
Migrantes (CETMI)

Intercambio internacional Cristiano de
Juventud (ICYE)

Committee on Society, Development and Peace (SODEPAX)	Commission pour la société, le développement et la paix (SODEPAX)
Representative of the Ecumenical Patriarchate of Constantinople	Représentation du Patriarcat oecuménique de Constantinople
Representative of the Moscow Patriarchate	Représentation du Patriarcat de Moscou

Ausschuss für Gesellschaft, Entwicklung und Frieden (SODEPAX)	Comisión para la Sociedad, el Desarrollo y la Paz (SODEPAX)
Vertretung des Ökumenischen Patriarchats von Konstantinopel	Representación del Patriarcado Ecuménico de Constantinopla
Vertretung des Patriarchats von Moskau	Representación del Patriarcado de Moscú

IV

<u>WORLD COUNCIL OF CHURCHES</u>

<u>CONSEIL OECUMENIQUE DES EGLISES</u>

<u>ÖKUMENISCHER RAT DER KIRCHEN</u>

<u>CONSEJO MUNDIAL DE IGLESIAS</u>

1. DIAGRAM OF STRUCTURES

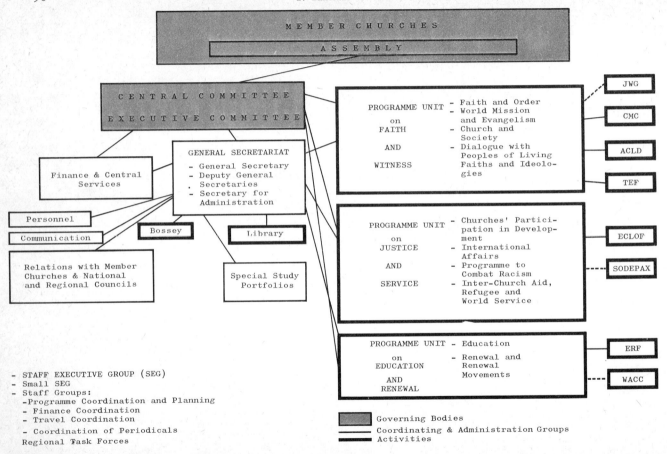

MEMBER CHURCHES

ASSEMBLY

CENTRAL COMMITTEE

EXECUTIVE COMMITTEE

GENERAL SECRETARIAT
- General Secretary
- Deputy General
. Secretaries
- Secretary for
  Administration

Finance & Central
Services

Personnel

Communication

Bossey

Library

Relations with Member
Churches & National
and Regional Councils

Special Study
Portfolios

PROGRAMME UNIT
on
FAITH
AND
WITNESS
- Faith and Order
- World Mission
  and Evangelism
- Church and
  Society
- Dialogue with
  Peoples of Living
  Faiths and Ideolo-
  gies

JWG

CMC

ACLD

TEF

PROGRAMME UNIT
on
JUSTICE
AND
SERVICE
- Churches' Partici-
  pation in Develop-
  ment
- International
  Affairs
- Programme to
  Combat Racism
- Inter-Church Aid,
  Refugee and
  World Service

ECLOF

SODEPAX

PROGRAMME UNIT
on
EDUCATION
AND
RENEWAL
- Education
- Renewal and
  Renewal
  Movements

ERF

WACC

- STAFF EXECUTIVE GROUP (SEG)
- Small SEG
- Staff Groups:
  - Programme Coordination and Planning
  - Finance Coordination
  - Travel Coordination
  - Coordination of Periodicals
Regional Task Forces

Governing Bodies
Coordinating & Administration Groups
Activities

1. ORGANIGRAMME

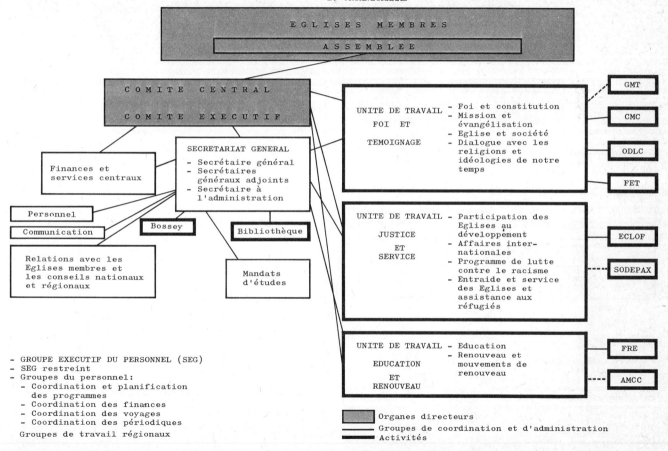

1. SCHEMATISCHE DARSTELLUNG DER STRUKTUR

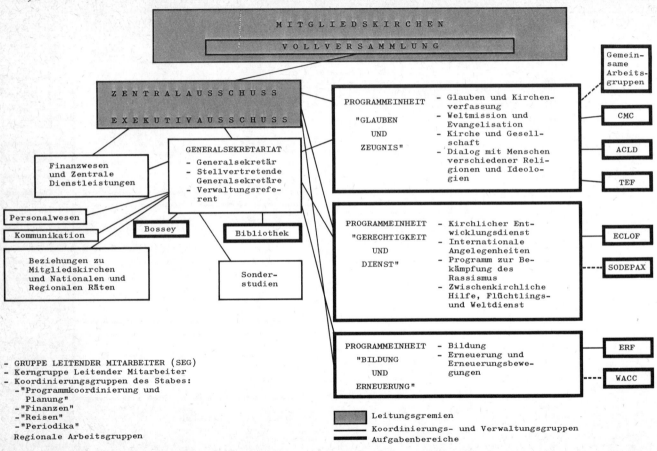

- GRUPPE LEITENDER MITARBEITER (SEG)
- Kerngruppe Leitender Mitarbeiter
- Koordinierungsgruppen des Stabes:
  - "Programmkoordinierung und Planung"
  - "Finanzen"
  - "Reisen"
  - "Periodika"
- Regionale Arbeitsgruppen

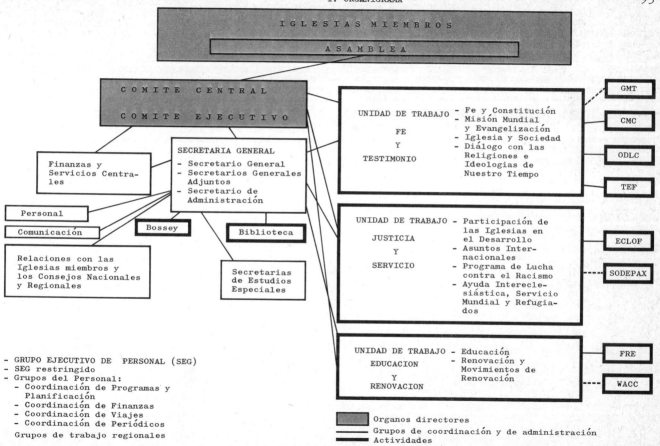

IGLESIAS MIEMBROS
ASAMBLEA

COMITE CENTRAL
COMITE EJECUTIVO

SECRETARIA GENERAL
- Secretario General
- Secretarios Generales Adjuntos
- Secretario de Administración

Finanzas y Servicios Centrales

Personal

Comunicación

Relaciones con las Iglesias miembros y los Consejos Nacionales y Regionales

Bossey

Biblioteca

Secretarias de Estudios Especiales

UNIDAD DE TRABAJO
FE Y TESTIMONIO
- Fe y Constitución
- Misión Mundial y Evangelización
- Iglesia y Sociedad
- Diálogo con las Religiones e Ideologías de Nuestro Tiempo

GMT
CMC
ODLC
TEF

UNIDAD DE TRABAJO
JUSTICIA Y SERVICIO
- Participación de las Iglesias en el Desarrollo
- Asuntos Internacionales
- Programa de Lucha contra el Racismo
- Ayuda Intereclesiástica, Servicio Mundial y Refugiados

ECLOF
SODEPAX

UNIDAD DE TRABAJO
EDUCACION Y RENOVACION
- Educación
- Renovación y Movimientos de Renovación

FRE
WACC

- GRUPO EJECUTIVO DE PERSONAL (SEG)
- SEG restringido
- Grupos del Personal:
  - Coordinación de Programas y Planificación
  - Coordinación de Finanzas
  - Coordinación de Viajes
  - Coordinación de Periódicos

  Grupos de trabajo regionales

Organos directores
Grupos de coordinación y de administración
Actividades

2. DETAILED LIST OF SECRETARIATS AND PROGRAMMES

PROGRAMME UNIT ON FAITH AND WITNESS

1. Commission on Faith and Order

2. Commission on World Mission and Evangelism (CWME)

Programmes

Urban Industrial Mission (UIM)

Rural Agricultural Mission

Education for Mission

Joint Action for Mission (JAM)

Ecumenical Sharing of Personnel (ESP)

Secretary for Evangelism

Secretary for Research and Relations with Orthodox

2. LISTE DES SECRETARIATS ET PROGRAMMES

UNITE "FOI ET TEMOIGNAGE"

1. Commission de foi et constitution

2. Commission de mission et d'évangélisation (CME)

Programmes

Mission en milieu urbain et industriel (MUI)

Mission en milieu rural

Education en vue de la mission

Unité d'action missionnaire (UAM)

Echange oecuménique de personnel (EOP)

Secrétaire à l'évangélisation

Secrétaire chargé de la recherche et des relations avec les orthodoxes

2. LISTE DER SEKRETARIATE UND PROGRAMME

PROGRAMMEINHEIT "GLAUBEN UND ZEUGNIS"

1. Kommission für Glauben und Kirchenverfassung

2. Kommission für Weltmission und Evangelisation (CWME)

   Programme

   Kirchlicher Dienst in der urbanen und industriellen Gesellschaft (UIM)

   Kirchlicher Dienst in ländlichen Gebieten

   Zurüstung für die Mission

   Gemeinsames Handeln in der Mission (JAM)

   Ökumenischer Mitarbeiteraustausch (ESP)

   Referent für Fragen der Verkündigung

   Referent für Forschung und Beziehungen zu den Orthodoxen

2. LISTA DE LAS SECRETARIAS Y PROGRAMAS

UNIDAD "FE Y TESTIMONIO"

1. Comisión de Fe y Constitución

2. Comisión de Misión Mundial y Evangelización (CMME)

   Programas

   Misión Urbana e Industrial (MUI)

   Misión Rural

   Educación para la Misión

   Acción Misionera Conjunta (AMC)

   Intercambio Ecuménico de Personal (IEP)

   Secretario de Evangelización

   Secretario de Investigación y de Relaciones con los Ortodoxos

Study Centres Collective Subscription Scheme	Abonnement collectif aux publications des centres d'études
International Review of Mission	International Review of Mission

Sponsored Agencies	**Institutions parrainées**
Christian Medical Commission (CMC)	Commission médicale chrétienne (CMC)
Theological Education Fund (TEF)	Fonds pour l'enseignement théologique (FET)
Agency for Christian Literature Development (ACLD)	Organisation de développement de la littérature chrétienne (ODLC)

3. Working Group on Church and Society	3. Groupe de travail "Eglise et société"
4. Portfolio on Dialogue with People of Living Faiths and Ideologies (DFI)	4. Secrétariat du dialogue avec les religions et idéologies de notre temps (DRI)
Consultation on the Church and the Jewish People (CCJP)	Comité pour l'Eglise et le peuple juif (CEPJ)

PROGRAMME UNIT ON JUSTICE AND SERVICE	UNITE "JUSTICE ET SERVICE"
1. Commission on Inter-Church Aid, Refugee and World Service (CICARWS)	1. Commission d'entraide et de service des Eglises et d'assistance aux réfugiés (CESEAR)
a) Sub-Commission on the Project System	a) Sous-commission du système des projets

Gemeinschaftsabonnement für die Veröffent-
lichungen der Studienzentren

International Review of Mission

Geförderte Einrichtungen

Christliche Gesundheitskommission (CMC)

Theologischer Ausbildungsfonds (TEF)

Christlicher Entwicklungsdienst für
Literatur (ACLD)

3. Arbeitsgruppe "Kirche und Gesellschaft"

4. Ressort "Dialog mit Menschen verschiedener Religionen und Ideologien"
(DFI)

Ausschuss für die Kirche und das Jü-
dische Volk (CCJP)

PROGRAMMEINHEIT "GERECHTIGKEIT UND DIENST"

1. Kommission für Zwischenkirchliche Hilfe,
Flüchtlings- und Weltdienst (CICARWS)

a) Unterkommission "Projektsystem"

Suscripción Colectiva a las Publicaciones
de los Centros de Estudio

International Review of Mission

Instituciones Patrocinadas

Comisión Médica Cristiana (CMC)

Fondo de Educación Teológica (FET)

Organismo para el Desarrollo de la
Literatura Cristiana (ODLC)

3. Grupo de Trabajo "Iglesia y Sociedad"

4. Secretaría para el Diálogo con las
Religiones e Ideologías de Nuestro
Tiempo (DRI)

Comité para la Iglesia y el Pueblo
Judío (CIPJ)

UNIDAD "JUSTICIA Y SERVICIO"

1. Comisión de Ayuda Intereclesiástica,
Servicio Mundial y Refugiados
(CAISMR)

a) Subcomisión del Sistema de Proyectos

Secretariat for Africa/Asia/Europe/ Latin America/Middle East	Secrétariat de l'Afrique/de l'Asie/ de l'Europe/de l'Amérique latine/ du Moyen Orient
Coordination of the Project System	Coordination du système des projets
Desk for the Registration and Analysis of Projects	Secrétariat d'enregistrement et d'analyse des projets
b) Direct Services Sub-Commission	b) Sous-commission des services directs
Personnel Desk	Secrétariat du personnel
Material Aid Desk	Secrétariat d'aide matérielle
Programme on Social Service	Secrétariat d'action sociale et diaconale
Health and Casa Locarno Programmes	Programmes "santé et Casa Locarno"
Ecumenical Sharing of Personnel (ESP)	Echange oecuménique de personnel (EOP)
Literature Programme	Programme d'aide aux publications
c) Refugee Sub-Commission	c) Sous-commission des réfugiés
d) Sub-Commission on Emergencies and Rehabilitation Programmes	d) Sous-commission de l'aide d'urgence et des programmes de reconstruction

Afrika-, Asien-, Europa-, Lateinamerika-, Nahost-Büro	Secretaría para Africa/Asia/Europa/América Latina/Oriente Medio
Koordinierung des Projektsystems	Coordinación del Sistema de Proyectos
Büro für Projekterfassung und -analyse	Oficina de Registro y Análisis de Proyectos
b) Unterkommission"Direct Services"	b) Subcomisión de Servicios Directos
Büro für Personalfragen	Oficina de Personal
Büro für Materialhilfe	Oficina de Ayuda Material
Ressort für Soziale Fragen und Diakonie	Secretaría de Acción Social y Diaconal
Programmbereich "Gesundheitsdienst und Casa Locarno"	Programas "Salud y Casa Locarno"
Ökumenischer Mitarbeiteraustausch (ESP)	Intercambio Ecuménico de Personal (IEP)
Literaturprogramm	Programa de Publicaciones
c) Unterkommission "Flüchtlingsdienst"	c) Subcomisión de Refugiados
d) Unterkommission "Katastrophenhilfe und Rehabilitationsprogramme"	d) Subcomisión de Ayuda de Urgencia y Programas de Reconstrucción

99

e) Finance Sub-Commission

Ecumenical Church Loan Fund (ECLOF)

Fund for Reconstruction and Reconciliation
in Indochina   1)

Secretariat for Migration   1)

Human Rights Resources Office for
Latin America   1)

2. Commission of the Churches on International Affairs (CCIA)

3. Commission on the Churches' Participation
in Development (CCPD)

Ecumenical Development Fund

Technical Services

Studies

---

1) These services are administratively
attached to CICARWS but responsible to
the Programme Unit on Justice and
Service

e) Sous-commission des finances

Fondation oecuménique pour l'aide aux
Eglises (ECLOF)

Fonds de reconstruction et de récon-
ciliation en Indochine   1)

Secrétariat des migrations   1)

Bureau des droits de l'homme en
Amérique latine   1)

2. Commission des Eglises pour les
affaires internationales (CEAI)

3. Commission de la participation des
Eglises au développement (CPED)

Fonds oecuménique de développement

Services techniques

Etudes

---

1) Ces services sont rattachés administra-
tivement à la CESEAR mais relèvent de
l'Unité "justice et service"

e) Unterkommission "Finanzen"

Ökumenischer Darlehensfonds (ECLOF)

Stiftung für Wiederaufbau und Versöhnung
in Indochina   1)

Sekretariat für Migration   1)

Büro für Menschenrechtsfragen in
Lateinamerika   1)

2. Kommission der Kirchen für Internationale Angelegenheiten (CCIA)

3. Kommission für Kirchlichen Entwicklungsdienst (CCPD)

Ökumenischer Entwicklungsfonds

Technische Hilfe

Studien

---

1) Diese Dienste sind in verwaltungs-
technischer Hinsicht CICARWS ange-
schlossen, unterstehen jedoch der Programmeinheit "Gerechtigkeit und Dienst"

e) Subcomisión de Finanzas

Fondo Ecuménico de Préstamos a las
Iglesias (ECLOF)

Fondo de Reconstrucción y Reconcili-
ación en Indochina   1)

Secretaría de Migraciones   1)

Oficina de Derechos Humanos para
América Latina   1)

2. Comisión de las Iglesias para Asuntos
Internacionales (CIAI)

3. Comisión sobre la Participación de.las
Iglesias en el Desarrollo (CPID)

Fondo Ecuménico de Desarrollo

Servicios Técnicos

Estudios

---

1) Estos servicios están unidos administra-
tivamente a la CAISMR, pero dependen de la
U nidad "Justicia y Servicio"

101

Development Education	Education en vue du développement
Documentation	Documentation

4. Commission on the Programme to Combat Racism (PCR)

   Special Fund to Combat Racism

5. Committee (of the RCC and the WCC) on Society, Development and Peace (SODEPAX)

PROGRAMME UNIT ON EDUCATION AND RENEWAL

1. Staff Working Group on Renewal

  a) Renewal and Renewal Movements

    Women's Desk

    Risk

  b) Ecumenical Youth Service (EYS)/World Youth Projects (WYP)

2. Staff Working Group on Education

4. Commission du programme de lutte contre le racisme (PLR)

   Fonds spécial de lutte contre le racisme

5. Commission (ECR/COE) pour la société, le développement et la paix (SODEPAX)

UNITE "EDUCATION ET RENOUVEAU"

1. Groupe de travail "renouveau"

  a) Renouveau et mouvements de renouveau

    Secrétariat de la femme

    Risk

  b) Service oecuménique de jeunes (SOJ)/ Projets d'entraide mondiale de jeunesse (PEMJ)

2. Groupe de travail "éducation"

Erziehung zur Entwicklungsverantwortung	Educación para el Desarrollo
Dokumentation	Documentación

4. <u>Kommission für das Programm zur Be-
kämpfung des Rassismus (PCR)</u>

   Sonderfonds zur Bekämpfung des Rassis-
mus

5. <u>Gemeinsamer Ausschuss (der R.-K.K.und
des ÖRK) für Gesellschaft, Entwicklung
und Frieden (SODEPAX)</u>

PROGRAMMEINHEIT "BILDUNG UND ERNEUERUNG"

1. <u>Arbeitsgruppe "Erneuerung"</u>

  a) Erneuerung und Erneuerungsbewegungen

     Büro "Frauenarbeit in Kirche und
     Gesellschaft"

     Risk

  b) Ökumenischer Jugenddienst/Weltjugend-
     projekte

2. <u>Arbeitsgruppe "Bildung</u>

---

4. <u>Comisión del Programa de Lucha
contra el Racismo (PLR)</u>

   Fondo Especial de Lucha contra el Racismo

5. <u>Comisión (ICR/CMI) para la Sociedad,
el Desarrollo y la Paz (SODEPAX)</u>

UNIDAD "EDUCACION Y RENOVACION"

1. <u>Grupo de Trabajo "Renovación"</u>

  a) Renovación y Movimientos de
     Renovación

     Oficina de la Mujer

     Risk

  b) Servicio Ecuménico para el Trabajo con
     la Juventud (SEJ)/ Proyectos para la
     Juventud Mundial (PJM)

2. <u>Grupo de Trabajo "Educación"</u>

Office of Education	Bureau de l'éducation
Family Ministries Office, Family Education	Bureau des ministères familiaux, Bureau de l'éducation familiale
Laity and Adult Education	Formation des laïcs et éducation des adultes
Scholarships Office	Secrétariat des bourses

GENERAL SECRETARIAT	SECRETARIAT GENERAL
Administration	Administration
Personnel Office	Service du personnel
Library	Bibliothèque
Portfolio for Biblical Studies	Secrétariat des études bibliques
Humanum Studies	Etudes sur l'humanum
Relations with Member Churches and National and Regional Councils	Relations avec les Eglises membres et les conseils nationaux et régionaux

Department of Communication	Département de communication
Press Section	Section "presse"

Büro für Bildungsfragen	Oficina de Educación
Ressort "Familienfragen"	Oficina de Ministerios Familiares, Oficina de Educación Familiar
Zurüstung von Laien und Erwachsenen- bildung	Formación de Laicos y Educación de Adultos
Stipendienbüro	Oficina de Becas

GENERALSEKRETARIAT	SECRETARIA GENERAL
Verwaltung	Administración
Personalbüro	Oficina de Personal
Bibliothek	Biblioteca
Ressort "Bibelstudien"	Secretaría de Estudios Bíblicos
Humanum-Studien	Estudios sobre "Humanum"
Beziehungen zu Mitgliedskirchen und Nationalen und Regionalen Räten	Relaciones con las Iglesias Miembros y los Consejos Nacionales y Regionales

Abteilung "Kommunikation"	Departamento de Comunicación
Pressebüro	Sección Prensa

Film and Visual Arts Section	Section "films et arts visuels "
Radio/TV Section	Section "radio-télévision "
Language Service	Service linguistique
Publications Section	Section "publications "

Ecumenical Institute, Bossey — **Institut oecuménique, Bossey**

Department of Finance and Central Services — **Département des finances et services centraux**

Accounts Section for Refugee Programme and Travel Loan Funds	Comptabilité "programme des réfugiés et prêts aux voyages"
Accounting, Treasury and Electronic Data Processing	Comptabilité, trésorerie et traitement électronique de l'information
Accounting Section	Section "comptabilité "
Treasury Section	Section "trésorerie"
Electronic Data Processing	Traitement électronique de l'information
Economat	Economat
Mail Service	Courrier

Büro für Film, Bild und Graphik	Sección Cinematografía y Artes Visuales
Rundfunk- und Fernsehbüro	Sección Radio y Televisión
Sprachendienst	Servicio Lingüístico
Verlagsbüro	Sección Publicaciones

Ökumenisches Institut, Bossey	**Instituto Ecuménico, Bossey**
Abteilung "Finanzwesen und Zentrale Dienstleistungen"	**Departamento de Finanzas y Servicios Centrales**
Rechnungsabteilung "Flüchtlingsprogramm und Reisedarlehen"	Sección Contabilidad del Programa de Refugiados y de Préstamos para Viajes
Vermögensverwaltung, Buchhaltung und Elektronische Datenverarbeitung	Contabilidad, Tesorería y Proceso Electrónico de la Información
Buchhaltung	Sección Contabilidad
Vermögensverwaltung und Zahlungen	Sección Tesorería
Elektronische Datenverarbeitung	Proceso Electrónico de la Información
Materialeinkauf und -verwaltung	Economato
Postdienst	Correo

Cleaning Service	Nettoyage
Building Supervision	Entretien et surveillance des locaux
Telephone Exchange	Standard
Telex Service	Télex
Duplication Section	Reproduction des documents
Park and Gardens	Parc et jardins
Reception and Visitors Service	Réception et visites guidées

Gebäudereinigung	Limpieza
Instandhaltung des Gebäudes	Mantenimiento y Vigilancia de los Locales
Telefonzentrale	Centralita
Telex	Telex
Vervielfältigungsabteilung	Reproducción de Documentos
Unterhaltung des Grundstücks	Parque y Jardines
Empfang und Besucherdienst	Recepción y Visitas Acompañadas

109

V

STUDIES

CHURCH AND SOCIETY

The Future of Humanity in a World of
Science-based Technology

Reports

Genetics and the Quality of Life

Population Policy, Social Justice
and the Quality of Life

Violence, Non-Violence and the Struggle
for Social Justice

FAITH AND ORDER

The Authority of the Bible

Baptism, Confirmation and Eucharist

Beyond Intercommunion

Catholicity and Apostolicity

Common Witness and Proselytism

Concepts of Church Unity and Models of
Church Union

V

ETUDES

EGLISE ET SOCIETE

L'avenir de l'homme et de la société dans
un monde technologique

Rapports

La génétique et la qualité de la vie

Politique démographique, justice sociale
et qualité de vie

La violence, la non-violence et la lutte
pour la justice sociale

FOI ET CONSTITUTION

L'autorité de la Bible

Baptême, confirmation et eucharistie

Au-delà de l'intercommunion

Catholicité et apostolicité

Témoignage commun et prosélytisme

Les conceptions de l'unité de l'Eglise
et les modèles d'union d'Eglises

V

<u>STUDIEN</u>

KIRCHE UND GESELLSCHAFT

Die Zukunft des Menschen und der Gesellschaft in einer wissenschaftlich-tech-
nischen Welt

<u>Berichte</u>

Genetik und die Qualität des Lebens

Bevölkerungspolitik, soziale Gerechtigkeit und Qualität des Lebens

Gewalt, Gewaltfreiheit und der Kampf
um soziale Gerechtigkeit

GLAUBEN UND KIRCHENVERFASSUNG

Die Autorität der Bibel

Taufe, Konfirmation und Eucharistie

Interkommunion oder Gemeinschaft?

Katholizität und Apostolizität

Gemeinsames Zeugnis und Proselytismus

Konzepte von Kirchen-Einheit und Modelle
von Kirchen-Union

V

<u>ESTUDIOS</u>

IGLESIA Y SOCIEDAD

El futuro del hombre y de la sociedad en
un mundo tecnológico

<u>Informes</u>

Genética y calidad de vida

Política demográfica, justicia social
y calidad de vida

La violencia, la no violencia y la lucha por
la justicia social

FE Y CONSTITUCION

La autoridad de la Biblia

Bautismo, confirmación y eucaristía

Más allá de la intercomunión

Catolicidad y apostolicidad

Testimonio común y proselitismo

Conceptos de la unidad de la Iglesia y
modelos de unión de iglesias

The Council of Chalcedon and its Significance for the Ecumenical Movement

Le Concile de Chalcédoine et sa signification pour le mouvement oecuménique

Giving Account of the Hope that is in us (Common Expression of Faith: Giving Account of the Hope that is in us, cf. I Peter 3:15)

Rendre raison de l'espérance qui est en nous (l'expression commune de la foi: rendre raison de l'espérance qui est en nous, cf. Pierre 3,15)

Ministry and Sacraments in the Church Local and Universal

Ministère et sacrements dans l'Eglise locale et dans l'Eglise universelle

The Ordained Ministry

Le ministère ordonné

The Ordained Ministry in Ecumenical Perspective

Le ministère ordonné dans la perspective oecuménique

Spirit, Order and Organization

Esprit, structure et organisation

The Unity of the Church and the Unity of Mankind

L'unité de l'Eglise et l'unité de l'humanité

Worship Today

Le culte aujourd'hui

WORLD MISSION AND EVANGELISM

MISSION ET EVANGELISATION

The Missionary Structure of the Congregation

La structure missionnaire de la paroisse

Patterns of Ministry and Theological Education

Formes de ministère et éducation théologique

The Role of Christians in Changing Human Institutions

Le rôle des chrétiens dans l'évolution des institutions humaines

Das Konzil von Chalcedon und seine Bedeutung
für die ökumenische Bewegung

Rechenschaft über die Hoffnung, die in uns
ist (Gemeinsamer Ausdruck des Glaubens:
Rechenschaft von der Hoffnung, die in uns
ist; vgl. 1. Petr. 3,15)

Amt und Sakramente in der lokalen und universalen Kirche

Das ordinierte Amt

Das ordinierte Amt in ökumenischer Per-
spektive

Geist, Ordnung und Organisation

Die Einheit der Kirche und die Einheit der
Menschheit

Gottesdienst heute

WELTMISSION UND EVANGELISATION

Die missionarische Struktur der Gemeinde

Formen kirchlichen Dienstes und theologische
Ausbildung

Die Rolle der Christen im Wandel der
Institutionen

El Concilio de Calcedonia y su significado para el movimiento ecuménico

Dar razón de la esperanza que hay en
nosotros (La expresión común de la fe:
dar razón de la esperanza que hay en
nosotros, cf. I Pedro 3:15)

Ministerio y sacramentos en la Iglesia
local y en la Iglesia universal

El ministerio ordenado

El ministerio ordenado en la perspectiva
ecuménica

Espíritu, estructura y organización

La unidad de la Iglesia y la unidad
de la humanidad

El culto en el día de hoy

MISION MUNDIAL Y EVANGELIZACION

La estructura misionera de la congregación local

Formas de ministerio y educación
teológica

El papel de los cristianos en las
instituciones humanas en transformación

Salvation Today	Le salut aujourd'hui
The Use of the Bible in Evangelism	Le rôle de la Bible dans l'évangélisation
The Word of God and the Church's Missionary Obedience	La Parole de Dieu et l'obéissance missionnaire de l'Eglise
The Word of God and the Living Faiths of Men	La Parole de Dieu et les croyances contemporaines
World Studies on Churches in Mission	Etudes mondiales sur les Eglises en mission

Das Heil der Welt heute

Die Bibel in der evangelistisch-missiona-
rischen Verkündigung

Das Wort Gottes und die missionarische
Verpflichtung der Kirche

Das Wort Gottes und der moderne nicht-
christliche Glaube

Weltweite Studien über Kirchen in der
Mission

La Salvación hoy

El papel de la Biblia en la evangelización

La Palabra de Dios y la obediencia
misionera de la Iglesia

La Palabra de Dios y las religiones
vivas del hombre

Estudio mundial sobre las iglesias en
misión

VI
LIST OF WCC MEMBER CHURCHES, ASSOCIATED CHURCHES AND ASSOCIATED COUNCILS (1)

1. MEMBER CHURCHES

ARGENTINA

Evangelical Church of the River Plata

Evangelical Methodist Church of Argentina

AUSTRALASIA

Methodist Church of Australasia

The United Church in Papua, New Guinea and the Solomon Islands

AUSTRALIA

Churches of Christ in Australia

The Church of England in Australia

———

(1) In each case, the title underlined is the official one.

VI
CONSEIL OECUMENIQUE DES EGLISES: EGLISES MEMBRES, EGLISES ASSOCIEES, CONSEILS ASSOCIES (1)

1. EGLISES MEMBRES

ARGENTINE

Eglise évangélique du Rio de la Plata

Eglise évangélique méthodiste d'Argentine

AUSTRALASIE

Eglise méthodiste d'Australasie

Eglise unie de Papouasie, de Nouvelle-Guinée et des îles Salomon

AUSTRALIE

Eglises du Christ en Australie

Eglise anglicane en Australie

———

(1) Les titres soulignés sont les titres officiels.

VI

ÖKUMENISCHER RAT DER KIRCHEN: MITGLIEDS-
KIRCHEN, ANGESCHLOSSENE KIRCHEN, ANGE-
SCHLOSSENE RÄTE (1)

1. MITGLIEDSKIRCHEN

ARGENTINIEN

Evangelische Kirche am La Plata

Argentinische Evangelisch-Methodistische Kirche

AUSTRALASIEN

Methodistische Kirche von Australasien

Vereinigte Kirche in Papua, auf Neu-
guinea und den Salomon-Inseln

AUSTRALIEN

Kirchen Christi in Australien

Kirche von England in Australien

---

(1) Offizielle Titel unterstrichen.

VI

CONSEJO MUNDIAL DE IGLESIAS: IGLESIAS
MIEMBROS, IGLESIAS ASOCIADAS, CONSEJOS
ASOCIADOS (1)

1. IGLESIAS MIEMBROS

ARGENTINA

Iglesia Evangélica del Río de la Plata

Iglesia Evangélica Metodista Argentina

AUSTRALASIA

Iglesia Metodista de Australasia

Iglesia Unida de Papua
Nueva Guinea e Islas Salomón

AUSTRALIA

Iglesias de Cristo en Australia

Iglesias Anglicana en Australia

---

(1) Los títulos subrayados son los títulos
oficiales

The Congregational Union of Australia	Union congrégationaliste d'Australie
The Presbyterian Church of Australia	Eglise presbytérienne d'Australie

AUSTRIA / AUTRICHE

Old Catholic Church of Austria	Eglise vieille-catholique d'Autriche
Evangelical Church of the Augsburg and Helvetic Confession in Austria	Eglise évangélique de la confession d'Augsbourg et de la confession helvétique en Autriche

BELGIUM / BELGIQUE

Protestant Church of Belgium	Eglise protestante de Belgique
Reformed Church of Belgium	Eglise réformée de Belgique

BRAZIL / BRESIL

Igreja Episcopal do Brasil Episcopal Church of Brazil	Eglise épiscopale du Brésil
Igreja Evangélica de Confissão Lutherana do Brasil Evangelical Church of Lutheran Confession in Brazil	Eglise évangélique de la confession luthérienne au Brésil
Igreja Evangélica Pentecostal "O Brasil para Cristo" The Evangelical Pentecostal Church "Brazil for Christ"	Eglise évangélique pentecôtiste "Brésil pour Christ"

Kongregationalistische Vereinigung von Australien	Unión Congregacionalista de Australia
Presbyterianische Kirche von Australien	Iglesia Presbiteriana de Australia
ÖSTERREICH	AUSTRIA
Alt-Katholische Kirche Österreichs	Iglesia Vieja Católica de Austria
Evangelische Kirche A.u.H.B. in Österreich	Iglesia Evangélica de la Confesión de Ausburgo y de la Confesión Helvética en Austria
BELGIEN	BELGICA
Protestantische Kirche von Belgien	Iglesia Protestante de Bélgica
Reformierte Kirche von Belgien	Iglesia Reformada de Bélgica
BRASILIEN	BRASIL
Bischöfliche Kirche von Brasilien	Iglesia Episcopal del Brasil
Evangelische Kirche L.B. in Brasilien	Iglesia Evangélica de la Confesión Luterana en el Brasil
Evangelische Pfingstkirche "Brasilien für Christus"	Iglesia Evangélica Pentecostal "Brasil para Cristo"

Igreja Metodista do Brasil
Methodist Church of Brazil

Igreja Reformada Latino Americana
The Latin American Reformed Church

BULGARIA

Bulgarian Orthodox Church

BURMA

Burma Baptist Convention

Church of the Province of Burma

CAMEROON

Evangelical Church of Cameroon

Presbyterian Church of Cameroon

Presbyterian Church in Cameroon

Union of Baptist Churches of Cameroon

CANADA

The Anglican Church of Canada

Eglise méthodiste du Brésil

Eglise réformée latino-américaine

BULGARIE

Eglise orthodoxe bulgare

BIRMANIE

Convention baptiste de Birmanie

Eglise de la province de Birmanie

CAMEROUN

Eglise évangélique du Cameroun

Eglise presbytérienne camerounaise

Eglise presbytérienne au Cameroun

Union des Eglises baptistes du Cameroun

CANADA

Eglise anglicane du Canada

Methodistische Kirche von Brasilien	Iglesia Metodista del Brasil
Lateinamerikanische Reformierte Kirche	Iglesia Reformada Latinoamericana

BULGARIEN

Bulgarische Orthodoxe Kirche

BIRMA

Birmanischer Baptistenbund

Kirche der Provinz Birma

KAMERUN

Evangelische Kirche von Kamerun

Kamerunische Presbyterianische Kirche

Presbyterianische Kirche in Kamerun

Union der Baptistenkirchen von Kamerun

KANADA

Anglikanische Kirche von Kanada

BULGARA

Iglesia Ortodoxa Búlgara

BIRMANIA

Convención Bautista de Birmania

Iglesia de la Provincia de Birmania

CAMERUN

Iglesia Evangélica del Camerún

Iglesia Presbiteriana Camerunesa

Iglesia Presbiteriana en Camerún

Unión de las Iglesias Bautistas de Camerún

CANADA

Iglesia Anglicana del Canada

121

Canadian Yearly Meeting of the Society of Friends	Convention annuelle canadienne de la Société des amis
Christian Church (Disciples of Christ)	Eglise chrétienne (Disciples du Christ)
The Evangelical Lutheran Church of Canada	Eglise évangélique luthérienne du Canada
The Presbyterian Church in Canada	Eglise presbytérienne au Canada
The United Church of Canada	Eglise unie du Canada

CENTRAL AFRICA   AFRIQUE CENTRALE

Church of the Province of Central Africa — Eglise de la province d'Afrique centrale

CHILE   CHILI

Evangelical-Lutheran Church in Chile — Eglise évangélique luthérienne au Chili

Pentecostal Church of Chili — Eglise pentecôtiste du Chili

Pentecostal Mission Church — Eglise missionnaire pentecôtiste

CHINA   CHINE

China Baptist Council — Conseil baptiste de Chine

Kanadische Jahresversammlung der Ge-sellschaft der Freunde	Convención Anual Canadiense de la Sociedad de los Amigos
Christliche Kirche (Jünger Christi)	Iglesia Cristiana (Discípulos de Cristo)
Evangelisch-Lutherische Kirche von Kanada	Iglesia Evangélica Luterana del Canadá
Presbyterianische Kirche in Kanada	Iglesia Presbiteriana en el Canadá
Vereinigte Kirche von Kanada	Iglesia Unida del Canadá

ZENTRALAFRIKA

Kirche der Zentralafrikanischen Provinz

CHILE

Evangelisch-Lutherische Kirche in Chile

Pfingstkirche von Chile

Pfingstkirchliche Mission

CHINA

Chinesischer Baptistenrat

AFRICA CENTRAL

Iglesia de la Provincia de Africa Central

CHILE

Iglesia Evangélica luterana en Chile

Iglesia Pentecostal de Chile

Misión Iglesia Pentecostal

CHINA

Consejo Bautista de China

Chung-Hua Chi-Tu Chiao-Hui
Church of Christ in China

Chung-Hua Sheng Kung Hui
Anglican Church in China

Hua Pei Kung Lu Hui
Congregational Church in North China

CONGO

Evangelical Church of the Congo

CYPRUS

Church of Cyprus

CZECHOSLOVAKIA

Ceskobratrska církev evangeliská
Evangelical Church of Czech Brethren

Ceskoslovenská církev husitská
Czechoslovak Hussite Church

Pravoslavná církev v CSSR
Orthodox Church of Czechoslovakia

Ref. krest. církev na Slovensku
Reformed Christian Church in Slovakia

Slezská církev evangeliska a.v.
Silesian Evangelical Church of the
Augsburg Confession

Eglise du Christ en Chine

Eglise anglicane en Chine

Eglise congrégationaliste de la Chine du
Nord

CONGO

Eglise évangélique du Congo

CHYPRE

Eglise de Chypre

TCHECOSLOVAQUIE

Eglise évangélique des frères tchèques

Eglise hussite tchécoslovaque

Eglise orthodoxe de Tchécoslovaquie

Eglise chrétienne réformée en Slovaquie

Eglise évangélique de la confession
d'Augsbourg en Silésie

Kirche Christi in China	Iglesia de Cristo en China
Anglikanische Kirche in China	Iglesia Anglicana en China
Kongregationalistische Kirche in Nord-china	Iglesia Congregacionalista de China del Norte

KONGO / **CONGO**

Evangelische Kirche des Kongo	Iglesia Evangélica del Congo

ZYPERN / **CHIPRE**

Kirche von Zypern	Iglesia de Chipre

TSCHECHOSLOWAKEI / **CHECOSLOVAQUIA**

Evangelische Kirche der Böhmischen Brüder	Iglesia Evangélica de los Hermanos Checoslovacos
Tschechoslowakische Hussiten-Kirche	Iglesia Husita Checoslovaca
Orthodoxe Kirche der Tschechoslowakei	Iglesia Ortodoxa de Checoslovaquia
Reformierte Kirche der Slowakei	Iglesia Cristiana Reformada en Eslovaquia
Schlesische Evangelische Kirche A.B.	Iglesia Evangélica de la Confesión de Ausburgo en Silesia

Slovenská evanjelicka církev a.v. v CSSR
Slovak Evangelical Church of the Augsburg
Confession in the CSSR

Eglise évangélique slovaque de la
confession d'Augsbourg en Tchécoslovaquie

DAHOMEY

The Protestant Methodist Church in Dahomey
and Togo

DAHOMEY

Eglise protestante méthodiste au
Dahomey-Togo

DENMARK

Det danske Baptistsamfund
The Baptist Union of Denmark

DANEMARK

Union baptiste du Danemark

Den evangelisk-lutherske Folkekirke i
Danmark
Evangelical Lutheran Church in Denmark

Eglise évangélique luthérienne du
Danemark

EAST AFRICA

Presbyterian Church of East Africa

AFRIQUE ORIENTALE

Eglise presbytérienne d'Afrique orientale

EGYPT

Coptic Orthodox Church

EGYPTE

Eglise orthodoxe copte

Evangelical Church - The Synod of the Nile

Eglise évangélique copte, Synode du Nil

Greek Orthodox Patriarchate of Alexandria

Patriarcat orthodoxe grec d'Alexandrie

ETHIOPIA

Ethiopian Orthodox Church

ETHIOPIE

Eglise orthodoxe éthiopienne

Slowakische Evangelische Kirche A.B. in der CSSR	Iglesia Evangélica Eslovaca de la Confesión de Ausburgo en Checoslavaquia

DAHOME

Protestantisch-Methodistische Kirche in Dahome-Togo	Iglesia Protestante Metodista en el Dahomey y en el Togo

DÄNEMARK

DAHOMEY

Baptistenunion von Dänemark	Unión Bautista de Dinamarca
Evangelisch-Lutherische Volkskirche in Dänemark	Iglesia Evangélica Luterana de Dinamarca

DINAMARCA

OSTAFRIKA

AFRICA ORIENTAL

Presbyterianische Kirche von Ostafrika	Iglesia Presbiteriana de Africa Oriental

ÄGYPTEN

EGIPTO

Koptische Orthodoxe Kirche	Iglesia Ortodoxa Copta
Koptische Evangelische Kirche (Nil-Synode)	Iglesia Evangélica Copta, Sínodo del Nilo
Griechisch-Orthodoxes Patriarchat von Alexandrien	Patriarcado Ortodoxo Griego de Alejandría

ÄTHIOPIEN

ETIOPE

Äthiopische Orthodoxe Kirche	Iglesia Ortodoxa Etíope

FINLAND

Suomen Evankelis-Luterilainen Kirkko
Evangelical Lutheran Church of Finland

FRANCE

Evangelical Church of the Augsburg
Confession of Alsace and Lorraine

Evangelical Lutheran Church of
France

Reformed Church of Alsace and Lorraine

Reformed Church of France

GABON

Evangelical Church of Gabon

FEDERAL REPUBLIC OF GERMANY

Catholic Diocese of the Old Catholics
in Germany

Moravian Church

Evangelical Church in Germany

FINLANDE

Eglise évangélique luthérienne de Finlande

FRANCE

Eglise de la confession d'Augsbourg
d'Alsace et de Lorraine

Eglise évangélique luthérienne de
France

Eglise réformée d'Alsace et de Lorraine

Eglise réformée de France

GABON

Eglise évangélique du Gabon

REPUBLIQUE FEDERALE D'ALLEMAGNE

Diocèse catholique des vieux-catholiques
en Allemagne

Eglise des frères moraves

Eglise évangélique en Allemagne

FINNLAND

Evangelisch-Lutherische Kirche von
Finnland

FRANKREICH

Kirche A.B. von Elsass und Lothringen

Evangelisch-Lutherische Kirche von
Frankreich

Reformierte Kirche von Elsass und
Lothringen

Reformierte Kirche von Frankreich

GABUN

Evangelische Kirche von Gabun

BUNDESREPUBLIK DEUTSCHLAND

Katholisches Bistum der Alt-Katholiken
in Deutschland

Evangelische Brüder-Unität

Evangelische Kirche Deutschland

FINLANDIA

Iglesia Evangélica Luterana de Finlandia

FRANCIA

Iglesia de la Confesión de Ausburgo
de Alsacia y Lorena

Iglesia Evangélica Luterana de Francia

Iglesia Reformada de Alsacia y Lorena

Iglesia Reformada de Francia

GABON

Iglesia Evangélica del Gabón

REPUBLICA FEDERAL DE ALEMANIA

Diócesis Católica de los Viejos Católicos
en Alemania

Iglesia de los Hermanos Moravos

Iglesia Evangélica en Alemania

Membership of the Evangelical Church
in Germany:

Evangelical Church in Baden
Evangelical Lutheran Church in Bavaria
Evangelical Church in Berlin-Brandenburg
Evangelical Church in Brunswick
Evangelical Church of Bremen
Evangelical Lutheran Church of Eutin
Evangelical Lutheran Church in the State of
Hamburg
Evangelical Lutheran Church of Hanover
Evangelical Church in Hesse and Nassau
Evangelical Church of Hesse Electorate-
Waldeck
Church of Lippe
Evangelical Lutheran Church in Lübeck
Evangelical-Reformed Church in Northwestern
Germany
Evangelical Lutheran Church in Oldenburg
United Protestant Evangelical Christian
Church of the Palatinate
Evangelical Church of the Rhineland
Evangelical Lutheran Church of Schaumburg-
Lippe
Evangelical Lutheran Church of Schleswig-
Holstein
Evangelical Church of Westphalia
Evangelical Church in Würtemberg

Mennonite Church

Eglises membres de l'EKD:

Eglise évangélique de Bade
Eglise évangélique luthérienne de Bavière
Eglise évangélique de Berlin-Brandebourg
Eglise évangélique luthérienne du Brunswick
Eglise évangélique de Brême
Eglise évangélique luthérienne d'Eutin
Eglise évangélique luthérienne de
l'Etat de Hambourg
Eglise évangélique luthérienne du Hanovre
Eglise évangélique de Hesse et de Nassau
Eglise évangélique de Hesse-
Waldeck
Eglise de Lippe
Eglise évangélique luthérienne de Lübeck
Eglise évangélique réformée d'Allemagne
du Nord-Ouest
Eglise évangélique luthérienne d'Oldenbourg
Eglise protestante évangélique chrétienne
unie du Palatinat
Eglise évangélique de Rhénanie
Eglise évangélique luthérienne de
Schaumbourg-Lippe
Eglise évangélique luthérienne du
Schleswig-Holstein
Eglise évangélique de Westphalie
Eglise évangélique du Wurtemberg

Union des communautés mennonites
allemandes

Mitgliedskirchen der EKD:

Evangelische Landeskirche in Baden
Evangelisch-Lutherische Kirche in Bayern
Evangelische Kirche in Berlin-Brandenburg
Evangelisch-Lutherische Landeskirche in
Braunschweig
Bremische Evangelische Kirche
Evangelisch-Lutherische Landeskirche Eutin
Evangelisch-Lutherische Kirche im Ham-
burgischen Staate
Evangelisch-Lutherische Landeskirche Hannovers
Evangelische Kirche in Hessen und Nassau
Evangelische Kirche von Kurhessen-Waldeck
Lippische Landeskirche
Evangelisch-Lutherische Kirche in Lübeck
Evangelisch-Reformierte Kirche in Nord-
westdeutschland
Evangelisch-Lutherische Kirche in Oldenburg
Vereinigte Protestantisch-Evangelisch-
Christliche Kirche der Pfalz
Evangelische Kirche im Rheinland
Evangelisch-Lutherische Landeskirche
Schaumburg-Lippe
Evangelisch-Lutherische Landeskirche
Schleswig-Holsteins
Evangelische Kirche von Westfalen
Evangelische Landeskirche in Württemberg

Vereinigung der Deutschen Mennonitenge-
meinden

Iglesias miembros de la EKD:

Iglesia Evangélica de Baden
Iglesia Evangélica Luterana de Baviera
Iglesia Evangélica de Berlín-Brandeburgo
Iglesia Evangélica Luterana de
Brunswick
Iglesia Evangélica de Brema
Iglesia Evangélica Luterana de Eutin
Iglesia Evangélica Luterana del Estado
de Hamburgo
Iglesia Evangélica Luterana de Hanover
Iglesia Evangélica de Hesse y Nassau
Iglesia Evangélica de Hesse-Waldeck
Iglesia de Lippe
Iglesia Evangélica Luterana de Lübeck
Iglesia Evangélica Reformada de
Alemania del Noroeste
Iglesia Evangélica Luterana de Oldenburgo
Iglesia Protestante Evangélica Cristiana
Unida del Palatinado
Iglesia Evangélica de Renania
Iglesia Evangélica Luterana de Schaum-
burgo-Lippe
Iglesia Evangélica Luterana de Schleswig-
Holstein
Iglesia Evangélica de Westfalia
Iglesia Evangélica de Würtemberg

Unión de las Comunidades Menonitas
Alemanas

GERMAN DEMOCRATIC REPUBLIC	REPUBLIQUE DEMOCRATIQUE ALLEMANDE
Federation of the Evangelical Churches in the GDR	Fédération des Eglises évangéliques en République démocratique allemande
Membership of the Federation of the Evangelical Churches in the GDR:	
Evangelical Church of Anhalt	Eglise évangélique d'Anhalt
Evangelical Church in Berlin-Brandenburg	Eglise évangélique de Berlin-Brandebourg
Evangelical Church of the Görlitz Region	Eglise évangélique du territoire ecclésiastique de Görlitz
Evangelical Church of Greifs-wald	Eglise évangélique de Greifswald
Evangelical Lutheran Church of Mecklenburg	Eglise évangélique luthérienne du Mecklembourg
Evangelical Church of the Province of Saxony	Eglise évangélique de la province ecclésiastique de Saxe
Evangelical Lutheran Church of Saxony	Eglise évangélique luthérienne de Saxe
Evangelical Lutheran Church in Thuringia	Eglise évangélique luthérienne de Thuringe
Moravian Church	Eglise des frères moraves
Federation of the Old Catholic Church in the GDR	Fédération de l'Eglise vieille-catholique en République démocratique allemande
GHANA	GHANA
Evangelical Presbyterian Church	Eglise presbytérienne évangélique
The Methodist Church, Ghana	Eglise méthodiste, Ghana

DEUTSCHE DEMOKRATISCHE REPUBLIK	REPUBLICA DEMOCRATICA ALEMANA
Bund der Evangelischen Kirchen in der Deutschen Demokratischen Republik	Federación de Iglesias Evangélicas en la República Democrática Alemana
Evangelische Landeskirche Anhalts	Iglesia Evangélica de Anhalt
Evangelische Kirche in Berlin-Brandenburg	Iglesia Evangélica de Berlín-Brandeburgo
Evangelische Kirche des Görlitzer Kirchengebietes	Iglesia Evangélica del Territorio Eclesiástico de Görlitz
Evangelische Landeskirche Greifswald	Iglesia Evangélica de Greifswald
Evangelisch-Lutherische Landeskirche Mecklenburgs	Iglesia Evangélica Luterana de Mecklemburgo
Evangelische Kirche der Kirchenprovinz Sachsens	Iglesia Evangélica de la Provincia Eclesiástica de Sajonia
Evangelisch-Lutherische Landeskirche Sachsen	Iglesia Evangélica Luterana de Sajonia
Evangelisch-Lutherische Kirche in Thüringen	Iglesia Evangélica Luterana de Turingia
Evangelische Brüder-Unität (Distrikt Herrnhut)	Iglesia de los Hermanos Moravos
Gemeindeverband der Alt-Katholischen Kirche in der Deutschen Demokratischen Republik	Federación de la Iglesia Vieja Católica en la República Democrática Alemana
GHANA	GHANA
Evangelische Presbyterianische Kirche	Iglesia Presbiteriana Evangélica, Ghana
Methodistische Kirche, Ghana	Iglesia Metodista, Ghana

Presbyterian Church of Ghana	Eglise presbytérienne du Ghana

GREECE

Ekklesia tes Ellados
Church of Greece

Hellenike Evangelike Ekklesia
Greek Evangelical Church

HONG KONG

The Church of Christ in China,
The Hong Kong Council

HUNGARY

Magyarországi Baptista Egyház
Baptist Church in Hungary

Magyarországi Evangélikus Egyház
Lutheran Church in Hungary

Magyarországi Reformatus Egyház
Reformed Church in Hungary

ICELAND

Evangelical Lutheran Church of Iceland

INDIA

Church of North India

GRECE

Eglise de Grèce

Eglise évangélique grecque

HONG-KONG

Eglise du Christ en Chine, Conseil
de Hong-Kong

HONGRIE

Eglise baptiste de Hongrie

Eglise luthérienne de Hongrie

Eglise réformée de Hongrie

ISLANDE

Eglise évangélique luthérienne d'Islande

INDE

Eglise de l'Inde du Nord

Presbyterianische Kirche von Ghana	Iglesia Presbiteriana de Ghana

GRIECHENLAND

GRECIA

Kirche von Griechenland	Iglesia de Grecia
Griechische Evangelische Kirche	Iglesia Evangélica Griega

HONGKONG

HONG-KONG

Rat der Kirche Christi in China, Hongkong	Iglesia de Cristo en China, Consejo de Hong-Kong

UNGARN

HUNGRIA

Baptistenkirche in Ungarn	Iglesia Bautista de Hungría
Evangelisch-Lutherische Kirche in Ungarn	Iglesia Luterana de Hungría
Reformierte Kirche in Ungarn	Iglesia Reformada de Hungría

ISLAND

ISLANDIA

Evangelisch-Lutherische Kirche von Island	Iglesia Evangélica Luterana de Islandia

INDIAN

INDIA

Kirche von Nordindien	Iglesia de la India del Norte

Church of South India	Eglise de l'Inde du Sud
Federation of Evangelical Lutheran Churches in India	Fédération des Eglises évangéliques luthériennes en Inde
Mar Thoma Syrian Church of Malabar	Eglise syrienne Mar Thoma de Malabar
The Orthodox Syrian Church, Catholicate of the East	Eglise orthodoxe syrienne, Catholicat d'Orient
The Samavesam of Telugu Baptist Churches	Convention des Eglises baptistes Telegu

INDONESIA   INDONESIE

Gereja Batak Karo Protestan Karo Batak Protestant Church	Eglise protestante Karo Batak
Gereja-Gereja Kristen Java Christian Churches of Java	Eglises chrétiennes de Java
Gereja Kalimantan Evangelis Kalimantan Evangelical Church	Eglise évangélique de Kalimantan
Gereja Kristen Jawi Wetan Christian Church of East Java	Eglise chrétienne de Java-Est
Gereja Kristen Injili di Irian Barat Evangelical Christian Church in West Irian	Eglise chrétienne évangélique en Irian occidental
Gereja Kristen Indonesia Indonesian Christian Church	Eglise chrétienne d'Indonésie
Gereja Kristen Pasundan Pasundan Christian Church	Eglise chrétienne de Pasundan

Kirche von Südindien	Iglesia de la India del Sur
Bund Evangelisch-Lutherischer Kirchen in Indien	Federación de Iglesias Evangélicas Luteranas en la India
Syrische Mar-Thoma-Kirche von Malabar	Iglesia Siria Mar Thoma de Malabar
Orthodoxe Syrische Kirche, Katholikat des Ostens	Iglesia Ortodoxa Siria, Catolicado de Oriente
Bund der Telugu-Baptisten-Gemeinden	Convención de las Iglesias Bautistas de Telegu

INDONESIEN	INDONESIA
Protestantische Karo-Batak-Kirche	Iglesia Protestante Karo Batak
Christliche Kirchen von Java	Iglesias Cristianas de Java
Evangelische Kirche auf Kalimantan	Iglesia Evangélica de Kalimantan
Christliche Kirche von Ostjava	Iglesia Evangélica del Este de Java
Christlich -Evangelische Kirche in Westirian	Iglesia Cristiana Evangélica en Irián Occidental
Indonesische Christliche Kirche	Iglesia Cristiana de Indonesia
Sundanesische Christliche Kirche (Westjava)	Iglesia Cristiana de Pasundan

<u>Gereja Kristen Sulawesi Tengah</u> Christian Church in Mid-Sulawesi	Eglise chrétienne du centre de Sulawesi
<u>Gereja Masehi Injili Minahasa</u> Christian Evangelical Church in Minahasa	Eglise chrétienne évangélique de Minahasa
<u>Gereja Masehi Injili di Timor</u> Protestant Evangelical Church in Timor	Eglise protestante évangélique à Timor
<u>Gereja Protestan di Indonesia</u> Protestant Church in Indonesia	Eglise protestante en Indonésie
<u>Gereja Protestan Maluku</u> Protestant Church of the Moluccas	Eglise protestante des Moluques
<u>Gereja Toraja</u> Toraja Church	Eglise Toraja
<u>Huria Kristen Batak Protestan</u> Protestant Christian Batak Church	Eglise chrétienne protestante Batak
<u>Banua Niha Keriso Protestan Nias</u> The Church of Nias	Eglise de Nias
<u>Gereja Kristen Protestan Simalungun</u> Simalungun Protestant Christian Church	Eglise chrétienne protestante Simalungun
<u>Huria Kristen Indonesia</u> Indonesian Christian Church	Eglise chrétienne d'Indónésie
<u>Gereja Masehi Injili Sangihe. Dan Talaud</u> <u>(GMIST)</u> Church of Sangi Talaud, Indonesia	Eglise des îles Sangi et Talaud, Indónésie

<u>IRAN</u>:

Synod of the Evangelical Church of Iran

<u>IRAN</u>

Synode de l'Eglise évangélique d'Iran

Christliche Kirche in Mittelsulawesi	Iglesia Cristiana del Centro de Sulawesi
Christlich-Evangelische Kirche in Minahasa	Iglesia Cristiana Evangélica de Minahasa
Christlich-Evangelische Kirche auf Timor	Iglesia Protestante Evangélica en Timor
Protestantische Kirche in Indonesien	Iglesia Protestante en Indonesia
Protestantische Kirche der Molukken	Iglesia Protestante de las Molucas
Toraja-Kirche	Iglesia Toraja
Protestantisch-Christliche Batak-Kirche	Iglesia Cristiana Protestante Batak
Kirche von Nias	Iglesia de Nias
Protestantisch-Christliche Kirche Simalungun	Iglesia Cristiana Protestante Simalungun
Indonesische Christliche Kirche	Iglesia Cristiana de Indonesia
Kirche der Sangi- und Talaud - Inseln, Indonesien	Iglesia de las islas Sangi y Taland, Indonesia

IRAN

Synode der Evangelischen Kirche von Iran	Sínodo de la Iglesia Evangélica del Irán

ITALY

Chiesa Evangelica Internazionale
The International Evangelical Church

Chiesa Evangelica Metodista d'Italia
Evangelical Methodist Church of Italy

Chiesa Evangelica Valdese
Waldensian Church

JAMAICA

The Moravian Church in Jamaica

The United Church of Jamaica and Grand
Cayman

JAPAN

Nippon Kirisuto Kyodan
The United Church of Christ in Japan

Japanese Orthodox Church

Nippon Sei Ko Kai
Anglican Episcopal Church in Japan

JERUSALEM

Greek Orthodox Patriarchate of Jerusalem

ITALIE

Eglise évangélique internationale

Eglise évangélique méthodiste d'Italie

Eglise évangélique vaudoise

JAMAÏQUE

Eglise morave en Jamaïque

Eglise unie de la Jamaïque et du Grand
Caïman

JAPON

Eglise unie du Christ au Japon

Eglise orthodoxe japonaise

Eglise anglicane épiscopale au Japon

JERUSALEM

Patriarcat orthodoxe grec de Jérusalem

ITALIEN	**ITALIA**
Evangelische Internationale Kirche	Iglesia Evangélica Internacional
Evangelisch-Methodistische Kirche von Italien	Iglesia Evangélica Metodista de Italia
Evangelische Waldenser-Kirche	Iglesia Evangélica Valdense
JAMAIKA	**JAMAICA**
Brüder-Unität auf Jamaika	Iglesia Morava en Jamaica
Vereinigte Kirche von Jamaika und Grand Cayman	Iglesia Unida de Jamaica y Gran Caimán
JAPAN	**JAPON**
Vereinigte Kirche Christi in Japan	Iglesia Unida de Cristo en el Japón
Japanische Orthodoxe Kirche	Iglesia Ortodoxa Japonesa
Anglikanisch-Bischöfliche Kirche in Japan	Iglesia Anglicana Episcopal en el Japón
JERUSALEM	**JERUSALEN**
Griechisch-Orthodoxes Patriarchat von Jerusalem	Patriarcado Ortodoxo Griego de Jerusalén

141

KENYA

Church of the Province of Kenya

The Methodist Church in Kenya

KOREA

The Korean Methodist Church

The Presbyterian Church in the Republic
of Korea

The Presbyterian Church of Korea

LEBANON

Armenian Apostolic Church

Union of the Armenian Evangelical
Churches in the Near East

LESOTHO

Lesotho Evangelical Church

LIBERIA

Lutheran Church in Liberia

KENYA

Eglise de la province du Kenya

Eglise méthodiste au Kenya

COREE

Eglise méthodiste de Corée

Eglise presbytérienne en République de
Corée

Eglise presbytérienne de Corée

LIBAN

Eglise apostolique arménienne

Union des Eglises évangéliques armé-
niennes au Proche-Orient

LESOTHO

Eglise évangélique du Lesotho

LIBERIA

Eglise luthérienne au Libéria

KENIA

Kirche der Provinz Kenia

Methodistische Kirche in Kenia

KOREA

Koreanische Methodistische Kirche

Presbyterianische Kirche in der Republik
Korea

Presbyterianische Kirche von Korea

LIBANON

Armenische Apostolische Kirche

Vereinigung der Armenischen Evangelischen
Kirchen im Nahen Osten

LESOTHO

Evangelische Kirche in Lesotho

LIBERIA

Lutherische Kirche in Liberia

KENIA

Iglesia de la Provincia de Kenia

Iglesia Metodista en Kenia

COREA

Iglesia Metodista de Corea

Iglesia Presbiteriana en la República
de Corea

Iglesia Presbiteriana de Corea

LIBANO

Iglesia Apostólica Armenia

Unión de las Iglesias Evangélicas
Armenias en el Cercano Oriente

LESOTHO

Iglesia Evangélica de Lesotho

LIBERIA

Iglesia Luterana en Liberia

MADAGASCAR

Church of Jesus Christ in Madagascar

Malagasy Lutheran Church

MALAYSIA AND SINGAPORE

The Methodist Church in Malaysia and
Singapore

MEXICO

Methodist Church of Mexico

NETHERLANDS

Algemene Doopsgezinde Sociëteit
General Mennonite Society

Evangelisch Lutherse Kerk
Evangelical Lutheran Church

De Gereformeerde Kerken in Nederland
The Reformed Churches in the Netherlands

Nederlandse Hervormde Kerk
Netherlands Reformed Church

Oud-Katholieke Kerk van Nederland
Old Catholic Church of the Netherlands

Remonstrantse Broederschap
Remonstrant Brotherhood

MADAGASCAR

Eglise de Jésus-Christ à Madagascar

Eglise luthérienne malgache

MALAISIE ET SINGAPOUR

Eglise méthodiste en Malaisie et à
Singapour

MEXIQUE

Eglise méthodiste du Mexique

PAYS-BAS

Société générale des mennonites

Eglise évangélique luthérienne

Eglises réformées aux Pays-Bas

Eglise réformée des Pays-Bas

Eglise vieille-catholique des Pays-Bas

Frères de la remonstrance

MADAGASKAR

Kirche Christi in Madagaskar

Madagassische Lutherische Kirche

MALAYSIA UND SINGAPUR

Methodistische Kirche in Malaysia und
Singapur

MEXIKO

Methodistische Kirche von Mexiko

NIEDERLANDE

Allgemeine Sozietät der Mennoniten

Evangelisch-Lutherische Kirche

Reformierte Kirchen in den Niederlanden

Niederländische Reformierte Kirche

Alt-Katholische Kirche der Niederlande

Remonstrantische Brüderschaft

MADAGASCAR

Iglesia de Jesucristo en Madagascar

Iglesia Luterana Malgache

MALASIA Y SINGAPUR

Iglesia Metodista en Malasia y
Singapur

MEXICO

Iglesia Metodista de México

PAISES BAJOS

Sociedad General de los Menonitas

Iglesia Evangélica Luterana

Iglesias Reformadas en los Países Bajos

Iglesia Reformada de los Países Bajos

Iglesia Vieja Católica de los Países
Bajos

Hermanos Remonstrantes

NEW CALEDONIA

Evangelical Church in New Caledonia
and the Loyalty Isles

NEW HEBRIDES

Presbyterian Church of the New Hebrides

NEW ZEALAND

Associated Churches of Christ in New
Zealand

The Baptist Union of New Zealand

Church of the Province of New Zealand

The Congregational Union of New
Zealand

The Methodist Church of New Zealand

The Presbyterian Church of New
Zealand

NIGERIA

Methodist Church, Nigeria

Nigerian Baptist Convention

NOUVELLE-CALEDONIE

Eglise évangélique en Nouvelle-
Calédonie et aux Îles Loyauté

NOUVELLES-HEBRIDES

Eglise presbytérienne des Nouvelles-
Hébrides

NOUVELLE-ZELANDE

Eglises unies du Christ en Nouvelle-
Zélande

Union baptiste de Nouvelle-Zélande

Eglise de la province de Nouvelle-Zélande

Union congrégationaliste de Nouvelle-
Zélande

Eglise méthodiste de Nouvelle-
Zélande

Eglise presbytérienne de Nouvelle-
Zélande

NIGERIA

Eglise méthodiste, Nigéria

Convention baptiste nigériane

NEUKALEDONIEN

Evangelische Kirche auf Neukaledonien
und den Loyalty-Inseln

NEUE HEBRIDEN

Presbyterianische Kirche der Neuen
Hebriden

NEUSEELAND

Vereinigte Kirchen Christi in Neuseeland

Baptistenunion von Neuseeland

Kirche der Provinz Neuseeland

Kongregationalistische Vereinigung
von Neuseeland

Methodistische Kirche von Neuseeland

Presbyterianische Kirche von Neuseeland

NIGERIA

Methodistische Kirche, Nigeria

Nigerianischer Baptistenkonvent

NUEVA CALEDONIA

Iglesia Evangélica en Nueva Caledonia
y en las Islas Lealtad

NUEVAS HEBRIDAS

Iglesia Presbiteriana de las Nuevas
Hébridas

NUEVA ZELANDIA

Iglesias de Cristo Asociadas en Nueva
Zelandia

Unión Bautista de Nueva Zelandia

Iglesia de la Provincia de Nueva
Zelandia

Unión Congregacionalista de Nueva
Zelandia

Iglesia Metodista de Nueva Zelandia

Iglesia Presbiteriana de Nueva
Zelandia

NIGERIA

Iglesia Metodista, Nigeria

Convención Bautista Nigeriana

The Presbyterian Church of Nigeria

Eglise presbytérienne du Nigéria

NORWAY

NORVEGE

Den Norske Kirke
Church of Norway

Eglise de Norvège

PAKISTAN

PAKISTAN

The Church of Pakistan

Eglise du Pakistan

United Presbyterian Church of
Pakistan

Eglise presbytérienne unie du
Pakistan

PHILIPPINES

PHILIPPINES

Philippine Independent Church

Eglise indépendante philippine

United Church of Christ in the Philippines

Eglise unie du Christ aux Philippines

The Evangelical Methodist Church in the
Philippines

Eglise évangélique méthodiste aux
îles Philippines

POLAND

POLOGNE

Autocephalic Orthodox Church in Poland

Eglise autocéphale orthodoxe en
Pologne

Kościoła Ewangelicko-Augsburskiego w Prl
Evangelical Church of the Augsburg
Confession in Poland

Eglise évangélique de la confession
d'Augsbourg en Pologne

Presbyterianische Kirche von Nigeria — Iglesia Presbiteriana de Nigeria

NORWEGEN — NORUEGA

Kirche von Norwegen — Iglesia de Noruega

PAKISTAN — PAQUISTAN

Kirche von Pakistan — Iglesia de Paquistan

Vereinigte Presbyterianische Kirche von Pakistan — Iglesia Presbiteriana Unida del Paquistan

PHILIPPINEN — FILIPINAS

Unabhängige Philippinische Kirche — Iglesia Filipina Independiente

Vereinigte Kirche Christi auf den den Philippinen — Iglesia Unida de Cristo en Filipinas

Evangelisch-Methodistische Kirche auf den Philippinen — Iglesia Evangélica Metodista en las Islas Filipinas

POLEN — POLONIA

Autokephale Orthodoxe Kirche in Polen — Iglesia Autocéfala Ortodoxa en Polonia

Evangelische Kirche A.B. in Polen — Iglesia Evangélica de la Confesión de Ausburgo en Polonia

Kościoła Polskokatolickiego w Prl
Polish Catholic Church in Poland

Eglise catholique polonaise en Pologne

Staro-Katolickiego Kościoła
Mariatowitow w Prl
Old Catholic Mariavite Church in Poland

Eglise vieille-catholique mariavite
en Pologne

RUMANIA

ROUMANIE

Biserica Evangelica Dupa Confesiunea
Dela Augsburg
Evangelical Church of the Augsburg Confession

Eglise évangélique de la confession
d'Augsbourg

Biserica Ortodoxá Romane
Rumanian Orthodox Church

Eglise orthodoxe roumaine

Biserica Reformatá Din România
Reformed Church of Rumania

Eglise réformée de Roumanie

Evangelical Synodal Presbyterial Church
of the Augsburg Confession in the Socialist
Republic of Rumania

Eglise évangélique presbytérienne-
synodale de la confession d'Augsbourg
en République socialiste de Roumanie

SAMOA

SAMOA

The Congregational Christian Church in
Samoa

Eglise chrétienne congrégationaliste
à Samoa

SIERRA LEONE

SIERRA LEONE

The Methodist Church, Sierra Leone

Eglise méthodiste, Sierra Leone

SOUTH AFRICA

AFRIQUE DU SUD

The Bantu Presbyterian Church of South
Africa

Eglise presbytérienne bantoue d'Afrique
du Sud

Polnische Katholische Kirche in Polen	Iglesia Católica Polonesa en Polonia
Alt-Katholische Kirche der Mariaviten in Polen	Iglesia Vieja Católica Mariavita en Polonia

RUMÄNIEN	RUMANIA
Evangelische Kirche A.B.	Iglesia Evangélica de la Confesión de Ausburgo
Rumänische Orthodoxe Kirche	Iglesia Ortodoxa Rumana
Reformierte Kirche von Rumänien	Iglesia Reformada de Rumania
Evangelische Synodal-Presbyterianische Kirche A.B. in der Sozialistischen Republik Rumänien	Iglesia Evangélica Presbiteriana Sinodal de la Confesión de Ausburgo en la República Socialista de Rumania

SAMOA	SAMOA
Kongregationalistisch-Christliche Kirche auf Samoa	Iglesia Cristiana Congregacionalista en Samoa

SIERRA LEONE	SIERRA LEONE
Methodistische Kirche, Sierra Leone	Iglesia Metodista, Sierra Leona

SÜDAFRIKA	SUDAFRICA
Presbyterianische Bantu-Kirche von Südafrika	Iglesia Presbiteriana Bantú de Sudáfrica

Church of the Province of South Africa

Eglise de la province d'Afrique du Sud

Evangelical Lutheran Church in Southern Africa - South-Eastern Region

Eglise évangélique luthérienne en Afrique australe, région sud-orientale

Evangelical Lutheran Church in Southern Africa - Transvaal Region

Eglise évangélique luthérienne en Afrique australe, région du Transvaal

The Methodist Church of South Africa

Eglise méthodiste d'Afrique du Sud

Moravian Church in South Africa

Eglise morave en Afrique du Sud

The Presbyterian Church of Southern Africa

Eglise presbytérienne d'Afrique australe

The United Congregational Church of Southern Africa

Eglise congrégationaliste unie d'Afrique australe

SPAIN

ESPAGNE

Spanish Evangelical Church

Eglise évangélique espagnole

SRI LANKA

SRI LANKA

The Anglican Church in Sri Lanka

Eglise anglicane à Sri Lanka

Methodist Church, Sri Lanka

Eglise méthodiste, Sri Lanka

Kirche der Provinz Südafrika	Iglesia de la Provincia de Sudáfrica
Evangelisch-Lutherische Kirche im südlichen Afrika- Südöstliche Region	Iglesia Evangélica Luterana en Africa Austral, Región Sudoriental
Evangelisch-Lutherische Kirche im südlichen Afrika - Transvaal - Region	Iglesia Evangélica Luterana en Africa Austral, Región de Transvaal
Methodistische Kirche von Südafrika	Iglesia Metodista de Sudáfrica
Brüder-Unität in Südafrika	Iglesia Morava en Sudáfrica
Presbyterianische Kirche des südlichen Afrika	Iglesia Presbiteriana del Africa Austral
Vereinigte Kongregationalistische Kirche des südlichen Afrika	Iglesia Congregacionalista Unida de Africa Austral

SPANIEN

Spanische Evangelische Kirche

SRI LANKA

Anglikanische Kirche in Sri Lanka

Methodistische Kirche, Sri Lanka

ESPANA

Iglesia Evangélica Española

SRI LANKA

Iglesia Anglicana en Sri Lanka

Iglesia Metodista, Sri Lanka

153

SWEDEN	SUEDE
Svenska Kyrkan Church of Sweden	Eglise de Suède
Svenska Missionsförbundet The Mission Covenant Church of Sweden	Eglise de la convention missionnaire de Suède
SWITZERLAND	SUISSE
Old Catholic Church of Switzerland	Eglise vieille-catholique de Suisse
Swiss Protestant Church Federation	Fédération des Eglises protestantes de la Suisse
SYRIA	SYRIE
The National Evangelical Synod of Syria and Lebanon	Synode évangélique national de Syrie et du Liban
Greek Orthodox Patriarchate of Antioch and All the East	Patriarcat grec-orthodoxe d'Antioche et de tout l'Orient
Syrian Orthodox Patriarchate of Antioch and All the East	Patriarcat orthodoxe syrien d'Antioche et de tout l'Orient
TAHITI	TAHITI
Evangelical Church of French Polynesia	**Eglise évangélique de Polynésie française**
TAIWAN	TAIWAN
Tai-Oan Ki-Tok Tiu-Lo Kau-Hoe The Presbyterian Church in Taiwan, Republic of China	Eglise presbytérienne à Taïwan, République de Chine

SCHWEDEN	**SUECIA**
Kirche von Schweden	Iglesia de Suecia
Schwedischer Missionsverband	Iglesia de la Convención Misionera de Suecia
SCHWEIZ	**SUIZA**
Christkatholische Kirche der Schweiz	Iglesia Vieja Católica de Suiza
Schweizerischer Evangelischer Kirchenbund	Federación de las Iglesias Protestantes de Suiza
SYRIEN	**SIRIA**
Evangelische Nationalsynode von Syrien und Libanon	Sínodo Evangélico Nacional de Siria y del Líbano
Griechisch-Orthodoxes Patriarchat von Antiochien und dem gesamten Morgenland	Patriarcado Griego-Ortodoxo de Antioquía y de todo el Oriente
Syrisch-Orthodoxes Patriarchat von Antiochien und dem gesamten Morgenland	Patriarcado ortodoxo Sirio de Antioquía y de todo el Oriente
TAHITI	**TAHITI**
Evangelische Kirche von Französisch-Polynesien	Iglesia Evangélica de la Polinesia Francesa
TAIWAN	**TAIWAN**
Presbyterianische Kirche auf Taiwan (Republik China)	Iglesia Presbiteriana en Taiwan, República de China

TANZANIA	**TANZANIE**
Church of the Province of Tanzania	Eglise de la province de Tanzanie
Evangelical Lutheran Church in Tanzania	Eglise évangélique luthérienne en Tanzanie
THAILAND	**THAILANDE**
The Church of Christ in Thailand	Eglise du Christ en Thaïlande
TOGO	**TOGO**
Evangelical Church of Togo	Eglise évangélique du Togo
TRINIDAD	**TRINITE**
The Presbyterian Church in Trinidad and Grenada	Eglise presbytérienne à la Trinité et à Grenade
TURKEY	**TURQUIE**
Ecumenical Patriarchate of Constantinople	Patriarcat oecuménique de Constantinople
UGANDA	**OUGANDA**
The Church of Uganda, Rwanda and Burundi	Eglise de l'Ouganda, du Rwanda et du Burundi
UNION OF SOVIET SOCIALIST REPUBLICS	**UNION DES REPUBLIQUES SOCIALISTES SOVIETIQUES**
Armenian Apostolic Church	Eglise apostolique arménienne

TANSANIA	**TANZANIA**
Kirche der Provinz Tansania	Iglesia de la Provincia de Tanzania
Evangelisch-Lutherische Kirche in Tansania	Iglesia Evangélica Luterana en Tanzania
THAILAND	**TAILANDIA**
Kirche Christi in Thailand	Iglesia de Cristo en Tailandia
TOGO	**TOGO**
Evangelische Kirche von Togo	Iglesia Evangélica del Togo
TRINIDAD	**TRINIDAD**
Presbyterianische Kirche auf Trinidad und Grenada	Iglesia Presbiteriana en Trinidad y Granada
TÜRKEI	**TURQUIA**
Ökumenisches Patriarchat von Konstantinopel	Patriarcado Ecuménico de Constantinopla
UGANDA	**UGANDA**
Kirche von Uganda, Ruanda und Burundi	Iglesia de Uganda, Rwanda y Burundi
UdSSR	**URSS**
Armenische Apostolische Kirche	Iglesia Apostólica Armenia

Eesti Evangeeliumi Luteri usu Kirik
Estonian Evangelical Lutheran Church

Georgian Orthodox Church

Latvijas Evangeliska-Luteriska
Baznica
Evangelical Lutheran Church of Latvia

Russian Orthodox Church

The Union of Evangelical Christian
Baptists of USSR

UNITED KINGDOM AND EIRE

ENGLAND

The Baptist Union of Great Britain
and Ireland

The Church of England

Churches of Christ in Great Britain and
Ireland

The Methodist Church

The Moravian Union

The Salvation Army

Eglise évangélique luthérienne d'Estonie

Eglise orthodoxe géorgienne

Eglise évangélique de Lettonie

Eglise orthodoxe russe

Union des baptistes chrétiens évangéliques de l'URSS

ROYAUME-UNI ET IRLANDE

ANGLETERRE

Union baptiste de Grande-Bretagne et
d'Irlande

Eglise d'Angleterre

Eglises du Christ en Grand-Bretagne et en
Irlande

Eglise méthodiste

Union morave

Armée du salut

Estnische Evangelisch-Lutherische Kirche	Iglesia Evangélica Luterana de Estonia
Georgische Orthodoxe Kirche	Iglesia Ortodoxa Georgiana
Evangelisch-Lutherische Kirche Lettlands	Iglesia Evangélica Luterana de Letonia
Russische Orthodoxe Kirche	Iglesia Ortodoxa Rusa
Allunionsrat der Evangeliumschristen-Baptisten, UdSSR	Unión de los Bautistas Cristianos Evangélicos de la URSS

VEREINIGTES KÖNIGREICH UND IRLAND   REINO UNIDO E IRLANDA

ENGLAND   INGLATERRA

Baptistenunion von Grossbritannien und Irland	Unión Bautista de Gran Bretana e Irlanda
Kirche von England	Iglesia de Inglaterra
Kirchen Christi in Grossbritannien und Irland	Iglesias de Cristo en Gran Bretaña e Irlanda
Methodistische Kirche	Iglesia Metodista
Brüder-Unität	Unión Morava
Heilsarmee	Ejército de Salvación

The United Reformed Church (England and Wales)	Eglise réformée unie (Angleterre et Pays de Galles)

IRELAND

The Church of Ireland

The Methodist Church in Ireland

The Presbyterian Church in Ireland

SCOTLAND

The Church of Scotland

The Congregational Union of Scotland

Episcopal Church in Scotland

United Free Church of Scotland

WALES

The Church in Wales

The Presbyterian Church of Wales

Union of Welsh Independents

IRLANDE

Eglise d'Irlande

Eglise méthodiste en Irlande

Eglise presbytérienne en Irlande

ECOSSE

Eglise d'Ecosse

Union congrégationaliste d'Ecosse

Eglise épiscopale en Ecosse

Eglise libre unie d'Ecosse

PAYS DE GALLES

Eglise au Pays de Galles

Eglise presbytérienne du Pays de Galles

Union des indépendants gallois

Vereinigte Reformierte Kirche
(England und Wales)

Iglesia Reformada Unida
(Inglaterra y País de Gales)

IRLAND
Kirche von Irland

IRLANDA
Iglesia de Irlanda

Methodistische Kirche in Irland

Iglesia Metodista en Irlanda

Presbyterianische Kirche in Irland

Iglesia Presbiteriana en Irlanda

SCHOTTLAND
Kirche von Schottland

ESCOCIA
Iglesia de Escocia

Kongregationalistische Vereinigung von
Schottland

Unión Congregacionalista de Escocia

Bischöfliche Kirche in Schottland

Iglesia Episcopal en Escocia

Vereinigte Freikirche von Schottland

Iglesia Libre Unida de Escocia

WALES
Kirche in Wales

PAIS DE GALES
Iglesia en el País de Gales

Presbyterianische Kirche von Wales

Iglesia Presbiteriana del País de
Gales

Union Walisischer Independenter

Unión de los Independientes Galeses

UNITED STATES OF AMERICA	ETATS-UNIS D'AMERIQUE
African Methodist Episcopal Church	Eglise méthodiste épiscopale africaine
African Methodist Episcopal Zion Church	Eglise méthodiste épiscopale africaine de Sion
American Baptist Churches in the U.S.A.	Eglises baptistes américaines aux Etats-Unis
American Lutheran Church	Eglise luthérienne américaine
The Antiochian Orthodox Christian Archdiocises of New York and all North America	Archidiocèse chrétien orthodoxe d' Antioche de New-York et de toute l' Amérique du Nord
Christian Church (Disciples of Christ)	Eglise chrétienne (Disciples du Christ)
Christian Methodist Episcopal Church	Eglise chrétienne méthodiste épiscopale
Church of the Brethren	Eglise des frères
Church of the East (Assyrian)	Eglise de l'Orient (assyrienne)
The Episcopal Church	Eglise épiscopale
Hungarian Reformed Church in America	Eglise réformée hongroise en Amérique
Lutheran Church of America	Eglise luthérienne en Amérique

USA	ESTADOS UNIDOS DE AMERICA
Afrikanische Methodistisch-Bischöfliche Kirche	Iglesia Metodista Episcopal Africana
Afrikanische Methodistisch-Bischöfliche Zions-Kirche	Iglesia Metodista Africana de Sión
Amerikanische Baptistenkirchen in den USA	Iglesias Bautistas Americanas en los Estados Unidos
Amerikanische Lutherische Kirche	Iglesia Luterana Americana
Antiochenisch-Orthodoxe Christliche Erzdiözese von New York und ganz Nordamerika	Arquidiócesis Cristiana Ortodoxa de Antioquía de Nueva York y de toda América del Norte
Christliche Kirche (Jünger Christi)	Iglesia Cristiana (Discípulos de Cristo)
Christliche Methodistisch-Bischöfliche Kirche	Iglesia Cristiana Metodista Episcopal
Kirche der Brüder	Iglesia de los Hermanos
Kirche des Ostens (Assyrisch)	Iglesia del Oriente (Asiriana)
Bischöfliche Kirche	Iglesia Episcopal
Ungarische Reformierte Kirche in Amerika	Iglesia Reformada Húngara en América
Lutherische Kirche in Amerika	Iglesia Luterana en América

Moravian Church in America - Northern Province	Eglise morave en Amérique, province du Nord
Moravian Church in America - Southern Province	Eglise morave en Amérique, province du Sud
National Baptist Convention of America	Convention baptiste nationale d'Amérique
National Baptist Convention, U.S.A., Inc.	Convention baptiste nationale des Etats-Unis, S.A.
The National Council of Communty Churches, U.S.A.	Conseil national des Eglises communautés, Etats-Unis
The Orthodox Church in America	Eglise orthodoxe en Amérique
Polish National Catholic Church of America	Eglise catholique nationale polonaise d'Amérique
Presbyterian Church in the United States	Eglise presbytérienne aux Etats-Unis
Reformed Church in America	Eglise réformée en Amérique
Religious Society of Friends	Société religieuse des amis
Friends General Conference	Conférence générale de la Société des amis
Friends United Meeting	Convention unie des amis

Brüder-Unität in Amerika - Nördliche Provinz	Iglesia Morava en América, Provincia del Norte
Brüder-Unität in Amerika - Südliche Provinz	Iglesia Morava en América, Provincia del Sur
Nationaler Baptistenbund von Amerika	Convención Nacional Bautista de América
Nationaler Baptistenbund USA, Inc.	Convención Nacional Bautista de los Estados Unidos, S.A.
Nationalrat der Community-Kirchen, USA	Consejo Nacional de las Iglesias Comunidades, Estados Unidos
Orthodoxe Kirche in Amerika	Iglesia Ortodoxa en América
Polnische Katholische Nationalkirche von Amerika	Iglesia Nacional Católica Polaca de América
Presbyterianische Kirche in den Vereinigten Staaten	Iglesia Presbiteriana en los Estados Unidos
Reformierte Kirche in Amerika	Iglesia Reformada en América
Religiöse Gesellschaft der Freunde	Sociedad Religiosa de los Amigos
Generalkonferenz der Freunde	Conferencia General de la Sociedad de los Amigos
Vereinigte Versammlung der Freunde	Convención Unida de los Amigos

The Romanian Orthodox Episcopate of America

Episcopat orthodoxe roumain d' Amérique

Russian Orthodox Greek Catholic Church of America

Eglise orthodoxe russe grecque catholique d'Amérique

Seventh Day Baptist General Conference

Conférence générale des baptistes du septième jour

United Church of Christ

Eglise unie du Christ

The United Methodist Church

Eglise méthodiste unie

The United Presbyterian Church in the United States of America

Eglise presbytérienne unie aux Etats-Unis d'Amérique

WEST AFRICA

AFRIQUE OCCIDENTALE

The Church of the Province of West Africa

Eglise de la province d'Afrique occidentale

WEST INDIES

ANTILLES

The Church in the Province of the West Indies

Eglise de la province des Antilles

The Methodist Church in the Caribbean and the Americas

Eglise méthodiste aux Caraïbes et aux Amériques

Moravian Church - Eastern West Indies Province

Eglise morave, province des Antilles orientales

YUGOSLAVIA

YOUGOSLAVIE

Reformatska Crke u SFRJ
The Reformed Church in Yugoslavia

Eglise réformée en Yougoslavie

Rumänisches Orthodoxes Bistum von Amerika	Episcopado Ortodoxo Rumano de América
Russisch-Orthodoxe Griechisch-Katholische Kirche von Amerika	Iglesia Ortodoxa Rusa Griega Católica de América
Generalkonferenz der Baptisten des Siebten Tages	Conferencia General de los Bautistas del Séptimo Día
Vereinigte Kirche Christi	Iglesia Unida de Cristo
Vereinigte Methodistische Kirche	Iglesia Metodista Unida
Vereinigte Presbyterianische Kirche in den Vereinigten Staaten von Amerika	Iglesia Presbiteriana Unida en los Estados Unidos de América

WESTAFRIKA	AFRICA OCCIDENTAL
Kirche der Provinz Westafrika	Iglesia de la Provincia de Africa Occidental

WESTINDIEN	ANTILLAS
Kirche in der Provinz Westindien	Iglesia de la Provincia de las Antillas
Methodistische Kirche in der Karibik und Mittel- und Lateinamerika	Iglesia Metodista en el Caribe y las Américas
Brüder-Unität - Westindische Provinz Ost	Iglesia Morava - Provincia de las Antillas Orientales

JUGOSLAWIEN	YUGOSLAVIA
Reformierte Kirche in Jugoslawien	Iglesia Reformada Yugoslava

Serbian Orthodox Church

Eglise orthodoxe serbe

Slovenska cv.-kr.. a.v. cirkev v. Juhuslavii
Slovak Evangelical Church of the Augusburg Confession in Yugoslavia

Eglise évangélique slovaque de la confession d'Augsbourg en Yougoslavie

ZAÏRE

Church of Christ in Zaïre - Community of Disciples

Church of Christ in Zaïre - Community of Christ the Light

Church of Christ in Zaïre - Mennonite Community in Zaïre

Church of Christ on Earth by the Prophet Simon Kimbangu

Evangelical Church of Zaïre

Presbyterian Church in Zaïre

ZAÏRE

Eglise du Christ au Zaïre, Communauté des disciples

Eglise du Christ au Zaïre, Communauté du Christ lumière

Eglise du Christ au Zaïre, Communauté mennonite au Zaïre

Eglise du Christ sur la terre par le prophète Simon Kimbangu

Eglise évangélique du Zaïre

Eglise presbytérienne au Zaïre

ZAMBIA

United Church of Zambia

ZAMBIE

Eglise unie de Zambie

OTHER CHURCHES

Eesti Evangeeliumi Luteri Usu Kirik (Stockholm)
Estonian Evangelical Lutheran Church

EGLISES EN EXIL

Eglise évangélique luthérienne d' Estonie (en exil)

Serbische Orthodoxe Kirche	Iglesia Ortodoxa Serbia
Slowakische Evangelisch-Christliche Kirche A.B. in Jugoslawien	Iglesia Evangélica Eslovaca de la Confesión de Ausburgo en Yugoslavia

ZAIRE

Kirche Christi in Zaire - Communauté des Disciples	Iglesia de Cristo en el Zaire, Communidad de los Discípulos
Kirche Christi in Zaire - Communauté du Christ Lumière	Comunidad de Cristo en el Zaire, Comunidad de Cristo Luz
Kirche Christi in Zaire - Communauté mennonite au Zaïre	Iglesia de Cristo en el Zaire, Comunidad Menonita en el Zaire
Kirche Christi auf Erden durch den Propheten Simon Kimbangu	Iglesia de Cristo sobre la Tierra por el Profeta Simón Kimbangu
Evangelische Kirche von Zaire	Iglesia Evangélica del Zaire
Presbyterianische Kirche in Zaire	Iglesia Presbiteriana en el Zaire

SAMBIA / ZAMBIA

Vereinigte Kirche von Sambia	Iglesia Unida de Zambia

KIRCHEN IM EXIL / IGLESIAS EN EXILIO

Estnische Evangelisch-Lutherische Kirche (im Exil)	Iglesia Evangélica Luterana de Estonia (en exilio)

Latvijas Evangeliská Luteriská Baznica
Latvian Evangelical Lutheran Church
(Ontario)

Eglise évangélique luthérienne lettonne
(en exil)

Lettische Evangelisch-Lutherische Kirche
(im Exil)

Iglesia Evangélica Luterana Letona
(en exilio)

2. ASSOCIATED CHURCHES

ALGERIA
Protestant Church of Algeria

ARGENTINA
United Evangelical Lutheran Church

BOLIVIA
Evangelical Methodist Church in Bolivia

CAMEROON
African Protestant Church

CHILE
The Methodist Church of Chile

CUBA
Methodist Church in Cuba

Presbyterian-Reformed Church in Cuba

EQUATORIAL GUINEA
Evangelical Church of Equatorial Guinea

2. EGLISES ASSOCIEES

ALGERIE
Eglise protestante d'Algérie

ARGENTINE
Eglise évangélique luthérienne unie

BOLIVIE
Eglise évangélique méthodiste en Bolivie

CAMEROUN
Eglise protestante africaine

CHILI
Eglise méthodiste du Chili

CUBA
Eglise méthodiste à Cuba

Eglise presbytérienne réformée à Cuba

GUINEE EQUATORIALE
Eglise évangélique de Guinée équatoriale

2. ANGESCHLOSSENE KIRCHEN	**2. IGLESIAS ASOCIADAS**
<u>ALGERIEN</u>	<u>ARGELIA</u>
Evangelische Kirche von Algerien	Iglesia Protestante de Argelia
<u>ARGENTINIEN</u>	<u>ARGENTINA</u>
Vereinigte Evangelisch-Lutherische Kirche	<u>Iglesia Evangélica Luterana Unida</u>
<u>BOLIVIEN</u>	<u>BOLIVIA</u>
Evangelische Methodistenkirche in Bolivien	<u>Iglesia Evangélica Metodista en Bolivia</u>
<u>KAMERUN</u>	<u>CAMERUN</u>
Protestantische Afrikanische Kirche	Iglesia Protestante Africana
<u>CHILE</u>	<u>CHILE</u>
Methodistische Kirche von Chile	<u>Iglesia Metodista de Chile</u>
<u>KUBA</u>	<u>CUBA</u>
Methodistische Kirche in Kuba	<u>Iglesia Metodista en Cuba</u>
Presbyterianisch-Reformierte Kirche in Kuba	<u>Iglesia Presbiteriana-Reformada en Cuba</u>
<u>ÄQUATORIALGUINEA</u>	<u>GUINEA ECUATORIAL</u>
Evangelische Kirche von Äquatorialguinea	Iglesia Evangélica de Guinea Ecuatorial

INDIA	**INDE**
Bengal-Orissa-Bihar Baptist Convention	Convention baptiste de Bengal-Orissa-Bihar
JAPAN	**JAPON**
The Korean Christian Church in Japan	Eglise chrétienne coréenne au Japon
LIBERIA	**LIBERIA**
Presbytery of Liberia	Synode du Libéria
NETHERLANDS ANTILLES	**ANTILLES NEERLANDAISES**
Protestantse Kerk von de Nederlandse Antillen Protestant Church of the Netherlands Antilles	Eglise protestante des Antilles néerlandaises
PERU	**PEROU**
The Methodist Church of Peru	Eglise méthodiste du Pérou
PORTUGAL	**PORTUGAL**
Igreja Evangélica Presbiteriana de Portugal Evangelical Presbyterian Church of Portugal	Eglise évangélique presbytérienne du Portugal
Igreja Lusitana Catolica Apostolica Evangélica Lusitanian Catholic-Apostolic Evangelical Church	Eglise catholique apostolique évangélique de Lusitanie

INDIEN

Baptistenkonvent von Bengal-Orissa-
Bihar

JAPAN

Koreanische Christliche Kirche in Japan

LIBERIA

Presbyterianische Synode von Liberia

NIEDERLÄNDISCHE ANTILLEN

Protestantische Kirche der Nieder-
ländischen Antillen

PERU

Methodistische Kirche von Peru

PORTUGAL

Evangelische Presbyterianische Kirche
Portugals

Lusitanische Katholische Apostolische
Evangelische Kirche

INDIA

Convención Bautista de Bengal-Orissa-
Bihar

JAPON

Iglesia Cristiana Coreana en el Japón

LIBERIA

Sínodo de Liberia

ANTILLAS NEERLANDESAS

Iglesia Protestante de las Antillas
Neerlandesas

PERU

Iglesia Metodista del Peru

PORTUGAL

Iglesia Evangélica Presbiteriana
de Portugal

Iglesia Lusitana Católica Apostólica
Evangélica

175

SPAIN

Spanish Reformed Episcopal Church

SUDAN

The Presbyterian Church in the Sudan

URUGUAY

The Evangelical Methodist Church in
Uruguay

ZAÏRE

Church of Christ in Zaïre - Episcopal
Baptist Community in Africa

ESPAGNE

Eglise réformée épiscopale d'Espagne

SOUDAN

Eglise presbytérienne au Soudan

URUGUAY

Eglise évangélique méthodiste en
Uruguay

ZAÏRE

Eglise du Christ au Zaïre
Communauté épiscopale baptiste en
Afrique (C.E.B.A.)

SPANIEN

Spanische Reformierte Bischöfliche
Kirche

SUDAN

Presbyterianische Kirche im Sudan

URUGUAY

Evangelisch-Methodistische Kirche in
Uruguay

ZAIRE

Kirche Christi in Zaire - Communauté
épiscopale baptiste en Afrique (C.E.B.A.)

ESPANA

Iglesia Española Reformada Episcopal

SUDAN

Iglesia Presbiteriana en el Sudán

URUGUAY

Iglesia Evangélica Metodista en el
Uruguay

ZAIRE

Iglesia de Cristo en el Zaire -
Comunidad Episcopal Bautista en Africa
(C.E.B.A.)

3. ASSOCIATED COUNCILS	3. CONSEILS ASSOCIES
Australian Council of Churches	Conseil australien des Eglises
Ecumenical Council of Austrian Churches	Conseil oecuménique des Eglises en Autriche
Burma Christian Council	Conseil chrétien birman
Canadian Council of Churches	Conseil canadien des Eglises
Ecumenical Council of Churches in the Czech Socialist Republic	Conseil oecuménique des Eglises en République socialiste tchécoslovaque
Ecumenical Council of Denmark	Conseil oecuménique du Danemark
Ecumenical Council of Finland	Conseil oecuménique de Finlande
Council of Christian Churches (GDR)	Conseil des Eglises chrétiennes en RDA
Council of Christian Churches in Germany (FRG)	Conseil des Eglises chrétiennes en Allemagne (RFA)
Hong Kong Christian Council	Conseil chrétien de Hong-Kong
Ecumenical Council of Hungarian Churches	Conseil oecuménique des Eglises hongroises
National Christian Council of India	Conseil chrétien national de l'Inde

3. ANGESCHLOSSENE RÄTE	3. CONSEJOS ASOCIADOS
Australischer Rat der Kirchen	Consejo Australiano de Iglesias
Ökumenischer Rat der Kirchen in Österreich	Consejo Ecuménico de Iglesias en Austria
Birmanischer Christenrat	Consejo Cristiano Birmano
Kanadischer Rat der Kirchen	Consejo Canadiense de Iglesias
Ökumenischer Kirchenrat in der Tschechischen Sozialistischen Republik	Consejo Ecuménico de Iglesias en la República Socialista Checoslovaca
Ökumenischer Rat von Dänemark	Consejo Ecuménico de Dinamarca
Ökumenischer Rat von Finnland	Consejo Ecuménico de Finlandia
Arbeitsgemeinschaft Christlicher Kirchen in der DDR	Consejo de Iglesias Cristianas en RDA
Arbeitsgemeinschaft Christlicher Kirchen in Deutschland	Consejo de Iglesias Cristianas en Alemania (RFA)
Christenrat von Hongkong	Consejo Cristiano de Hong-Kong
Ökumenischer Rat Ungarischer Kirchen	Consejo Ecuménico de las Iglesias Húngaras
Nationaler Christenrat von Indien	Consejo Nacional Cristiano de la India

Council of Churches in Indonesia	Conseil des Eglises en Indonésie
The National Christian Council of Japan	Conseil chrétien national du Japon
Council of Churches of Malaysia and Singapore	Conseil des Eglises de Malaisie et de Singapour
Council of Churches in the Netherlands	Conseil des Eglises aux Pays-Bas
National Council of Churches in New Zealand	Conseil national des Eglises en Nouvelle-Zélande
National Council of Churches in the Philippines	Conseil national des Eglises aux Philippines
Polish Ecumenical Council	Conseil oecuménique polonais
Christian Council of Rhodesia	Conseil chrétien de Rhodésie
The South African Council of Churches	Conseil sud-africain des Eglises
Swedish Ecumenical Council	Conseil oecuménique suédois
National Christian Council of Sri Lanka	Conseil chrétien national de Sri Lanka
British Council of Churches	Conseil britannique des Eglises

Rat der Kirchen in Indonesien	Consejo de Iglesias en Indonesia
Nationaler Christenrat von Japan	Consejo Nacional Cristiano del Japon
Rat der Kirchen von Malaysia und Singapur	Consejo de Iglesias de Malasia y Singapur
Rat der Kirchen in den Niederlanden	Consejo de Iglesias en los Países Bajos
Nationaler Kirchenrat in Neuseeland	Consejo Nacional de Iglesias en Nueva Zelandia
Nationaler Kirchenrat in den Philippinen	Consejo Nacional de Iglesias en Filipinas
Polnischer Ökumenischer Rat	Consejo Ecuménico Polaco
Christenrat von Rhodesien	Consejo Cristiano de Rhodesia
Südafrikanischer Rat der Kirchen	Consejo Sudafricano de Iglesias
Schwedischer Ökumenischer Rat	Consejo Ecuménico Sueco
Nationaler Christenrat von Sri Lanka	Consejo Nacional Cristiano de Sri Lanka
Britischer Rat der Kirchen	Consejo Británico de Iglesias

<u>National Council of the Churches of
Christ in the U.S.A.</u>

Ecumenical Council of Churches in
Yugoslavia

Conseil national des Eglises du
Christ aux Etats-Unis

Conseil oecuménique des Eglises en
Yougoslavie

Nationalrat der Kirchen Christi in
den Vereinigten Staaten von Amerika

Ökumenischer Kirchenrat in Jugoslawien

Consejo Nacional de las Iglesias de
Cristo en los Estados Unidos

Consejo Ecuménico de Iglesias en
Yugoslavia

Explanatory Note

- In the following section the English terms
are arranged in alphabetical order according
to the first letter of the main concept, e.g.
'community development' will be found under
'development'.

- When the translation of a term is given
under a different entry (e.g. lay academy
See under: lay training centre) it should
be looked for under the word with its
initial letter underlined (in this case
'training').

- Each English term translated carries a
number. Alphabetical indexes for the other
three languages will be found at the end of
the book giving the reference number of the
corresponding English term.

- In the case of titles and abbreviations,
the number given in the indexes refers to
the page on which a particular entry
appears.

- A detailed list of the structures, secretariats and programmes of the World Council
of Churches is given in chapter IV, p. 419.

- It should be noted that in French, German
and Spanish the job titles given refer to
the post and not to the person occupying
it. They are therefore given here in the
masculine gender and will vary if the post
is held by a woman, e.g. 'Director of

Notice explicative

- Dans le chapitre qui suit, les termes anglais
sont classés par ordre alphabétique selon
la première lettre du concept clé (exemple:
"community development" est classé sous
"development").

- Lorsque l'un de ces termes renvoie à une
deuxième expression (exemple: "lay academy
See under: lay training centre"), on trouvera celle-ci sous le mot dont la première
lettre est soulignée (ici: sous "training").

- Chaque terme anglais traduit est précédé
d'un numéro. Les index alphabétiques
français, allemand et espagnol qui se
trouvent à la fin du livre renvoient, pour
chacun des termes énumérés, au numéro
du mot anglais correspondant.

- Dans le cas des "titres et abréviations",
les numéros indiqués dans les index renvoient aux pages où figurent ces titres et
abréviations.

- Un organigramme du Conseil oecuménique des
Eglises, et la liste complète de ses
secrétariats et programmes, figurent au
chapitre IV, p. 419.

- On notera enfin qu'en français, en allemand
et en espagnol, les titres professionnels
sont toujours indiqués par rapport aux
postes et figurent au masculin. Lorsqu'on
voudra se référer à la personne qui occupe

Hinweise für die Benutzung

- Die im nachstehenden Kapitel "Terminologie" an erster Stelle erscheinenden englischen Begriffe sind alphabetisch geordnet, und zwar nach dem ersten Buchstaben des Hauptbegriffes. 'Community development' findet man so zum Beispiel unter dem Stichwort 'development'.

- Bei Querverweisen (Beispiel: lay academy See under: lay training centre) ist der erste Buchstabe des Stichwortes, unter dem die Übersetzung zu finden ist, unterstrichen (in diesem Fall: t - training).

- Alle englischen Begriffe sind numeriert. Die in den drei alphabetischen Registern (Französisch - Deutsch - Spanisch) am Ende des Buches jeweils angegebene Nummer bezieht sich auf den entsprechenden englischen Begriff.

- Im Falle von Titeln und Abkürzungen bezeichnet die im alphabetischen Register angegebene Nummer die Seite, auf der der gesuchte Titel oder die entsprechende Abkürzung zu finden ist.

- Eine schematische Darstellung der Struktur und eine vollständige Liste der Sekretariate und Programme des Ökumenischen Rates der Kirchen enthält Kapitel IV, S. 420.

- Die in Französisch, Deutsch und Spanisch angegebenen Berufsbezeichnungen beziehen

Explicación del uso

- En el capítulo siguiente, los términos en inglés están clasificados por órden alfabético, teniendo en cuenta la primera letra del concepto principal (ejemplo: "community development" está clasificado por "development").

- Cuando uno de los términos remite a otra expresión (ejemplo: lay academy See under: lay training centre"), se encontrará la misma bajo la palabra cuya primera letra ha sido subrayada (en este caso: bajo "training").

- Cada término en inglés con sus traducciones está precedido de un número. Cada uno de los términos de los índices alfabéticos en francés, alemán y español que se encuentran al final del libro, remite al número de la palabra en inglés correspondiente.

- En el caso de "títulos y abreviaturas", los números indicados en los índices remiten a las páginas en las que figuran esos títulos y abreviaturas.

- En el capítulo IV, pag. 420 figuran un organigrama del Consejo Mundial de Iglesias y la lista completa de sus secretarías y programas.

- Obsérvese que en francés, alemán y español, los títulos profesionales se indican siempre en relación a los cargos y figuran

Personnel' will be either 'directeur du personnel' or 'directrice du personnel'.

le poste, il conviendra naturellement
d'utiliser, selon les cas, le masculin
ou le féminin (exemple:"Director of
Personnel" se traduira par "directeur du
personnel" ou "directrice du personnel").

sich auf den jeweiligen Posten, nicht auf
die Person, die diesen Posten innehat. Sie sind
daher in der maskulinen Form angegeben und
müssen abgewandelt werden, wenn eine Frau den
entsprechenden Posten innehat. Beispiel:
Director of Personnel - Personaldirektor -
Personaldirektorin.

en masculino. Cuando se haga mención a
la persona que ocupa el cargo, deberá
utilizarse, por supuesto, según del caso,
el masculino o el femenino (ejemplo:
"Director of Personnel" se traducirá
por "director de personal" o "directora de
personal").

VII ALPHABETICAL LIST OF VOCABULARY (1)	VII TERMINOLOGIE (1)	VII TERMINOLOGIE (1)	VII TERMINOLOGIA (1)
1 Aborigines	aborigènes (mpl), autochtones (mpl)	Aborigenes (mpl), Ureinwohner (mpl) (=-bevölkerung/f/)	aborígenes (mpl), autóctonos (mpl)
2 abortion	avortement (m); interruption (f) de grossesse	Schwangerschafts-abbruch (m); Abtreibung (f)	aborto (m); interrupción (f) del embarazo
3 abortion counselling	information (f) sur l'interruption de grossesse	Schwangerschafts-konfliktberatung (f), Schwangerschafts-abbruchberatung (f)	asesoramiento (m) sobre la interrupción del embarazo
4 abortion on eugenic/ medico-social/ ethical indications	interruption (f) de grossesse sur indications eugéniques/médicales/ sociales/morales	Schwangerschafts-abbruch (m) aufgrund eugenischer/ medizinischer/sozialer/ethischer Indikation	interrupción (f) del embarazo por indicaciones eugénicas/médicas/ sociales/morales
5 induced abortion	avortement (m) provoqué	induzierter Abort (m)	aborto (m) provocado
academy			
6 evangelical academy	académie (f) évangélique	Evangelische Akademie	academia (f) evangélica
lay academy - See under: lay training centre			

(1) See "Explanatory Note", p. 183   (1) Voir "Notice explicative", p. 183   (1) Siehe 'Hinweise für die Benutzung' S. 184   (1) Véase "Explicación del uso", pag. 184

7 accidia (extreme state of spiritual sloth and despondency)	acédia (f) (terme ascétique, désigne l'état ultime de l'abat- tement de l'esprit)	Acedia (f) (Aszetischer Begriff zur Bezeichnung ab- soluter geistlicher Trägheit)	acedia (f) (Término ascético que indica el grado más bajo del abati- miento del espíritu)
8 accommodation	compromis (m), entente (f)	Entgegenkommen (n), Verständigung (f)	entendimiento (m); término (m) medio
accountability 9 mutual accounta- bility	engagement (m) libre- ment assumé de la part des Eglises de se rendre compte mutuellement de leur vie et témoignage	Bereitschaft (f) zur verbindlichen gegen- seitigen Rechen- schaft	compromiso (m) por parte de las iglesias de rendirse cuenta mutuamente de su fe y testimonio
10 action-reflection programme	programme (m) "action-réflexion"	kombiniertes Stu- dien- und Aktions- programm (n)	programa (m) de acción y reflexión

See also: manpower, labour

11 active population,
    work force,
    labour force
	population (f) ac-
	tive, forces (fpl)
	de travail
		Erwerbsbevölkerung
		(f), Erwerbsperso-
		nen (fpl), Erwerbs-
		tätige (mpl)
			población (f) activa,
			mano de obra (f),
			número (m) de obreros,
			fuerza (f) de
			trabaj (=laboral)

12 acculturation	acculturation (f)	Akkulturation (f)	aculturación (f)
13 addicts	toxicomanes (mpl)	Suchtkranke (mpl)	toxicómanos (mpl)
14 drug addicts	toxicomanes (mpl) (victimes de la drogue)	Drogenabhängige (mpl)	Toxicómanos (mpl), drogadictos (mpl)

admission (general, limited, reciprocal) - See under: communion

15 advancement (within a grade)	avancement (m) (à l'intérieur d'une classe)	Beförderung (f) (innerhalb einer Gehaltsgruppe)	ascenso (m) (dentro de una misma categoría)
16 adventure playground	jardin (m) Robinson	Abenteuerspiel-platz (m)	parque (m) infantil
17 adviser	conseiller (m)	Berater (m)	asesor (m)
18 young adviser /WCC Assembly/	jeune conseiller (m) /Assemblée du COE/	junger Berater (m) /ÖRK-Vollversamm-lung/	asesor (m) juvenil /Asamblea del CMI/

advisory service - See under: counselling service

19 Afrikaans /South Africa/	afrikaans(langue/f/ afrikaner)/Afrique du Sud/	Afrikaans/Süd-afrika/	africaans (idioma /f/africander) Sudáfrica/
20 Afrikaner /South Africa/	afrikaner (adj. m et f), Afrikaner (m) /Afrique du Sud/	afrikaanisch, Afrikaaner (m) /Südafrika/	africander (adj. m y f), africander (m) (Sudáfrica/
21 Afro-Americans	Afro-américains (mpl)	Afroamerikaner (mpl)	afroamericanos (mpl)
22 after-care	1. post-cure (f) 2. aide (f) post-pénitentiaire	1. Nachbehandlung (f) 2. Resozialisierungs-hilfe (f)	1. tratamiento (m) posthostpitalario; asistencia (f) posthostpitalaria 2. ayuda (f) post-penitenciaria
23 Agape (a fellowship meal follow-ing the ancient and historical	agape (f) (1. repas fraternel commémorant la der-nière cène de Jésus	Agape (f) (1. Liebesmahl: im Anschluss an das Abendmahl	ágape (f) (1. comida frater-nal conmemorando la última cena de Jesús

	christian practice and tradition; administration of the bread only 2. fellowship meal: not Holy Communion) agency	2. repas fraternel, sans relation avec la Sainte Cène)	2. Gemeinschaftsmahl: keine Verbindung mit dem Abendmahl)	2. comida fraternal, sin relación con la Santa Cena)
24	funding agency	institution (f) (= organisme /m/) de financement	finanzierende Organisation (f)	institución (f) (=organismo /m/) de financiación
25	fund-raising agency	institution (f) collectrice (organisme /m/ collecteur) de fonds	kapitalbeschaffende Stelle (f)	organismo (m) para la obtención de fondos
26	related (inter-related) agencies /CICARWS/	institutions (fpl) (=organismes /mpl/) d'entraide en relation (=en liaison) avec la CESEAR	Organisationen (fpl) (=Verbände /mpl/) in (Arbeits-)Verbindung mit CICARWS	instituciones (fpl) (=organismos /mpl/) de ayuda mutua en relación con la CAISMR
27	(church) service agencies, (church) relief agencies	institutions (fpl) d'entraide (ecclésiastiques), organismes (m) de secours (ecclésiastiques) (on a dit aussi parfois : agences /fpl/ de service, de secours)	(kirchliche) Hilfswerke (npl)	instituciones (fpl) de servicio (eclesiásticas), organismos (mpl) de socorro (eclesiásticos)
28	Sponsored Agencies /CWME/	institutions (fpl) parrainées /CME/	geförderte Einrichtungen (fpl) /CWME/	instituciones (fpl) patrocinadas /CMME/

191

| 29 | voluntary agency (=organization) | institution (f) (organisation/f/) bénévole (privée); oeuvre (f) privée | freiwilliges Hilfswerk (n); freies (i.S. v. nichtöffentlich, privat) Hilfswerk (n) | institución (f) (=organización/f/) (privada) de trabajo voluntario; obra (f) privada |

aid

30	foreign aid	aide (f) étrangère (=extérieure)	Auslandshilfe (f)	ayuda (f) extranjera (=exterior)
31	inter-church aid	entraide (f) des Eglises	zwischenkirchliche Hilfe (f)	ayuda (f) intereclesiástica
32	material aid	aide (f) matérielle	Materialhilfe (f), Hilfsgüter (npl)	ayuda (f) material
33	tied aid	aide (f) conditionnelle (=liée)	gebundene Hilfe (f)	ayuda (f) condicionada (=vinculada)
34	untied aid	aide (f) inconditionnelle (=non liée)	ungebundene Hilfe (f)	ayuda (f) no condicionada (=desvinculada)

aide

| 35 | nursing aide | aide-soignant (m) | Krankenpflegehelferin (f) | ayudante/=auxiliar /m/ (m) de enfermeria |
| 36 | rural medical aide | auxiliaire (m) médical rural | ländlicher Gesundheitshelfer (m) | ayudante (m) (=auxiliar/m/) medicina rural |

aim

| 37 | Aim of the Commission on Faith and Order "The aim of the Commission is to | But de la Commission de foi et constitution "Le but de la Commission est de pro- | Ziel der Kommission für Glauben und Kirchenverfassung "Ziel der Kommission ist es, die Einheit | Propósito de la Comisión de Fe y Constitución "El propósito de la Comisión es |

proclaim the oneness of the Church of Jesus Christ and to call the churches to the goal of visible unity in one faith and one eucharistic fellowship, expressed in worship and in common life in Christ, in order that the world may believe."

clamer l'unité de l'Eglise de Jésus-Christ et d'appeler les Eglises à rendre visible cette unité en une seule foi et une seule communauté eucharistique, s'exprimant dans le culte et la vie commune en Christ, afin que le monde croie."

der Kirche Jesu Christi zu verkündigen und die Kirchen aufzurufen zu dem Ziel der sichtbaren Einheit in einem Glauben und einer eucharistischen Gemeinschaft, die ihren Ausdruck im Gottesdienst und im gemeinsamen Leben in Christus findet, damit die Welt glaube."

proclamar la unidad de la Iglesia de Jesucristo y exhortar a las iglesias a hacer visible esta unidad en una misma fe y en una sola comunión eucarística, expresada en el culto y en la vida común en Cristo, para que el mundo crea."

38 Aim of the Conference on World Mission and Evangelism "Its aim is to assist the Christian community in the proclamation of the Gospel of Jesus Christ, by word and deed, to the whole world to the end that all may believe in him and be saved."

But (m) de la Conférence de mission et d'évangélisation "Elle a pour but d'aider la communauté chrétienne à proclamer l'Evangile de Jésus-Christ au monde entier, par la parole et par l'action, afin que tous puissent croire en lui et être sauvés."

Zielsetzung der Konferenz für Weltmission und Evangelisation "Sie soll die Gemeinschaft der Christen in ihrem Bemühen unterstützen, das Evangelium von Jesus Christus in Wort und Tat der ganzen Welt zu verkündigen, damit alle Menschen an ihn glauben und gerettet werden."

Propósito (m) de la Conferencia de Misión Mundial y Evangelización "Su propósito es el de ayudar a la comunidad cristiana a proclamar el Evangelio de Jesucristo en el mundo entero, por medio de la palabra y la acción, para que todos crean en El y sean salvos."

39 aims and functions, functions and purposes

buts (mpl) et fonctions (fpl)

Ziele (mpl) und Aufgaben (fpl)

metas (fpl) (=propósitos/mpl/) y funciones (fpl)

40 anamnesis (remembrance, memorial. In biblical and liturgical usage, never 'commemoration' in the sense of recalling a completed past event but the act of 'calling to mind' what is now present before God, a commitment of ourselves to God, a recollection that we are in his presence)	anamnèse (f) (réminiscence, mémorial. Dans la Bible et la liturgie ce n'est point une commémoration, souvenir d'un passé révolu, mais un rappel de ce qui est présent devant le Père, l'acte de se référer à Dieu, de se rappeler devant Dieu)	Anamnese (f) (Erinnerung, Memorial. In der Bibel und Liturgie nicht im Sinne einer Erinnerung an eine "vergangene Vergangenheit", sondern als Vergegenwärtigung dessen, was vor Gott ist; der Akt des sich auf Gott Berufens, sich vor Gott Erinnerns)	anamnesis (f) (=anamnesia/f/) (Reminiscencia. rememoración. En la Biblia y en la liturgia no se trata de una conmemoración como recuerdo de un pasado ya superado, sino de lo que está presente delante del Padre, el acto de referirse a Dios, de recordar delante de Dios)
41 anaphora (uplifting of the elements. Central part of the Eastern Eucharistic Liturgy, corresponding to the Roman 'canon')	anaphore (f) (élévation des dons. Partie centrale de la liturgie eucharistique orientale qui correspond au Canon romain)	Anaphora (f) (Darbringung, Elevation der Gaben. Hauptteil der orthodoxen eucharistischen Liturgie, der dem römischen Messkanon entspricht)	anáfora (f) (Elevación de los dones. Parte central de la liturgia eucarística oriental que corresponde al Canon romano)
42 ANC:African National Congress/South Africa/	ANC: Congrès (m) national africain /Afrique du Sud/	ANC: Afrikanischer Nationalkongress (m) /Südafrika/	ANC: Congreso (m) Nacional Africano /Sudáfrica/
43 ANC:African National Council /Rhodesia/	ANC: Conseil (m) national africain /Rhodésie/	ANC: Afrikanischer Nationalrat (m) /Rhodesien/	ANC: Consejo (m) Nacional Africano /Rhodesia/

44 anthropomorphosis (denotes the fact of the incarnation, God becomes man)	anthropomorphose (f) (désigne le fait de l'incarnation. Dieu devient homme)	Anthropomorphose (f) (bezeichnet das Ereignis der Inkarnation. Gott wird Mensch)	antropomórfosis (f) (se refiere al hecho de la encarnación. Dios se hace hombre.
45 apartheid, "separate development"	apartheid (m), "développement (m) séparé"	Apartheid (f), "getrennte (=eigenständige)Entwicklung"	apartheid (m), "desarrollo (m) separado"
46 petty apartheid /South Africa/	apartheid (m) quotidien/Afrique du Sud/(l'apartheid tel qu'il se manifeste au niveau des relations quotidiennes entre les groupes raciaux)	"Petty Apartheid" (f) /Südafrika/ (Gesamtheit der Kontakt-/bzw. Distanzverhältnisse zwischen den Rassengruppen, die durch Gesetz geregelt sind)	apartheid (m) diario /Sudáfrica/ (apartheid (m) a nivel de las relaciones cotidianas entre los grupos raciales)
47 apocatastasis (Origen's view of the final restoration of all creatures)	apocatastase (f) (théorie d'Origène sur la restauration finale de toutes les créatures)	Apokatastasis (f) (Theorie des Origenes über die vollkommene Wiederherstellung der Schöpfung am Weltende)	apocatástasis (f) (Teoría de Orígenes sobre la restauración final de todas las criaturas)

Apocrypha - See under: biblical studies

47 apophatic (apophatic or negative theology uses negative terms to speak of God)	apophatique (La théologie apophatique, négative, procède par négation de toute définition de Dieu)	apophatisch (Die apophatische - verneinende - Theologie arbeitet mit Verneinungen jeder Definition Gottes)	apofático (La teología apofática, negativa, procede a través de negaciones de toda definición de Dios)
49 appeal	appel (m) de fonds	Spendenaufruf (m)	solicitud (f) de recursos (=de fondos)

195

50 applicant	candidat (m)	Stellenbewerber (m), Bewerber (m)	candidato (m), solicitante (m)
51 application	candidature (f), demande (f) d'emploi	Stellengesuch (n), Bewerbung (f)	candidatura (f), solicitud (f) (=demanda /f/) de empleo
52 application form	formule (f) (=formulaire/m/) de demande d'emploi	Bewerbungsformular (n)	formulario (m) (de solicitud de empleo)
53 application for membership /WCC/	demande (f) d'admission /COE/	Antrag (m) auf Mitgliedschaft, /ÖRK/	solicitud (f) de admisión (=de ingreso) /CMI/
54 approach	manière (f) d'envisager, approche (f), vision (f), optique (f); point (m) de vue; conception (f); méthode (f) d'approche	Betrachtungsweise (f); Einstellung (f); Denken (n), Konzeption (f); Ansatz (m), Methode (f)	manera (f) de encarar, enfoque (m), visión (f), óptica (f); punto (m) de vista; concepción (f); procedimiento (m) (=método/m/) de estudio
55 archetype (ideal pattern of things and beings. The Fathers regard Christ as the divine archetype of man)	archétype (m) (prototype idéal des choses et des êtres. Chez les Pères le Christ est l'Archétype divin de l'homme)	Archetyp (m) (Idealer Prototyp der Dinge und Lebewesen. Für die Kirchenväter ist Christus der göttliche Archetyp des Menschen)	arquetipo (m) (Prototipo ideal de las cosas y de los seres. Según los Padres, Cristo es el Arquetipo divino del hombre)
56 area orientation (=briefing)	session (f) de préparation, stage (m) d'initiation (aux conditions locales)	auslandskundliche Vorbereitung (f)	curso (m) de información (=de orientación)

arms

57 arms control	contrôle (m) de l'armement	Rüstungskontrolle (f)	control (m) de armamentos
58 arms limitation, limitation of armaments	limitation (f) des armements	Rüstungsbeschränkungen (f)	limitación (f) de armamentos
59 arms race	course (f) aux armements	Wettrüsten (n), Rüstungswettlauf (m)	carrera (f) de armamentos (=armamentista)
60 arrivals, intake /migration/	entrées (fpl), arrivées (fpl), somme (f) (=nombre /m/) des entrées /migration/	Zugänge(mpl), Zugang (m) /Migration/	entradas (fpl), llegadas (fpl), número (m) de entradas /migración/
61 Assembly /WCC,CEC/	Assemblée (f) /COE, KEK/	Vollversammlung (f) /ÖRK, KEK/	Asamblea (f) /CMI, KEK/
62 to assert (=enforce) one's rights	faire valoir ses droits	seine Rechte wahrnehmen	hacer valer sus derechos, defender sus derechos

assistance

63 technical assistance	assistance (f) technique	technische Hilfe (f)	asistencia (f) técnica
64 assistant	assistant (m), adjoint (m)	Assistent (m)	auxiliar (m), ayudante (m)
65 Assistant to ...	assistant (m) du ...	Referent (m) im ... (Generalsekretariat, in der Abteilung...)	Ayudante (m) del ...
66 medical assistant	assistant (m) médical	"medizinischer Assistent", Hilfsarzt (m) /Entwicklungsländer/	ayudante (m)(=auxiliar (m) de medicina

197

awareness
awareness-building - See under: consciousness-raising

growth of awareness - See under: awakening of consciousness

67 backlash,
   white backlash
   /USA/

durcissement (m)
(des blancs)/Etats-
Unis/ (violente ré-
action anti-noire
provoquée par les
demandes, jugées
excessives, de la
minorité noire)

weisser 'backlash'
/USA/ (scharfe Re-
aktion der Weissen
auf die als über-
trieben erachteten
Forderungen der
schwarzen Minder-
heit)

endurecimiento (m)
(de los blancos)
/Estados Unidos/
(violenta reacción
antinegra provo-
cada por las exi-
gencias de la
minoría negra, con-
sideradas excesivas)

balance
68   Unappropriated
     Balance /CICARWS/

solde (m) non affec-
té /CESEAR/

nichtzugewiesener
Gewinnvortrag (m),
Dispositionsfonds
(m) /CICARWS/

saldo (m) no asig-
nado /CAISMR/

69 to ban /South Africa/
   (through 'banning
   orders' which ban
   individuals from
   normal social con-
   tact, restricting
   their freedom of
   movement, con-
   fining them to one
   district etc.)

placer sous l'effet
d'interdits, bannir
/Afrique du Sud/
(le "ban" ou "ban-
nissement" est un
ordre individuel qui
détermine un lieu
et un horaire fixes
de résidence; ou
l'interdiction de
pénétrer dans cer-

bannen, mit dem
Bann belegen, Bann-
verfügungen erlas-
sen /Südafrika/
(eine mit dem Bann
belegte Person un-
terliegt den fol-
genden Beschrän-
kungen ihrer Frei-
heitsrechte: Zu-
weisung eines be-

proscribir/Sudá-
frica/ (Las órdenes
de proscripción
/=de interdicción/
/"banning orders"/
son órdenes indivi-
duales que prohiben
a una persona resi-
dir en un lugar o
zona mencionados,
o ausentarse de

tains lieux; ou celle d'appartenir à certaines organisations, ou de rencontrer certains types de personnes)	stimmten Wohnsitzes mit festgelegten Ausgehzeiten; Verbot, bestimmte Orte aufzusuchen oder bestimmten Organisationen anzugehören oder mit bestimmten Personen zusammenzutreffen)	ellas, o asistir a reuniones, o pertenecer a determinadas organizaciones, o comunicarse con determinadas personas)

Bantustan - See under: homeland

baptisme

70 baptism by affusion	baptême (m) dans l'eau vive	Taufe (f) durch Begiessen	bautismo (m) por afusión
71 baptism by immersion	baptême (m) par immersion	Taufe (f) durch Untertauchen	bautismo (m) por inmersión
72 baptism by sprinkling	baptême (m) par aspersion	Taufe (f) durch Besprengen	bautismo (m) por aspersión
73 adult baptism	baptême (m) des adultes	Erwachsenentaufe (f)	bautismo (m) de adultos
74 believers baptism	baptême (m) des croyants, baptême (m) des professants	Taufe (f) von Gläubigen	bautismo (m) de creyentes
75 infant baptism, paedobaptism	pédobaptisme (m), baptême (m) des enfants	Kindertaufe (f)	bautismo (m) de niños

baptismal

| 76 baptismal order, order of baptism | service (m) de baptême | Tauforordnung (f) | servicio (m) de bautismo |

77 baptismal service   service (m) de   Taufgottesdienst (m)   servicio (m) de
                        baptême   bautismo

Bible

Bible Correspondence Courses - See under: biblical studies

Bible Societies - See under: biblical studies

Bible study   - See under: biblical studies

Bible study enabler - See under: biblical studies

Bible study groups - See under: biblical studies

Bible study leader - See under: biblical studies

Bible study leadership development - See under: biblical studies

Bible study outlines - See under: biblical studies

Bible study tools - See under: biblical studies

   Daily Bible Reading Notes - See under: biblical studies

   distribution of the Bible - See under: biblical studies

   selections from the Bible- See under: biblical studies

biblical

biblical scholars - See under: biblical studies

78 biblical studies

The <u>canon</u> of the Bible includes both the Old Testament and the New Testament. It must be noted, however, that the canon of the original Hebrew text of the Old Testament (the <u>Masora</u>)is shorter than the most famous Greek translation of the Old Testament (the <u>Septuagint</u>). The latter includes also what Catholics call the <u>Deutero-Canonical books</u> and what Protestants usually call the <u>Apocrypha</u> . Besides these additional books included in the Septuagint there is another large body of <u>intertestamental writings</u>. They include what Protestants usually call the <u>Pseudepigrapha</u> (while Catholics call them "the <u>Apocrypha</u>"). To the intertestamental literature belong also e.g. the <u>Qumran documents</u>. There are <u>New Testament Apocrypha</u> such as the many apocryphal gospels, which are not included in Bible editions.

In <u>Bible study</u> done by individuals or <u>Bible study groups</u> a biblical text or theme is examined within its <u>literary and historical context</u> (<u>exegesis</u>) and the group attempts to discern what is <u>God's Word</u> through this particular text or theme for the readers in today's situation. For group work it is good to have a <u>Bible study leader</u> (or, better still, <u>Bible study enabler</u>) and with a view to this <u>Bible study leadership development</u>, training courses or <u>Bible study enablers</u>, have to be conducted . For individual and sometimes also corporate reading <u>Daily</u>

recherche (f) biblique

Le <u>canon</u> de la Bible comprend l'Ancien Testament et le Nouveau Testament. Il faut relever toutefois que le canon du texte original hébreu de l'Ancien Testament (la <u>masorah</u>) est plus court que la traduction grecque la plus connue de l'Ancien Testament (la version des <u>septante</u>). Cette dernière comprend également ce que les catholiques appellent les <u>livres deutérocanoniques</u> et que les protestants désignent généralement par <u>apocryphes</u>. A côté de ces livres supplémentaires contenus dans la version des septante, il existe un nombre important d'<u>écrits intertestamentaires</u>. Ceux-ci comprennent les livres que les protestants appellent communément les <u>pseudépigraphes</u>, et les catholiques les apocryphes. Les <u>manuscrits de Qumran</u>, par exemple, font aussi partie de la littérature intertestamentaire. Il existe également des <u>apocryphes du Nouveau Testament</u> (<u>néo-testamentaires</u>), tels les nombreux évangiles apocryphes, qui ne figurent pas dans les éditions de la Bible.

Dans les <u>études bibliques</u> entreprises individuellement ou en groupes (<u>groupes d'étude/s/ biblique/s/</u>), le texte ou le thème biblique choisi est examiné dans son <u>contexte littéraire et historique</u> (<u>exégèse</u>). A travers ce texte ou ce thème particuliers, le groupe s'efforce de discerner la <u>parole de Dieu</u> telle qu'elle s'adresse aux lecteurs d'aujourd'hui. Pour le travail en groupe, il est bon d'avoir un <u>animateur d'études bibliques</u> et d'envisager la

Bibelforschung (f)

Zum Kanon der Bibel gehören das Alte wie auch das Neue Testament. Der Kanon des Alten Testaments im hebräischen Urtext (die Masora) ist jedoch kürzer als die berühmteste griechische Übersetzung des Alten Testaments (die Septuaginta). Zur Septuaginta gehören auch diejenigen Schriften, die im katholischen Sprachgebrauch deuterokanonische Bücher, im protestantischen hingegen allgemein Apokryphen genannt werden. Neben diesen zusätzlichen Büchern, die die Septuaginta enthält, gibt es noch eine grosse Zahl von Schriften, die die Brücke zwischen Altem und Neuem Testament herstellen. Zu ihnen gehören die von den Protestanten als Pseudepigraphen (von den Katholiken hingegen als Apokryphen) bezeichneten Schriften und die Qumranschriften. Es gibt neutestamentliche Apokryphen, beispielsweise die zahlreichen apokryphen Evangelien, die in unseren Bibelausgaben nicht enthalten sind.

In den Bibelstudien, die man allein oder in Bibelstudiengruppen vornimmt, wird ein bestimmter Text oder ein Thema aus der Bibel in seinem literarischen und zeitgeschichtlichen Zusammenhang untersucht (Exegese); dabei versucht man, anhand eines solchen Textes oder Themas die Bedeutung von Gottes Wort für den Leser heute zu erkennen. Bei der Gruppenarbeit kann ein Bibelstudienleiter oder Bibelstudien-"Befähiger" wichtige Hilfen geben, und es gibt spezielle Kurse zur Heranbildung von Bibelstudienleitern oder Bibelstudien-"Befähigern". Für die private oder gemeinschaftliche Lektüre

investigación (f) bíblica

El canon de la Biblia incluye el Antiguo y el Nuevo Testamento. Se ha de notar, sin embargo, que el canon del texto original en hebreo del Antiguo Testamento (la Masora) es más corto que el de la traducción griega más conocida (la Septuaginta). Esta última incluye además los libros que los católicos denominan Deuterocanónicos y que los protestantes llaman por lo general Apócrifos. Además de estos libros adicionales, figuran en la Septuaginta numerosos escritos intertestamentarios. Entre ellos encontramos los que los protestantes denominan generalmente Pseudoepígrafos y los católicos Apócrifos. A la literatura intertestamentaria pertenecen también, por ejemplo, los manuscritos de Qumrán. Existen apócrifos neotestamentarios tales como los numerosos evangelios apócrifos, que no figuran en las ediciones de la Biblia.

En los estudios bíblicos llevados a cabo individualmente o en grupo (grupo de estudio bíblico), se examina el texto o tema bíblico dentro de su contexto literario e histórico (exégesis) y el grupo procura discernir, a través de este texto o tema particular, cuál es la Palabra de Dios para los lectores contemporáneos. Es conveniente que el grupo de trabajo cuente con un líder de estudios bíblicos o, mejor aún, con animadores de estudios bíblicos, previendo para este fin la formación de líderes de estudios bíblicos (se organizan cursos de prepara-

Bible Reading Notes are published, Bible correspondence courses are organized and Bible study tools such as biblical work books or vocabularies, different translations and paraphrases, concordances and commentaries published. Many groups also use Bible study outlines with an introduction to the text, questions and themes for study.

Bible Societies work for the translation, printing and distribution of the Bible and selections from the Bible in the different language areas of the world. In the Roman Catholic church an Office for Common Bible Work has been created which is part of the Secretariat for Promoting Christian Unity and which works closely with the United Bible Societies (UBS). There is also a Roman Catholic World Federation for Biblical Apostolate which does work similar to the Bible Societies and fosters the distribution and reading of the Bible among Roman Catholics. Due to this collaboration between the UBS and the Roman Catholic Church most translations are now made on a fully ecumenical basis and a Common Bible has been published which contains the Old and New Testament canon according to the Revised Standard Version as well as the Deutero-Canonical books. In Bible translation there is at the moment a tendency to abandon formal correspondence translation and to make dynamic equivalence translations. This means that the receptor language is taken as seriously as the source language. Such dynamic equivalence translations in

formation d'animateurs d'études bibliques (on organise à cet effet des cours de formation d'animateurs d'études bibliques). Pour faciliter la lecture individuelle et quelquefois aussi collective, des notes pour la lecture quotidienne de la Bible sont publiées, des cours bibliques par correspondance sont organisés et du matériel d'étude(s)biblique(s), qui comprend des dictionnaires bibliques ou lexiques (vocabulaires), différentes traductions et paraphrases, des concordances et des commentaires, est également publié. De nombreux groupes utilisent aussi des cahier bibliques (manuels d'études bibliques) contenant une introduction au texte, des questions et un plan d'étude.

Les sociétés bibliques travaillent à la traduction, à l'impression et à la diffusion de la Bible et de livres de la Bible dans les différentes régions linguistiques du globe. Un Bureau pour le travail biblique oecuménique a été créé au sein de l'Eglise catholique romaine; il fait partie du Secrétariat pour l'unité des chrétiens et travaille en étroite relation avec l'Alliance biblique universelle (ABU). Il existe également une Fédération catholique mondiale pour l'apostolat de la Bible qui accomplit un travail comparable à celui des sociétés bibliques et encourage la diffusion et la lecture de la Bible chez les catholiques romains. Grâce à cette collaboration de l'ABU et de l'Eglise catholique romaine, la plupart des traductions se font aujourd' hui sur une base entièrement oecuménique et

werden Notizen zur täglichen Bibellektüre
herausgegeben, Korrespondenzkurse für das
Bibelstudium veranstaltet und Arbeitshilfen
wie Arbeitsbücher zur Bibel, Wörterbücher,
verschiedene Übersetzungen und Paraphrasen,
Konkordanzen und Kommentare veröffentlicht.
Viele Gruppen benutzen auch Arbeitspläne
zum Bibelstudium, die eine kurze Einführung
in den gewählten Text, Fragen und bestimmte
Aufgabenstellungen für die Untersuchung enthalten.

Die Bibelgesellschaften sind für Übersetzung,
Druck und Verbreitung der Bibel und Aus-
züge aus der Bibel in den verschiedenen
Sprachgebieten der Welt zuständig. Im Rahmen
des Sekretariats für die Einheit der Christen
hat die Katholische Kirche ein Büro für ökumenische Bibelarbeit, das mit dem Weltbund
der Bibelgesellschaften (UBS) eng zusammen-
arbeitet. Daneben gibt es die Katholische
Weltvereinigung für das Bibelapostolat, die
in ähnlicher Weise wie die Bibelgesellschaften tätig ist und Verbreitung und Lektüre
der Bibel unter römisch-katholischen Christen
fördert.

Dank dieser Zusammenarbeit zwischen dem Weltbund der Bibelgesellschaften und der Römisch-
Katholischen Kirche beruhen die meisten Übersetzungen heute auf einer uneingeschränkt
ökumenischen Grundlage; so wurde z.B. in Englisch
und Französisch eine Gemeinsame Bibel (engl.:
Common Bible, franz.: Traduction oecuménique
de la Bible - TOB) herausgegeben, die den alt-
und neutestamentlichen Kanon gemäss der "Revised Standard Version" wie auch die deutero-

ción de animadores de estudios bíblicos).
Para facilitar la lectura personal, y a
veces también colectiva, se publican
notas de lectura bíblica diaria, se
organizan cursos bíblicos por correspondencia y se publican materiales de
estudio bíblico, tales como diccio-
narios o vocabularios bíblicos, distintas traducciones y paráfrasis, concor-
dancias y comentarios. Muchos grupos
emplean también manuales de estudios
bíblicos (cuadernos bíblicos) con una
introducción al texto, preguntas y
ejercicios.

Las Sociedades Bíblicas se ocupan de la
traducción, impresión y distribución
de la Biblia y de libros de la Biblia
en las diversas regiones linguísticas
del mundo. En la Iglesia Católica
Romana se creó una Oficina para el
Trabajo Bíblico Ecuménico que forma
parte del Secretariado para la Promoción
de los Cristianos y trabaja en estrecha
relación con las Sociedades Bíblicas
Unidas. Existe también una Federación
Mundial Católica Romana para el Aposto-
lado Bíblico, que realiza un trabajo similar al de las Sociedades Bíblicas y pro-
mueve la distribución y lectura de la
Biblia entre los católicos romanos. Gracias
a esta colaboración entre la SBU y la
Iglesia Católica Romana, la mayoría
de las traducciones se hacen ahora sobre
una base enteramente ecuménica
y se ha publicado una Common Bible inglesa
que contiene al canon del Antiguo y del

the common language of the people are especially important for evangelism, while other translations are needed for liturgical use and biblical studies.

In the biblical studies done mostly by biblical scholars but also for instance by the "Equipe de recherche biblique" in France and other parts of the world the Bible is studied by different methods. Usually a distinction is made between exegesis(which examines what the author of a text intended to say to the first readers of the text in their particular milieu) and hermeneutics (in which an attempt is made to bridge the time and culture gap and to translate and interpret the message of the text for today). Biblical studies in the West have been strongly oriented towards the literary and historic reading (or criticism) of the Bible. In literary criticism, the different literary genres have been examined, distinguishing, for instance, between wisdom literature, prophetic literature, apocalyptic literature, etc. In critical studies of form and tradition an attempt is made to see how the texts originated, how an oral or written tradition grew up and how it was transmitted. Redactional historical (or critical) studies examine what theological, polemical, didactic, liturgical, etc. emphasis the final redactor wanted to make. In all these historic critical studies of the Bible the distinction between tradition and redaction is therefore important and the Bible is read essentially in a diachronic way. More recently there has been much emphasis on a synchronic way of

une Common Bible anglaise a été publiée, qui contient le canon de l'Ancien et du Nouveau Testaments selon la Revised Standard Version ainsi que les livres deutérocanoniques. En français, la TOB (traduction oecuménique de la Bible) est en cours de réalisation. Le Nouveau Testament a paru en 1972 et la publication de la Bible entière est prévue pour 1975. En matière de traduction de la Bible, on tend aujourd'hui à abandonner le principe de la correspondance (=de l'équivalence)formelle au profit de traductions selon le principe de l'équivalence dynamique. En d'autres termes, on accorde autant d'intérêt à la langue réceptrice qu'à la langue originale. Si ces traductions en langue courante selon le principe de l'équivalence dynamique revêtent une importance particulière pour l'évangélisation, il y a lieu de recourir à d'autres traductions pour l'usage liturgique et les études bibliques.

Dans la recherche biblique entreprise la plupart du temps par des biblistes (=spécialistes des sciences bibliques), mais aussi par exemple par les Equipes de recherche biblique en France et par des groupes équivalents dans d'autres pays, la Bible est étudiée selon différentes méthodes. On distingue généralement entre l'exégèse (qui examine ce que l'auteur d'un texte a voulu dire aux premiers lecteurs/=destinataires/du texte dans leur milieu particulier) et l'herméneutique (qui s'efforce de franchir le fossé du temps et de la

kanonischen Schriften enthält. Bei der
Übersetzung der Bibel geht man heute mehr
und mehr ab von der Übersetzungsform der
"formalen Entsprechung" und in zunehmendem
Masse hin zur Übersetzungsweise der "dynamischen Gleichwertigkeit". Dies bedeutet,
dass man der Zielsprache dieselbe Bedeutung
beimisst wie der Ausgangssprache. Solche
dynamischen Gleichwertigkeits-Übersetzungen
in die Umgangssprache der Menschen sind be-
sonders wichtig für die Verkündigung, wohin-
gegen andere Übersetzungsformen für den
Gottesdienst und die Bibelforschung notwen-
dig sind.

In der Bibelforschung, die hauptsächlich von
Bibelforschern, aber z.B. auch von den
"Equipes de recherche biblique" in Frankreich
und in anderen Teilen der Welt betrieben wird,
bedient man sich verschiedener Methoden. Gewöhnlich unterscheidet man dabei zwischen
der Exegese (wo untersucht wird, was der Ver-
fasser des Textes den ursprünglichen Lesern
dieses Textes in ihrem geschichtlich-sozi-
alen Milieu sagen wollte) und der Hermeneutik
(d.h. dem Versuch, Zeitabstand und kulturelle
Unterschiede zu überbrücken und die Botschaft
des Textes für die Menschen heute zu über-
setzen und zu interpretieren). Die Bibelforschung im Westen war in besonderem Masse
auf die literarisch-historische Forschung
(oder Kritik) abgestellt. In der Literarkri-
tik werden die verschiedenen Literatur-"Gat-
tungen" untersucht, wobei man z.B. zwischen
den Weisheitsbüchern, den Prophetensprüchen
und den Apokalypsen unterscheidet. In den
form- und überlieferungskritischen Unter-

Nuevo Testamento, según la Revised
Standard Version, así como los libros
Deuterocanónicos. En la traducción de
la Biblia existe actualmente la ten-
dencia a abandonar el principio de la
equivalencia formal y a aplicar el de la
equivalencia dinámica, es decir que se da
tanta importancia al idioma receptor como
al idioma original. Esas traducciones
en idioma corriente según el principio
de la equivalencia dinámica, revisten
una especial importancia para la evangelización, mientras que se requiere otro
tipo de traducciones para el empleo
litúrgico y para los estudios bíblicos.

En la investigación bíblica emprendida por
especialistas en ciencias bíblicas y
también, por ejemplo, por los Equipos
de Investigación Bíblica en Francia y
otras partes del mundo, se estudia la
Biblia con diferentes métodos. Por lo
general se hace una distinción entre
la exégesis (que estudia lo que el autor
de un texto quiso decir a los primeros lectores
/=destinatarios/ del texto en su medio
particular) y la hermenéutica (que procura salvar la distancia entre tiempo y
cultura y traducir e interpretar el
mensaje del texto en términos contemporáneos). La investigación bíblica en Occi-
dente ha sido claramente orientada hacia
la lectura (o crítica) literaria e histórica
de la Biblia. En lo que concierne a la
crítica literaria se han estudiado los
diversos géneros literarios, haciéndose
una distinción entre literatura sapiencial,

reading the Bible by taking the text as it
is given to us and by applying the methods
of structural analysis to biblical exegesis.

In the Orthodox churches and the churches in
the East in general much more emphasis is
laid on the liturgical reading of the Bible
and biblical meditation. An attempt is often
made there to go there beyond the literal
meaning to a symbolic and typological meaning
of the texts.

culture et de traduire et interpréter le
message du texte en termes contemporains).
En Occident, la recherche biblique a été
nettement orientée vers la lecture (ou
critique) littéraire et historique de la
Bible. Dans le cadre de la critique littéraire,
on a examiné les différents genres littéraires;
c'est ainsi que l'on distingue par exemple
le genre sapiential, le genre prophétique, le
genre apocalyptique, etc. Dans les études
critiques des formes et de la tradition, on
s'efforce de rechercher comment les textes
ont vu le jour, comment une tradition orale
ou écrite s'est développée et comment elle
a été transmise. Dans les études historiques
(ou critiques) de rédaction, on examine les
points théologiques, polémiques, didactiques,
liturgiques, etc. que le rédacteur du texte
final a voulu mettre en évidence. Dans toutes
ces études historico-critiques de la Bible
par conséquent, la distinction entre tradition et rédaction est importante et la
Bible est lue essentiellement dans une perspective diachronique. Plus récemment, on a
beaucoup mis l'accent sur une lecture syn-
chronique de la Bible en prenant le texte
tel qu'il se présente et en appliquant à
l'exégèse biblique les méthodes de l'analyse
structurale.

Dans les Eglises orthodoxes et les Eglises
d'Orient en général, on accorde une place
bien plus importante à la lecture liturgique
de la Bible et à la méditation biblique. On
s'y efforce souvent d'aller au-delà du sens
littéral et d'atteindre au sens symbolique
et typologique des textes.

suchungen versucht man festzustellen, wie
ein Text entstanden ist, wie sich eine
mündlich oder schriftlich geprägte Tradition
herausgebildet hat und wie sie überliefert
wurde. In den redaktionsgeschichtlichen (oder
-kritischen) Forschungen untersucht man,
welche theologischen, polemischen, didaktischen,
liturgischen Schwerpunkte der Redaktor des
Textes setzen wollte. In allen diesen ge-
schichtskritischen Untersuchungen der Bibel
ist die Unterscheidung zwischen Überlieferung
und Redaktion daher von Bedeutung, und die
Bibel wird im wesentlichen diachronisch untersucht. In jüngerer Zeit hat man besonderes
Gewicht auf eine synchronische Erforschung der
Bibel gelegt; d.h., der Text wird in der uns
heute zum Lesen angebotenen Form untersucht,
wobei man in der Bibelexegese die Methoden
der Strukturanalyse anwendet.

In den orthodoxen Kirchen und ganz allgemein
in den Kirchen des Ostens legt man sehr viel
mehr Gewicht auf die Lesung der Bibel im
Gottesdienst und auf die biblische Meditation.
Man versucht dort häufig, in den Texten über
die wortwörtliche Bedeutung hinaus einen
symbolischen und typologischen Sinngehalt
zu erkennen.

profética y apocalíptica, etc. En los
estudios críticos de las formas y de la
tradición se procura comprender cómo se
originaron los textos, cómo se desarrolló
una tradición oral o escrita y cómo fue
transmitida. En los estudios históricos
(o críticos) de redacción se examina cuál
fue el énfasis teológico, polémico,
didáctico, litúrgico,etc. que quiso dar
el redactor final. Por lo tanto, en todos estos estudios históricos críticos
de la Biblia, es importante la distinción
entre tradición y redacción y se lee la
Biblia esencialmente en forma diacrónica.
Recientemente se dió mucho énfasis a una
lectura sincrónica de la Biblia, tomando
el texto tal como se presenta y aplicando
los métodos del análisis estructuralista
a la exégis bíblica.

En las iglesias ortodoxas y generalmente
en las iglesias orientales se da mayor
importancia a la lectura litúrgica de
la Biblia y a la meditación bíblica. Se
procura a menudo superar el significado
literal y lograr un significado simbólico y
tipológico de los textos.

209

biblical vocabularies - See under: biblical studies

biblical work books - See under: biblical studies

bibliography

79 select biblio- graphy	bibliographie (f) sommaire	ausgewählte Biblio- graphie (f)	síntesis (f) biblio- gráfica
80 biocide	biocide (m)	Biozid (m)	biocidio (m)
81 birth control	régulation (f) des naissances	Geburtenkontrolle (f)	regulación (f) (=con- trol /m/) de la nata- lidad
82 birth rate	taux (m) de natalité	Geburtenrate (f)	tasa (f) de natalidad

bishop - See under: threefold ministry

83 black, blacks	noir (m), noirs (mpl)	Schwarzer (m), Schwarze (mpl)	negro (m), negros (mpl)
84 black Americans	Américains (mpl) noirs	schwarze Amerikaner (mpl)	norteamericanos (mpl) negros, estadouniden- ses (mpl) negros
85 black power	pouvoir (m) noir	Black Power (f)	poder (m) negro
86 black soul	héritage (m) noir; authenticité (f) .(=génie /m/) noir(e); sensibilité (f) noire (telle qu'elle s'exprime à travers les blues)	Black Soul (f)	herencia (f) negra; autenticidad (f) (=genio /m/ negro); sensibilidad (f) negra
87 blackness	négritude (f)	Négritude (f); "Afrikanität"(f) (Selbstverständnis /n/ der Schwarzen)	negritud (f)

88 board	conseil (m), comité (m) directeur (=de direction); commission (f)	leitendes Gremium (n), Vorstand (m), Kuratorium (n), Ausschuss (m)	consejo(m), junta (f), junta(f) directiva, comité (m) de dirección
89 Board of ECLOF	Conseil (m) de fondation (=Conseil/m/) de l'ECLOF	ECLOF-Verwaltungsrat (m)	Consejo (m) de l'ECLOF
90 Board of the Ecumenical Institute, Bossey	Comité (m) de direction de l'Institut oecuménique, Bossey	Kuratorium (n) des Ökumenischen Instituts Bossey	Consejo (m) Directivo del Instituto Ecuménico, Bossey
91 Board of the Fund for Reconstruction and Reconciliation in Indochina	Comité (m) directeur du Fonds de reconstrucion et de réconciliation en Indochine	Verwaltungsrat (m) der Stiftung für Wiederaufbau und Versöhnung in Indochina	Comité (m) Director del Fondo de Reconstrucción y Reconciliación en Indochina
92 Advisory Appeals Board /WCC/	Commission (f) consultative de recours /COE/	Beratender Ausschuss (m) für Berufungsanträge /ÖRK/	Comisión (f) Consultiva de Apelaciones /CMI/
93 Advisory Disciplinary Board /WCC/	Commission (f) disciplinaire consultative /COE/	Beratender Ausschuss (m) für Disziplinarfragen /ÖRK/	Comisión (f) Disciplinaria Consultiva /CMI/
94 Classification Board /WCC/	Commission (f) de classification (des emplois) /COE/	Ausschuss (m) für die Arbeitsplatzklassifizierung /ÖRK/	Comisión (f) de Clasificación (de los cargos) /CMI/
95 editorial board	comité (m) de rédaction	Redationsausschuss (m)	consejo (m) de redacción

96 body	organe (m),organis-me (m), institu-tion (f), conseil (m)	Körperschaft (f), Gremium (n), Or-gan (n)	órgano (m), organis-mo(m), cuerpo (m)
97 book review	critique (f) d'ouvrages	Buchbesprechung (f), Rezension (f)	crítica (f) de libros
98 border industry policy /South Africa/	politique (f) des in-dustries fronta-lières /Afrique du Sud/	Programm (n) der "Grenzindustrien" /Südafrika/	política (f) de las industrias fronterizas /Sudáfrica/
99 brain drain	exode (m) des compé-tences (=des cer-veaux)	brain drain (Ab-wanderung qualifi-zierter Wissen-schaftler)	éxodo (m) de intelec-tuales, fuga (f) de "cerebros"
100 briefing	séance (f) de mise au courant (=d'o-rientation), briefing (m)	Informationsbe-sprechung (f), Briefing (n)	sesión (f) de in-formación (=orien-tación)
101 press briefing	mise (f) au courant de la presse	Informationsge-spräch (n) mit Journalisten	información (f) de prensa
budget			
102 General Budget /WCC/	budget (m) général /COE/	Allgemeiner Haus-halt (m)/ÖRK/	Presupuesto (m) General /CMI/
103 Operating Budget /CWME/	budget d'exploita-tion /CME/	Jahreshaushalt (m) /CWME/	Presupuesto (m) de Funcionamiento /CMME/
104 Programme and Research Budget /PCR/	budget (m) "pro-gramme et recherche" /PLR/	Programm- und For-schungshaushalt (m) /PCR/	Presupuesto (m) para Programa e Investigacion /PLR/

business cycle - See under: economic cycle

camp

105	settlement camp; transit camp	camp (m) de réin_stallation; camp (m) de transit	Auffanglager (n); Durchgangslager (n)	campamento (m) de tránsito; aloja-miento (m) provi-sional
106	(voluntary) work camp	chantier (m)	Aufbaulager (n)	campamento (m) de trabajo (voluntario)

canon - <u>See</u> <u>under</u>: <u>bi</u>blical studies

capital

107	capital intensive	à fort emploi de capital, à forte composante-capital, à fort(e) coeffi-cientde (=teneur en) capital	kapitalintensiv	de alto coeficiente de capital, que re-quiere mucho çapital, con utilización in-tensiva de capital
108	capital transfer	transfert (m) de(s) capitaux	Kapitaltransfer (m)	transferencia (f) de capital

mobilization (=procurement=raising) of capital - <u>See</u> <u>under</u>: <u>f</u>und raising

care

109	curative care	soins (mpl) curatifs	kurative Gesund-heitspflege (f)	asistencia (f) cura-tiva
110	hospital-centred care	soins (mpl) hospi-taliers	Krankenhausversor-gung (f)	asistencia (f) hospitalaria
111	intensive care unit	service (m) de réanimation, service (m) de soins inten-sifs	Intensivstation (f) Intensivpflege-station (f)	servicio (m) de asistencia intensiva

112	out-patient care	soins (mpl) ambula-toires, consultations (fpl) externes	ambulante Kranken-versorgung (f)	asistencia (f) am-bulatoria
113	pastoral care	pastorale (f)/ mi-nistère (m) pastoral/	Seelsorge (f)	cuidado (m) (=aten-ción (f) = ser-vicio /m/)
114	physician-orien-ted care	soins (mpl) privés	ärztliche Versor-gung(f), ärztliche Betreuung(f)	asistencia (f) mé-dica profesional
115	preventive care	soins (mpl) pré-ventifs	vorbeugende Ge-sundheitspflege (f)	asistencia (f) pre-ventiva
116	primary secondary tertiary care	soins (mpl) pri-maires/secondaires/tertiaires	primäre/sekundäre/tertiäre Pflege-dienste (mpl)	asistencia (f) pri-maria/secundaria/terciaria
117	carrying capacity /ecology/	capacité (f) limite /écologie/	Belastbarkeit (f) /Ökologie/	capacidad (f) de carga /ecología/
118	cartoon	1. dessin (m) sa-tirique; caricature (f) 2. dessin (m) animé	1. Karikatur (f), Cartoon (m) 2. Zeichentrick-film (m)	1. caricatura (m); 2. dibujos (mpl) animados
	case			
119	case study	méthode (f) (=étude /f/) des cas; étude (f) de cas; mono-graphie (f)	Fallstudie (f)	método (m) de caso; estudio (f) de caso; monografía (f)
120	case work	case-work (m), tra-vail (m) social in-dividualisé	Einzelfallhilfe (f), Einzelhilfe (f)	servicio (m) social de caso

121 family case work	travail (m) social familial, thérapie (f) familiale	familienzentrierte Einzel(fall)hilfe (f)	servicio (m) social de caso a nivel de la familia
122 cassette machine	appareil (m) à cassettes	Kassettenrecorder (M)	grabador (m) (=magnetófono/m/) de cassette
123 cataphatic (cataphatic or affirmative theology proceeds by way of affirmation and, knowing God in what He in His essence is not, produces only an incomplete knowledge of God)	cataphatique (La théologie cataphatique, positive procède par affirmation et conduit à une connaissance de Dieu forcément incomplète car elle le connaît dans ce qu'il n'est pas, dans son essence qui reste radicalement inconnaissable)	cataphatisch (Die cataphatische - positive - Theologie arbeitet mit Affirmationen und führt zu einer Kenntnis Gottes, die zwangsläufig unvollkommen ist, da sie ihn in dem erkennt, was er nicht ist, in seinem Wesen, das radikal unerfassbar bleibt)	catafático (La teología catafática, positiva, procede a través de afirmaciones y conduce a un conocimiento de Dios incompleto, pues lo conoce en aquello que El no es, permaneciendo su esencia totalmente incongnoscible)
124 catharsis (ascetic term denoting an attempt at purification)	catharsis (f) (terme ascétique qui désigne un effort de purification)	Katharsis (f) (Aszetischer Begriff, der das Bemühen um (innere) Reinigung bezeichnet)	catarsis (f) (Término ascético que significa un esfuerzo de purificación)
celebration			
common celebration - See under: communion			
125 chairman, chairwoman	président (m), présidente (f)	Vorsitzender (m), Vorsitzende (f)	presidente (m/f), presidenta (f)

126 Chairman of Programme Unit on...	président (m) de l'Unité "..."	Vorsitzender (m) der Programmeinheit "..."	Presidente (m) de la Unidad "..."
127 Vice-Chairman of the Programme Unit on ...	vice-président (m) de l'Unité "..."	Stellvertretender Vorsitzender (m) der Programmeinheit "..."	vicepresidente (m) de la Unidad "..."
128 challenge	mise (f) en question, contestation (f), mise (f) à l'épreuve; défi (m), gageure (f), stimulant (m); interpellation (f), mise (f) en demeure, appel (m) (à l'action), exigence (f); objectif (m) (à atteindre), tâche (f)	Infragestellung (f); Herausforderung (f); Auseinandersetzung (f):Aufgabe (f)	poner en duda (= en tela de juicio), poner a prueba; impugnación (f), desafío (m), reto (m), acicate (m); intimación (f), exigencia (f), interpelación (f), exhortación (f); tarea (f) (= trabajo (m)=misión/f/) apasionante (=exaltante); objetivo (m)
129 to challenge	mettre en doute, contester; interpeller, mettre en demeure, inciter à; appeler à, inviter à	(etw., jem.) in Frage stellen; (jem.) herausfordern; (jem.)aufrufen zu, auffordern	poner en duda (=en tela de juicio); desafiar, retar, impugnar; interpelar, intimar, exhortar; invitar a, incitar a
change			
130 patterns of change	modèles (mpl) (=formes/fpl/) de changement	Formen (fpl) des Wandels	modalidades (fpl) (=pautas/fpl/) de cambio

131	social change	mutation (f) (=trans-formation/f/) sociale	gesellschaftliche Veränderungen (fpl); sozialer Umbruch; sozialer Wandel	cambio (m) social
132	technological change	changement (m) technique	technologischer Wandel (m)	cambio (m) tecno-lógico
133	charisma, charismata, charism, charisms See also: spiritual gifts gifts of the Spirit	charisme (m), charismes (mpl) Voir aussi sous: dons spirituels, dons de l'Esprit	Charisma (n), Charismata (Charismen)(npl) Siehe auch: geistliche Gaben, Gaben des Geistes, Gnadengaben	carisma (m), carismas (mpl) Véase también: dones espirituales, dones del Espíritu
134	chicanos /USA/ (immigrants to the USA from Central America)	chicanos (mpl)/Etats-Unis/ (ressortissants d'Amérique centrale - Mexique, Porto Rico, Cuba - ayant immigré aux Etats-Unis)	Chicanos /USA/ (Einwanderer aus Mittelamerika (Mexiko, Puerto Rico, Kuba))	chicanos (mpl) /Estados Unidos/ (originarios de Centroamérica - México, Puerto Rico, Cuba - emigrados a los Estados Unidos)

child spacing - See under: family spacing

135	chrismation (or confirmation) (laying-on of hands, performed after water-baptism)	chrismation (f) (ou: confirmation /f/= imposition des mains accomplie après le baptême d'eau)	Chrismation (f) (oder: Konfirmation /f/ = Handauflegung nach der Taufe)	crismación (f) (o confirmación /f/ = imposición de manos después del bautismo de agua)
136	Christendom	chrétienté (f)	Christenheit (f)	cristiandad (f)
137	Christianity	christianisme (m)	Christentum (n)	cristianismo (m)

217

138 christophoric (Christ bearing, "until you take the shape of Christ, Gal.4:19; the life I now live is not my life but the life which Christ lives in me",Gal. 2:20)	christophore (porteur du Christ, "afin que le Christ soit formé en vous /Gal.4, 19/, ce n'est plus moi qui vis, mais c'est le Christ qui vit en moi" /Gal. 2, 20/)	Christophorus (m) (Träger Christi, "bis dass Christus in euch eine Gestalt gewinne" /Gal. 4, 19/; "Ich lebe aber, doch nun nicht ich, sondern Christus lebt in mir" /Gal. 2, 20/)	cristóforo (Quien lleva a Cristo; para "que Cristo sea formado en vosotros"/Gal. 4:19/; "y ya no vivo yo, mas vive Cristo en mí"/Ga. 2:20/)

church

139 church constitution	constitution (f) de l'Eglise	Kirchenverfassung (f)	constitución de la Iglesia
140 church discipline	discipline (f) de l'Eglise, règlement (m) (=règles/fpl/) de l'Eglise	Kirchenzucht (f), Kirchenordnung (f)	disciplina (f) eclesiástica, cánones (mpl) (=normas/fpl/) de la Iglesia

church fellowship - See under: fellowship

141 church government	1. autorités (fpl) de l'Eglise 2. discipline (f) ecclésiastique (=de l'Eglise)	1. Kirchenregiment (n), Kirchenleitung 2. Kirchenordnung (f)	1. autoridades (fpl) eclesiásticas (= de la Iglesia) 2. disciplina (f) eclesiástica
142 church leader	dirigeant (m) (=responsable/m/)d'Eglise, personnalité (f) ecclésiastique	(führende)kirchliche Persönlichkeit (f), Kirchenführer (m)	dirigente (m) eclesiástico, responsable (m) de Iglesia, personalidad (f) eclesiástica
143 church order	1. discipline (f) ecclésiastique (= de l'Eglise) 2. ordre (m) ecclésiastique	1.Kirchenordnung (f) 2. Kirchenverfassung (f)	1. disciplina (f) de la Iglesia (=eclesiásti 2. orden (m) eclesiástico

144	episcopal church order	ordre (m) épiscopal, épiscopat (m)	bischöfliche Kirchenverfassung (f)	orden (m) episcopal
145	presbyteral church order	ordre (m) presbytéral, presbytérat (m)	presbyterianische Kirchenverfassung (f)	orden (m) presbiteral
146	church structures	structures (fpl) ecclésiastiques	kirchliche Strukturen (fpl)	estructuras (fpl) eclesiásticas

church union - See under: union

church unity - See under: unity

147	Ancient Church	Eglise (f) ancienne	Alte Kirche (f)	Iglesia (f) Antigua
148	Associate Member Church	Eglise (f) membre associée	angeschlossene Mitgliedskirche	iglesia (f) miembro asociada
149	charismatic church	Eglise (f) charismatique	charismatische Kirche (f)	iglesia (f) carismática
150	Confessing Church	Eglise (f) confessante	Bekennende Kirche (f)	Iglesia (f) Confesante
151	Early Church; Primitive Church	Eglise (f) primitive	frühe Kirche (f), Urgemeinde (f), Urkirche (f) (R.-K.)	Iglesia (f) Primiva
152	Eastern Orthodox Churches	Eglises (fpl) orthodoxes byzantines	östlich-orthodoxe Kirchen (fpl), Ostkirchen	iglesias (fpl) ortodoxas bizantinas
153	free churches	Eglises (fpl) libres; Eglises (fpl) non conformistes	Freikirchen (fpl)	iglesias (fpl) libres
154	house church	réunion (f) de maison	Hauskirche (f)	iglesia (f) en casa de familia

155	local church	Eglise (f) locale	Ortsgemeinde (f)	iglesia (f) local
156	majority church, national church, people's church	Eglise (f) multitudiniste	Volkskirche (f)	iglesia (f) multitudinaria
157	member church	Eglise (f) membre	Mitgliedskirche (f)	iglesia (f) miembro
158	Oriental Orthodox Churches	Eglises (fpl) orthodoxes orientales	orientalisch-orthodoxe Kirchen (fpl), östliche Kirchen	iglesias (fpl) ortodoxas orientales
159	receiving church	Eglise (f) d'accueil	aufnehmende (= empfangende) Kirche (f)	iglesia (f) que recibe (=de recepción = de acogida)
160	the Reformation churches	Eglises (fpl) issues de la Réforme	reformatorische Kirchen (fpl)	iglesias (fpl) provenientes de la Reforma
161	The Reformed churches	Eglises (fpl) réformées	reformierte Kirchen (fpl)	iglesias (fpl) reformadas
162	regional (=provincial) church	Eglise (f) régionale	Landeskirche	iglesia (f) regional
163	sending church	Eglise (f) d'envoi	sendende Kirche (f)	iglesia (f) que envía
164	silent churches	Eglises (fpl) du silence	die schweigenden Kirchen (fpl)	iglesias (fpl) del silencio
165	state church	Eglise (f) d'Etat	Staatskirche (f)	iglesia (f) oficial
166	underground church	Eglise (f) souterraine	Untergrundkirche (f)	iglesia (f) subterránea ; rebelde
167	Universal Church	Eglise (f) universelle	universale Kirche (f)	Iglesia (f) Universal

168 clearing house	centre (m) d'information et de documentation; centre (m) d'échanges	Clearinghouse (n)	centro (m) de intercambio de información
169 clinic	dispensaire (m) service(m) de consultations)	Behandlungszentrum (n), Ambulatorium (n)	dispensario (m), policlínica (f) servicio (m) de consultas
170 mobile clinic	dispensaire (m) mobile/=itinétrent)	fahrbare Klinik (f); mobiles Ambulatorium (n)	dispensario (m) móvil
171 satellite clinic	dispensaire (m) satellite	Aussenstation (f), Aussenambulatorium (n), Zubringerambulatorium (n),	policlínica (f) (= dispensario /m/) satélite
172 cloning	bouturage (m) cellulaire, cloning (m)	Klonen (n)	formación (f) de clonas
173 coercion	contrainte (f)	Zwang (m), Druck (m)	coacción (f)
174 co-existence	coexistence (f)	Koexistenz (f)	coexistencia (f)
175 co-humanity	cohumanité (f)	Mitmenschlichkeit (f)	cohumanidad (f)
176 co-liturgist (one who shares in Christ's priestly ministry)	co-liturge (m) (participant au ministère sacerdotal du Christ)	Mit-Zelebrant (m) (Teilhaber am Opferamt Christi)	coliturgo (m) (Participante en el ministerio sacerdotal de Cristo)
177 collective bargaining	négociations (fpl) collectives	Tarifverhandlungen (fpl)	negociaciones (fpl) colectivas

college

theological college - See under: theological school

178	colour bar	barrière (f) de la couleur, "colour bar"(f)	Rassenschranke (f)	"barrera (f) de color"
179	the coloured	1. personnes (fpl) de couleur 2. métis (mpl)/Afrique du Sud/	1. Farbige (mpl) 2. Mischlinge (mpl) /Südafrika/	1. personas (fpl) de color 2. mestizos (mpl) /Sudáfrica/
	commission			
180	Plenary Commission /Faith and Order/	Commission (f) plénière /Foi et constitution/	Plenum (n) der Kommission /Glauben und Kirchenverfassung/	Comisión (f) Plenaria /Fe y Constitución/
181	Standing Commission /Faith and Order/	Commission (f) permanente /Foi et constitution/	Ständige Kommission /Glauben und Kirchenverfassung/	Comisión (f) Permanente /Fe y Constitución/
182	commissioner /CCIA/	membre (m) de la Commission /CEAI/	Kommissionsmitglied (n) /CCIA/	comisionado (m), miembro (m) de la Comisión /CIAI/
183	commissioner at Large /CCIA/	membre (m) (de la commission) par mandat spécial/CEAI/	Kommissionsmitglied (n) zur besonderen Verwendung (ZbV)/CCIA/	comisionado (m) por mandato especial/CIAI/
184	"Committed to Fellowship"	"Engagés au service de la communauté fraternelle"	"Verpflichtet auf Gemeinschaft"	"Al servicio de la causa de la comunidad", "Comprometidos para la comunidad"
185	committee	comité (m), commission (f)	Ausschuss (m)	comité (m), comisión (f)
186	Ad Hoc Committee on Youth /Staff Working Group on Renewal/	Comité (m) ad hoc de jeunesse /Groupe de de travail "renouveau"/	Ad-Hoc-Ausschuss (m) "Jugendarbeit" /Arbeitsgruppe "Erneuerung"/	Comité (m) Ad Hoc para el Trabajo con la Juventud /Grupo de Trabajo "Renovación"/

187	Advisory Committee /CEC/	Comité (m) consultatif /KEK/	Beratender Ausschuss (m) /KEK/	Comité (m) Asesor /KEK/
188	Audit Scrutiny Sub-Committee /Finance Committee of the WCC Central Committee/	Sous-comité (m) des vérificateurs de comptes /Comité des finances du Comité central, COE/	Unterausschuss (m) zur Kontrolle des Berichts der Rechnungsprüfer /Finanzausschuss des ÖRK-Zentralausschusses/	Subcomité (m) de Auditoría/ Comité de Finanzas del Comité Central, CMI/
189	Business Committee /WCC Assembly/	Comité (m) directeur de l'Assemblée /Assemblée du COE/	Lenkungsausschuss (m) der Vollversammlung /ÖRK-Vollversammlung/	Comité (m) Directivo de la Asamblea /Asamblea del CMI/
190	Central Committee /WCC/	Comité (m) central /COE/	Zentralausschuss (m) /ÖRK/	Comité (m) Central /CMI/
191	Communication Committee	Comité (m) de la communication	Kommunikationsausschuss (m)	Comité (m) de Comunicación
192	Credentials Committee /WCC Central Committee and Assembly/	Comité (m) de vérification des pouvoirs /Comité central et Assemblée du COE/	Ausschuss (m) für Beglaubigungsschreiben/ÖRK, ÖRK-Zentralausschuss und Vollversammlung/	Comité (m) de Verificación de Poderes (=Credenciales) /Comité Central y Asamblea del CMI/
193	Executive Committee /WCC, CCIA, CWME, PCR/	Comité (m) exécutif /COE, CEAI, CME, PLR/	Exekutivausschuss (m) /ÖRK, CCIA, CWME, PCR/	Comité (m) Ejecutivo /CMI, CIAI, CMME, PLR/
194	Finance Committee /WCC Executive Committee, Central Committee and Assembly/	Comité (m) des finances /Comité éxécutif, Comité central et Assemblée du COE/	Finanzausschuss (m) /Exekutivausschuss, Zentralausschuss und Vollversammlung des ÖRK/	Comité (m) de Finanzas /Comité Ejecutivo, Comité Central y Asamblea del CMI/

195	Health Committee /CICARWS/	Comité (m) du Programme de santé /CESEAR/	Gesundheitsausschuss (m) /CICARWS/	Comité (m) del Programa de Salud /CAISMR/
196	House Committee /Ecumenical Centre/	Comité (m) des affaires internes /Centre oecuménique/	Ausschuss (m) für interne Angelegenheiten/Ökumenisches Zentrum /	Comité (m) de Asuntos Internos/Centro Ecuménico/
197	Housing Committee /WCC/	Comité (m) des questions de logement /COE/	ÖRK-Wohnungsausschuss (m)	Comité (m) de Vivienda /CMI/
198	Humanum Consultative Committee	Comité (m) consultatif des Études sur l'humanum	Beratender Ausschuss (m) für die Humanum-Studien	Comité (m) Consultivo de Estudios sobre "Humanum"
199	National ECLOF Committee	comité (m) national de l'ECLOF	nationales ECLOF-Komitee (n)	comité (m) nacional del ECLOF
200	Nominations Committee /WCC Assembly/	Comité (m) des désignations /Assemblée du COE/	Nominierungsausausschuss (m) /ÖRK-Vollversammlung/	Comité (m) de Nombramientos /Asamblea del CMI/
201	Nominations and Staffing Committee /WCC Executive Committee and Central Committee/	Comité (m) des désignations /Comité exécutif et Comité central du COE/	Nominierungsausschuss (m) /ÖRK-Exekutivausschuss und Zentralausschuss/	Comité (m) de Nombramientos /Comité Ejecutivo y Comité Central del CMI/
202	Policy Reference Committee /WCC Central Committee and Assembly/	Comité (m) d'examen des directives /Comité central et Assemblée du COE/	Weisungsausschuss (m) für Grundsatzfragen /ÖRK Zentralausschuss und Vollversammlung/	Comité (m) de Estudio de Asuntos Generales /Comité Central y Asamblea del CMI/

203	Press and Broad-casting Committee /WCC Assembly/	Comité (m) de la presse et de la radio -télévision /Assemblée du COE/	Ausschuss (m) für Presse, Rundfunk und Fernsehen /ÖRK-Vollversammlung/	Comité (m) de Prensa, Radio y Televisión /Asamblea del CMI/
204	Priorities Committee /Central Committee/	Comité (m) des priorités /Comité central/	Prioritätenaus-schuss (m)/Zentral-ausschuss/	Comité (m) de Priori-dades/Comité Central/
205	Programme Guide-lines Committee /WCC Assembly/	Comité (m) d'orien-tation du programme /Assemblée du COE/	Ausschuss (m) für Programmrichtlinien /ÖRK-Vollversamm-lung/	Comité (m) de Orien-tación de Programas /Asamblea del CMI/
206	Reference Committee /WCC Central Committee and Assembly/	Comité (m) d'examen /Comité central et Assemblée du COE/	Weisungsausschuss (m)/ÖRK-Zentralaus-schuss und Vollver-sammlung /	Comité (m) de Estudio /Comité Cen-tral y Asamblea del CMI/
207	Scholarships Committee /Staff Working Group on Education/	Comité (m) des bourses /Groupe de travail "éducation"/	Stipendienausschuss (m) /Arbeitsgruppe "Bildung"/	Comité (m) de Becas /Grupo de Trabajo "Educación/
208	(Steering) Committee/SODEPAX/	Comité (m) (direc-teur)/SODEPAX/	(Lenkungs)Ausschuss (m) /SODEPAX/	Comité (m) (de Dirección)/SODEPAX/
209	Unit Committee	Comité (m) d'unité, Comité (m) de l' Unité "..."	Ausschuss (m) der Einheit, Ausschuss (m) der Programm-einheit	Comité (m) de la Unidad "..."
210	Work Groups and Message Committee /WCC Assembly/	Comité (m) "message et groupes de tra-vail"/Assemblée du COE/	Ausschuss (m) für die Arbeitsgruppen und die Botschaft der Vollversammlung	Comité (m) "Grupos de Trabajo y Redacción del Men-saje"/Asamblea del CMI/

211	Working Committee /Faith and Order/	Comité (m) de travail /Foi et constitution/	Arbeitsausschuss (m) /Glauben und Kirchenverfassung/	Comité (m) de Trabajo /Fe y Constitución/
212	Worship Committee /WCC, WCC Assembly/	Comité (m) des cultes /COE, Assemblée du COE/	Gottesdienstausschuss (m) /ORK, ÖRK-Vollversammlung/	Comité (m) de Cultos /CMI, Asamblea del CMI/
213	communal living	vie (f) en groupe, vie (f) communautaire	gemeinschaftsbezogenes Leben (n)	vida (f) en comunidad (=comunitaria)
214	commune	commune (f)	Wohngemeinschaft (f), Kommune	comuna (f)
215	to communicate, to take communion	communier	das Abendmahl empfangen, feiern	comulgar
216	communicatio idiomatum, perichoresis (the mutual exchange of properties between the two natures in Christ in the unity of their life in Him as the unique hypostasis of the Logos)	communication (f) des idiomes, périchorèse (f) (échange des propriétés entre les deux natures en Christ dans l'unité de leur vie en fonction de l'unique hypostase du Verbe)	Communicatio idiomatum (f), Idiomenkommunikation (f), Perichorese (f) (Austausch der Eigenschaften zwischen den beiden Naturen in Christus in der Einheit ihres Lebens im Dienste der einzigartigen Hypostase des fleischgewordenen Wortes)	comunicación de los idiomas, pericoresis (f) (Intercambio de las propiedades entre las dos naturalezas en Cristo en la unidad de su vida como la hipostasis unica del Verbo)
217	communicator	informateur (m)	Kommunikator (m)	informante (m); relator (m)

218 Communion (Koinonia) (1)

Man is created in and for communion with
God. In losing this, his whole relationship with his fellow men and with his
natural environment is disturbed. In
Jesus Christ, God renews the communion
in both dimensions.

The eucharist is the sacramental event
in which this renewed communion is both
celebrated and enacted, by the power
of the Holy Spirit. Our sharing at the
Lord's table thus inseparably involves
communion both with God and with our
fellow men, in Jesus Christ. It is
the eschatological sign of universal
salvation.

Communion indicates the goal to be
achieved by the ecumenical movement.
This term describes the fellowship
willed by Christ. The following terms
refer to different practices.

1. Admission: The term "admission"
   refers to those cases where a Church,
   in celebrating the eucharist, admits
   to the table members of other
   Churches. Such admission may be

(1) Definitions taken from Faith and
    Order, Louvain 1971, Study Reports
    and Documents

Communion (Koinonia) (1)

L'homme est créé dans la communion de
Dieu et en vue de cette communion avec
lui. En la perdant, il bouleverse
l'ensemble de ses relations avec ses
semblables et avec la nature qui l'en-
toure. En Jésus-Christ, Dieu restaure
cette communion dans ses deux dimensions.

L'eucharistie est l'événement sacramentel
dans lequel cette communion renouvelée
est célébrée et accomplie par la puissance
du Saint-Esprit. Notre participation à
la table sainte implique donc à la fois
la communion avec Dieu et avec notre
prochain en Jésus-Christ. Elle est le
signe eschatologique du salut universel.

Le terme de communion indique le but vers
lequel tend le mouvement oecuménique. Il
désigne la communion voulue par le Christ.

On distingue les
pratiques suivantes:
1. L'admission: on parle d'"admission"
   lorsqu'une Eglise, célébrant l'eucharistie, admet à sa table des membres
   d'autres Eglises. L'admission peut
   être limitée, générale ou réciproque.

(1) Terminologie empruntée au rapport de la
    Conférence mondiale de Foi et constitu-
    tion, Louvain, août 1971

Gemeinschaft (koinonia)   (1)

Der Mensch wurde in der Gemeinschaft
mit Gott und für diese geschaffen.
Wenn er sie verliert, ist seine gesamte
Beziehung zu seinen Mitmenschen und zu
seiner natürlichen Umwelt gestört. In
Jesus Christus erneuert Gott die Gemeinschaft in beiden Dimensionen.

Die Eucharistie ist das sakramentale Ge-
schehen, in dem diese erneuerte Gemeinschaft durch die Kraft des Heiligen Geistes gefeiert wie auch bewirkt wird.
Unsere Teilhabe am Tisch des Herrn
schliesst somit, in Jesus Christus, un-
trennbar die Gemeinschaft mit Gott und
mit unseren Mitmenschen ein. Die Eucharistie ist das eschatologische Zeichen des
universalen Heils.

Gemeinschaft bezeichnet das von der ökumenischen Bewegung zu erreichende Ziel.
Dieser Begriff beschreibt die von Christus
gewollte Gemeinschaft. Die folgenden Begriffe verweisen auf verschiedene Prak-
tiken.

1. Zulassung: Der Begriff "Zulassung"

---

(1) Die vorstehenden Begriffsbestimmungen
 wurden dem Band Löwen 1971, Studienbe-
 richte und Dokumente der Sitzung der
 Kommission für Glauben und Kirchenverfassung, hrsg. von Konrad Raiser, Bei-
 heft zur Ökumenischen Rundschau 18/19,
 (Stuttgart, 1971), S.57 ff. entnommen

Comunión (koinonía)   (1)

"El hombre es creado en y para la comunión
con Dios. Al perderla, se altera el conjunto de sus relaciones con sus semejantes
y con la naturaleza que le rodea. En
Jesucristo, Dios renueva esta comunión en
ambas dimensiones.

La eucaristía es el acontecimiento sacramental en el que se celebra y cumple, por el
poder del Espíritu Santo esta comunión
renovada. Nuestra participación en la mesa
del Señor implica, pues, tanto la comunión
con Dios como con nuestro prójimo en
Jesucristo. Es el signo escatológico de
la salvación universal.

El término comunión indica la meta que se
ha propuesto el movimiento ecuménico.
Designa la comunión querida por Cristo. Se
distinguen las siguientes prácticas:

1.   Admisión: Se habla de"admisión"

---

(1) Definiciones tomadas del Informe de
 la Conferencia Mundial de Fe y Constitución, Lovaina, agosto de 1971

limited, general or reciprocal.

Limited admission: This term can mean
either (i) exceptional admission for
pastoral reasons which is the ground
of all exceptional cases in Orthodox
and Roman Catholic practice, or (ii)
limited admission in a wider sense,
based on the awareness that every
baptized Christian belongs fundamen-
tally to the one communion of the
Church and is directed towards his
sanctification in the body of Christ.

General admission: This is the regular
practice of a great number of Protestant
Churches. There are, however, different
forms. On the one hand, there is the
practice of a number of Protestant
Churches by which they invite to the
Holy Communion baptized and communicant
members of other Churches. On the
other hand, there is the practice of
a number of other Protestant Churches
(and of groups within the former) by
which the invitation is given to
"all who love the Lord Jesus".

Reciprocal admission (= intercommunion):
This term may be used for two types
of situation: (i) the establishment
of intercommunion by agreement between
two Churches, usually in geographically
different regions, and without any
question of organic union being raised;
(ii) when two Churches are committed to

Admission limitée: celle-ci revêt
deux formes: a) l'admission exceptionnelle
pour des raisons pastorai... c'est le cas
de toutes les célébrations except-
tionnelles pratiquées dans l'Eglise
orthodoxe et l'Eglise catholique romaine; b) l'admission limitée dans un
sens plus large: celle-ci se fonde
sur la reconnaissance du fait que
tout chrétien baptisé appartient fon-
damentalement à la communion unique de
l'Eglise et est appelé à sa sanctification dans le corps du Christ.

Admission générale: cette pratique est
celle de la plupart des Eglises protestantes. Il faut cependant distinguer
entre a) la pratique de certaines
Eglises protestantes qui invitent à la
Sainte Cène les membres baptisés et
communiants des autres Eglises; b) la
pratique d'un certain nombre d'autres
Eglises protestantes (et de certains
groupes parmi les premières citées sous a))
qui adressent leur invitation à "tous
ceux qui aiment le Seigneur Jésus".

Admission réciproque (= intercommunion):
on parle d'admission réciproque: a)
lorsque deux Eglises, généralement si-
tuées dans des régions géographiques
différentes, établissent entre elles
l'intercommunion aux termes d'un accord
sans poser la question de l'union organique; b) lorsque deux Eglises se sont
engagées à réaliser l'union organique,

bezieht sich auf solche Fälle, in denen eine Kirche bei der Feier der Eucharistie Glieder anderer Kirchen zum
Tisch des Herrn zulässt. Eine solche
Zulassung kann begrenzt, allgemein
oder gegenseitig sein.

Begrenzte Zulassung: Dieser Begriff
kann entweder bedeuten 1. ausnahms-
weise Zulassung aus seelsorgerlichen
Gründen, wie dies bei allen ausser-
gewöhnlichen Fällen in der orthodoxen
und römisch-katholischen Praxis der
Fall ist, oder 2. begrenzte Zulassung
in einem weiteren Sinne, die auf dem
Bewusstsein beruht, dass jeder getaufte Christ grundsätzlich zu der einen
Gemeinschaft der Kirche gehört und
auf seine Heiligung im Leibe Christi
ausgerichtet ist.

Allgemeine Zulassung: Diese Praxis wird
von einer grossen Zahl protestantischer
Kirchen allgemein befolgt. Es bestehen
hier jedoch unterschiedliche Formen.
Einerseits gibt es die Praxis einer
Reihe protestantischer Kirchen, die
getaufte und abendmahlsberechtigte
Glieder anderer Kirchen zum Abend-
mahl einladen. Andererseits gibt es
die Praxis einer Reihe anderer protestantischer Kirchen (und Gruppen innerhalb
der zuerst genannten Kirchen), die "alle,
die den Herrn Jesus liebhaben", einladen.

Gegenseitige Zulassung (= Interkommunion):

cuando una iglesia, al celebrar la
eucaristía, admite a su mesa a los
miembros de otras iglesias. La admisión
puede ser limitada, general o recíproca.

Admisión limitada: Este término puede
significar: a) la admisión excepcional
por motivos pastorales: es el caso de
todas las celebraciones excepcionales
de la Iglesia Ortodoxa y de la Iglesia Católica Romana; b) la admisión limitada en un
sentido más amplio, basada en el reconocimiento del hecho de que todo cristiano bau-
tizado pertenece fundamentalmente a la
comunión única de la Iglesia, habiendo sido
llamado a su santificación en el cuerpo
de Cristo.

Admisión general: Es la práctica de
la mayoría de las iglesias protestantes.
Es necesario distinguir sin embargo
entre a) la práctica de
algunas iglesias protestantes que invitan a la Santa Cena a los miembros
bautizados y comulgantes de otras iglesias y b) la práctica de algunas de las
otras iglesias protestantes (y de algunos
grupos de las citadas en el apartado a))
que dirigen su invitación a "todos los
que aman al Señor Jesús".

Admisión recíproca (= intercomunión):
Se habla de admisión recíproca: a)
cuando dos iglesias, situadas generalmente
en regiones geográficas diferentes,
establecen la intercomunión por medio
de un acuerdo

work for organic union, sometimes
within a specific period, and enter
into relationship on the ground
that the causes of division between
them have, in principle, been removed.

2. <u>Common Celebration</u>: By this term
we designate a form of concelebration
by ministers of different confessions
on behalf of occasional gatherings
of their people, each of the participants being aware of his bringing
to the celebration whatever he has
received of faith and of ministry,
together with his repentence for dis-
unity, his commitment to the over-
coming of this, and his hope in the
unity and fulness that is Christ's
will.

3. <u>Intercelebration</u>: This term is
suggested for those cases where two
or more separated Churches are prepared reciprocally to allow their
ministers to preside at their
eucharistic worship.

parfois à une date déterminée, et
qu'elles décident de célébrer l'intercommunion, partant du principe que les
causes de la division qui les sépare
ont été écartées.

2. <u>La célébration commune</u>: la célébration
commune est une certaine forme de con-
célébration présidée par des ministres de
confessions différentes, lors de rassemble-
ments occasionnels de leurs membres,
chacun des participants étant conscient
d'apporter à cette célébration la part
de foi et de ministère qu'il a reçue,
sa repentance à cause de la désunion,
son engagement à dépasser ce stade, et
son espérance en l'unité et en la pléni-
tude qui sont la volonté du Christ.

3. <u>L'intercélébration</u>: on suggère d'employer
ce terme chaque fois que deux ou plusieurs
Eglises séparées sont disposées à autoriser
réciproquement leurs ministres à présider
leur célébration eucharistique.

Dieser Begriff kann auf zwei verschiedene Situationen angewandt werden: a) auf die Herstellung der Interkommunion durch Übereinkunft zwischen zwei Kirchen, gewöhnlich in verschiedenen geographischen Bereichen und ohne Zusammenhang mit der Frage einer organischen Vereinigung; b) wenn zwei Kirchen sich verpflichtet haben, für eine organische Union zu arbeiten, zuweilen innerhalb eines festgelegten Zeitraums, und in diese Beziehung auf der Grundlage ein
Ursachen für die Spaltung zwischen ihnen im Prinzip beseitigt worden sind.

2. Gemeinsame Zelebration: Mit diesem Begriff bezeichnen wir eine Form der Konzelebration von Geistlichen verschiedener Konfessionen bei gelegentlichen Zusammenkünften von Gliedern ihrer Kirchen, wobei sich jeder der Beteiligten bewusst ist, dass er all das mit in diese Feier hineinbringt, was er an Glauben und Amt empfangen hat, zusammen mit seiner Busse für die Spaltung, seiner Verpflichtung für deren Überwindung und seiner Hoffnung auf die Einheit und Fülle, die Christi Wille ist.

3. Interzelebration: Dieser Begriff wird für solche Fälle vorgeschlagen, in denen zwei oder mehrere getrennte Kirchen bereit sind, gegenseitig den Trägern des geistlichen Amtes zu erlauben, ihren eucharistischen Gottesdienst zu leiten.

entre ellas, sin plantear la cuestión de la unión orgánica; b) cuando dos iglesias que se han comprometido a trabajar por su unión orgánica, a veces dentro de un plazo determinado, deciden celebrar la intercomunión sobre la base de que las causas de la división que existe entre ellas, han sido, en principio, superadas.

2. Celebración común: Con esta expresión designamos una modalidad de concelebración presidida por ministros de confesiones distintas en reuniones ocasionales de sus miembros. Cada participante sabe que aporta a la celebración lo que ha recibido de fe y ministerio, además de su arrepentimiento por la desunión y su compromiso de superarla, así como su esperanza por alcanzar la unidad y la plenitud conforme a la voluntad de Cristo.

3. Intercelebración: Se sugiere el empleo de este término cada vez que dos o más iglesias separadas están dispuestas a autorizar recíprocamente a sus ministros a presidir su celebración eucarística.

	English	French	German	Spanish
218	communion (koinonia) See pp. 227-231	communion (f) (koinonia); communion (f), Sainte Cène (f) Voir pp. 227-231	Gemeinschaft (f) (Koinonia); Communio (f); Abendmahl (n) Siehe S.228ff.	comunión (f) (koinonía); comunión (f), Santa Cena (f) Véase pag. 228
219	Holy Communion	Sainte Cène (f)	Abendmahl (n)	Santa Cena (f)
220	service of Holy Communion	service (m) de Sainte Cène	Abendmahlsgottesdienst (m)	servicio (m) de Santa Cena
221	to administer Holy Communion	distribuer la Sainte Cène	das Abendmahl austeilen (=reichen)	administrar la Santa Cena
222	community	1. collectivité (f) 2. Communité (f); communauté (f) humaine	Gemeinschaft (f)	1. colectividad (f) 2. comunidad (f)
223	community centre	centre (m) de rencontres, centre (m) socio-culturel; centre (m) de loisirs; centre (m) social	1. Sozialzentrum (n), 2. Freizeitzentrum (n)	centro (m) comunitario; centro (m) de reuniones, centro (m) sociocultural; centro (m) recreativo, centro (m) social
	community development - See under: development			
224	community of faith	communauté (f) de foi	Glaubensgemeinschaft (f)	comunidad (f) de fe
225	community organization	organisation (f) communautaire	Gemeinwesenorganisation (f)	organización (f) comunitaria
226	basic community (= group)	communauté (f) de base (=de vie), groupe (m) de base	Basisgruppe (f), Basisgemeinschaft (f), Basisgemeinde (f)	comunidad (f) de base, grupo (m) de base

227	caring community	communauté (f) diaconale (=caritative)	Gemeinschaft (f) (=Gemeinde/f/) für andere	comunidad (f) diaconal
228	healing community	communauté (f) porteuse de guérison, communauté (f) thérapeutique	heilende Gemeinschaft (f) (=Gemeinde)	comunidad (f) generadora de salud, comunidad (f) terapéutica
229	saving community	communauté (f) porteuse de salut (=salvatrice)	Gemeinde (f) als Heilsvermittlerin	comunidad (f) salvífica
230	servant community	communauté (f) servante	dienende Gemeinschaft (f) (=Gemeinde)	comunidad (f) de servicio
231	underground community	communauté (f) souterraine	"Underground"-Gemeinschaft (f)	comunidad (f) subterránea; - rebelde
232	worshipping community	communauté (f) chrétienne (=des fidèles); communauté (f) de prière; assemblée (f) liturgique	gottesdienstliche Gemeinschaft (f), anbetende Gemeinde (f)	comunidad (f) de adoración
233	world community (context: DFI) =By world community we do not mean mere interdependence of men and nations, but an order that enables communities to live together crea-	communauté (f) mondiale (contexte:DRI) =Par l'expression communauté mondiale, nous ne désignons pas la simple interdépendance des hommes et des nations, mais un ordre grâce auquel les communautés peuvent vivre	Weltgemeinschaft (f) (Kontext: DFI) = Mit Weltgemeinschaft meinen wir nicht bloss die Interdependenz von Menschen und Nationen, sondern eine Ordnung, die es Gemeinschaften ermöglicht, in Ge-	comunidad (f) mundial (contexto:DRI) =Por comunidad mundial entendemos una estructura que permite a las comunidades vivir juntas de manera creadora en justicia y en paz para su mutuo enriquecimiento y no una

tively in justice and peace for their mutual enrichment...It should be conceived of as a community of communities. World community is not only the sum of individual human beings; it is composed of communities of diverse kind and a variety of societal structures, some natural, some historically and culturally determined, some freely contracted (eg. ethnic, linguistic, religious, political). (cf. Christian - Jewish Consultation, Geneva 1972)

ensemble de manière créatrice dans la justice et la paix, pour leur mutuel enrichissement... Cette communauté mondiale doit se concevoir comme une communauté de communautés; car elle est davantage que la somme de plusieurs individus: elle se compose de communautés de formes diverses et de structures sociales différentes, certaines naturelles, d' autres déterminées par l'histoire et la culture, d' autres encore créées librement (telle les communautés ethniques, linguistiques, religieuses, politiques).

rechtigkeit und Frieden kreativ zusammenleben... Weltgemeinschaft sollte man als eine Gemeinschaft von Gemeinschaften verstehen. Weltgemeinschaft ist nicht nur die Summe der einzelnen Menschen, die in ihr leben; sie setzt sich vielmehr zusammen aus Gemeinschaften verschiedener Art und vielfältigen gesellschaftlichen Strukturen, die teils auf natürliche Weise entstanden, teils durch Geschichte und Kultur determiniert oder auch aus freiem Willen ihrer Glieder geschaffen worden sind (z.B. Sprachgemeinschaften, ethnische, religiöse politische Gemeinschaften).

mera interdependencia de hombres y naciones... Esta comunidad mundial debe concebirse como una comunidad de comunidades. La comunidad mundial es no sólo la suma de individuos: se compone de comunidades de distinto tipo y de estructuras sociales diferentes, algunas naturales, otras determinadas por la historia y la cultura, otras creadas libremente (por ejem. las comunidades étnicas, lingüísticas, religiosas, políticas).

234 commuting

1. migration (f) frontalière
2. migration (f) alternante (= pendulaire = journalière)

Pendeln (n), Pendelwanderung (f)

1. migración (f) fronteriza
2. migración (f) diaria

235 Composite Statement of Needs /WCC finance/	inventaire (m) général des besoins /finances du COE/	Rahmenaufstellung (f) des Finanzbedarfs /Finanzwesen,ÖRK/	inventario (m) general de necesidades /finanzas del CMI/
236 compound /South Africa/ (enclosure in which African miners live for the duration of their contract, requiring special permission to leave is·)	"compound" (m) /Afrique du Sud/ (enceinte ou vivent les mineurs africains pendant la durée de leur contrat et dont ils ne peuvent sortir sans autorisation spéciale)	Compound (m) /Südafrika/ (abgetrennte, umzäunte Siedlungen, in denen die afrikanischen Minenarbeiter während der Dauer ihres Arbeitsvertrages wohnen, und die sie nur mit Sondergenehmigungen verlassen dürfen)	"compound" (m) /Sudafrica/ (lugar donde viven los mineros africanos durante el período de su contrato y del que no pueden salir sin una autorización especial)
237 compounder	préparateur (m) en pharmacie	Apothekengehilfe (m)	auxiliar (m) (=mancebo/m/) de farmacia
238 concern(s)	intérêt (m); affaire(s) (mpl); préoccupation (f), souci (m); inquiétude (f), anxiété (f); question (f), problème (m); tâche (f); responsabilité (f), sens (m) des responsabilités	Interesse (n), Beschäftigung (f) mit; Sorge (f); Aufgabe (f), Verantwortung(-sbewusstsein)(f, n), Engagement (n)	interés (m): asunto(s) (m); precopucación (f); inquietud (f); ansiedad (f); cuestión (f), problema (m); tarea (f); responsabilidad (f), sentido (m) de responsabilidad
239 conciliarity	conciliarité (f)	Konziliarität	conciliaridad (f)
240 conciliar movement	mouvement (m) conciliaire	konziliare Bewegung (f)	movimiento (m) conciliar

concord

	English	French	German	Spanish
241	Book of Concord (Luth.)	Livre (m) de concorde (recueil officiel des symboles de l'Eglise luthérienne /1580/ dont la "Formule" est le dernier des écrits)	Konkordienbuch (n)	Libro (m) de Concordia (colección oficial de los símbolos de la Iglesia Luterana /1580/, cuyo último escrito es la "Fórmula")
242	Formula of Concord (Luth.)	Formule (f) de concorde	Konkordienformel (f)	Fórmula (f) de Concordia

concordance - See under: biblical studies

	English	French	German	Spanish
243	conference	conférence (f)	Konferenz (f)	conferencia (f)
244	Conference on World Mission and Evangelism	Conférence (f) de mission et d'évangélisation	Konferenz (f) für Weltmission und Evangelisation	Conferencia (f) de Misión Mundial y Evangelización
245	Regional Conference	conférence (f) régionale	Regionalkonferenz (f)	conferencia (f) regional
246	World Conference on Faith and Order	Conférence (f) mondiale de Foi et constitution	Weltkonferenz (f) für Glauben und Kirchenverfassung	Conferencia (f) Mundial de Fe y Constitución
247	confession	confession (f)	Konfession (f), Bekenntnis (n)	confesión (f)
248	confession of faith	confession (f) de foi	Glaubensbekenntnis (n)	confesión (f) de fe
249	confession of sins	confession (f) des péchés	Beichte (f)	confesión (f) de los pecados

confessional

250	confessional documents, doctrinal standards (of the Ev. Luth. Church)	livres (mpl) symboliques (de l'Eglise év. luth.)	Bekenntnisschriften (fpl) (der ev.-luth. Kirche)	documents (mpl) confesionales, posiciones (fpl) doctrinales (de la Iglesia Ev. Luterana)
251	world confessional families	familles (fpl) confessionnelles mondiales	weltweite Bekenntnisfamilien (fpl), Konfessionsfamilien (fpl)	familias (fpl) confesionales mundiales
252	confessionalism	attachement (m) excessif à une confession donnée, particularisme (m) confessionnel (= religieux)	Konfessionalismus (m)	confesionalismo (m)

confirmation - See under: chrismation

253	congregation	paroisse (f); assemblée (f), communauté (f)	Gemeinde (f); Versammlung (f)	parroquia (f); asamblea (f), congregación (f)
254	local congregation	paroisse (f) locale	Ortsgemeinde (f)	congregación (f) local
255	mixed congregation	paroisse (f) (racialement) mixte	gemischtrassige Gemeinde (f)	congregación (f) (racialmente) mixta
256	conscientious objection	objection (f) de conscience	Wehrdienst-, Kriegsdienstverweigerung (f) aus Gewissensgründen	objeción (f) de conciencia

257	conscientious objector	objecteur (m) de conscience	Wehrdienst-, Kriegs-dienstverweigerer(m)	objetor (m) de conciencia
258	conscientization /Paolo Freire/ consciousness	conscientisation (f) /Paolo Freire/	Bewusstseinsbildung (f) (conscientização /f/) /Paolo Freire/	concientización (f) /Paolo Freire/
259	consciousness - raising, awareness-building	développement (m) (=formation /f/)de la conscience, sensibilisation (f)	Bewusstseinsbildung (f)	desarrollo (m) de la conciencia, sensibilización (f)
260	awakening of consciousness, realization, growth of awareness	éveil (m) de la conscience, prise (f) de conscience	Bewusstwerden (n)	toma (f) de conciencia, despertar (m) de la conciencia
261	critical consciousness	conscience (f) critique	kritisches Bewusstsein (n)	conciencia (f) crítica
262	consecration	consécration (f)	Konsekration (f)	consagración (f)
263	constituency	1. mandants (mpl), milieux (mpl) intéressés 2. membres (mpl), Eglises membres (fpl) et conseils (mpl) associés/COE/	1. Mitglieder (npl), interessierte Kreise (mpl) Einflussbereich (m) 2. Mitgliedschaft (f), Mitgliedskirchen (fpl) und angeschlossene Räte(mpl) /ÖRK/	1. mandantes (mpl), esfera (f) de influencia 2. miembros (mpl), iglesias (fpl) miembros y consejos (mpl) asociados /CMI/
264	Constitution and Rules of the World Council of Churches	Constitution (f) et règlement (m) du Conseil oecuménique des Eglises	Verfassung (f) und Satzungen (fpl) des Ökumenischen Rates der Kirchen	Constitución (f) y Reglamentos (mpl) del Consejo Mundial de Iglesias

265	consultant	conseiller (m), expert-conseil (m); consultant (m)	Berater (m)	asesor (m), consultor (m)
266	Special Consultant to the Office of Education	conseiller (m) spécial auprès du Bureau de l'éducation	Sonderberater (m) beim Büro für Bildungsfragen	Asesor (m) Especial de la Oficina de Educación
267	consultation	colloque (m); conférence (f)	Konsultation (f); Konferenz (f)	consulta (m), coloquio (m); conferencia (f)
268	joint consultation	concertation (f)	Mitarbeitergespräch (n)	coconsulta (s)
	contraception			
269	methods of contraception (=of birth control)	méthodes (fpl) anticonceptionnelles (=contraceptives)	empfängnisverhütende (antikonzeptionelle) Methoden (fpl)	métodos (mpl) anticonceptivos (=contraceptivos = anticoncepcionales)
270	contraceptives	moyens (mpl) contraceptifs, contraceptifs (mpl)	empfängnisverhütende Mittel (npl), Verhütungsmittel (npl), Kontrazeptiva (npl)	anticonceptivos (mpl) contraceptivos(mpl), medios (mpl) contraceptivosos
271	contraceptive counselling	information (f) contraceptive	Empfängnisverhütungsberatung (f)	asesoramiento (m) (=información/f/) contraceptivo(a)
	contributions			
272	financial contributions	contributions (fpl) financières, dons (mpl) en espèces	finanzielle Beiträge (mpl); Geldspenden (fpl)	contribuciones (fpl) financieras, donaciones (fpl) en efectivo

273	contributions in kind, contributed goods	dons (mpl) en nature	Sachleistungen (fpl), Sachspenden (fpl)	contribuciones (fpl) en especie
274	coordinator	coordonnateur (m), coordinateur /m/	Koordinator (m)	coordinador (m)
275	Coordinator of the Project System /CICARWS/	coordinateur (m) du Système des projets /CESEAR/	Koordinator (m) für das Projektsystem /CICARWS/	Coordinador (m) del Sistema de Proyectos /CAISMR/
276	Coordinator of Refugee Services /CICARWS/	coordinateur (m) des services auprès des réfugiés /CESEAR/	Koordinator (m) für den Flüchtlings- dienst /CICARWS/	Coordinador (m) de los Servicios para Refugiados /CAISMR/
278	Associate Youth Coordinator /Staff Working Group on Renewal/	coordinateur (m) adjoint des activi- tés de jeunesse /Groupe de travail "renouveau"/	Beigeordneter Koor- dinator (m) für Ju- gendarbeit /Arbeits- gruppe "Erneuerung"/	Coordinador (m) Ad- junto del Trabajo con la Juventud/ Grupo de Trabajo "Renovación"/
279	Finance Coordinator /Education and Re- newal/	coordinateur (m) des questions financières /Edu- cation et renouveau/	Koordinator (m) für das Finanzwesen /Bildung und Erneu- erung/	Coordinador (m) de Asuntos Financieros /Educación y Reno- vación/
280	Personnel Coordi- nator /Education and Renewal/	coordinateur (m) des questions du person- nel /Education et renouveau/	Koordinator (m) für Personalfragen/Bil- dung und Erneuerung/	Coordinador (m) de Asuntos del Per- sonal
281	Youth Coordinator /Staff Working Group on Renewal/	coordinateur (m) des activités de jeunesse /Groupe de travail "re- nouveau"/	Koordinator (m) für Jugendarbeit /Ar- beitsgruppe "Er- neuerung"/	Coordinador (m) del Trabajo con la Ju- ventud /Grupo de Renovación"/

242

correspondent

282	national corres-pondent	correspondant (m) national	Nationalkorrespondent (m)	corresponsal (m) nacional
283	council	1. conseil(m) 2. concile (m)	1. Rat (m) 2. Konzil (n)	1. consejo (m) 2. concilio (m)
284	council in working relationship with the WCC	conseil (m) en relation de travail avec le COE	Rat (m) in Arbeits-verbindung mit dem ÖRK	consejo (m) en re-lación de trabajo con el CMI
285	Affiliated Council, Council affiliated to the CWME	conseil (m) affilié, conseil (m) affilié à la CME	affiliierter Rat (m), angegliederter Rat /CWME/	consejo (m) afiliado, consejo (m) afiliado a la CMME
286	Associate Council (of the WCC)	conseil (m) associé (au COE)	assoziierter Rat (m), angeschlossener Rat (m) /ÖRK/	consejo (m) asociado (al CMI)
287	"truly universal council"	"concile (m) authen-tiquement univer-sel"	"wahrhaft universales Konzil"	"concilio (m) verda-deramente universal"

councelling

288	counselling (=adviso-ry) service	service (m) de con-sultation (=d'orien-tation=d'aide)	Beratungsdienst (m)	servicio (m) de asesoramiento (=de orientación=de ayuda =consultivo)
289	family counselling (=guidance)	consultation (f) fa-miliale	Familienberatung (f)	orientación (f) fa-miliar
290	legal counselling (=advice)	(service /m/de) con-sultations (fpl) juridiques	Rechtsberatung (f)	(servicio /m /de) asesoramiento (m) jurídico
291	marriage coun-selling	consultation(s) (f) conjugale(s), conseils (mpl) con-jugaux	Eheberatung (f)	consultas (fpl) ma-trimoniales (= con-yugales)

292	marriage coun-selling service	service (m) de consultations conjugales (=conseils conjugaux)	Eheberatungsdienst (m)	servicio (m) de consultas matrimoniales (=conyugales)
293	pre-marital (=pre-marriage) counselling	consultation(s) (f) prémaritale(s) (=prénuptiale/s/)	voreheliche Beratung (f)	consultas (fpl) prematrimoniales (=prenupciales)
294	counsellor	conseiller (m)	Berater (m)	consejero (m)
295	counter-culture	contre-culture (f)	Gegenkultur (f)	contracultura (f)
296	counterpart; counterpart agency counterpart group	partenaire (m); organisme (m) homologue (=de contre-partie), groupe (m) homologue (=de contre-partie)	Partner (m); Counterpart-Organisation (f), Counterpart-Gruppe (f)	contraparte (f); organización (f) homóloga, grupo (m) homólogo
297	counterpart staff	personnel (m) de l'organisme (=du groupe) homologue	Counterpart-Personal (n)	personal (m) de la organización homóloga (=del grupo homólogo)
	country			
298	receiving country; country of immigration	pays (m) d'accueil; pays (m) d'immigration	Aufnahmeland (n); Einwanderungsland (n)	país (m) de acogida (=de recepción); país (m) de inmigración
299	sending country; country of origin; emigration country	pays (m) de départ; pays (m) d'origine; pays (m) d'émigration	Abgabeland (n); Herkunftsland (n), Auswanderungsland (n)	país (m) de origen; país (m) de emigración
300	coverage	couverture (f); portée (f); reportage (m)	Berichterstattung (f)	cobertura(f), campo (m) de aplicación, alcance (m); atención (f) dedicada (por la prensa, la radio, la televisión) a un asunto

CPE - See under : clinical pastoral education

CPT - <u>See</u> <u>under</u>: clinical pastoral <u>training</u>

301 craftsman   artisan (m)   Handwerker (m)   artesano (m)
<u>See also</u>: <u>w</u>orker

crafts and trade - <u>See</u> <u>under</u>: handicrafts

302	crèche, day-nursery credit	crèche (f)	Kinderkrippe (f)	crèche (f), casa (f) cuna
303	credit union	caisse (f) de crédit (=d'épargne et de crédit), caisse (f) populaire	Spar- und Darlehens-kasse (f)	caja (f) de présta-mos y ahorro
304	stand-by credit	crédit (m) "stand-by" (=de prompte assistance finan-cière)	Bereitschaftskredit (m)	crédito (m) de disponibilidad inmediata, crédi-to (m) "stand by"
305	creed	confession (f) de foi	Glaubensbekenntnis(n)	credo (m)
306	Apostles' Creed	symbole (m) des Apôtres	Apostolikum (n), Apostolisches Glaubensbekenntnis (n)	símbolo (m) de los Apóstoles
307	Athanasian Creed	symbole (m) d' Athanase	Athanasium (n), Athanasianisches Glaubensbekenntnis (n)	Credo (m) de Ata-nasio

crop

308	cash crop	culture (f) de rapport (=commerciale)	gewerblicher Anbau (m)	cultivo (m) comer-cial (=para comer-cialización=de ex-portación)
309	feed crop	culture (f) fourragère	Futterbau (m)	cultivo (m) forrajero

310 industrial crop	culture (f) industrielle	gewerblicher Anbau (m)	cultivo (m) industrial
311 curative institution	établissement (m) de soins	kurative Einrichrichtung (f)	establecimiento (m) de asistencia médica
312 curriculum	programme (m) scolaire, programme (m) d'études	Lehrplan (m), Unterrichtsplan (m), Curriculum (n)	programa (m) (=plan) (m) de estudios

day care centre - See under: day home

day-nursery - See under: crèche

313 deacon

Since there are considerable differences between the various traditions in the functions and significance assigned to the diaconal office, the following notes offer simply a rough guide to certain important differences in a field where changes are taking place, in practice and in terminology.

In the Orthodox Church the diaconate is a permanent and separate, mainly liturgical, ministry which also may include pastoral and administrative functions. In some cases a deacon proceeds to the priesthood.

In the Roman Catholic Church the diaconate is the lowest degree of the consecrated hierarchy in the Church's visible structure. It has traditionally been conferred only on those proposing to go forward to the priesthood but the Second Vatican Council initiated a restoration of the diaconate as a permanent office serving the people by the liturgy, preaching and works of charity, and opened it to 'men of mature years even if they be married'.

In the Anglican Communion the deacon is a man commissioned and ordained to a ministry of preaching, teaching, pastoral care and service, usually for a period of a year, in preparation for the priesthood.

diacre (m et f)

Les fonctions du diaconat, et la portée qu'on lui confère, diffèrent considérablement d'une tradition confessionnelle à l'autre. Dans les remarques qui suivent, nous indiquons très brièvement quelques-unes des principales différences existant dans ce domaine, actuellement en pleine évolution tant sur le plan de la pratique que de la terminologie.

Dans l'Eglise orthodoxe, le diaconat est un ministère permanent et indépendant. Les fonctions du diacre sont essentiellement liturgiques. Parfois aussi, elles peuvent être d'ordre pastoral ou administratif. Dans certains cas, le diacre peut accéder au sacerdoce.

Dans l'Eglise catholique romaine, le diaconat est le degré inférieur dans la hiérarchie consacrée de l'Eglise. Traditionnellement, l'ordre diaconal n'était conféré qu'à ceux qui se destinaient au sacerdoce. Récemment, le Concile oecuménique Vatican II a entrepris de rétablir le diaconat en tant qu'office propre et permanent et en a ouvert l'accès "à des hommes mûrs, même mariés":le diacre est appelé à servir le peuple de Dieu "dans la 'diaconie' de la liturgie, de la Parole et de la charité".

Dans la communion anglicane, le diacre exerce le ministère de la prédication, de l'enseignement, de la pastorale et du service, généralement pendant une

Diakon (m), Diakonin (f)

Funktionen und Bedeutung des diakonischen
Amtes werden in den einzelnen Traditionen
sehr unterschiedlich bewertet. Die nachstehenden Notizen sollen daher lediglich auf
einige wesentliche Unterschiede auf einem
Gebiet verweisen, in dem sich in Praxis und
Sprachgebrauch ein Wandel vollzieht. (Aus-
führlich s. hierzu die Kapitel "Diakon",
"Diakonie" in: 'Taschenlexikon Religion
und Theologie' und 'Die Religion in Geschichte und Gegenwart (RGG)' - Bibliographie.)

In der orthodoxen Kirche ist der Diakonat
ein selbständiges, in erster Linie litur-
gisches Amt auf Lebenszeit, das auch seel-
sorgerliche und administrative Funktionen
umfassen kann. In einigen Fällen ist der
Diakonat auch nur Zwischenstation auf
dem Weg zum Priesteramt.

In der römisch-katholischen Kirche ist
der Diakonat der zweitunterste der höheren Weihegrade in der kirchlichen
Hierarchie. Das diakonische Amt wurde ehe-
mals nur jenen übertragen, die sich auf das
Priesteramt vorbereiteten. Das Zweite Vati-
kanische Konzil hat jedoch den Diakonat
als Amt auf Lebenszeit wiederhergestellt
und 'ihn auch verheirateten Männern in
reiferen Jahren' zugänglich gemacht. Der
Diakon dient den Menschen durch die Diakonie der Liturgie, des Wortes und der
Liebe.

In der anglikanischen Kirche wird der Diakon

diácono (m y f)

Existen diferencias considerables entre
las distintas tradiciones con respecto
a las funciones y al alcance del oficio
de diácono. En las notas siguientes se
esbozan algunas de las principales diferencias que existen en este campo, actualmente en evolución tanto a nivel prác-
tico como de terminología.

En la Iglesia Ortodoxa el diaconado es un
ministerio permanente e independiente,
principalmente litúrgico, que comprende
a veces también funciones pastorales y
administrativas. En algunos casos, el
diácono puede llegar a ser sacerdote.

En la Iglesia Católica Romana el diaconado es el grado inferior en la jerarquía
consagrada de la Iglesia. Tradicionalmen-
te el orden diaconal sólo se confería a
aquellas personas destinadas al sacerdocio,
pero el Concilio Vaticano II emprendió la
tarea de restablecer el diaconado como un
oficio permanente abierto a los hombres
de edad madura aunque fueren casados . El
diácono está llamado a servir a su pueblo
a través de la liturgia, la predicación
de la Palabra y la caridad.

En la Comunión Anglicana el diácono es
un hombre ordenado, que ejerce un ministerio de predicación, enseñanza, pastoral y
servicio, por un período de un año generalmente, antes de llegar a ser sacerdote.

En la Iglesia Luterana el diácono es un
hombre ordenado o no, que pertenece a una

In Lutheran Churches a deacon is a man be-
longing to an institution or community
who is specially trained for specific
services (social, educational, administrative, medical or ecclesiastical) and then,
with or without ordination, performs such
services professionally on behalf of his
Church, in a church organization, Christian
society, or public administration.

In the Reformed and Presbyterian Churches,
a deacon is a man or woman elected by
the congregation to attend to the
stewardship of church funds and to social
action.

In Congregational and Baptist and other
Churches, a deacon is a man or woman
appointed to assist in worship, pastoral
care and administration.

année, avant d'accéder au sacerdoce.
Il est ordonné à ce ministère.

Dans les Eglises luthériennes, le diacre,
ordonné ou non, est rattaché à une institution ou à une communauté. Il a reçu une formation spécifique en vue d'accomplir un service
donné (dans le domaine social, éducatif,
administratif, médical ou ecclésiastique).
Il accomplit ce service au nom de son
Eglise dans un organisme rattaché à une
Eglise, dans un organisme chrétien ou
même dans un secteur administratif public.

Dans les Eglises réformées et presbytériennes,
le diacre ou la diacre, élus par la paroisse,
ont pour tâche de gérer les fonds de l'E-
glise ou d'animer l'action sociale.

Dans les Eglises congrégationalistes
et baptistes, et dans plusieurs autres,
le diacre ou la diacre sont désignés pour
accomplir diverses tâches dans le cadre
du culte, de la pastorale et de l'administration.

314 deaconess

The name given in many traditions to a
woman who performs some permanent ministry
of service, in some cases as a member of
an order or community, in others indepen-

diaconesse (f)

Dans la plupart des traditions confession-
nelles, la diaconesse exerce un ministère
diaconal permanent. Le plus souvent elle
est membre d'un ordre ou d'une communauté;

zum Amt der Wortverkündigung, der Lehre, der Seelsorge und des Dienstes berufen und ordiniert; er übt dieses Amt in Vorbereitung zum Priesteramt gewöhnlich für die Dauer eines Jahres aus.

In den lutherischen Kirchen gehört der Diakon einer bestimmten Institution oder Gemeinschaft an und erhält eine besondere Ausbildung für bestimmte Dienste (im Sozial- und Bildungswesen, in der Verwaltung, auf dem Gebiet der Krankenpflege oder zur Wahrnehmung bestimmter Funktionen innerhalb der Kirche); als ordinierter oder auch nichtordinierter Diakon leistet er diese Dienste in einer kirchlichen Organisation, einer christlichen Einrichtung oder in der öffentlichen Verwaltung hauptamtlich im Namen seiner Kirche.

In den reformierten und presbyterianischen Kirchen werden Männer oder Frauen von der Gemeinde in das diakonische Amt gewählt; sie sind für die Verwaltung kirchlicher Mittel und soziale Fragen zuständig.

In den kongregationalistischen, baptististischen und anderen Kirchen werden Männer oder Frauen in das diakonische Amt berufen, um in Gottesdienst, Seelsorge oder Verwaltung helfend tätig zu sein.

Diakonisse (f)

Mit 'Diakonisse' bezeichnet man in vielen Traditionen eine Frau, die ein dienend-fürsorgerisches Amt auf Lebenszeit ausübt. In vielen Fällen ist sie Mitglied eines Ordens

institución o comunidad. Recibe una formación especial para un servicio determinado (social, docente, administrativo, médico o eclesiástico). Cumple este servicio profesional en nombre de su Iglesia, en un organismo vinculado a la Iglesia, en una sociedad cristiana o incluso en la administración pública.

En la Iglesia Reformada y Presbiteriana puede ser diácono un hombre o una mujer. La congregación lo elige para cumplir la tarea de administrar los fondos de la Iglesia o tareas de acción social.

En la Iglesia Congregacionalista y Bautista y en otras puede ser diácono un hombre o una mujer. Se le designa para cumplir distintas tareas dentro del marco del culto, del cuidado pastoral y de la administración

diaconisa (f)

En la mayoría de las tradiciones confesionales, la diaconisa ejerce un ministerio permanente de servicio (diaconal). En algunos casos es miembro de una orden o

251

dently and attached to a church. Some
churches are now opening up new
ministries for deaconesses, given them
the status of deacon or bringing them
into the ordained ministry.

mais parfois aussi, elle accomplit ce
ministère au nom de l'Eglise, à titre individuel. Certaines Eglises invitent
par ailleurs les diaconesses à être or-
données diacres et à devenir membres
du clergé.

oder einer Gemeinschaft, doch kann sie im Namen ihrer Kirche auch unabhängig tätig sein. Darüber hinaus fordern manche Kirchen die Diakonissen auf, sich zu Diakoninnen ordinieren zu lassen und ein geistliches Amt zu übernehmen.

comunidad, pero a veces cumple ese ministerio en nombre de una iglesia, a título personal. Por otra parte, algunas iglesias invitan a las diaconisas a ordenarse como diáconos, y a llegar a ser miembros del clero.

315 decision-making	prise (f) de(s) décisions(s)	eine Entscheidung (f) treffen	adopción (f) de decisiones
316 decision-making process	formation (f) des décisions, processus (m) de décision(s)	Entscheidungsprozess (m)	procedimiento (m) para la adopción de decisiones, procedimiento (m) resolutorio

shared decision-making - See under: joint management

317 dehumanization	déshumanisation (f)	Entmenschlichung (f) Enthumanisierung (f)	deshumanización (f)
318 to dehumanize	déshumaniser, priver de sa dignité d'homme, aliéner	entmenschlichen, enthumanisieren, jem. seiner Menschenwürde berauben	deshumanizar
319 delegate	délégué (m)	Delegierter (m)	delegado (m)
320 fraternal delegate /WCC Assembly/	délégué (m) fraternel /Assemblée du COE/	befreundeter Delegierter (m) /ORK-Vollversammlung/	delegado (m) fraternal /Asamblea del CMI/
321 young delegate /WCC Assembly/	jeune délégué (m) /Assemblée du COE/	junger Delegierter (m) /ORK-Vollversammlung/	delegado (m) juvenil /Asamblea del CMI/

delivery-vehicle system - See under: nuclear arms

322 demonstrator /development/	moniteur(m), animateur (m)/développement/	Animateur (m), Demonstrator (m) /Entwicklung/	monitor (m), animador (m)/desarrollo/
323 demythologizing	démythologisation (f), démythisation (f)	Entmythologisierung (f)	desmitologización (f)

324 denomination	dénomination (f)	Denomination (f)	denominación (f)
325 denominational	dénominationnel	denominationell	denominacional
326 denominationalism	attachement (m) excessif à une dénomination donnée, particularisme (m) religieux	Denominationalismus (m), Konfessionalismus (m)	denominacionalismo (m)
327 departures, outflow /migration/	sortie(s) (f) /migration/	Abgänge (mpl), Abgang (m) /Migration/	salidas (fpl)/migración/
328 to deport, to expel	expulser	ausweisen	expulsar
329 the deprived	démunis (mpl), défavorisés (mpl)	die Besitz- und Rechtlosen (mpl)	los despojados (mpl) los excluidos (mpl), los desfavorecidos (mpl)
330 desacralisation	désacralisation (f),	Entsakralisierung (f)	desacralización (f)
331 to desegregate	déségréguer, abolir la ségrégation	desegregieren, die Rassentrennung (= Rassendiskriminierung) aufheben	abolir la segregación
332 desegregation	déségrégation (f), abolition (f) de la ségrégation	Desegregation (f), Aufhebung (f) der Rassentrennung	abolición (f) de la segregación
333 deserter	déserteur (m)	Deserteur (m)	desertor (m)
334 design	modèle (m), projet (m); maquette (f)	Plan (m), Entwurf (m)	diseño (m), croquis (m), proyecto (m), plano (m)
335 desk	secrétariat (m)	Büro (n)	secretaría (f)

deterrence

336	policy of mutual deterrence	politique (f) de dissuasion mutuelle	Politik (f) der gegenseitigen Abschreckung	política (f) de disuasion mutua
337	deterrent	moyen (m) de dissuasion; force(s)(f) de dissuasion	Abschreckungsmittel (n); Abschreckungswaffen (fpl)	medio (m) de disuasión
338	detribalization	détribalisation (f) (désintégration des sociétés tribales)	Detribalisierung (f) (Desintegration der Stämme)	destribalización (f) (desintegración de las sociedades tribales)

Deutero-Canonical Books - See under: biblical studies

developer

339	rural developer	animateur (m) (=moniteur/m/) rural	Entwicklungshelfer (m) in ländlichen Gebieten, landwirtschaftlicher Entwicklungshelfer (m)	animador (m) rural
340	development (the interrelated process of economic growth, social justice and self-reliance)	développement (m) (processus au sein duquel la croissance économique, la justice sociale et l'autonomie se trouvent indissociablement liées)	Entwicklung (f) (der Prozess, in dem wirtschaftliches Wachstum, soziale Gerechtigkeit und Eigenverantwortung in unauflöslichem Zusammenhang stehen)	desarrollo (m) (proceso en el que están estrechamente relacionados el crecimiento económico, la justicia social y la autonomía)
341	development according to kind	politique (f) du développement séparé	Politik (f) der "getrennten Entwicklung"	poíítica (f) del desarrollo separado

342 development education, education for development	éducation (f) en vue du développement	entwicklungspolitische Bewusstseinsbildung (f), Entwicklungspädagogik (f), (Erziehung zur) Entwicklungsverantwortung (f)	educación (f) para el desarrollo
343 development pattern	modèle (m) (=schéma /m/ = formule /f/) de développement	Entwicklungsmodell (n)	modelo (m) (=pauta /f/) de desarrollo
344 development scheme	plan (m) de développement	Entwicklungsplan	plan (m) de desarrollo
345 development worker	coopérant; animateur (m); praticien (m) du développement	Entwicklungshelfer (m)	animador (m), líder (m) de programas de desarrollo, cooperador (m) en cuestiones de desarrollo
346 church-sponsored development work	oeuvre (f) de développement des Eglises	kirchliche Entwicklungsarbeit (f), kirchlicher Entwicklungsdienst (m)	trabajo (m) de desarrollo de las iglesias
347 community development	développement (m) communautaire (= des collectivités); animation (f) des collectivités	Gemeinwesenaktivierung (f), Gemeinwesenentwicklung (f), kommunale Entwicklung(f), kommunale Selbsthilfe (f) (-projekte/npl/)	desarrollo (m) de la comunidad (= comunitario)

	English	French	German	Spanish
348	community development worker	animateur (m) /développement communautaire/	Animateur (m) /Gemeinwesenentwicklung/	animador (m)/desarrollo comunitario/, líder (m) de trabajo en comunidades
349	integrated (=balanced) development	développement (m) global (=harmonisé)	integrierte Entwicklung (f)	desarrollo (m) integrado (=armónico=equilibrado)
350	"Partners in Development" (Report of the Commission on International Development by Lester B. Pearson)	"Vers une action commune pour le développement du tiers-monde" (rapport de la Commission du développement international, par Lester B. Pearson)	Der Pearson-Bericht: Bestandsaufnahme und Vorschläge für Entwicklungspolitik (Bericht der Kommission für Internationale Entwicklung, von Lester B. Pearson)	"El desarrollo: empresa común" (Informe de la Comisión de Desarrollo Internacional, por Lester B. Pearson)
351	rural development	animation (f) rurale	Ländliche Entwicklung (f), landwirtschaftliche Entwicklungsförderung (f)	animación (f) rural (fomento de la comunidad rural)

separate development - See under: apartheid

diachronic way of reading the Bible - See under: biblical studies

	English	French	German	Spanish
352	diaconal year (voluntary year of Christian social service)	année (f) diaconale (service bénévole d'un an, de type diaconal, accompli dans l'Eglise)	Diakonisches Jahr (freiwilliges Dienstjahr im Bereich der Diakonie)	año (m) de servicio social voluntario
353	diaconate See also: deacon (an order of	diaconat (m) Voir aussi sous: diacre (l'un des trois	Diakonat (n) Siehe auch: Diakon (Bestandteil des	diaconado (m) Véase también: diácono (orden de diácono;

ministers in the Church or the ministry performed by deacons and diaconesses)	ordres du ministère: l'ordre diaconal; le ministère diaconal; le ministère exercé par le diacre, la diacre et la diaconesse)	dreifach gestuften Amtes; das diakonische Amt; Gesamtheit der durch die Kirche organisierten oder getragenen Dienste sozialer Hilfe; Gesamtheit der Amtsträger der Diakonie)	ministerio diaconal; ministerio ejercido por el diácono, la diácona y la diaconisa)
354 diakonia (the practical service of the Church and the individual Christian, following Christ's example and in obedience to him, and in confirmation of the Gospel of God's love in Christ)	diaconie (f) (1. terme spécifique désignant le service chrétien au sens théologique, l'existence chrétienne à l'image de celle du Christ 2. service organisé /dans une Eglise/)	Diakonie (f) (der biblisch begründete Dienst helfender Liebe der Kirche; Präsenz der Gemeinde im sozialen Bezugsfeld)	diaconía (f) (1. Término específico que significa servicio cristiano 2. Servicio organizado /en una iglesia/)
dialogue			
355 dialogue with primal world views	dialogue (m) avec les visions premières du monde	Dialog (m) mit ursprünglichen Weltbildern	diálogo (m) con las concepciones primeras del mundo
356 Buddhist-Christian dialogue	dialogue (m) entre bouddhistes et chrétiens	buddhistisch-christlicher Dialog (m)	diálogo (m) entre budistas y cristianos
357 Hindu-Christian dialogue	dialogue (m) entre hindous et chrétiens	hinduistisch-christlicher Dialog (m)	diálogo (m) entre hindúes y cristianos
358 inter-faith dialogue	1. dialogue (m) entre religions (=inter-	1. interreligiöser Dialog (m)	1. diálogo (m) entre religiones (=inter-

259

		religieux) 2. dialogue (m) inter- confessionnel	2. interkonfessio- neller Dialog (m)	religioso) 2. diálogo (m) inter- confesional
359	inter-religious dialogue	dialogue (m) entre religions (=inter- religieux)	interreligiöser Dialog (m)	diálogo (m) entre religiones (= interre- ligioso)
360	intra-religious dialogue	dialogue (m) intra- religieux	intra-religiöser Dialog (m)	diálogo (m) intra- religioso
361	Jewish-Christian dialogue	dialogue (m) judéo- chrétien	jüdisch-christlicher Dialog (m)	diálogo (m) judeo- cristiano
362	Marxist-Christian dialogue	dialogue (m) entre marxistes et chré- tiens	marxistisch-christ- licher Dialog (m)	diálogo (m) cristia- no marxista
363	Muslim-Christian dialogue	dialogue (m) islamo- chrétien	muslimisch-christ- licher Dialog (m)	diálogo cristiano- islámico
364	diet	ration (f)alimentaire régime (m) alimen- taire	1. Nahrung (f), Er- nährung (f) 2.Diät (f), Schon- Krankenkost (f)	1. dieta (f) 2. régimen (m) ali- mentario (=dietético)
365	Director /WCC,Bossey/	directeur (m) /COE, Bossey/	Direktor (m) /ÖRK, Bossey/	Director (m) /CMI, Bossey/
366	Director for Biblical Studies	directeur (m) du Secrétariat des études bibliques	Direktor (m) des Ressorts "Bibel- studien	Director (m) de la Secretaría de Estu- dio Bíblicos
367	Director of the Department of Finance and Central Services	directeur (m) du Département des finances et services centraux	Direktor (m) der Abteilung "Finanz- wesen und Zentrale Dienstleistungen"	Director (m) del Departamento de Finanzas y Servicios Centrales

368	Director of the Humanum Studies	directeur (m) des Etudes sur l'humanum	Direktor (m) der Humanum-Studien	Director (m) de Estudios sobre "Humanum"
369	Director of Personnel /WCC/	directeur (m) du personnel /COE/	Personaldirektor (m) /ÖRK/	Director (m) de Personal /CMI/
370	Director for Studies /CEC/	directeur (m) des études /KEK/	Studiendirektor (m) /KEK/	Director (m) de Estudios /KEK/
371	acting director	directeur (m) intérimaire (=par intérim)	Amtierender Direktor (m)	director (m) interino
372	Assistant Director /Bossey, WCC/	1. directeur (m) adjoint /Bossey, COE/ 2. assistant (m) du directeur, sous-directeur (m)	1. Stellvertretender Direktor (m) /Bossey, ÖRK/ 2. Persönlicher Referent (m) des Direktors	1. Director (m) Adjunto /Bossey, CMI/ 2. ayudante (m) del director
373	Associate Director of Personnel /WCC/	directeur (m) adjoint du personnel /COE/	Beigeordneter Personaldirektor (m) /ÖRK/	Director (m) Adjunto de Personal /CMI/
374	Associate Director /CMC, Bossey/	directeur (m) adjoint /CMC, Bossey/	Beigeordneter Direktor (m) /CMC, Bossey/	Director (m) Adjunto /CMI, Bossey/
375	Deputy Director /CWME, CICARWS, CCPD/	directeur (m) adjoint /CME, CESEAR, CPED/	Stellvertretender Direktor (m) /CWME, CICARWS, CCPD/	Director (m) Adjunto /CMME, CAISMR, CPID/
376	Deputy Director of Central Services	directeur (m) adjoint, chargé des Services centraux/Département des finances et services centraux/	Stellvertretender Direktor (m) der Abteilung "Finanzwesen und Zentrale Dienstleistungen" (mit besonderer Zu-	Director (m) Adjunto, encargado de los Servicios Centrales /Departamento de Finanzas y Servicios Centrales/

         ständigkeit für die
zentralen Dienst-
leistungen")

377	Deputy Director for Finance, Accounts and EDP	directeur (m) adjoint, chargé de la Section "comptabilité, trésorerie et traitement électronique de l'information" /Département des finances et services centraux/	Stellvertretender Direktor (m) der Abteilung "Finanwesen und Zentrale Dienstleistungen" (mit besonderer Zuständigkeit für die Vermögensverwaltung, Buchhaltung und Elektronische Datenverarbeitung)	Director (m) Adjunto, encargado de la Sección Contabilidad, Tesorería y Proceso Electrónico de la Información/ Departamento de Finanzas y Servicios Centrales/
378	disarmament	désarmement (m)	Abrüstung (f)	desarme (m)
	disease			
379	deficiency diseases	maladies (fpl) de carence	Mangelkrankheiten (fpl)	enfermedades (fpl) carenciales
380	dispensary	dispensaire (m); centre (m) de distribution de médicaments	Poliklinik(f); Ambulatorium (n), Verteilungsstelle (f) für Medikamente	dispensario (m)

distribution of health services - See under: health care delivery

381	diviner	devin-guérisseur (m)	Wahrsager (m)	adivino (m) curandero (m)
	doctrinal			
382	doctrinal authority	autorité (f) doctrinale	Lehrautorität (f)	autoridad (f) doctrinal

doctrinal standards/ of the Ev.Luth. Church/ → See under: confessional documents

383	doctrine	doctrine (f)	Lehre (f)	doctrina (f)
384	agreement on doctrine, doctrinal accord	accord (m) doctrinal	Übereinstimmung (f) der Lehre, Lehrkonkordie (f), Lehrvereinbarung (f)	acuerdo (m) doctrinal
385	doxology (liturgical formula of praise to God)	doxologie (f) (formule liturgique de glorification)	Doxologie (f) (Liturgische Formel der Verherrlichung)	doxología (f) (fórmula litúrgica de glorificación)
386	dropout rate	taux (m) de déperdition scolaire	Prozentsatz (m) der vorzeitigen Schulabgänger (=Dropouts /mpl/)	porcentaje (m) de deserción (=de abandono) escolar
387	dropouts	élèves (mpl) ayant abandonné (=déserté) l'école en cours d'études, abandons (mpl) scolaires	Dropouts (mpl), vorzeitige Schulabgänger (mpl)	alumnos (mpl) que han abandonado (=desertado) la escuela
388	ecocide	écocide (m)	Ökozid (m), Umweltmord (m)	ecocidio (m)
389	ecological balance	équilibre (m) écologique	ökologisches Gleichgewicht (n)	equilibrio (m) ecológico
390	ecologist	écologiste (m)	Ökologe (m)	ecólogo (m)

391 ecology	écologie (f)	Ökologie (f)	ecología (f)
392 economic (=business) cycle; (over-all) economic situation	conjoncture (f)	Konjunktur (f)	coyuntura (f)
economy			
393 cash economy	économie (f) monétaire	Geldwirtschaft (f)	economía (f) monetaria
394 production economy	économie (f) de production	Produktionswirtschaft (f)	economía (f) de producción
395 subsistence economy	économie (f) de subsistance	Subsistenzwirtschaft (f),Bedarfsdeckungswirtschaft(f)	economía (f) de subsistencia
396 economy of the Holy Spirit (dispensation of the Holy Spirit)	économie (f) du Saint-Esprit (dispensation du Saint-Esprit)	Oikonomie (f) des Heiligen Geistes (das planvolle Heilshandeln des Heiligen Geistes)	economía (f) del Espíritu Santo (dispensación del Espíritu Santo)
397 ecosystem	écosystème (m)	Ökosystem (n)	ecosistema (m)
398 ecumenics	sciences (fpl) oecuméniques	Ökumene-Wissenschaft (f), ökumenische Theorie (f)	disciplina (f) que estudia el ecumenismo
399 editor	1. directeur (m) (d'un journal, d'une revue) 2. rédacteur (m); rédacteur (m) en chef	1. Herausgeber (m) 2. Schriftleiter (m), Chefredakteur (m)	1. director (m) (de un diario o revista) 2. redactor (m) responsable

400	Editor of One World /Communication/	rédacteur (m) de la revue "One World" /Communication/	Herausgeber (m) von "One World" /Kommunikation/	Redactor (m) de la revista "One World" /Comunicación/
401	education	éducation (f); enseignement (m); formation (f); instruction (f)	Erziehung (f); Bildungswesen (n), Bildungsarbeit (f), Bildung (f) und Ausbildung	educación (f), enseñanza (f); formación (f); instrucción (f)

education for development - See under: development education

402	adult education	formation (f) des adultes	Erwachsenenbildung (f)	educación (f) de adultos
403	basic education	éducation (f) de base	Grundbildung (f)	educación (f) básica
404	Christian education	éducation (f) chrétienne; formation (f) chrétienne, catéchèse (f)	christliche Erziehung (f); christliche Bildungsarbeit (f), Erziehung (f) in christlicher Verantwortung	educación (f) cristiana; formación (f) cristiana, catequesis (f)
405	church education	enseignement (m) dispensé dans les établissements religieux	kirchliche Bildungsarbeit (f), kirchliches Bildungswesen (n)	enseñanza (f) impartida en los establecimientos religiosos

clinical pastoral education - See under: clinical pastoral training

406	community education	éducation (f) communautaire; enseignement (m) communautaire	Erziehung (f) zur Gemeinschaft, gemeinschaftsbezogene Erziehung (f)	educación (f) comunitaria; enseñanza (f) comunitaria

407	formal education	éducation (f) institutionnalisée, enseignement (m) scolaire	institutionelle Erziehung (f), Schul- und Bildungswesen (n)	educación (f) formal
408	general education	éducation (f) générale; enseignement (m) général	Allgemeinbildung (f)	educación (f) general; enseñanza (f) general
409	informal education; socialization	éducation (f) non institutionnalisée; socialisation (f)	nichtinstitutionelle Erziehung (f), Sozialisation (f)	educación (f) informal; socialización (f)
410	integrated education	éducation (f) globale (=intégrée)	ganzheitliche Bildung (f)	educación (f) global (=integral)
411	liberating education	éducation (f) libératrice	befreiende Bildung (f)	educación (f) liberadora
412	lifelong education, continuous education	éducation (f) permanente, formation (f) permanente (=continue)	permanente (=ständige) Weiterbildung (f)	educación (f) permanente, formación (f) permanente (=continua)
413	nonformal education	éducation (f) extra-scolaire	ausserschulische Bildung(-sarbeit)(f)	educación (f) no formal
414	popular education	éducation (f) populaire	Volksbildung (f)	educación (f) popular
415	"Seeing Education Whole"	"pour une vision (f) (=conception/f/) globale de l'éducation"	Konzept (n) der integralen (=ganzheitlichen) Bildung	"Hacia una concepción (f) global de la educación"
416	self-education	éducation (f) autonome, autodidactisme (m), étude (f) personnelle (=libre)	Selbstunterricht (m), Autodidaktik (f)	autoeducación (f)

417	social education	éducation (f) sociale	soziale Bewusstseins-bildung (f); Gemein-schaftskunde (f)	educación (f) social
418	special (=remedial) education (=training)	pédagogie (f) thérapeutique	Heilerziehung (f), Heilpädagogik (f)	enseñanza (f) especial
419	theological education (=training)	formation (f) théologique	theologische Ausbildung (f)	formación (f) teológica
420	educator	enseignant (m); éducateur (m), pédagogue (m)	Pädagoge (m); Lehrer (m)	enseñante (m); educador (m), pedagogo (m)
421	Embargo: for release after plenary action	Diffusion autorisée après la séance plénière	Sperrfrist (f): Frei nach Beschlussfassung im Plenum	No difundir hasta después de la sesión plenaria
422	Embargo:for release against delivery	Diffusion autorisée après la présentation en séance (plénière)	Sperrfrist: Frei nach Vorlage in der Sitzung (im Plenum)	No difundir hasta su presentación en la sesión (plenaria)
423	Embargo: for release at...	Ne pas diffuser avant le...	Sperrfrist : Frei ab...	No difundir antes del...
424	emergency	situation (f) d'urgence	Notstand (m), Notlage (f)	emergencia (f), situación (f) de emergencia (= de urgencia), situación (f) excepcional (=crítica)

425	emergency aid (=relief)	aide (f) (=secours /m/) d'urgence	Katastrophenhilfe (f), Nothilfe (f), Soforthilfe (f)	ayuda (f) (=socorro /m/) de urgencia
426	emergency telephonic help	service (m) de secours par télé-phone	Telefonseelsorge (f)	servicio (m) de socorro por teléfono

emigration - See under: external migration

427	employee	salarié(m), em-ployé (m)	Arbeitnehmer (m)	empleado (m), obrero (m), asalariado (m)
428	employer	employeur (m)	Arbeitgeber	empleador (m)
429	employment agency	bureau (m) de placement	Arbeitsvermittlung (f)	oficina (f) de colocaciones
430	empowerment	éducation (f) en vue de l'autodétermi-nation (= de la participation)	Befähigung (f) zur Selbstbestimmung; Beteiligung (f) an der Macht	capacitación (f) para el ejercicio de la libre determinación (= de la participación)

empowerment of the family - See under: famuly power

enterprise

431	private enterprise	entreprise (f) privée	Privatunternehmen (n)	empresa (f) privada
432	public enterprise	entreprise (f) publique	öffentliches Unter-nehmen (n)	empresa (f) pública
433	enthusiasts	illuminés (mpl)	Schwärmer (mpl)	iluminados (mpl)
434	environment	1. environnement (m), milieu (m) humain 2. milieu (m) physique (=naturel)	Umwelt (f)	medio (m), medio (m) ambiente

435	deterioration of the environment	dégradation (f) de l'environnement	Umweltzerstörung (f)	deterioro (m) del medio
436	global environment	environnement (m) global	globale Umwelt (f)	medio (m) global

human environment - See under: habitat

437	protection of the environment	protection (f) de l'environnement	Umweltschutz (f)	protección (f) del medio
438	environmental sanitation	hygiène (f) du milieu	Umwelthygiene (f)	higiene (f) (=saneamiento/m/) del medio
439	epiclesis (Explicit invocation of the Holy Spirit in the Eastern Liturgy: the action of the Holy Spirit which precedes any manifestation of Christ)	épiclèse (f) (invocation spéciale de l'Esprit Saint dans la liturgie orientale. Par extension: l'action de l'Esprit Saint précédant toute manifestation du Christ)	Epiklese (f) (Besondere Anrufung des Heiligen Geistes in der Liturgie. Im weiteren Sinne: Wirken des Heiligen Geistes, das jeder Manifestierung Christi vorausgeht)	epiclesis (f) (Invocación especial del Espíritu Santo en la liturgia oriental. Por extensión: la acción del Espíritu Santo que precede a toda manifestación de Cristo)

epicscopate

440	historic episcopate	épiscopat (m) historique	historisches Bischofsamt (n)	episcopado (m) histórico
441	eschatology (doctrine of the last things)	eschatologie (f) (doctrine sur les choses dernières)	Eschatologie (f) (Lehre von den letzten Dingen)	escatología (f) (Doctrina sobre las últimas cosas)

ethics

442	contextual ethics	éthique (f) contextuelle	kontextuelle Ethik (f) ("Situationsethik"/f/)	ética (f) contextual

Eucharist - See also: communion

443 Eucharist, Lord's Supper, Liturgy	eucharistie (f), Sainte Cène (f), liturgie (f)	Eucharistie (f), Abendmahl (n), Liturgie (f)	eucaristía (f), Santa Cena (f), liturgia (f)
eugenics			
444 negative eugenics	eugénique (f) négative	negative Eugenik (f)	eugenesia (f) negativa
445 positive eugenics	eugénique (f) positive	positive Eugenik (f)	eugenesia (f) positiva
446 evangelicals	évangéliques (mpl)	Evangelikale (mpl)	evangélicos (m) conservadores
447 conservative evangelicals	évangéliques (mpl) conservateurs	konservative Evangelikale (mpl)	evangélicos (mpl) conservadores
448 evangelism	évangélisation (f)	Verkündigung (f)	evangelización (f)
449 evangelization	évangélisation (f), annonce (f) de l'Evangile	Evangelisation (f); Verkündigung (f) des Evangeliums	evangelización (f)
450 exclusiveness	exclusivisme (m)	Ausschliesslichkeit (f), Exklusivität	exclusivismo (m)
451 executive	directeur (m), cadre (m), responsable (m)	leitender Mitarbeiter (m)	director(m), responsable (m); ejecutivo (m)

executive staff - See under: managerial staff

exegesis - See under: biblical studies

	expectations			
452	rising expectations	montée (f) des espoirs	steigende Erwartungen (fpl)	aspiraciones (fpl) crecientes, aumento (m) de esperanzas
	to expel - <u>See</u> <u>under</u>: <u>d</u>eport			
453	extension, extension work	vulgarisation (f)	Fortbildung (f), Extension (f)	extensión (f), divulgación (f), vulgarización (f), difusión (f)
454	extension service	service (m) de vulgarisation	Fortbildungseinrichtung (f)	servicio (m) de extensión
455	extension worker	vulgarisateur (m)	Entwicklungsberater (m)	vulgarizador (m)
456	agricultural (=rural) extension	vulgarisation (f) agricole	landwirtschaftliche Beratung (f), landwirtschaftliche Fortbildung (f), Extension (f)	extensión (f) agrícola
457	facilitator	animateur (m)	Animateur (m)	animador (m)

458 faith and religion (context:DFI)

Some difficulty may be caused in the context of Dialogue by the use of terms like religion and faith, either in the singular or the plural.

Religion and faith may be used interchangeably in some languages but not in others, and the translation will therefore vary according to the different contexts.

The word religion itself may mean personal faith, or a system of thought and ritual, the historic phenomena involving creed, cultus and culture, or one aspect of life as different from others.

Faith may mean belief and trust in God, and loyalty to traditional doctrines and communal values. Faith, for the Christian, involves both belief in his relationship to God through Jesus Christ, and a way of understanding God, man and the world.

Living faiths here implies "faiths by which men and women actually live - enduring values which provide guidance and direction for millions of people". (based on reports in Living Faiths and the Ecumenical Movement, WCC, 1971)

foi (f) et religion (f) (context: DRI)

Dans le contexte du dialogue, l'emploi des termes religion et foi soulève parfois des difficultés.

Dans certaines langues, les termes religion (angl. religion) et foi (angl. faith) sont interchangeables, dans d'autres non.

Le mot religion peut désigner soit la foi personnelle, soit un système de pensée et de rites, les phénomènes historiques qui englobent à la fois la confession de foi, le culte, la culture, soit un aspect de la vie considéré comme étant distinct des autres.

Le mot anglais faith peut s'utiliser au singulier ou au pluriel. Dans le premier cas, il se traduira en français par foi; dans le second cas, par religions, convictions religieuses.

Le mot foi peut signifier croyance et confiance en Dieu, et attachement aux doctrines traditionnelles et aux valeurs communes. Pour le chrétien, la foi est en même temps sa croyance dans sa relation avec Dieu par Jésus-Christ, et une manière de concevoir Dieu, l'homme et le monde.

L'expression anglaise living faiths, traduite en français par religions de notre temps, désigne ici les convictions religieuses qui orientent véritablement la vie des homme d'aujourd'hui - les valeurs permanentes qui donnent une orientation et un but à des millions de gens. (cf. Living Faiths and the Ecumenical Movement, WCC, 1971)

Glauben (m) und Religion (f) (Kontext: DFI)

Die Übersetzung der Begriffe Glauben (engl. faith) und Religion (engl. religion) bereitet mitunter Schwierigkeiten. Die Worte Religion und Glauben sind in einigen Sprachen austauschbar, in anderen nicht.

Das Wort Religion kann persönlicher Glauben bedeuten, ein System von Lehren und Riten, eine Tradition, die Glaubensbekenntnis, Kultus und Kultur umschliesst.

Das Wort faith(s) wird im Englischen im Singular und Plural benutzt. Im erstereren Fall übersetzt man es ins Deutsche mit Glauben, im letzteren mit Religionen oder Glauben als Oberbegriff für verschiedene Religionen. Das Wort Glauben kann Glauben an Gott, Vertrauen in Ihn bedeuten, das Festhalten an überlieferten Lehren und Werten. Glauben heisst für den Christen die Überzeugung, mit Gott durch Jesus Christus verbunden zu sein; Glauben impliziert eine bestimmte Art und Weise, Gott, die Menschen und die Welt zu begreifen.

Der englische Ausdruck living faiths im Titel "Portfolio on Dialogue with People of Living Faiths and Ideologies" wird wie folgt übersetzt: Ressort "Dialog mit Menschen verschiedener Religionen und Ideologien"; living faiths bezeichnet hier die religiösen Überzeugungen, die das Leben der Menschen massgeblich bestimmen - die bleibenden Werte, die für das Leben von Millionen von Menschen richtungsweisend sind. (Zusammengestellt nach Berichten in: Living Faiths and the Ecumenical Movement, WCC, 1971)

fe (f) y religión (f) (contexto: DRI)

El empleo de los términos religión y fe en el contexto de Diálogo presenta a veces algunas dificultades.

En algunos idiomas los términos religión (inglés: religion) y fe (inglés: faith) son intercambiables, en otros no y su traducción varía por lo tanto según los diferentes contextos.

La palabra religión puede designar tanto la fe personal como un sistema de pensamiento y de ritos, los fenómenos históricos que abarcan al mismo tiempo la confesión de fe, el culto, la cultura, o un aspecto de la vida considerado diferente de los demás.

La palabra inglesa faith puede ser utilizada en singular o en plural. En el primer caso, se traducirá al español por fe; en el segundo por religiones, convicciones religiosas.

La palabra fe puede significar creencia y confianza en Dios, y fidelidad a las doctrinas tradicionales y a los valores comunes. Para el cristiano, significa tanto su creencia en su relación con Dios a través de Jesucristo como una manera de comprender a Dios, al hombre y al mundo.

La expresión inglesa living faiths, traducida al español por religiones de nuestro tiempo significa aquí las convicciones religiosas que hoy dan sentido a la vida de los hombres, los valores permanentes que orientan y dirigen a millones de personas. (cf. Living Faiths and the Ecumenical Movement, WCC, 1971)

273

family

459	family (=family life) education	éducation (f) familiale	Vorbereitung (f) zum Leben in der Familie	educación (f) familiar

family guidance - <u>See under</u>: family <u>counselling</u>

460	family limitation	limitation (f) des naissances	Geburtenregelung (f) (=-beschränkung/f/)	limitación (f) de los nacimientos
461	family ministry	pastorale (f) des familles; ministère (m) familial (=auprès des familles)	Familienseelsorge (f)	pastoral (f) de la familia, ministerio (m) familiar
462	family organization	association (f) familiale	Familienbund (m) (= -organisation/f/ = -verband/m/)	asociación (f) familiar
463	family planning	planification (f) de la famille	Familienplanung (f)	planificación (f) de la familia
464	family planning clinic	centre (m) de planification (=planning) familial(e)	Zentrum (n) für Familienplanung	centro (m) de planificación de la familia
465	family (=child) spacing	espacement (m) des naissances	Planung (f) der Geburtenfolge	espaciamiento (m) de los nacimientos
466	extended family	famille (f) élargie	erweiterte Familie (f)	familia (f) extensa
467	joint family	grande famille (f)	Grossfamilie (f)	familia (f) amplia
468	nuclear family	famille (f) nucléaire	Kernfamilie (f)	familia (f) nuclear

469 reunion of families, uniting families	regroupement (m) des familles	Familienzusammen-führung (f)	reunión (f) (=reencuentro /m/) de familias
470 small family	famille (f) restreinte	Kleinfamilie (f)	familia (f) reducida
471 feature article	article (m) de fond; reportage (m) (journalistique)	Feature (n)	artículo (m) de fondo; reportaje (m) (en un periódico)
472 feed-back	rétroaction(f), effet (m) rétroactif; information (f) en retour	Rückkoppelung (f) Feed-back(n), Rückfluss (m) (von Informationen, Erfahrungen)	retroacción (f) efecto (m) retroactivo; retroinformación (f), conexión (f)
473 feeding	alimentation (f)	Nahrungsaufnahme (f), Fütterung (f)	alimentación (f)
474 supplementary feeding (=food)	alimentation (f) (=aliment /m/) d'appoint	Zusatzernährung (f) (=-nahrung/f/)	alimentación (f) (=alimento /m/) complementaria(◦)
475 feeding centre (=station)	centre(m) de secours alimentaires	Speisungszentrum (n)	centro (m) de ayuda alimentaria, comedor (m) (=en situaciones de urgencia)
476 fellowship	1. communauté (f); communauté (f) fraternelle 2. communion (f)	1. Gemeinschaft (f); brüderliche Gemeinschaft (f) 2. Gemeinschaft(koinonia)	1. comunidad (f); comunidad (f) fraternal 2. comunión (f)
477 church fellowship(Leuenberg Agreement:	communion (f) ecclésiale (Accord de Leuenberg:	Kirchengemeinschaft (f) (Leuenberger Konkordie:	comunión (f) eclesial (Acuerdo de Leuenberg:

275

Church fellow-ship means that, on the basis of the consensus they have reached in their under-standing of the Gospel, churches with different confessional positions accord each other fellow-ship in word and sacrament and strive for the fullest possible cooperation in witness and ser-vice to the world)	La communion eclésiale signifie que les Eglises de tradi-tions confessionnelles différentes, se fondant sur l'accord auquel elles sont parvenues dans la compréhen-sion de l'Evangile, se déclarent mu-tuellement en communion quant à la prédication et à l'administra-tion des sacrements et s'efforcent de par-venir à la plus grande unité possi-ble dans le témoi-gnage et le service envers le monde)	Kirchengemeinschaft bedeutet, dass Kirchen ver-schiedenen Bekennt-nisstandes aufgrund der gewonnenen Über-einstimmung im Ver-ständnis des Evan-geliums einander Gemeinschaft an Wort und Sakra-ment gewähren und eine möglichst gros-se Gemeinsamkeit in Zeugnis und Dienst an der Welt erstreben)	La comunión eclesial significa que las iglesias de tradiciones con-fesionales diferen-tes, basándose en el consenso que han alcanzado en su com-prensión del Evangelio, se declaran mutua-mente en comunión en cuanto a la pre-dicación y a la administración de los sacramentos y se esfuerzan por lograr la mayor cooperación posible en el testimonio y servicio al mundo)
478 pulpit and table fellowship, pulpit and altar fellowship (See also: church fellowship)	communion (f) (ecclésiale) quant à la prédication et la Cène	Kanzel- und Abend-mahlsgemeinschaft (f), Tisch- und Kanzel-gemeinschaft (f), Altar- und Kanzel-gemeinschaft (f)	Comunión (f) de púlpito y altar
479 feminism	féminisme (m)	Feminismus (m)	feminismo (m)
480 feminist movement; feminist group	mouvement (m) féministe; groupe (m) féministe	Frauenbewegung (f); Frauengruppe (f)	movimiento (m) feminista; grupo (m) feminista

field

481 field officer	collaborateur (m) (=responsable /m/) des bureaux extérieurs (=sur les lieux =sur le terrain)	Mitarbeiter (m) im Aussendienst	colaborador (m) (= responsable/m/) sobre el terreno (=de las oficinas exteriores)
482 field staff	personnel (m) des bureaux extérieurs, collaborateurs (mpl) sur les lieux	Mitarbeiter (mpl) im Aussendienst, Aussendienstpersonal (n), Personal (n) der Aussenstellen	personal (m) de campo (=de las oficinas exteriores)
483 field study	étude (f) sur le terrain	Feldstudie (f)	estudio (m) sobre el terreno
484 field work	travaux (mpl) (=activité /f/) sur le terrain	Aussendienst (m)	trabajo(m) (=actividad/f/) sobre el terreno

film

485 film strip	film (m) fixe (=à vues fixes); série (f) de diapositives	Stehfilm (m) Bildband (n); Lichtbildreihe (f)	serie (f) de diapositivas
486 animated film	film (m) d'animation; dessin (m) animé	Trickfilm (m); Zeichentrickfilm (m)	dibujos (mpl) animados
487 feature film, feature-length film	grand film (m), long métrage (m)	Feature-Film (m)	película (f) principal, largo metraje (m)
488 full-length film	long métrage (m)	Spielfilm (m)	(película de) largo metraje (m)
489 short film	court métrage (m)	Kurzfilm (m)	(película de) corto metraje (m)

490 first fruit	prémices (fpl)	Erstlingsgabe (f)	primicias (fpl)
491 flyer	prospectus (m), dépliant (m), feuillet (m) d'information	Faltprospekt (m)	volante (m)
foetal			
492 foetal abnormalities	malformations(fpl) foetales	fötale Anomalien (fpl)	malformaciones (fpl) (=anomalías /fpl/) fetales
493 foetal diagnosis	diagnostic (m) foetal	Fötaldiagnose (f)	diagnóstico (m) fetal
494 folder	1. dépliant (m) 2. dossier (m)	1. Faltprospekt (m) 2. Arbeitsmappe (f)	1. folleto (m) (plegable) 2. carpeta (f)
495 follow-up	suite (f) à donner à (une conférence); maintien (m) de contacts	Nachkontakte (mpl); Nacharbeit (f)	etapa (f) de continuación de(una conferencia); mantener y fortalecer contactos (=relaciones)
496 follow-up action	action (f) consécutive (=complémentaire)	Nacharbeit (f), Weiterführung (f) der Arbeit; Kontrolle (f); Auswertung	medidas (fpl)(=acción /f/) complementaria(s); actividad (f) consecutiva
497 follow-up course	stage (m) (=cours /m/) de perfectionnement	Fortbildungskurs (m)	curso (m) (=cursillo /m/) de perfeccionamiento
498 food	nourriture (f); aliment (m), denrée (f) (=produit/m/) alimentaire	Lebensmittel (n), Nahrungsmittel (n)	alimento (m), producto (m) alimenticio

499 food additive	additif (m) alimentaire	Lebensmittelzusatz (m)	aditivo (m) alimentario
500 food aid	aide (f) alimentaire	Nahrungsmittelhilfe (f)	ayuda (f) alimentaria
501 food crops	cultures (fpl) vivrières	Nutzpflanzenanbau (m)	huertas (fpl), cultivos (mpl) de plantas comestibles
502 food demand	demande (f) alimentaire	Nahrungsmittelnachfrage (f)	demanda (f) de alimentos
503 food hygiene	hygiène (f) alimentaire	Ernährungshygenie (f)	higiene (f) de la alimentación
504 food (=nutritional) requirements	besoin (mpl) alimentaires	Nahrungsmittelbedarf (m)	necesidades (fpl) alimentarias (=nutricionales)
505 food shortage	pénurie (f) alimentaire	Nahrungsmittelknappheit (f)	escasez (f) de alimentos
506 food statistics	statistique(f) alimentaire	Nahrungsmittelstatistik (f)	estadística (f) alimentaria
507 food supply	disponibilités (fpl) (=ressources/fpl/) alimentaires	Lebensmittelvorrat (m)	suministros (mpl) de alimentos
508 food technology	technologie (f) alimentaire	Lebensmitteltechnologie (f)	tecnología (f) alimentaria
509 world food situation	situation (f) alimentaire mondiale	Welternährungssituation (f)	situación (f) alimentaria mundial
force			
510 use of force	recours (m) à la force	Anwendung (f) von Gewalt	recurrir al uso de la fuerza; uso (m) de la fuerza

511 legitimate use of force	légitime recours (m) à la force	legitime Anwendung (f) von Gewalt	uso (m) legítimo de la fuerza
512 foreshadowing, foretaste	préfiguration (f), prémices (fpl)	Abschattung (f), Erstlingsgabe (f)	prefiguración (f)
513 form criticism /biblical studies/	critique (f) des formes /études bibliques/	Formkritik (f) /Bibelstudien/	crítica (f) de la forma /estudios bíblicos/
514 forum	tribune (f), forum (m); table (f) ronde	Forum (n), öffentliche Diskussion (f); Podiumsdiskussion (f)	foro (m), mesa (f) redonda
515 fringe benefits	indemnités (fpl) et avantages (mpl) divers	freiwillige Sozialleistungen (fpl) der Betriebe	prestaciones (fpl) suplementarias; ventajas (fpl) sociales
frontier			
516 frontier conference /Bossey/	colloque (m) interdisciplinaire (entre théologiens et spécialistes d'autres disciplines) /Bossey/	interdisziplinäres Kolloquium (n) (Teilnehmer: Theologen und Vertreter anderer Disziplinen)/Bossey/	coloquio (m) interdisciplinario(entre teólogos y especialistas de otras disciplinas) /Bossey/
517 frontiers of faith	confins (mpl) de la foi	Grenzen (fpl) des Glaubens	fronteras (fpl) de la fe
518 frontiers between faith and unfaith	aux confins (mpl) (=frontières /fpl/) de la foi	an den Grenzen (fpl) von Glauben und Unglauben	en las fronteras (fpl) de la fe
519 frontiers of the Church	fronts (mpl) nouveaux de l'Eglise	Pionieraufgaben(fpl) der Kirche	nuevas fronteras (fpl) de la Iglesia

520	frontiers of mission	fronts (mpl) nouveaux de la mission	Pionieraufgaben(fpl) der Mission	nuevas fronteras (fpl) de la misión
521	frontier work	1. activité (f) d'avant-garde (=de pionnier =expérimentale) 2. activités (fpl) interdisciplinaires (entre théologiens et spécialistes d' autres disciplines) /Bossey/	1. Pionierarbeit (f), bahnbrechende, wegbereitende Tätigkeit (f) 2. interdisziplinäre Studien- (= Forschungs-)-arbeit (von Theologen und Vertretern anderer Disziplinen)/Bossey/	1. actividad (f) de vanguardia 2. actividades (fpl) interdisciplinarias(entre teólogos y especialistas de otras disciplinas)/Bossey/
	frontier worker			
522	movement of frontier workers	migration (f) frontalière	Pendeln (n), Pendelwanderung (f)	migración (f) fronteriza
	functions and purposes - See under: aims and functions			
	fund			
523	fund raising, mobilization (= procurement = raising) of capital	mobilisation (f) de fonds (=capitaux)	Kapitalbeschaffung (f)	movilización (f) de fondos (=del capital)
524	earmarked funds, designated money	crédits (mpl) (=fonds /mpl/) affectés (=spéciaux =réservés)	zweckgebundene Mittel (npl), zweckbestimmte Gelder (npl)	créditos (mpl) (=fondos/mpl/) reservados (=especiales
525	Joint ICEM/WCC Revolving Travel Loan Fund	Fonds (m) mixte de roulement CIME/COE "prêts aux voyages"	Gemeinsamer JCEM-ÖRK-Reisedarlehens-Umlauffonds (m)	Fondo (m) Mixto de Rotación CIME/ CMI "Préstamos para Viajes"
526	operating fund	fonds (m) d'exploitation	Betriebskapital(n)	fondo (m) de explotación (=de funcionamiento)

527	Provident Fund of the WCC	Fondation (f) de prévoyance du COE	Versorgungskasse (f) des ÖRK	Fondo (m) de Previsión del CMI
528	Restricted Capital Fund /Office of Education/	Fonds (m) inaliénable /Bureau de l'éducation/	Nutzniessungsfonds (m) /Büro für Bildungsfragen/	Fondo (m) no Disponible /Oficina de Educación/
529	Retirement and Social Welfare Fund for the Staff of the WCC, Retirement Fund	Fondation (f) de retraite et des oeuvres sociales en faveur du personnel du COE, Fondation (f) de retraite	Pensionskasse (f) des ÖRK	Fondo (m) de Retiro y de Previsión Social en beneficio del Personal del CMI, Fondo (m) de Retiro
530	revolving fund, revolving loan fund	fonds (m) de roulement; fonds (m) autonome de prêts, fonds (m) d'avances remboursables	Umlauffonds (m), Kreditumlauffonds (m)	fondo (m) rotatorio (=de rotación); fondo (m) automáticamente renovable; fondos (mpl) para préstamos
531	Travel Assistance Fund /WCC/	Fonds (m) d'aide aux voyages /COE/	Reisezuschussfonds (m) /ÖRK/	Fondo (m) de Ayuda para Viajes/CMI/
532	Travel Loan Fund /WCC, CICARWS/	Fonds (m) de prêts aux voyages /COE, CESEAR/	Reisedarlehensfonds (m) /ÖRK, CICARWS/	Fondo (m) de Préstamos para Viajes/CMI, CAISMR/
533	trust fund	fonds (m) de dépôt, fonds (m) d'affectation spéciale	Treuhandfonds (m)	fondo (m) fiduciario, fondo (m) de depósito, asignación (f) especial
534	working capital fund	fonds (m) de roulement (=d'exploitation)	Betriebskapital (n)	fondo (m) de operaciones (= de explotación)

535	Working Capital Fund /CWME/	Fonds (m) des disponibilités /CME/	Betriebskapital (n) /CWME/	Fondo (m) de Reserva para Funcionamiento /CMME/
536	fundamentalists	fondamentalistes (mpl)	Fundamentalisten (mpl)	fundamentalistas (mpl)
537	futurologist	futurologue (m)	Futurologe (m)	futurólogo (m)
538	futurology	futurologie (f)	Futurologie (f)	futurología (f)

gap

539	credibility gap	crise (f) de confiance	Vertrauenskrise (f)	crisis (f) de confianza, margen (m) de credibilidad
540	food gap	déficit (m) alimentaire	Nahrungsmitteldefizit (n), Lebensmitteldefizit (n)	déficit (m) alimentario
541	rich-poor gap	fossé (m) (=écart/m/) entre riches et pauvres	Abstand (m) (=Kluft /f/) zwischen den reichen und den armen Ländern, Gefälle (n) zwischen Industrie- und Entwicklungsländern	separación (f) (=brecha /f/ = desigualdad /f/) entre ricos y pobres
542	gathering and sending (of the Church)	rassemblement et envoi (de l'Eglise)	Versammlung und Sendung (der Kirche)	reunión y envío (de la Iglesia)

gene

543	gene pool	banque (f) de gènes	Genpool (m)	banco (m) de genes, banco (m) de material genético
544	gene transplantation	transplantation (f) des gènes	Gentransplantation (f)	transplante (m) de genes
545	defective genes	gènes (mpl) défectueux	anomale Gene (npl)	genes (mpl) anómalos (=anormales; defectuosos)

genetic

546	genetic burden	fardeau (m) génétique	genetische Belastung (f)	carga (f) genética
547	genetic constitution	constitution (f) génétique	genetische Konstitution (f)	constitución (f) genética
548	genetic correction	correction (f) génétique	Genkorrektur (f)	corrección (f) genética
549	genetic counselling	consultation (f) génétique	genetische Beratung (f)	asesoramiento (m) genético
550	genetic defect	anomalie (f) génétique	genetischer Schaden (m)	anomalía (f) (=defecto /m/) genética(o)
551	genetic disorder	trouble (m) génétique	genetische Störung (f)	trastorno (m) (=perturbación /f/ =afección /f/) genético(a)
552	genetic endowment	patrimoine (m) (=caractères/mpl/) héréditaire(s)	Erbanlagen (fpl)	patrimonio (m) genético

553 genetic information	information (f) génétique	genetische Information (f)	información (f) genética
554 genetic tailoring	patrimoine (m) génétique sur mesure	genetisch massgeschneidertes Individuum (n)	"ingeniería"(f) (=manipulación /f/) genética
555 genetical engineering	manipulation (f) génétique	Genmanipulation (f)	manipulación (f) genética
556 genetics	génétique (f)	Genetik (f)	genética (f)
557 genocide	génocide (m)	Völkermord (m)	genocidio (m)
558 genotype	génotype (m)	Genotyp (m)	genotipo (m)
559 GNP - Gross National Product	PNB - produit national brut (m)	Bsp - Bruttosozialprodukt (n)	PNB - producto nacional bruto (m)
560 gift	don (m)	Spende (f)	donación (f)
561 spiritual gifts, gifts of the Spirit See also: charismata	dons (mpl) spirituels, dons (mpl) de l'Esprit Voir aussi sous: charismes	geistliche Gaben (fpl), Gaben des Geistes, Gnadengaben (fpl) Siehe auch: Charismata	dones (mpl) espirituales, dones (mpl) del Espíritu Véase también: carismas

government

562 local government	administration (f) locale	Kommunalverwaltung (f)	administración (f) local, autoridades (fpl) locales
563 urban government	municipalité (f) (=administration /f/ municipale)	Stadtverwaltung(f)	municipio (m) ayuntamiento (m), municipalidad (f)

grace

564	infusion of grace	infusion (f) de la grâce	Eingiessung (f) der Gnade	infusión (f) de la gracia
565	means of grace	moyens (mpl) de grâce	Gnadenmittel (npl)	medios (mpl) de gracia
566	grade	classe (f)	Gehaltsgruppe (f)	categoría (f)

grain

567	high yielding varieties of grain	variété (fpl) de céréales à haut rendement (=hautement productives de céréales)	Hochleistungs-Getreidesorten (fpl)	variedades (fpl) de cereales de gran rendimiento (=altamente productivas de cereales)
568	grant	1. don (m); subside (m), subvention (f), indemnité (f) 2. bourse (f) d'études, allocations (fpl) d'études	1. Zuwendung(f), Zuschuss (m) 2. Stipendium (n), Studienhilfe (f)	1. donación (f); subvención (f), subsidio (m) 2. beca (f) de estudios, subsidios (mpl) para estudios
569	block grant	don (m) global; subvention (f) globale	Rahmenzuschuss (m)	donación (f) global; subvención (f) global
570	initial grant	don (m) initial; subvention (f) initiale	Initialzuschuss (m)	donación (f) inicial; subvención (f) inicial
571	'green revolution'	"révolution verte"	"Grüne Revolution"	"revolución verde"

group

572	group areas /South Africa/	zones (fpl) de regroupement/Afrique du Sud/ (secteurs	Gruppengebiete (npl) /Südafrika/ (bestimmten Rassengrup-	zonas (fpl) homogéneas/Sudáfrica/ (reservadas a al-

	réservés à certains groupes raciaux)	pen vorbehaltene Wohngebiete)	gunos grupos racia-les)
573 Group Areas Act /South Africa/	loi (f) sur la ré-sidence des groupes raciaux /Afrique du Sud/	Gruppengebietsge-setz (n), Gesetz (n) über getrennte Wohngebiete, /Süd-afrika/	ley (f) sobre las zonas homogéneas reservadas a los distintos grupos raciales /Sudáfrica/
574 group therapy	thérapie (f) de groupe	Gruppentherapie (f)	terapia (f) de grupo
575 group work	travail (m) (social) de groupe	Gruppenarbeit (f)	trabajo (m) social de grupo
576 Advisory Group on Urban Industrial Mission /CWME/	Groupe (m) consulta-tif de la Mission en milieu urbain et industriel /CME/	Beratungsgruppe (f) für den kirchlichen Dienst in der ur-banen und indu-striellen Gesell-schaft/CWME/	Grupo (m) Asesor de Misión Urbana e Industrial (CMME)
577 Core Group /UIM/	Groupe (m) restreint /MUI/	Kerngruppe (f) /UIM/	Grupo (m) Reducido /MUI/
domestic group - See under: household			
578 facilitating group	groupe (m) d'ani-mation	Animationsgruppe (f)	grupo (m) de ani-mación
579 informal (=un-official = spon-taneous) group	groupe (m) informel (=sauvage)	informelle Gruppe(f), Spontangruppe (f)	grupo (m) informal (=espontáneo)
580 marginal groups	groupes (mpl) mar-ginaux	Marginalgruppen (fpl), Randgruppen (fpl)	grupos (mpl) mar-ginales

581	marginalized groups	groupes (mpl) margi-nalisés	marginalisierte Gruppen (fpl)	grupos (mpl) (mpl) marginados
582	Regional Contact Group	Groupe (m) régional de liaison /MUI/	Regionale Verbindungsgruppe (f) /UIM/	Grupo (m) Regional de Contacto /MUI/
583	Small Staff Executive Group /WCC/	Groupe (m) exécutif restreint du personnel /COE/	Kerngruppe (f) Leitender Mitarbeiter /ÖRK/	Grupo (m) Ejecutivo Reducido de Personal/CMI/
584	Staff Executive Group (SEG)/WCC/	Groupe (m) exécutif du personnel (SEG)/COE/	Gruppe (f) Leitender Mitarbeiter (SEG)/ÖRK/	Grupo (m) Ejecutivo de Personal (SEG) /CMI/
585	Staff Group on Coordination of Periodicals /WCC/	Groupe (m) de coordination des périodiques /COE/	ÖRK- Koordinierungsgruppe (f) "Periodika"/ÖRK/	Grupo (m) de Coordinación de las Publicaciones Periódicas /CMI/
586	Staff Group on Finance Coordination /WCC/	Groupe (m) de coordination des finances /COE/	ÖRK-Koordinierungsgruppe (f) "Finanzen"/ÖRK/	Grupo (m) de Coordinación de Finanzas /CMI/
587	Staff Group on Programme Coordination and Planning /WCC/	Groupe (m) de coordination et de planification des programmes /COE/	ÖRK-Koordinierungsgruppe (f) "Programmkoordinierung und Planung"/ÖRK/	Grupo (m) de Coordinación y Planificación de Programas /CMI/
588	Staff Group on Travel Coordination /WCC/	Groupe (m) de coordination des voyages /COE/	ÖRK-Koordinierungsgruppe (f) "Reisen" /ÖRK/	Grupo (m) de Coordinación de Viajes /CMI/
589	study group	groupe (m) d'étude	Studiengruppe (f)	grupo (m) de estudios
590	working group	groupe (m) de travail	Arbeitsgruppe (f)	grupo (m) de trabajo

growth

591	balanced growth	croissance (f) équilibrée	ausgewogenes (= gleichgewichtiges) Wachstum (n)	crecimiento (m) equilibrado
592	exponential growth	croissance (f) exponentielle	exponentielles Wachstum (n)	crecimiento (m) exponencial
593	"Limits to Growth"	"Limites à la croissance"	"Grenzen des Wachstums"	"límites del crecimiento"
594	optimum growth rate	taux (m) de croissance optimal	optimale Wachstumsrate (f)	tasa (f) óptima de crecimiento
595	self-sustaining growth	croissance (f) auto-entretenue	sich selbsttragendes Wachstum (n)	crecimiento (m) autosostenido
596	zero growth	croissance (f) zéro (=nulle)	Null-Wachstum (n)	crecimiento (m) nulo (=cero)

habitat

597	human habitat; human environment	habitat (m) humain; milieu (m) humain, environnement (m)	Habitat (n) des Menschen; Umwelt(f) des Menschen	habitat (m) humano; medio (m) humano
598	hagiophany (denotes any manifestation of holiness, from agios =holy)	hagiophanie (f) (vient de "agios", saint, et désigne toute manifestation de la sainteté)	Hagiophanie (f) (von gr. "hagios": heilig; bezeichnet jede Ausserung der Heiligkeit)	hagiofanía (f) (Viene de agios, santo y se refiere a cualquier manifestación de la santidad)

handicapped

599	the mentally handi-capped	handicapés (mpl) mentaux	geistig Behinderte (mpl)	incapacitados (mpl) (=impedidos /mpl/) mentales, personas (fpl) con impedimentos mentales
600	the physically handicapped	handicapés (mpl)	körperlich Be-hinderte (mpl)	físicamente dis-minuidos (=impedidos) (mpl), personas (fpl) con impedimentos físicos
601	handicrafts, crafts and trades	artisanat (m)	Handwerk (n)	artesanía (f)
602	Head of Treasury Section /Finance and Central Ser-vices/	chef (m) de la Section trésorerie /Finances et ser-vices centraux/	Leiter (m) der Ab-teilung "Vermögens-verwaltung und Zahlungen"/Finanz-wesen und Zentrale Dienstleistungen/	Jefe (m) de la Sección Tesorería /Finanzas y Servi-cios Centrales/
603	headquarters of the WCC	siège (m) du COE	ÖRK-Zentrale (f)	sede (f) del CMI
604	health (physical, mental and social well-being)	santé (f) (bien-être physique, men-tal et social)	Gesundheit (f) (Zu-stand des körper-lichen, seelischen und sozialen Wohlbe-findens)	salud (f)(bienestar físico, mental y social)
605	health---	---de santé (=sani-taire); --- d'hygiène; --- médical	--- Gesundheits---, --- gesundheitlich; --- medizinisch	--- de la salud (=sanitario); --- de sanidad; --- médico

606 health assistant	assistant (m) sanitaire	Gesundheitsassistent (m)	ayudante (m) (=auxiliar /m/) sanitario
607 health care	soins (mpl) médicaux	Gesundheitspflege (f); Gesundheitsversorgung (f)	asistencia (f) sanitaria
608 health care delivery, distribution of health services	distribution (f) des soins médicaux	Bereitstellung (f) von Gesundheitsdiensten	prestación (f) de asistencia sanitaria
609 health care system	système (m) sanitaire	Gesundheitswesen(n)	sistema (m) de asistencia sanitaria
610 health care unit	unité (f) sanitaire	Gesundheitsversorgungseinheit (f)	servicio (m) de asistencia sanitaria
611 health centre	centre (m) sanitaire (=de soins = médical)	Gesundheitszentrum (n)	centro (m) sanitario (=de asistencia médica)
612 health education	éducation (f) sanitaire, éducation (f) pour la santé	Gesundheitsaufklärung und -erziehung (f)	educación (f) (=enseñanza /f/) sanitaria, educación (f) para la salud
613 health planning	planification (f) sanitaire	Gesundheitsplanung (f)	planificación (f) sanitaria
614 health post	poste (m) de secours	Sanitätsposten (m), Krankenstation (f)	puesto (m) de socorro
615 health record	fiche (f) (=dossier /m/) médical(e)	Krankengeschichte (f), Krankenblatt (n); Anamnese (f)	historia (f) clínica

616	health regulations	règlement (m) sanitaire	Gesundheitsvorschriften (fpl)	reglamento (m) sanitario
617	health team	équipe (f) soignante	Gesundheitsteam (n)	equipo (m) sanitario (=de salud)
618	health visitor	visiteur (m) sanitaire	Gesundheitsbesucher (m), Gesundheitsaufseher (m)	visitador (m) sanitario
619	health worker(s)	travailleur (m) (= agent/m/) sanitaire, personnel(s) (m) de santé, personnel (m) soignant, soignants (mpl)	Gesundheitspersonal (n); Angehöriger (m) des Pflegedienstes, Pflegepersonal (n)	trabajador (m) sanitario, sanitario(m) personal (m) sanitario
620	basic health services	services (mpl) sanitaires de base	elementare Gesundheitsversorgung (f)	servicios (mpl) sanitarios básicos (=generales)
621	community health	santé (f) de la collectivité	Gesundheit (f) der Gemeinschaft	salud (f) de la colectividad
622	community health care	soins (mpl) médicaux des collectivités (=au service des collectivités)	gemeinschaftsbezogene Gesundheitspflege (f)	asistencia (f) sanitaria de la comunidad (=de la colectividad)
623	comprehensive health care	action (f) sanitaire globale, soins(mpl) de santé globaux	ganzheitliche Gesundheitspflege (f)	asistencia (f) sanitaria total
624	family health	santé (f) de la famille	Gesundheit (f) der Familie	salud (f) de la familia

625	integrated health care	soins (mpl) médicaux intégrés	integrierte Gesundheitspflege (f)	asistencia (f) sanitaria integrada
626	maternal and child health (MCH)	protection (f) maternelle et infantile (PMI)	Gesundheitshilfe (f) für Mutter und Kind, Mutterschutz (m)	higiene (f) maternoinfantil (=de la madre y el niño) (HMI)
627	national health plan	plan (m) national de santé	staatlicher Gesundheitsplan (m)	plan (m) nacional de salud; plan (m) sanitario nacional
628	hearing	1. enquête (f) publique 2. réunion (f) d'information-débat /Assemblée du COE/	1. Hearing (n), Anhörung (f), öffentliche, parlamentarische Untersuchung (f) 2. Hearing (Informationsgespräch) /ÖRK-Vollversammlung/	1. audiencia (f); juicio (m) oral 2. consulta (f); sesión (f) de información y discusión /Asamblea del CMI/
629	herbalist	herboriste (m)	Kräuterkundiger (m), Kräuterarzt (m)	herbolario (m)

hermeneutics - See under: biblical studies

630	hesychasm (quietness, recollection in inner peace; ascetic mystical method of achieving interiority /the Kingdom of God within you, Lk.17:21/	hésychasme (m) (vient de "hésychie": silence, recueillement dans la paix intérieure. Méthode ascétique et mystique de l'intériorisation /"le Royaume est au-dedans de vous", Luc 17, 21/ et de la	Hesychasmus (m) (Von gr. "hesychie": Ruhe, Stille, Sammlung im inneren Frieden. Aszetische und mystische Methode der Verinnerlichung /"Das Reich Gottes ist inwendig in euch", Luk.17,27/	hesicasmo (m) (Viene de "hesyjie": silencio, recogimiento en la paz interior. Método ascético y místico de la introspección/"El Reino dentro de vosotros está", Luc. 17:21/ y de

and private prayer; a hesychast is one who practices this method)	prière du coeur)	und des Gebets des Herzens)	la oración del corazón)
631 Hispanic-Americans	Hispano-américains (mpl)	Hispano-Amerikaner (mpl)	hispanoamericanos (mpl)

historic reading (=criticism) - See under: bibilical studies

home

632 home care, domiciliary services	service (m) de soins et d'aide à domicile	Hauspflege (f)	servicio (m) de atención a domicilio
633 home for unmarried mothers and children	foyer (m) d'accueil pour mères célibataires	Heim (n) für alleinstehende Mütter	hogar (m) para madres solteras
634 children's home (=hostel)	maison (f) d'enfants, home (m) pour enfants	Kinderheim (n), Erziehungsheim (n)	hogar (m) infantil
635 day home (for children), day care centre	garderie (f) d'enfants, halte-garderie (f)	Kindertagesheim (n)	guardería (f)
636 nursing home for old people; residential home for old people	centre (m) de soins pour personnes âgées	Altenpflegestätte (f)	centro (m) de asistencia para ancianos
637 old people's home, old folk's home	maison (f) de retraite, home (m) pour personnes âgées	Altenwohnheim (n), Altenheim (n)	hogar (m) para ancianos, asilo (m) de ancianos

638 homeland/South Africa/ (African reserve, formerly called Bantustan)	foyer (m) national /Afrique du Sud/ (réserve africaine, autrefois appelée Bantoustan)	"homeland"(n)/Süd-afrika/ (Reservat (m) für Schwarzafrikaner, früher Bantustan genannt)	"territorio"(m) patrio"/Sudáfrica/ (reserva africana, antes llamada Bantoustan)

horizontal approach in voluntary service - See under: voluntary service

hospital

639 hospital administrator	administrateur (m) hospitalier	Krankenhausverwal-ter (m)	administrador (m) de hospital
640 referral hospital	hôpital (m) central	Zentralkrankenhaus (n) Überweisungskranken-haus (n)	hospital (m) central
641 household, domestic group	communauté (f)(de vie)	Wohngemeinschaft (f)	comunidad (f) (de vida)
642 mixte household	ménage (m) (=foyer /m/) mixte	Mischehe (f)	matrimonio (m) mixto

hovels - See under: shanties

human

643 being human and becoming human	l'être et le devenir humains, l'humain (=l'humanité) et son accomplissement (=sa réalisation)	Mensch sein und wer-den	el ser y devenir humanos, lo humano (= la humanidad) y su realización

644 illiteracy	analphabétisme (m)	Analphabetismus (m), Analphabetentum (n)	analfabetismo (m)
645 the illiterate	analphabètes (mpl)	Analphabeten (mpl)	analfabetos (mpl)
646 illness episode	épisode (m) morbide	Krankheitsereignis (n)	episodio (m) patológico

immigrant worker - See under: migrant worker

immigration

647 immigration laws (=legislation)	législation (f) sur l'immigration	Einwanderungsgesetze (npl), Einwanderungsgesetzgebung (f)	leyes (fpl) de inmigración, legislación (f) sobre inmigración
648 selective immigration	migration (f) sélective	selektive Einwanderung (f)	migración (f) selectiva

inclusive

649 racially inclusive community	communauté (f) racialement pluraliste	rassisch pluralistische Gemeinschaft (f)	comunidad (f) racialmente pluralista
650 inclusiveness	universalité (f) (=tous en un)	umfassender Charakter (m), Inklusivität (f)	pluralismo (m) (= todos en uno)
651 racial inclusiveness	pluralisme (m) racial	rassischer Pluralismus (m)	pluralismo (m) racial

income

652 distribution of income	répartition (f) des revenus	Einkommensverteilung (f)	distribución (f) (=repartición /f/) de la renta

653 indigenization   indigénisation (f)   Indigenisierung (f),   indigenización (f)
Einheimischwerdung(f)

    industrial

654 industrial chaplain   aumônier (m) en mi-   Industriepfarrer (m)   capellán (m)
lieu industriel   (= - pastor/m/)   industrial (= en
medio industrial)

    industrial democracy - See under: participation in management

    industrial relations - See under: labour relations

655 influx,   influx (m) (=apport   Zustrom (m),   contingente (m)
    inflow   /m/) migratoire   Zuwanderung (f)   (de inmigrantes),
entradas (fpl) de
inmigrantes, corriente
(f) de inmigración

656 influx control/South   contrôle (m) de l'   Zuzugskontrollen   restricciones (fpl)
    Africa/   afflux (=de l'immigra-   (fpl) (Einschrän-   a la entrada de
    (restriction of   tion) des Africains   kung/f/ des Rechts   personas (a la corrien-
    the movement   (dans les zones ur-   Schwarzer auf freie   te de africanos hacia
    of Africans   baines)/Afrique du   Umsiedlung in die   las zonas urbanas)
    into the cities)   Sud/   Städte) /Südafrika/   /Sudáfrica/

656a insight(s)   discernement (m),   Einsicht (f);   discernimiento (m),
intuition (f);   Wissen (n);   intuición (f);
approche (f)(intui-   Vorstellung (f) von;   conocimiento (m)(in-
tive), connaissance (f)   Ansatz (m);   tuitivo); com-
(intuitive), intelli-   Kenntnisse (fpl)   prensión (f);
gence (f)(des choses);   perspectivas (fpl);
perspectives (fpl);   percepciones (fpl);
vues (fpl), per-   puntos (mpl) de
ceptions (fpl); con-   vista, opiniones (fpl);
ceptions (fpl);   experiencias (fpl)
données (fpl) acquises,
expériences (fpl)

intake- See under: arrivals

| 657 | caloric intake | ration (f) calorique (=calorifique) | Kalorienzufuhr (f) | ración (f) calórica, ingestión (f) de calorías |

intercelebration - See under: communion

intercommunion - See under: communion

intertestamental writings - See under: biblical studies

658 Jesus people	"Jesus people" (mpl)	Jesus People (mpl)	"Jesus people"(mpl)
659 job	emploi (m), fonction (f), poste (m)	Beschäftigung (f), Beruf (m), Arbeitsplatz (m)	empleo (m), función (f), puesto (m)
660 job classification	classification (f) des fonctions (=emplois)	Arbeitsplatzklassifizierung (f)	clasificación (f) de los empleos
661 job description	description (f) de(s) fonction(s) (=emplois)	Arbeitsplatzbeschreibung (f), Tätigkeitsbeschreibung (f)	descripción(f) de las funciones (=del empleo
662 job evaluation	évaluation (f) des fonctions (=emplois)	Arbeitsplatzbewertung (f)	evaluación (f) del trabajo
663 job fragmentation policy /South Africa/	politique (f) de la décomposition du travail (= des tâches)/Afrique du Sud/ (décomposition d'une tâche cohérente - autrefois exécutée par un blanc - en une série d'opérations élémentaires, indépendantes les unes des autres, que l'on confie à plusieurs noirs)	Politik (f) der "job fragmentation" (= Arbeitszerlegung) /Südafrika/ (Aufspaltung eines einheitlichen Arbeitsprozesses, für den ein Weisser verantwortlich war, in eine Reihe elementarer, unselbständiger Arbeitsvorgänge, die Schwarzen übertragen werden)	política(f) de descomposición del trabajo (= de las tareas) /Sudáfrica/ (descomposición de una tarea coherente -ejecutada anteriormente por un blanco- en una serie de operaciones elementales, independientes unas de otras, que se confían a varios africanos)
664 job performance	exécution (f) du travail (=des tâches)	Leistung (f)	actuación (f) en el trabajo

665 job requirement	qualification (f) professionnelle exigée	berufliche Anforderungen (fpl)	calificación (f) profesional requerida, condiciones (fpl) requeridas, idoneidad (f) requerida
666 job reservation policy /South Africa/	politique (f) (=principe /m/)de la réservation des emplois/ (visant à réserver aux blancs la plupart des emplois qualifiés) /Afrique du Sud/	Politik (f) der "job reservation", Arbeitsplatzreservierung (f) (Reservierung qualifizierter Arbeitsplätze vornehmlich für Weisse) /Südafrika/	política (f) de "reserva de empleos" (consiste en reservar a los blancos los oficios mejor remunerados que exigen calificaciones y dejar a los trabajadores africanos sólo las ocupaciones mal remuneradas, que no exigen calificación) /Sudáfrica/
667 job rotation, reassignment (within the same firm)	mutation (f) (systématique) de la main-d'oeuvre (à l'intérieur d'une même entreprise)	innerbetrieblicher Arbeitsplatzwechsel (m)	rotación (f) de las tareas (en una misma empresa)
668 dual jobholding	double occupation (f)	Doppelbeschäftigung (f)	doble ocupación (f), doble empleo (m)

669 kairos ('opportune time' and the irruption of such times into historical time)	kairos (m) ("temps favorable", irruptions de ces "temps" dans le temps historique)	Kairos (m) (Günstige, erfüllte Zeit; Einbrüche dieser"Zeiten" in die historische Zeit)	kairos (m) "Tiempo favorable", irrupciones de este tipo de "tiempo" en el tiempo histórico)
670 kenotic (from kenosis /cf. Phil.2:7/: the abasement and humility veiling the divinity of the Logos in his incarnation)	kénotique (vient de kénose: abaissement, voile d'humilité dont est voilée la divinité du Verbe dans son incarnation /cf. Phil. 2,7/)	Kenose (f), kenotisch (Herablassung, Entäusserung; Schleier des Menschseins, der die Göttlichkeit des Wortes in seiner Inkarnation verhüllt /vgl. Phil. 2,7/)	kenótico (Viene de kénosis: sumisión,velo de humildad con el que está velada la divinidad del Verbo en su encarnación /cf. Fil. 2:7/)
671 kerygma (public announcement or proclamation; the content of the Church's preaching and teaching directed to the evangelization and conversion of non-Christians)	kerygma (m) kérygme (m) (annonce; contenu de la prédication catéchétique de l'Eglise en vue de l'évangélisation et de la conversion des non-croyants)	Kerygma (n) (Botschaft. Inhalt der Verkündigung der Kirche im Blick auf die Evangelisation und Bekehrung der Nichtglaubenden)	kerygma (m) (Anuncio.Contenido de la predicación catequética de la Iglesia con objeto de evangelizar y convertir a los no creyentes)
672 kindergarten, nursery school	école (f) maternelle, jardin (m) d'enfants	Kindergarten (m)	kindergarten (m), jardin (m) de infantes
673 Kingdom of God	royaume (m) de Dieu	Reich (n) Gottes	reino (m) de Dios

674 Kingship of God	royauté (f) de Dieu	Königsherrschaft (f) Gottes	realeza (f) de Dios
675 know-how	savoir-faire (m)	Know-how (n)	conocimientos (mpl) técnicos o tecnológicos, técnica (f) operatoria, modo (m) operatorio

koinonia - See under: communion

labour, labour force - See under: manpower

          See also: active population

676 labour contract	contrat (m) de travail	Arbeitsvertrag (m)	contrato (m) de trabajo
677 labour exporting countries	Pays (m) fournisseur (de main-d'oeuvre)	Abgabeland (n)	país (m) proveedor de mano de obra
678 labour intensive	à fort emploi de main-d'oeuvre, à forte composante-main-d'oeuvre, à fort(e) coefficient de (=teneur en) main-d'oeuvre	arbeitsintensiv	de alto coeficiente de mano de obra

679 labour mobility	mobilité (f) de la main-d'oeuvre	Arbeitskräftemobilität (f)	movilidad (f) de la mano de obra
680 labour relations; industrial relations	relations (fpl) du travail; relations sociales (=humaines) dans l'entreprise	Beziehungen (fpl) zwischen den Sozialpartnern	relaciones (fpl) laborales; sicología (f) industrial

labour shortage - See under: manpower shortage

681 labour surplus	excédent (m) de main-d'oeuvre	Arbeitskräfteüberschuss (m) (=überhang/m/)	excedente (m) de mano de obra
682 contract labour system /South Africa/	système (m) de la main-d'oeuvre sous contrat (=contractuelle) /Afrique du Sud/	System (n) der Kontraktarbeit (=Vertragsarbeit) /Südafrika/	sistema (m) de mano de obra por contrato /Sudáfrica/
683 free movement of labour	libre circulation (f) des travailleurs (=de la main-d'oeuvre)	Freizügigkeit (f) der Arbeitskräfte	libre circulación (f) de los trabajadores (=de la mano de obra)
684 migratory labour system /South Africa/	système (m) du travail temporaire (=saisonnier) /Afrique du Sud/	System (n) der Saisonarbeit /Südafrika/	sistema (m) de mano de obra migratoria /Sudáfrica/
685 organized labour	travailleurs (mpl) syndiqués	gewerkschaftlich organisierte Arbeiterschaft	trabajadores (mpl) organizados
686 turnover of labour	rotation (f) (=renouvellement /m/= mouvements /mpl/ de la main d'oeuvre	Fluktuation (f) (Zahl der Zu- und Abgänge innerhalb eines Betriebes)	rotación (f) del personal (=de la mano de obra) cambio voluntario de empresa por

los obreros,
desplazamiento
de los obreros a
otros sitios de
trabajo)

laity centre - See under: lay training centre

land

687 land right(s), land title right(s)	droit(s) (m) foncier(s), droits (mpl) de propriété foncière	Recht (n) auf Grund- besitz, Eigentums- rechte (npl) an Grund und Boden	derecho(s) (m) a la propiedad de la tierra
688 Land Tenure Act /Rhodesia/	loi (f) sur le régime foncier /Rhodésie/	Landbesitzgesetz (n), Gesetz (n) über das Eigentum an Grund und Boden /Rhodesien/	ley (f) de tenencia de tierras/Rhodesia/
689 land use	utilisation (f) des terres (=du sol)	Bodenbenutzung (f)	uso (m) del suelo

language

690 language policy	politique (f) lin- guistique	Sprachenpolitik (f)	política (f) lingüística

receptor language - See under: biblical studies

source language - See under: biblical studies

law

691	international humanitarian law	droit (m) international humanitaire	internationales humanitäres Recht (n)	derecho (m) internacional humanitario
692	rule of law	primauté (f) (= règne /m/) du droit; régime (m) de droit	Herrschaft (f) des Rechtes	imperio (m) de la ley; régimen (m) de derecho
693	laying on of hands	imposition (f) des mains	Handauflegung (f)	imposición (f) de manos
694	layout	mise (f) en page	Layout (n)	compaginación (f)
695	leader	chef (m) (de file), meneur (m), leader (m); personnalité (f); responsable (m), cadre (m); animateur (m)	Leiter (m); führende Persönlichkeit (f); Führungskraft (f)	líder (m), jefe (m), conductor (m), caudillo (m); personalidad (f); responsable (m), dirigente (m); animador (m)
696	leadership	conduite (f), direction (f), leadership (m), autorité (f); animation (f); cadres (mpl), encadrement (m)	Führung (f), Leitung (f); Führungskräfte (fpl)	liderazgo (m), dirección (f), conducción (f); caudillaje (m); jefatura (f); animación (f); dirigentes (mpl)
697	learning, learning process	apprentissage (m)	Lernen (n), Lernprozess (m)	aprendizaje (m)
698	lifelong learning	apprentissage (m) permanent	lebenslanges Lernen (n)	aprendizaje (m) permanente

legal advice - See under: legal counselling

leisure

699	organization of leisure activities (=recreational activities)	organisation (f) des loisirs	Freizeitgestaltung (f)	actividades (fpl) recreativas
700	Leuenberg Agreement/Lutheran - reformed Churches/	Accord (m) de Leuenberg /Eglises luthéro-réformées/	Leuenberger Konkordie (f) /lutherische-reformierte Kirchen/	Acuerdo (m) de Leuenberg /Iglesia Luterana-Iglesia Reformada/
701	life expectation	espérance (f) de vie	Lebenserwartung (f)	esperanza (f) (=expectativa/f/) de vida

literacy

702	literacy training	alphabétisation (f)	Alphabetisierung (f)	alfabetización (f)
703	functional literacy programme	programme (m) d' alphabétisation fonctionnelle	Programm zur funktionalen Alphabetisierung (f)	programa (m) de alfabetización functional

literary genres - See under: biblical studies

literary and historic reading (=criticism) - See under: biblical studies

literate

704	the semi-literate	semi-alphabètes (mpl)	Semialphabeten (mpl)	semialfabetos (mpl)

literature

apocalyptic literature - See under: biblical studies

prophetic literature - See under: biblical studies

wisdom literature - See under: biblical studies

Liturgy - See under: Eucharist

705	experimental liturgy	liturgie (f) ex-périmentale	experimentelle Liturgie (f)	liturgia (f) ex-perimental
	loan			
706	loan agreement	accord (m) de prêt	Kreditabkommen (n)	acuerdo (m) (=con-venio/m/) de préstamo
707	loan contract	contrat (m) de prêt	Kreditvertrag (m)	contrato (m) de préstamo
708	loan guarantee	cautionnement (m), garantie (f)	Bürgschaft (f)	contrato (m) de garantía, garan-tía (f)
709	hard loan	prêt (m) assorti de conditions ri-goureuses	harter Kredit (m)	préstamo (m) en condiciones gravosas
710	preferential loan	prêt (m) préférentiel	Vorzugsanleihe (f)	préstamo (m) preferencial
711	soft loan	prêt (m) assorti de conditions favorables	weicher Kredit (m)	préstamo (m) (en condiciones) fa-vorable(s)

Lord's Supper - See under: Eucharist

307

712 to celebrate the Lord's Supper	célébrer la Sainte Cène	das Abendmahl feiern	celebrar la Santa Cena
713 to partake of the Lord's Supper	prendre la Sainte Cène	das Abendmahl empfangen	tomar la Santa Cena
714 Lordship of Christ	seigneurie (f) du Christ	Herrschaft (f) Christi	Señorío (m) de Cristo
715 lump sum	somme (f) (=versement /m/) forfaitaire (=global/e/)	Pauschalbetrag (m)	suma (f) (=cantidad /f/) global fija
716 magisterium /R.C. Church/	magistère (m) /Eglise cath.rom./	Lehramt (n) /R.-K. Kirche/	magisterio (m) /Iglesia Cat.Rom./
717 maladjusted children	enfants (mpl) inadaptés	verhaltensauffällige Kinder (mpl)	niños (mpl) inadaptados
718 malnutrition, nutritional deficiencies	malnutrition (f), carence (f) alimentaire	Mangelernährung (f)	malnutrición (f), carencia (f) alimentaria
719 protein and energy malnutrition	malnutrition (f) protéique et énergétique	Protein-Kalorien-Mangelernährung (f)	malnutrición (f) proteínica y energética
720 management	direction (f): administration (f); gestion (f) (d'entreprise); aménagement (m)	Unternehmensführung (f), Unternehmensleitung (f), Management (n)	dirección (f); administración (f); gestión (f); negociatión (f); manejo (m);

721	joint management, shared decision-making	cogestion (f)	(qualifizierte) Mitbestimmung (f)	cogestión (f)
722	middle management	cadres (mpl) moyens	mittleres Management (n), leitende Angestellte (mpl)	cuadros (mpl) ejecutivos intermedios
723	personnel management	gestion (f) du personnel	Personalverwaltung (f)	administración (f) de personal
724	top management	cadres (mpl) supérieurs (=dirigeants/mpl/)	Führungsspitze (f)	cuadros (mpl) ejecutivos superiores (=dirigentes/mpl/)
725	manager	administrateur (m); directeur (m), cadre (m)	Geschäftsführer (m), Manager (m)	administrador (m); director (m)
726	Publications Manager /Communication/	directeur (m) des publications /Communication/	Verlagsleiter (m) /Kommunikation/	Director (m) de Publicaciones /Comunicación/
727	managerial (=executive) staff	personnel (m) d'encadrement	leitende Angestellte (mpl)	personal (m) de dirección
728	manpower, labour, labour force	main-d'oeuvre (f)	Arbeitskräfte (fpl)	mano de obra (f)
729	manpower pool	réservoir (m) de main-d'oeuvre	Arbeitskräftereservoir (n)	reserva (f) de mano de obra
730	manpower reserves (=resources)	ressources (fpl) humaines, réserve (f) de main-d'oeuvre	verfügbare Arbeitskräfte (fpl), Arbeitskräftepotential (n)	recursos (mpl) humanos, reserva (f) de mano de obra

731 manpower (=labour) shortage	pénurie (f) de main-d'oeuvre	Arbeitskräfte- mangel (m)	escasez (f) de mano de obra

marriage

732 marriage counsellor	conseiller (m) conjugal	Eheberater (m)	consejero (m) matrimonial
733 marriage guidance clinic	établissement (m) (=centre/m/) de consultations con- jugales (= de conseils conjugaux)	Eheberatungsstel- le (f)	centro (m) de orientación matri- monial
734 marriage preparation (course)	(cours de) pré- paration (f) au mariage	Ehevorbereitung (f)	curso (m) de preparación matri- monial
735 inter-racial marriage	mariage (m) inter- racial	gemischtrassige Ehe (f)	matrimonio (m) interracial
736 mixed marriage	mariage (m) mixte	Mischehe (f)	matrimonio (m) mixto

Masora - See under: biblical studies

MCH - See under: maternal and child health

medical

737 medical mission	mission (f) médicale	ärztliche Mission (f)	misión (f) médica
738 medical worker(s)	travailleur (m) médical	medizinisches Per- sonal (n)	trabajador (m) de servicios auxi- liares médicos

739	church related medical work	services (mpl) médicaux rattachés aux Eglises (=chrétiens)	kirchliche (christliche) Gesundheitsdienste (mpl)	servicios (mpl) médicos que dependen de las iglesias (=cristianos)

medicine

740	community medicine	médecine (f) des collectivités	gemeindebezogene Medizin (f), gemeinschaftsbezogene Medizin (f)	medicina (f) de la comunidad
741	comprehensive medicine	médecine (f) globale (=totale)	ganzheitliche Medizin	medicina (f) total
742	preventive medicine	médecine (f) préventive	Präventivmedizin (f), prophylaktische Medizin (f)	medicina (f) preventiva

meeting

743	Joint Meeting of the Presidium and the Advisory Committee /CEC/	Réunion (f) commune du Présidium et du Comité consultatif /KEK/	Gemeinsame Tagung (f) des Präsidiums und des Beratenden Ausschusses /KEK/	Reunión (f) Conjunta del Presidium y del Comité Asesor /KEK/
744	Week of Meetings /WCC/	Semaine (f) de rencontres /COE/	Informationsgespräche (npl) der leitenden Mitarbeiter /ÖRK/	semana (f) de Reuniones /CMI/
745	membership	qualité (f) de membre, appartenance (f) à ...; composition (f); membres (mpl)	Mitgliedschaft (f)	calidad (f) de miembro; afiliación (f); miembros (mpl)

746 metanoia (change of mind, turnabout, conversion)	metanoïa (f) (revirement intellectuel, retournement, conversion)	Metanoia (f) (Geistige Umkehr, Bekehrung, Busse)	metanoia (f) (Cambio brusco intelectual, conversión)
migrant			
747 migrant worker; emigrant worker; immigrant worker	travailleur (m) migrant; travailleur (m) émigré; travailleur (m) immigré	ausländischer Arbeitnehmer (m), Fremdarbeiter (m) /CH/	trabajador (m) migrante; emigrante (m); inmigrante (m)
748 migrant workers fellowships (=associations)	associations (fpl) (=groupements/mpl/ =amicales/fpl/) de migrants	Zusammenschlüsse (mpl) ausländischer Arbeitnehmer	asociaciones (fpl) de migrantes
749 woman migrant	femme (f) immigrée (=migrante)	ausländische Arbeitnehmerin (f)	mujer (f) inmigrante (=migrante)
migration			
750 migration policy	politique (f) de la migration (=migratoire)	Ausländerpolitik (f)	política (f) de migración
751 clandestine (=illegal) migration	migration (f) clandestine	illegale Migration (f)	migración (f) clandestina (=ilegal)
752 external migration, emigration	migration (f) externe, émigration (f)	Aussenwanderung (f)	migración (f) externa, emigración (f)
753 internal migration	migration (f) interne	Binnenwanderung (f)	migración (f) interna

754	movement of migration; flow of migration, migration stream	mouvement (m) migratoire; flux (mpl) migratoires, courant (m) migratoire	Wanderungsbewegung (f); Wanderungsstrom (m)	movimiento (m) migratorio; flujo (m) migratorio, corriente (f) migratoria
755	net migration	solde (m) migratoire, migration (f) nette (différence entre les entrées et sorties)	Wanderungssaldo (m), Nettowanderung (f) (Differenz zwischen Zugängen und Abgängen)	saldo (m) migratorio, migración (f) neta (diferencia entre entradas y salidas)
756	return migration, re-migration	migration (f) de retour	Rückwanderung (f)	migración (f) de retorno
757	rural migration (=exodus), rural-urban migration	exode (m) rural	Landflucht (f), Entsiedlung (f) ländlicher Räume	éxodo (m) rural, migración (f) rural interna
758	seasonal migration	migration (f) saisonnière	saisonale (=saisonbedingte) Migration (f)	migración (f) estacional
759	volume of migration, gross migration	volume (m) migratoire, migration (f) totale (total des entrées et des sorties)	Bruttowanderung (f) (Gesamtheit der Zugänge und Abgänge)	migración (f) total (total de entradas y salidas)

minister - See also: threefold ministry

760	non-professional minister	pasteur (m) non professionnel	nebenberuflicher Pfarrer (m), nicht-professioneller Geistlicher (m)	pastor (m) no profesional
761	part-time minister	pasteur (m) à temps partiel	nebenamtlicher Pfarrer (m)	pastor (m) con dedicación parcial

313

762 ministry	ministère (m)	(geistliches) Amt (n), Dienst (m)	ministerio (m)
763 ministry for conflict situations	ministère (m) dans les situations de conflit	der Auftrag (der Kirchen), in Konfliktsituationen zu vermitteln	ministerio (m) para situaciones de conflicto
764 ministry of the laity	ministère (m) des laïcs	Laienamt (n)	ministerio (m) del laicado
765 ministry of reconciliation	ministère (m) de réconciliation	Amt (n) der Versöhnung	ministerio (m) de reconciliación
766 authentication of ministry	validation (f) du ministère	Validierung (f) (=Legitimierung/f/) der Ämter	validación (f) (=legitimación/f/ = autenticación /f/) del ministerio
767 crisis intervention ministry	ministère (m) d'intervention en cas de crise	der Auftrag (der Kirchen), in Krisensituationen zu vermitteln	ministerio (m) de intervención en situaciones de crisis
768 experimental ministries	ministères (mpl) expérimentaux	experimentelle Pfarrämter (npl)	ministerios (mpl) experimentales
769 full-time professional ministry	ministère (m) professionnel à plein temps	hauptberufliches Amt (n)	ministerio (m) profesional con dedicación exclusiva
770 healing ministry	ministère (m) de guérison	heilendes Amt (n)	servicio (m) de la salud, ministerio (m) de la salud
771 mutual recognition of ministries	reconnaissance (f) mutuelle des ministères	gegenseitige Anerkennung (f) der Ämter	reconocimiento (m) mutuo de los ministerios

772	ordained ministry	ministère (m) or-donné	ordiniertes Amt (n)	ministerio (m) ordenado
773	part-time ministry	ministère (m) à temps partiel	nebenberufliches Amt (n)	ministerio (m) con dedicación parcial
774	pastoral ministry	ministère (m) pastoral	seelsorgerlicher Dienst (m)	ministerio (m) pastoral
775	patterns of ministry	formes (fpl) de ministère	Formen (fpl), Gestalt (f) des Amtes, Amtsstruk-turen (fpl)	formas (fpl) de ministerio
776	preaching ministry	ministère (m) de la Parole	Amt (m) der Wort-verkündigung	ministerio (m) de la predicación
777	redemptive ministry of Christ	oeuvre (f) rédemp-trice du Christ	Erlösungswerk (n) Christi	ministerio (m) (=obra/f/) redentor(a) de Cristo
778	special ministry	ministère (m) spécialisé	Spezialdienste (mpl), spezieller Dienst (m)	ministerio (m) especializado
779	teaching ministry, teaching office	ministère (m) de l'enseignement (= de la catéchèse)	Lehramt (n)	ministerio (m) docente
780	team ministry	ministère (m) en équipe (=d'équipe)	Gruppenpfarramt (n), Teampfarramt (n)	ministerio (m) de equipo
781	threefold ministry: bishop, priest/minister (=pres-byter), deacon	triple ministère (m): évêque (m), prêtre (m)/pasteur (m) (=presbytre/m/), diacre (m)	Dreiteilung (f) des Amtes, dreifach gestuftes Amt (n): Bischof (m),Priester (m)/Pfarrer(m) (=Pres-byter /m/), Diakon (m)	triple ministerio (m): obispo (m), sacerdo-te (m)/ministro (m) (=presbítero /m/), diácono (m)

315

782	unification of ministries	unification (f) des ministères	Vereinheitlichung (f) der Ämter	unificación (f) de los ministerios

urban ministry - See under: urban mission

783	tent-making ministry	ministère (m) du "faiseur de tentes", ministère (m) non professionel	"Zeltmacher-Amt" (n), nicht-professionelles Amt (n), "Geistlicher Dienst im weltlichen Beruf"	ministerio (m) no profesional
784	miscegenation	métissage (m)	Rassenmischung (f)	mestizaje (m)
785	missio Dei, mission of God	missio Dei, mission (f) de Dieu	missio Dei, Mission (f) Gottes	missio Dei, misión (f) de Dios
786	missiology	missiologie (f)	Missionstheologie (f), Theologie (f) der missionarischen Verkündigung	misiología (f)

mission

787	mission agency	société (f) (=organisme /m/)missionnaire	Missionsgesellschaft (f)	organización (f) misionera
788	mission board	département (m) missionnaire	Missionsgesellschaft (f); Missionsleitung (f); Missionsabteilung (f)	junta (f) de misiones
789	Mission in Six Continents	Mission sur les six continents	Mission in sechs Kontinenten	Misión en el mundo entero
790	home mission	mission (f) intérieure	innere Mission (f)	misión (f) interior (=nacional)

791	industrial mission	mission (f) dans l'industrie, ministère (m) dans l'industrie	kirchlicher Dienst(m) in der industriellen Gesellschaft	misión (f) en medio industrial (=en la industria), ministerio (m) en medio industrial (= en la industria)
792	Joint Action for Mission (JAM)	Unité d'action missionnaire (UAM)	Gemeinsames Handeln in der Mission (JAM)	Acción Misionera Conjunta (AMC)
793	oneness in mission	Unité dans la mission	Einheit in der Mission	Unidad en la misión
794	overseas mission	mission (f) extérieure	äussere Mission (f)	misión (f) exterior (= extranjera)
795	prophetic, priestly and royal mission	mission (f) prophétique, sacerdotale et royale	prophetischer, priesterlicher und königlicher Auftrag (m)	misión (f) profética, sacerdotal y real
796	urban mission; urban ministry	mission (f) en milieu urbain, mission (f) urbaine; ministère (m) en milieu urbain	kirchlicher Dienst (m) in der urbanen Gesellschaft	misión (f) urbana, misión (f) en medio urbano; ministerio (m) en medio urbano

missionary

797	missionary council	conseil (m) de la mission	Missionsrat (m)	consejo (m) misionero
798	missionary outreach	rayonnement (m) missionnaire	Ausstrahlung (f) der Mission	proyección (f) misionera
799	missionary society	société (f) missionnaire (= de la mission)	Missionsgesellschaft (f)	sociedad (f) misionera

missioner

800	industrial missioner	équipier (m) en milieu industriel /mission dans l'industrie/	Mitarbeiter (m) im kirchlichen Dienst in der industriellen Gesellschaft	colaborador (m) en medio industrial /misión en medio industrial/
801	moderator	1. modérateur (m) (d'un synode) 2. président (m) (d'une séance, d'une réunion)	Vorsitzende(r)	1. moderador (m) (de una iglesia) 2. moderador (m) (de una reunión)

money

designated money - See under: earmarked funds

802	moratorium	moratoire (m)	Moratorium (n)	moratoria (f)

mortality

803	mortality rate	taux (m) de mortalité	Sterberate (f)	tasa (f) de mortalidad
804	infant mortality	mortalité (f) infantile	Säuglingssterblichkeit (f); Kindersterblichkeit (f)	mortalidad (f) infantil

movement

movement of frontier workers - See under: frontier worker

805	charismatic movement	mouvement (m) charismatique	charismatische Bewegung (f)	movimiento (m) carismático

806	Jesus movement	mouvement (m) de Jésus	Jesus-Bewegung (f)	movimiento (m) "Jesús"
807	renewal movement	mouvement (m) de renouveau	Erneuerungsbewegung (f)	movimiento (m) de renovación
808	spiritual movement	mouvement (m) charismatique	charismatische Bewegung (f)	movimiento (m) carismático
809	mystagogy (initiation into the mysteries)	mystagogie (f) (initiation aux mystères)	Mystagogie (f) (Einführung in die /heiligen/ Geheimnisse)	mistagogia (f) (Iniciación a los misterios)
810	nation-building	édification (f) du pays (=de la nation)	Aufbau (m) der Nation	construcción (f) de un país (=de una nación)
811	the needy	déshérités (mpl), économiquement faibles (mpl)	Arme (mpl), Notleidende (mpl)	los económicamente débiles (mpl)
812	neighbourhood help scheme	entraide (f) "bon voisinage"	Nachbarschaftshilfe (f)	ayuda (f) de buena vecindad

New Testament Apocrypha - See under: biblical studies

news

813 news bulletin	bulletin (m) d'in- formation	Nachrichten (fpl); Nachrichtenbulle- tin (n)	boletín (m) de noticias
814 newsletter	circulaire (f), bulletin (m) (d'in- formation)	Informationsblatt (n), Rundschreiben (n)	circular (f), boletín (m) de información
815 "News Round up" /EPS/	"Survol du calen- drier" (de janvier, février etc.) /SOEPI/		
816 noncooperation	refus (m) de coo- pérer	Kooperationsver- weigerung (f)	no cooperación (f)
817 non-growth	non-croissance (f)	Null-Wachstum (n)	estancamiento (m) (del crecimiento)
818 non-nuclear weapon state	Etat (m) non doté d'armes nucléaires	nicht-atomarer Staat (m)	Estado (m) que no posee armas nu- cleares
819 non-violence	non-violence (f)	Gewaltfreiheit (f)	no violencia (f)
820 principled non- violence	non-violence (f) comme principe d'action	Prinzip (n) der Gewaltfreiheit	no violencia (f) como principio de acción
non-violent			
821 non-violent action	action (f) non violente	gewaltfreie Aktion (f)	acción (f) no violenta
822 non-violent change	changement (m) non violent	gewaltfreie Ver- änderungen (fpl)	cambio (m) no violento

823 non-violent coercion	contrainte (f) non violente	gewaltfreier Zwang (m)	coacción (f) no violenta
824 non-violent movement	mouvement (m) non violent	gewaltfreie Bewegung (f)	movimiento (m) no violento
825 non-white, non-whites	non-blanc (m), non-blancs (mpl)	Nichtweisser (m), Nichtweisse (mpl)	no blanco (m), no blancos (mpl)
826 Not for attribution	Ne pas citer la source	nicht zu zitieren	No citar la fuente
827 Not for publication	Non destiné à la publication	nicht zur Veröffentlichung bestimmt	No se autoriza la publicación

nuclear

828 nuclear arms race	course (f) aux armes nucléaires	atomares (=nukleares) Wettrüsten (n) (=Rüstungswettlauf /m/)	carrera (f) de armamentos nucleares
829 nuclear-free zone	zone (f) dénucléarisée	atomwaffenfreie Zone (f)	zona (f) desnuclearizada
830 nuclear stockpiles	stocks (mpl) (=arsenaux /mpl/) d'armes nucléaires	Nuklearwaffenarsenale (npl)	existencias (fpl) (=stock /m/) de armas nucleares
831 nuclear test ban	interdiction (f) des essais nucléaires	Verbot (n) von Kernversuchen (Nuklearversuchen = Kernwaffenversuchen)	prohibición (f) (=proscripción /f/) de los ensayos nucleares
832 nuclear test stop	suspension (f) (=arrêt /m/) des essais (=expériences) nucléaires	Einstellung (f) der Kernversuche, Nuklearteststop (m)	suspensión (f) de los ensayos nucleares

833 nuclear warhead	ogive (f) nucléaire	Atomsprengkopf (m)	cabeza (f) nuclear de combate
834 nuclear-weapon power	puissance (f) dotée d'armes nucléaires	Nuklearmacht (f)	Potencia (f) que posee armas nucleares (=dotada de armas nucleares), Potencia (f) nuclear
835 delivery-vehicle system of nuclear weapons	vecteur (m) d'armes nucléaires	nuklearer Waffenträger (m)	sistema (m) de vehículos portadores de armas nucleares, sistema (m) de transporte (=portador)
836 stockpiling of nuclear weapons	accumulation (f) d'armes nucléaires	Akkumulierung (f) von Nuklearwaffen	almacenamiento (m) de armas nucleares

nurse

837 auxiliary nurse	infirmière (f) auxiliaire	Schwesternhelferin (f)	enfermera (f) auxiliar
838 community nurse	infirmière (f) des collectivités	Gemeindeschwester (f)	enfermera (f) comunitaria (= de la colectividad)
839 enrolled nurse	infirmière (f) diplômée	examinierte (diplomierte) Krankenschwester (f)	enfermera (f) titulada
840 public health nurse	infirmière (f) de la santé publique	Krankenschwester (f) (im öffentlichen Gesundheitsdienst)	enfermera (f) de salud pública

nursery school - See under: kindergarten

841	nursing	soins (mpl) infirmiers	Krankenpflege (f), Pflegedienst (m)	enfermería (f)
842	community nursing	soins (mpl) infirmiers des collectivités	Gemeindegesundheitspflege (f)	enfermería (f) de la colectividad (=comunitaria/f/)
	nurture			
843	Christian nurture	éducation (f) chrétienne	christliche Erziehung (f)	educación (f) cristiana
844	nutrition	1. nutrition (f) 2. alimentation (f)	1. Ernährung (f) 2. Nahrung (f)	1. nutrición (f) 2. alimentación (f)
845	nutrition education	éducation (f) alimentaire	Ernährungslehre (f)	educación (f) alimentaria

nutritional

nutritional deficiencies - See under: malnutrition

846	nutritional programme	programme (m) alimentaire	Ernährungsprogramm (n)	programa (m) nutricional (=alimentario)

nutritional requirements - See under: food requirements

847	nutritional research	recherche (f) nutritionnelle	Ernährungsforschung (f)	investigación (f) nutricional

848 observer	observateur (m)	Beobachter (m)	observador (m)
849 delegated observer /WCC Assembly/	observateur (m) délégué /Assemblée du COE/	Beobachter-Delegierter (m) /ÖRK-Vollver-versammlung/	observador (m) delegado /Asamblea del CMI/

occupational

850 occupational classi-fication	classification (f) (=nomenclature) des professions	Berufssystematik (f)	clasificación (f) profesional
851 occupational gui-dance	orientation (f) professionnelle	Berufsberatung (f)	orientación (f) profesional
852 offenders	délinquants (mpl)	Straffällige (mpl)	delincuentes (mpl)

office

Office for Common Bible Work - See under: biblical studies

853 Personnel Office /WCC/	Service (m) du personnel (m) /COE/	Personalbüro (n) /ÖRK/	Oficina (f) del Personal /CMI/

teaching office - See under: teaching ministry

854 threefold office of Christ	triple office (m) du Christ	dreifaches Amt (n) Christi	triple oficio (m) de Cristo
855 officer	fonctionnaire (m); chef (m), responsable (m); collaborateur (m)	1. Amtsträger (m) 2. Referent (m)	funcionario (m); jefe (m), responsable (m)

856 Officers 1. of the WCC, of the Central Committee 2. of a Commission	Bureau (m) 1. du Comité central du COE 2. d'une commission	1. die leitenden Amtsträger (mpl) des Zentralaus- schusses des ÖRK 2. Vorstand (m) einer Kommission	Mesa (f) 1. del Comité Central del CMI 2. de una comisión
857 Press Officer for the English Language /Communication/	chargé (m) de presse, Section de langue anglaise /Communication/	Pressereferent (m) für den englischen Sprachraum /Kommunaktion/	Encargado (m) de Prensa, Sección Idioma Inglés /Comunicación/
858 Press Officer for the French Language /Communication/	chargé (m) de presse, Section de langue française /Communication/	Pressereferent (m) für den franzö- sischen Sprach- raum /Kommunikation/	Encargado (m) de Prensa, Sección Idioma Francés /Comunicación/
859 Senior News Officer /Communication/	chef (m) de l'information /Communication/	Leiter (m) der Nachrichtenredak- tion /Kommunika- tion/	Jefe (m) de Información /Comunicación/
860 old people, the elderly	troisième âge (m), personnes (fpl) âgées	alte Menschen (mpl)	ancianos (mpl), personas (fpl) ancianas
861 old people's club, social centre (for old people)	club (m) du troisième âge	Altentagesstätte (f)	club (m) para ancianos
opportunities			
862 educational opportunities	chances (fpl) d'accès à l'éducation	Bildungschancen (fpl)	oportunidades (fpl) (=posibilidades/fpl/) de acceso a la edu- cación

863	equal opportunities	égalité (f) des chances	Chancengleich-heit (f)	igualdad (f) de oportunidades (=posibilidades)
864	oppressive situation	situation (f) d' oppression	Unterdrückung (f)	situación (f) de opresión
865	'opting out'	démission (f), fuite (f)	Verzicht (m), Aufgabe (f) (eines Vorhabens, Rechtes etc.)	desistir; abandonar
866	order of service	ordre (m) du culte, ordre (m) de service	Gottesdienstord-nung (f)	orden (m) del culto, orden (m) del servicio reli-gioso
867	ordination	ordination (f), ordination-consé-cration (f), consécration (f)	Ordination (f), (Priester-)Weihe (f), Einsetzung (f)	ordenación (f), consagración (f)
868	episcopal ordi-nation	ordination (f) épiscopale	bischöfliche Ordi-nation (f)	ordenación (f) episcopal

organization

869	Organizations in consultative status with the United Nations Economic and Social Council	organisations (fpl) ayant le statut con-sultatif auprès du Conseil économique et social des Nations Unies	Organisationen (fpl) mit beratendem Sta-tus beim Wirtschafts-und Sozialrat der Vereinten Nationen	organizaciones (fpl) reconocidas como entidades consul-tivas ante el Consejo Económi-co y Social de las Naciones Unidas
870	Non-Governmental Organizations (NGO)	organisations (fpl) non gouvernementales (ONG)	Nichtstaatliche Or-ganisationen (NGOs) (fpl)	organizaciones (fpl) no gubernamentales (ONG)

871 non-profit making organization	organisation (f) à but non lucratif	gemeinnützige Organisation (f), Organisation (f) ohne Erwerbscharakter	organización (f) sin fin lucrativo
872 otherness	altérité (f)	Anderssein (n), Verschiedenheit (f)	alteridad (f)
outflow - See under: departures			
873 'overforeignization' (over-population of a country by foreigners)	emprise (f) (=surpopulation /f/) étrangère; pénétration (f) étrangère	Überfremdung (f)	superpoblación (f) extranjera
874 pamphlet	brochure (f)	Broschüre (f)	folleto (m), fascículo (m)
875 panel	groupe (m) d'étude (=d'experts); table (f) ronde	Ausschuss (m); Podiumsgespräch (n) (=diskussion /f/)	grupo (m) especial (=de expertos); mesa (f) redonda, panel (m)
paraphrase - See under: biblical studies			

327

parenthood

876	planned parenthood	planification (f) de la famille	Familienplanung (f)	planificación (f) de la familia
877	responsible parenthood	parenté (f) responsable (=volontaire)	verantwortliche Elternschaft (f), verantwortete Elternschaft (f)	paternidad (f) responsable
878	parish	paroisse (f) (circonscription ecclésiastique)	Gemeinde (f) (Kirchenkreis)	parroquia (f) (circunscripción eclesiástica)
879	participation (in management), industrial democracy	participation (f)	Mitbestimmung (f)	participación (f), democracia (f) industrial
880	participation in change programme	programme (m) de la participation au changement	Programm (n) "Teilnahme am Wandel"	programa (m) de participación en el cambio
881	peoples participation in development	participation (f) populaire au développement	partizipatorische Entwicklung (f)	participación (f) popular en el desarrollo
882	particularism	particularisme (m)	Partikularismus (m)	particularismo (m)
883	particularity	particularité (f), spécificité (f), originalité (f)	Eigenart (f), Besonderheit (f), Unverwechselbarkeit (f)	particularidad (f), originalidad (f)
884	partnership	coopération (f) (sur la base d'une con-	Partnerschaft (f)	cooperación (f) (que resulta de un acuerdo

	certation égali- taire entre parte- naires), collaboration (f) dans l'égalité (entre hommes et femmes), action (f) solidaire		entre iguales), colaboración (f) (sobre una base de igualdad), participación (f) solidaria
885 partnership in mission	(Vers une) action apostolique commune, (vers une) action commune dans la mission	Partnerschaft in der Mission	participación solidaria en la misión
886 partnership in obedience	(Vers une) action commune dans l'obéissance	Partnerschaft im Gehorsam	participación solidaria en obediencia
887 mature partner- ship	(Vers une) action responsable commune	Beziehung (f) zwischen mündigen Partnern (=mün- digen Kirchen)	participación solidaria y respon- sable
888 pass, reference-book /South Africa/	laissez-passer (m) /Afrique du Sud/	Pass (m) /Südafrika/	pase (m), libreta (f) de referencia /Sudáfrica/
889 Pass Laws /South Africa/	lois (fpl) sur les laissez-passer /Afrique du Sud/	Passgesetze (npl) /Südafrika/	leyes (fpl) de pases/ /Sudáfrica/
890 pastoral care, pastoral ministry, pastoralia	pastorale (f), ministère (m) pastoral	Seelsorge (f)	cuidado (m)(=aten- ción /f/ = servicio /m/) pastoral, ministerio (m) pasto- ral, pastoral (f)

329

patient

| 891 | in-patient | malade (m) hospi-
talisé | stationärer
Patient (m) | enfermo (m) (=paciente/m/
hospitalizado |
| 892 | out-patient | malade (m) externe | ambulanter
Patient (m) | enfermo (m)
(=paciente /m/)
externo (=de am-
bulatorio =de consul-
torio) |

peace

893	peace-keeping ac- tivities	maintien (m) de la paix	Friedenssicherung (f)	mantenimiento (m) de la paz
894	peace research	recherche (f) sur la paix	Friedensforschung (f)	investigación (f) sobre la paz
895	pentecostal movement	mouvement (m) pentecôtiste	Pfingstbewegung (f)	movimiento (m) pentecostal
896	pentecostalist	pentecôtiste(m)	Pfingstler (m)	pentecostal (m)
897	"People in the News" /EPS/	"Personnalités" /SOEPI/		
898	performance appraisal	évaluation (f) de la performance (=du travail)	Leistungsbewer- tung (f)	evaluación (f) de la actuación en el trabjo

perichoresis - See under: communicatio idiomatum

| 899 | "Periscope"
/EPS/ | "En bref"
/SOEPI/ | | |

permit

900	entry permit	permis (m) d'entrée	Einreisege-nehmigung (f)	permiso (m) de entrada
901	exit permit /South Africa/ (precludes re-entry into the country)	autorisation (f) de sortie /Afrique du Sud/ (autorisation spé-ciale accordée à certaines personnes jugées indésirables par le gouverne-ment, et qui leur interdit de rentrer dans le pays)	Ausreisegenehmi-gung (f) /Südafrika/ (Abschiebung po-litischer Gegner durch Gewährung spezieller Aus-reisegenehmi-gungen, die eine Rückkehr aus-schliessen)	permiso (m) de salida /Sudáfrica/ (autorización especial otorgada a algunas personas consideradas indesea-bles por el gobier-no que les pro-hibe regresar al país)
902	residence permit	permis (m) de séjour	Aufenthaltser-laubnis (f) (=ge-nehmigung /f/)	permiso (m) (=autorización /f/) de residencia
903	work (=labour =employment) permit	permis (m) de tra-vail	Arbeitserlaubnis (f)	permiso (m) de trabajo

personnel

904	personnel policy	politique (f) du personnel	Personalpolitik (f)	política (f) del personal
905	auxiliary per-sonnel	personnel (m) auxiliaire	Hilfspersonal (n)	personal (m) auxiliar
906	expatriate per-sonnel	personnel (m) étranger	ausländisches Per-sonal(n)	personal (m) extranjero
907	middle level personnel	personnel (m) de niveau moyen (=de	Personal (n) der mittleren Ebene	personal (m) de categoría inter-

		niveau intermé- diaire)	(=Laufbahn), nach- geordnetes medizi- nisches Personal (n), paramedizinisches Personal (n)	media
908	operational per- sonnel	personnel (m) d'exécution	Projektpersonal (n)	personal (m) de ejecución
909	paramedical per- sonnel	personnel (m) paramédical	paramedizinisches Personal (n)	personal (m) paramédico
910	phenotype	phénotype (m)	Phänotyp (m)	fenotipo (m)
911	the pilgrim people of God	le peuple de Dieu en marche	das Volk Gottes unterwegs, das wandernde Gottes- volk	el pueblo peregri- no de Dios

planning

912	comprehensive planning	planification (f) globale	integrale Planung (f)	planificación (f) integral
913	national/regional/ local planning	aménagement (m) du territoire (au niveau national, régional, local)	Raumplanung (f), Raumordnung (f)	planificación (f) del espacio (a nivel nacional, regional, local)
914	town planning, urban planning	urbanisme (m), planification (f) ur- baine,	Stadtplanung (f), Städteplanung (f), Urbanistik (f)	urbanismo (m), planificación (f) urbana
915	platform	principes (mpl) de base, plateforme (f)	Grundsätze (mpl), Standpunkt (m),	principios (mpl) fundamentales,

	programme (f), déclaration (f) de principes	Plattform (f), Grundsatzerklärung (f)	plataforma (f), programa (m), declaración (f) de principios
916 pledges	contributions (fpl) annoncées; engagements (mpl) financiers	(finanzielle) Zusagen (fpl)	promesas (fpl) de contribuciones, contribuciones (fpl) prometidas
917 pleroma (fullness, plenitude, completion; used of spiritual things the Church is the pleroma of Christ /Eph. 1:23/)	plérome (m) (plénitude, accomplissement; s' applique aux choses spirituelles; l' Eglise est le plérome du Christ /Eph. 1, 23/)	Pleroma (n) (Fülle, Erfüllung, auf geistliche Dinge bezogen. Die Kirche ist das Pleroma Christi /Eph. 1, 23/)	pleroma (m) (Plenitud, cumplimiento. Se aplica a las cosas espirituales. La Iglesia es el pleroma de Cristo /Ef. 1:23/)
918 pneumatophoric (bearing the Holy Spirit)	pneumatophore (porteur de l'Esprit Saint)	Pneumatophor (m) (Träger des Heiligen Geistes)	pneumatóforo (m) (Quien lleva en sí al Espíritu Santo)
919 policy	politique (f) générale, orientation (f); attitude (f); plan (m)(d'action), système (m); lignes (fpl) directrices, lignes-forces (fpl); principes (mpl) de base; méthode (f) (d'action); objectif(s) (m)	Politik (f); Konzept (m), Konzeptionen (fpl); Richtlinien (fpl); Grundprinzipien (npl), Grundsatzentscheidungen (fpl); Zielsetzung (f)	política (f) general, orientación (f); actitud (f); plan (m) (de acción), sistema (m); directrices (fpl), normas (fpl); principios (mpl) básicos; método (m) (de acción); objetivo(s) (m)

920 pollution absorbtive capacity	capacité (f) d'absorption de la pollution	Absorptionsfähigkeit (f) für Schadstoffe	capacidad (f) de absorción de la contaminación

population

921 population control	régulation (f) de la population	kontrolliertes Bevölkerungswachstum (n)	regulación (f) de la población
922 population density	densité (f) de la population	Bevölkerungsdichte (f)	densidad (f) de la población
923 population explosion	explosion (f) démographique	Bevölkerungsexplosion (f)	explosión (f) demográfica
924 population growth	accroissement (m) de la population, croissance (f) démographique	Bevölkerungswachstum (n)	crecimiento (m) de la población (=demográfico)
925 population policy	politique (f) démographique	Bevölkerungspolitik (f)	política (f) demográfica
926 population pressure	poussée (f) démographique	Bevölkerungsdruck (m)	presión (f) demográfica
927 population pyramid	pyramide (f) des âges	Bevölkerungspyramide (f)	pirámide (f) de población
928 optimum population (=population optimum)	population (f) optimale	optimale Bevölkerung (f)	óptimo (m) de población
929 planning of population growth	planification (f) de l'accroissement de la population	Planung (f) des Bevölkerungswachstums	planificación (f) del crecimiento de la población

930 portfolio	1. charge (f), fonctions (fpl), portefeuille (m) (ministériel) 2. portefeuille (m) (investissements, titres)	1. Ressort (n), Geschäftsbereich (m), (Minister)Portefeuille (n) 2. (Anlagen-, Aktien-)Portefeuille (n)	1. cargo (m), funciones (fpl), cartera (f) (ministerial) 2. cartera (f) (inversiones, títulos)
931 special study portfolio /WCC/	mandat (m) d'étude /COE/	Ressort (n) "Sonderstudien"/ÖRK/	secretaría (f) de estudios especiales /CMI/

poverty line - <u>See</u> <u>under</u>: <u>s</u>ubsistence level

power

932 power politics	politique (f) de force	Machtpolitik (f)	política (f) de fuerza
933 power relationships	relations (fpl) de pouvoir	Machtverhältnisse (npl)	relaciones (fpl) de poder (=basadas en la fuerza)
934 power structures	structures (fpl) de pouvoir	Machtstrukturen (fpl)	estructuras (fpl) de poder
935 power struggle	lutte (f) pour le pouvoir	Machtkampf (m)	lucha (f) por el poder
936 power transfer	transfert (m) (=passation /f/) du (des) pouvoir(s)	Machtverlagerung (f), Übertragung (f) der Macht	transferencia (f) del (de los) poder(es)
937 countervailing power	contre-pouvoir (m)	Gegenmacht (f)	contrapoder (m)

335

938   family power

(Refers to both the positive and negative influences the family exerts on its members and on society; recent studies show the family to be under strain, and therefore enfeebled; hence the empowerment of the family, the restoration of the family to full effectiveness; the empowered family is the one which can exert family power.

In its most simple usage refers to the social and political impact families have when united in family groups - U.S. = family clusters)

"pouvoir (m) familial", influence (f) de la famille

(Par l'expression "family power", on désigne l'influence, négative ou positive, que la famille exerce sur ses membres et sur la société. De récentes études sociologiques ont montré que la famille, aujourd'hui soumise à diverses tensions, voyait son rôle s'affaiblir. D'ou la notion de "renforcement du rôle de la famille", du "rétablissement des fonctions de la famille".

Au sens plus étroit du terme, "family power" désigne l'influence sociopolitique que les familles sont susceptibles d'exercer lorsqu'elles se constituent en asso-

---

Familiale Funktion (f)

(Positiver und negativer Einfluss der Familie auf die Familienmitglieder und die Gesellschaft. Familiensoziologische Studien sprechen von einem Funktionsverlust der Familie. "Family power" impliziert davon ausgehend eine Wiederherstellung der familialen Funktionen/Funktionsfähigkeit.

Im engeren Sinne der sozio-politische Einfluss von Familiengruppen)

---

poder (m) familiar, influencia (f) de la familia

(La expresión "family power", se refiere a la influencia negativa o positiva que ejerce la familia sobre sus miembros y sobre la sociedad. Estudios sociológico recientes revelan que la familia se encuentra sometida actualmente a diversas tensiones que debilitan su influencia. De ahí la noción de "fortalecimiento del papel de la familia", y de "restablecimiento de las funciones de la familia".

En un sentido más restringido, "family power" significa la influencia sociopolítica que las familias pueden ejercer cuando se constituyen en asociaciones o gru-

		ciations ou groupe- ments familiaux /aux Etats-Unis: "family clusters"/)		pos familiares /en los Estados Unidos :"family clusters"/)
939	sharing of power(s)	partage (m) du(des) pouvoir(s)	Teilhabe (f) an der Macht	participación (f) en el (=del) poder
940	the powerful	détenteurs (mpl) (=tenants /mpl/) du pouvoir, puissants (mpl)	die Mächtigen (mpl), die Herrschenden (mpl)	poderosos (mpl)
941	the powerless	sans-pouvoir (mpl)	die Machtlosen (mpl)	los que no tienen poder (mpl), los desprovistos (mpl) de poder
942	powerlessness	1. non-pouvoir (m) 2. impuissance (f)	Machtlosigkeit (f)	1. carencia (f) de poder 2. impotencia (f)

pregnancy

943	termination of pregnancy	interruption (f) de grossesse	Schwangerschafts- abbruch (m)	interrupción (f) del embarazo

presbyter - See under: threefold ministry

944	President /WCC/	président (m) /COE/	Präsident (m) /ÖRK/	presidente (m) /CMI/
945	Honorary Presi- dent /WCC/	président (m) d'honneur /COE/	Ehrenpräsident (m) /ÖRK/	presidente (m) de honor /CMI/
946	Presidium /WCC, CEC/	1. collège (m) présidentiel /COE/ 2. présidium (m) /KEK/	Präsidium (n) /ÖRK, KEK/	presidium (m) /CMI, KEK/

337

priest - See under: threefold ministry

| 947 | worker priest | prêtre (m) ouvrier | Arbeiterpriester (m) | cura (m) obrero |

priesthood

948	the priesthood of all believers	sacerdoce (m) de tous les croyants	Priestertum (n) aller Gläubigen	sacerdocio (m) universal (=de todos los creyentes)
949	royal priesthood	sacerdoce (m) royal	königliches Priestertum (n)	sacerdocio (m) real
950	primal See also: world view	premier, fondamental, archétype, originel, traditionnel	erst(e), grundlegend, Ur~, ursprünglich, traditionell	primero, fundamental, básico, tradicional, primigenio, original
951	principalities and powers	autorités et puissances, autorités et pouvoirs	Mächte und Gewalten, Reiche und Gewalten	autoridades y potestades

prisoner

| 952 | discharged prisoners | anciens détenus (mpl) | Strafentlassene (mpl) | presos (mpl) puestos en libertad |
| 953 | treatment of prisoners | traitement (m) des détenus | Behandlung (f) der Gefangenen | tratamiento (m) de los presos |

privacy

| 954 | invasion of privacy | immixtion (f) (=ingérence /f/) dans la vie privée | Einbruch (m) in die Privatsphäre | injerencia (f) (=intromisión /f/) en la vida privada |

955 probation	probation (f) (sursis avec mise à l'épreuve)	Bewährungshilfe (f)	régimen (m) de libertad vigilada, libertad (f) condicional con régimen de prueba
956 pro-existence (=living for others)	pro-existence (f)	Proexistenz (f)	proexistencia (f) (=vivir para otros)

professional qualifications - See under: vocational qualifications

957 profile	dossier (m); portrait (m), notice (f) biographique	Informationsschrift (f), Porträt (n), Kurzbiographie (f); Profil (n)	antecedentes (mpl), características (fpl); semblanza (f), resúmen (m) biográfico

programme

958 Programme Askings /CWME/	demandes (fpl) de soutien de programmes /CME/	Programmforderungen (fpl) /CWME/	Pedidos (mpl) para Programas /CMME/
959 Ecumenical Youth Programmes (EYS and WYP) /Finances/	Programmes (mpl) oecuméniques de jeunesse(SOJ et PEMJ) /Finances/	Ökumenische Jugendprogramme (npl) (EYS und WYP) /Finanzwesen/	Programas (mpl) Ecuménicos de la Juventud (SEJ y PMJ) /Finanzas/
960 Health Programme /CICARWS/	Programme (m) de santé /CESEAR/	Gesundheitsprogramm (n) /CICARWS/	Programa (m) de Salud /CAISMR/
961 Service Programme /CICARWS/	Programme (m) annuel de service /CESEAR/	Jahresarbeitsprogramm (n) /CICARWS/	Programa (m) Anual de Servicio /CAISMR/

962 Scholarships Programme /Staff Working Group on Education/	Programme (m) des bourses /Groupe de travail "éducation"/	Stipendienprogramm (n) /Arbeitsgruppe "Bildung"/	Programa (m) de Becas /Grupo de trabajo "Educación"/

project

963 project aid (=assistance)	aide (f) liée à des projets	Projekthilfe (f)	ayuda (f) para proyectos específicos
964 project analyst	analyste (m) de projets	Referent (m) für Projektanalyse, Projektanalytiker (m)	analista (m) de proyectos
965 project application	demande (f) de projet, demande (f) d'inscription sur la Liste des projets /CESEAR/	Projektantrag (m)	solicitud (f) de proyecto, solicitud (f) de inscripción en la Lista de proyectos /CAISMR/
966 project approval	approbation (f) d'un projet	Projektbewilligung (f)	aprobación (f) de un proyecto
967 project holder (=sponsor)	responsable (m) de(s) projet(s)	Projektträger (m)	responsable (m) del (de los) proyecto(s)
968 project liability /CICARWS/	couverture (f) initiale du projet /CESEAR/	Projekthaftung (f) /CICARWS/	subvención (f) inicial para proyectos /CAISMR/
969 Project Liability Fund /CICARWS/	Fonds (m) de disponibilités pour les projets /CESEAR/	Projektdeckungsmittelfonds (m) /CICARWS/	Fondo (m) Disponible para Proyectos /CAISMR/

970 Project List /CICARWS/	Liste (f) des projets /CESEAR/	Projektliste (f) /CICARWS/	Lista (f) de proyectos /CAISMR/
971 project management, administration of projects	gestion (f) de(s) projet(s)	Projektleitung (f) (= -führung /f/)	gestión (f) de proyectos
972 project manager	directeur (m) de projet	Projektleiter (m)	director (m) de proyecto
973 project operation	exécution (f) (=mise /f/ en oeuvre) d'un projet	Durchführung (f) eines Projektes	ejecución (f) de un proyecto
974 project planning	planification (f) des projets	Projektplanung (f)	planificatión (f) de proyectos
975 project preparation	préparation (f) (=élaboration /f/) des projets	Projektvorberei- tung (f) (=-aus- arbeitung /f/)	preparación (f) (=elaboración /f/) de los proyectos
976 project processing; project procedure	traitement (m) ad- ministratif des projets	Projektbearbei- tung (f)	tramitación (f) de los proyectos
977 project screening group	groupe (m) de sélection des projets	Projektauswahl- gruppe (f)	grupo (m) de selección de pro- yectos
978 project-sponsoring Churches	Eglises (fpl) res- ponsables de(s) projet(s)	die für (die) Pro- jekte verantwort- lichen Kirchen (fpl)	iglesias (fpl) res- ponsables de (de los) proyecto(s)
979 appraisal (=eva- luation) of pro- jects	évaluation (f) des projets	Projektauswertung (f) (= -evaluierung /f/)	evaluación (f) de los proyectos

980	follow-up project	projet (m) consécutif; projet (m) complémentaire	Anschluss-, Ergänzungsprojekt (n)	proyecto (m) consecutivo; proyecto (m) complementario
981	identification of projects	détermination (f) des projets	Projektfindung (f)	determinación (f) de proyectos
982	multi-purpose project	projet (m) à fins multiples (=polyvalent)	Vielzweckprojekt (n)	proyecto (m) de propósitos múltiples
983	non-project aid	aide (f) hors projet	nicht-projektgebundene Hilfe (f)	ayuda (f) no destinada a proyectos específicos
984	package (=integrated) project	projet (m) global	Verbundprojekt (n)	proyecto (m) global (=de conjunto)
985	pilot project	projet (m) pilote	Modellvorhaben (n) Musterprojekt (n)	proyecto (m) piloto
986	pre-project study	étude (f) préalable (au projet)	Projekt(vor)studie (f), Vorgutachten (n)	estudio (f) previo (al proyecto)
987	programme project (A programme project is an activity, proposed for a limited period of time, which grows out of and is in line with the established programme and policy of the	projet (m) de programme (Le projet de programme est une activité proposée pour une période limitée. Il se situe dans la ligne du programme et de la politique générale du Conseil oecuménique, dont	Programmprojekt (n) (Ein Programmprojekt ist eine für einen begrenzten Zeitabschnitt geplante Tätigkeit, die sich aus dem festgelegten Programm und der Zielsetzung des ÖRK ergibt und damit in Einklang steht, die	proyecto (m) de programa (Un proyecto de programa es una actividad propuesta para un período determinado de tiempo, que proviene del programa y de la política del Consejo Mundial y sigue su línea. No es

	World Council, which is not financed by the General Budget and which is carried on under the direction of a unit or sub-unit or directly under the General Secretariat, under the general control of the Central Committee... The main sources of support for programme projects shall be individuals, foundations and church agencies. Uppsala Report, p. 375)	il émane. Il n'est pas financé par le budget général et son exécution, entreprise sous la direction d'une unité ou d'une section, ou du secrétariat général lui-même, est placée sous le contrôle du Comité central... Les principales sources de soutien des projets de programme sont des particuliers, des fondations ou des organismes ecclésiastiques. Rapport d'Upsal, p. 363)	nicht durch den Allgemeinen Haushalt finanziert wird und die - unter allgemeiner Aufsicht des Zentralausschusses - unter der Leitung einer Abteilung oder eines Referates oder des Generalsekretärs durchgeführt wird... Die Hauptquellen der Mittel für Programm-Projekte sollen Einzelpersonen, Stiftungen und kirchliche Werke oder Stellen sein. Bericht aus Uppsala 68, S. 394)	financiado por el Presupuesto General y el Comité Central controla su ejecución, cuya dirección está a cargo de una unidad o sección o del Secretario General mismo. Las principales fuentes de sostén de los proyectos de programa son particulares, fundaciones u organismos eclesiásticos. 'Uppsala Report' pag. 375)
988	regular project	projet (m) ordinaire	laufendes Projekt (n)	proyecto (m) ordinario (=corriente)
989	screening of projects	choix (m) (=sélection /f/) des projets	Projektauswahl (f)	selección (f) de proyectos

990	self-help project	projet (m) d'auto-assistance (=d' assistance au développement autonome)	Selbsthilfepro-jekt (n)	proyecto (m) de ayuda al desarrollo autónomo
991	social service (=community ser-vice) project	projet (m) de service social	Sozialdienst-Pro-jekt (n)	proyecto (m) de servicio social
992	supervision of projects	contrôle (m) de l'exécution des projets	Projektbeobachtung (f)	supervisión (f) de proyectos
993	ecumenical work project	chantier (m) oecuménique	ökumenisches Auf-baulager (n)	campamento (m) de trabajo ecuménico
994	promotion (to a higher grade), upgrading	promotion (f) (à une classe supé-rieure)	Beförderung (f) (in eine höhere Gehalts-gruppe)	ascenso (m) (a una categoría superior)
995	provincialism	particularisme (m)	Provinzialismus (m), 'Kirchturmpolitik'	provincialismo (m)

Pseudepigrapha - See under: biblical studies

996	publisher	éditeur (m)	1. Verlag (m) 2. Verleger (m)	editor (m)
997	quality of life	qualité (f) de la vie	Qualität (f) des Lebens, Lebens-qualität (f)	calidad (f) de la vida

Qumran documents - See under: biblical studies

998	quota fixing, quota system /USA/	contingentement (m), système (m) des quotas	Kontingentierung (f)	sistema (m) de contingentes (= de cuotas)
999	racial barriers	barrières (fpl) de race	Rassenschranken (fpl)	barreras (fpl) raciales
1000	racialist, racist	raciste	rassistisch	racista

realization - See under: awakening of consciousness

reassignment - See under: job rotation

recreational activities - See under: leisure

redactional historical (=critical) studies - See under: biblical studies

reference book - See under: pass

1001	refresher course	cours (m) de per-fectionnement (=recyclage /m/)	Fortbildungs(=Um-schulungs)kurs (m)	curso (m) de perfeccio-namiento; curso (m) de actualización

refugee

1002	refugee service	service (m) auprès des réfugiés	Flüchtlingsdienst (m)	servicio (m) para refugiados

1003 refugee work	activité (f) auprès des réfugiés	Flüchtlingsarbeit (f)	trabajo (m) de ayuda a los refugiados
1004 regularisation (of status)	régularisation (f)	Legalisierung (f)	regularización (f)
1005 rehabilitation	1. rééducation (f) physique (d'un malade) 2. rééducation (f) professionnelle (d'un ancien malade), réadaptation (f) professionnelle, recyclage (m) (d'un travailleur) 3. reclassement (m) social (d'un ancien détenu) 4. réinstallation (f) (de réfugiés, de personnes déplacées) 5. reconstruction (f), relèvement (m)(d'un pays après la guerre)	1. medizinische Rehabilitation (f) 2. berufliche Rehabilitation (f) 3. Resozialisierung (f) 4. Wiedereingliederung (f) (von Flüchtlingen) 5. Wiederaufbau (m) (eines Landes nach einem Krieg)	1. rehabilitación (f) (=readaptación /f/) física (de un enfermo) 2. rehabilitación (f) profesional (de un ex enfermo), rehabilitación (f) profesional (de un trabajador) 3. rehabilitación (f) social (de un ex preso) 4. reinstalación (f) (de refugiados) 5. rehabilitación (f) (=reconstrucción /f/) (de un país después de una guerra)
1006 Reign of God	règne (m) de Dieu	Gottesherrschaft (f)	reinado (m) de Dios
1007 For immediate release	Diffusion immédiate autorisée	Zur Veröffentlichung freigegeben, Zur Veröffentlichung frei	Se autoriza su difusión

1008	press release	communiqué (m) de presse	Pressemitteilung (f), Pressekommuniqué (n)	comunicado (m) de prensa

relief

1009	relief supplies	secours (mpl)	Hilfsgüter (npl)	socorro (m)
1010	relief work	oeuvre (f) (=action /f/) de secours	Nothilfe (f), Katastrophenhilfe (f)	acción (f) (=servicio /m/) de socorro
1011	relief worker(s)	secouriste (m), personnel (m) de secours	Katastrophenhelfer (m)	personal (m) de socorro

religion - See under: faith and religion

1012	to repatriate /migration/	rapatrier /migration/	abschieben /Migration/	repatriar /migración/

representations

1013	to make representations (to a governement)	1. faire des représentations (à un gouvernement); entreprendre des démarches (auprès d'un gouvernement) 2. protester (auprès d'un gouvernement)	1. (bei einer Regierung) vorstellig werden, Schritte (bei einer Regierung) unternehmen 2. (bei einer Regierung) Protest erheben	1. hacer representaciones (ante un gobierno); iniciar gestiones (ante un gobierno) 2. protestar (ante un gobierno)
1014	Reprinted by kind permission of...	Reproduit avec l'aimable autorisation de...	Nachdruck mit freundlicher Genehmigung des...	Reproducido con la amable autorización de ...

reserve

1015	General Reserve /WCC General Budget/	réserve (f) générale /budget général du COE/	Allgemeiner Rück-lagenfonds (m) /Allgemeiner Haus-halt, ÖRK/	reserva (f) gene-ral /Presupuesto General del CMI/
1016	Special Reserve /WCC General Budget/	réserve (f) spé-ciale /budget géné-ral du COE/	Sonderrücklagen-saldo (m) /Allge-meiner Haushalt, ÖRK/	reserva (f) espe-cial /Presupuesto General del CMI/
1017	resettlement	réinstallation (f) (de réfugiés, de personnes déplacées)	Umsiedlung (f), Wiederansied-lung (f)	reinstalación (f) (de refugiados)
1018	residential areas (=districts)	zones (fpl) d'habitat	Wohngebiete (npl)	zonas (fpl) de vivienda

resister

1019	draft resister	insoumis (m); réfractaire (m)	Wehrdienstdeser-teur (m)	prófugo (m)
1020	war resister	opposant (m) (=résistant /m/) à la guerre	Kriegsgegner (m)	opositor (m) a la guerra

resources

1021	finite resources	ressources (fpl) finies (=limitées)	begrenzte Ressour-cen (fpl)	recursos (mpl) limitados
1022	non-renewable resources	ressources (fpl) naturelles non renouvelables	nicht erneuerbare natürliche Ressour-cen	recursos (mpl) na-turales no reno-vables

1023 retraining	recyclage (m) (formation nouvelle)	Umschulung (f)	reeducación (f) profesional, reciclaje (m), readiestramiento (m), reorientación (f)
1024 revival, revivalism	réveil (m), revivalisme (m)	Erweckungsbewegung (f)	avivamiento (m)
1025 revivalist	revivaliste (m)	Anhänger (m) der Erweckungsbewegung	predicador (m) del avivamiento

right

1026 fundamental rights	droits fondamentaux (mpl)	Grundrechte (npl)	derechos fundamentales (mpl)
1027 fundamental human rights	droits (mpl) fondamentaux de l'homme	grundlegende Menschenrechte (npl)	derechos (mpl) fundamentales del hombre

human rights - <u>See</u> <u>under</u>: <u>Universal</u> Declaration of Human Rights

1028 human rights and fundamental freedoms	droits (mpl) de l'homme et libertés (fpl) fondamentales	Menschenrechte (npl) und Grundfreiheiten (fpl)	derechos (mpl) y libertades (fpl) fundamentales del hombre
1029 role-playing	jeu (m) de rôles	Rollenspiel (n)	"role-playing" (m)

Roman Catholic World Federation for the Biblical Apostolate - <u>See</u> <u>under</u>: biblical studies

rule

1030 Rule of God	règne (m) (=souveraineté /f/) de Dieu	Gottesherrschaft (f)	gobierno (m) de Dios

1031	Staff Rules and Regulations /WCC/	Statut (m) et règle-ment (m) du per-sonnel /COE/	Personalordnung (f) /ÖRK/	Estatuto (mpl) y Reglamento (m) del Personal /CMI/

rural

| 1032 | rural area | zone (f) rurale | ländliches Gebiet (n) | zona (f) rural |
| 1033 | rural development | développement (m) rural | ländliche Ent-wicklung (f) | desarrollo (m) rural |

rural exodus - See under: rural migration

| 1034 | rural planning | planification (f) rurale (=aménage-ment /m/ rural) | ländliche Planung (f) | planificación (f) rural |
| 1035 | rural settlements | 1. habitat (m) rural 2. aggloméra-tions (fpl) rurales | ländliche Wohnge-biete (npl) | aglomeraciones (fpl) rurales |

| 1036 | sacralisation | sacralisation (f) | Sakralisierung (f) | sacralización (f) |
| 1037 | sacramental fasting (refraining from all celebration of Holy Commu-nion e.g. during the time of a conference) | jeûne (m) sacramen-tal (suspension de toute célébration eucharistique, par ex. pendant la durée d'une conférence) | sakramentales Fa-sten (n) (Enthal-tung von allen A-bendmahlsfeiern z.B. für die Dauer einer Konferenz) | ayuno (m) sacra-mental (suspensión de toda cele-bración eucarística, por ejem. durante una conferencia) |

salary

1038	salary review	révision (f) des salaires	Überprüfung (f) der Gehälter	revisión (f) de los salarios
1039	salary structure	grille (f) (=structure /f/) des salaires	Gehaltsstruktur (f)	estructura (f) de los salarios

salvation

1040	God's plan of salvation	plan (m) de salut de Dieu	Heilsplan (m) Gottes	plan (m) de salvación de Dios
1041	order of salvation	ordre (m) du salut	Heilsordnung (f)	orden (m) de la salvación

school

1042	school attendance	scolarité (f), fréquentation (f) scolaire; scolarisation (f)	Schulzeit (f), Schulbesuch (m)	escolaridad (f), asistencia (f) escolar
1043	comprehensive school	école (f) polyvalente	Gesamtschule (f)	escuela (f) polivalente
1044	theological school (=college)	faculté (f) de théologie, école (f) de théologie, établissement (m) théologique	theologische Fakultät (f), theologische Hochschule (f), kirchliche Hochschule (f)	facultad (f) de teología; escuela (f) de teología
1045	schooling	enseignement (m) (=instruction /f/) scolaire	Unterricht (m); Ausbildung (f), Schulung (f)	preparación (f) escolar, enseñanza (f) (=instrucción /f/) escolar

1046 Secretariat of the Commission on Faith and Order	Secrétariat (m) de la Commission de foi et constitution	Sekretariat (n) der Kommission für Glauben und Kirchenverfassung	Secretaría (f) de la Comisión de Fe y Constitución
1047 secretary	1. secrétaire (m) 2. procès-verbaliste (m), rapporteur (m), secrétaire (m) (d'une commission)	1. Sekretär (m), Referent (m) 2. Berichterstatter (m) Schriftführer (m), Protokollführer (m) (eines Ausschusses)	1. secretario (m) 2. secretario (m) de actas, ponente (m), secretario (m) (de una comisión)
1048 secretary for...	secrétaire (m) à... (=auprès de...= chargé de...)	Referent (m) für...	secretario (m) de...
1049 Secretary for Administration /General Secretariat/	secrétaire (m) à l'administration /Secrétariat général/	Verwaltungsreferent (m) /Generalsekretariat/	Secretario (m) de Administración /Secretaría General/
1050 Secretary for Africa/Asia/ Europe/Latin America /CICARWS/	secrétaire (m) à l'Afrique/à l'Asie/ à l'Europe/ à l' Amérique latine /CESEAR/	Referent (m) für Afrika/Asien/ Europa/Latein- amerika /CICARWS/	Secretario (m) para Africa/Asia/Europa/ América Latina /CAISMR/
1051 Secretary for the Ecumenical Development Fund /CCPD/	secrétaire (m) chargé du Fonds oecuménique de développement /CPED/	Referent (m) für den Ökumenischen Entwicklungsfonds /CCPD/	Secretario (m) del Fondo Ecuménico de Desarrollo /CPID/
1052 Secretary for Emergencies and Rehabilitation /CICARWS/	secrétaire (m) à l' aide d'urgence et à la reconstruction /CESEAR/	Referent (m) für Katastrophenhilfe und Rehabilitations- programme/CICARWS/	Secretario (m) de Ayuda de Urgencia y de Reconstrucción /CAISMR/

1053 Secretary for Evangelism /CWME/	secrétaire (m) à l'évangélisation /CME/	Referent (m) für Fragen der Verkündigung /CWME/	Secretario (m) de Evangelización /CMME/
1054 Secretary, Office of Family Ministries /Staff Working Group on Education/	secrétaire (m) Bureau des ministères familiaux /Groupe de travail "éducation"/	Referent (m) für Familienfragen /Arbeitsgruppe "Bildung"/	Secretario (m), Oficina de Ministerios Familiares /Grupo de Trabajo "Educación"/
1055 Secretary for Film and Visual Arts /Communication/	secrétaire (m) chargé des films et arts visuels /Communication/	Referent (m) für Film, Bild und Graphik /Kommunikation/	Secretario (m) Encargado de Cinematografía y Artes Visuales /Comunicación/
1056 Secretary for the Language Service /Communication/	chef (m) du Service linguistique /Communication/	Leiter (m) des Sprachendienstes /Kommunikation/	Jefe (m) del Servicio Lingüístico /Comunicación/
1057 Secretary for Material Aid /CICARWS/	secrétaire (m) à l'aide matérielle /CESEAR/	Referent (m) für Materialhilfe /CICARWS/	Secretario (m) de Ayuda Material /CAISMR/
1058 Secretary for Migration /CICARWS/	secrétaire (m) à la migration /CESEAR/	Referent (m) für Migration /CICARWS/	Secretario (m) de Migración /CAISMR/
1059 Secretary for Programme /PCR/	secrétaire (m) au programme /PLR/	Programmreferent (m) /PCR/	Secretario (m) de Programa /PLR/
1060 Secretary for Radio and TV /Communication/	secrétaire (m) chargé de la radio-télévision /Communication/	Referent (m) für Rundfunk- und Fernsehen /Kommunikation/	Secretario (m) de los Servicios de Radio y Televisión /Comunicación/

353

	English	Français	Deutsch	Español
1061	Secretary for Research and Relations with Orthodox /CWME/	secrétaire (m) chargé de la recherche et des relations avec les orthodoxes /CME/	Referent für Forschung und Beziehungen zu den Orthodoxen /CWME/	Secretario (m) de Investigación y de las Relaciones con los Ortodoxos /CMME/
1062	Secretary for Scholarships /Staff Working Group on Education/	secrétaire (m) chargé des bourses /Groupe de travail "éducation"/	Stipendienreferent (m) Referent (m) für Stipendien /Arbeitsgruppe "Bildung"/	Secretario (m) de Becas /Grupo de Trabajo "Educación"/
1063	Secretary for Studies /CWME/	secrétaire (m) aux études /CME/	Studienreferent (m) /CWME/	Secretario (m) de Estudios /CMME/
1064	Acting General Secretary /WCC/	secrétaire (m) général intérimaire /COE/	Amtierender Generalsekretär (m) /ÖRK/	Secretario (m) General Interino /CMI/
1065	Area Secretary /CICARWS/	secrétaire (m) régional /CESEAR/	Gebietsreferent (m) /CICARWS/	Secretario (m) Regional /CAISMR/
1066	Deputy General Secretary /WCC/	secrétaire (m) général adjoint /COE/	Stellvertretender Generalsekretär (m) /ÖRK/	Secretario (m) General Adjunto /CMI/
1067	Editorial Secretary /Communication/	secrétaire (m) rédacteur /Communication/	Leiter (m) des Redaktionsbüros /Kommunikation/	Secretario (m) Redactor /Comunicación/
1068	Executive Secretary /for the Consultation on the Church and the Jewish People/	secrétaire (m) exécutif /Comité pour l'Eglise et le peuple juif/ /chargé de la pré-	Exekutivsekretär (m) /Ausschuss für die Kirche und das Jüdische Volk/ /für die Fünfte Vollversammlung/	Secretario (m) Ejecutivo /Comité para la Iglesia y el Pueblo Judío/ /encargado de la

	/for the Fifth Assembly/ /in the Secretariat of the Commission on Faith and Order/	paration à la cinquième Assemblée/ /Secrétariat de la Commission de foi et constitution/	/im Sekretariat der Kommission für Glauben und Kirchenverfassung/	preparación de la Quinta Asamblea/ /Secretaría de la Comisión de Fe y Constitución/
1069	Executive Secretary to the Ecumenical Church Loan Fund	secrétaire (m) exécutif, Fondation oecuménique pour l'aide aux Eglises	Geschäftsführer (m) des Ökumenischen Darlehensfonds	Secretario (m) Ejecutivo, Fondo Ecuménico de Préstamos a las Iglesias
1070	General Secretary /WCC, CEC/	secrétaire (m) général /COE, KEK/	Generalsekretär (m) /ÖRK, KEK/	Secretario (m) General /CMI, KEk/
1071	Research Secretary /PCR/	secrétaire (m) à la recherche /PLR/	Forschungsreferent (m) /PCR/	Secretario (m) de Investigación /PLR/

section

1072	Development Section /ECLOF/	Section (f) "développement"/ECLOF/	Abteilung (f) für Entwicklungshilfe /ECLOF/	Sección (f) de Préstamos para el Desarrollo /ECLOF/
1073	General Section /ECLOF/	Section (f) "prêts généraux"/ECLOF/	Abteilung (f) für allgemeine Darlehenshilfe /ECLOF/	Sección (f) de Préstamos Generales /ECLOF/
1074	secularization	sécularisation (f)	Säkularisierung (f), Verweltlichung (f)	secularización (f)
1075	secularism	sécularisme (m)	Säkularismus (m)	secularismo (m)

seeds

1076	improved seeds	semences (fpl) améliorées	hochwertiges Saatgut (n)	semillas (fpl) mejoradas
1077	to segregate	ségréguer	segregieren, nach Rassen trennen	segregar
1078	segregation	ségrégation (f), séparation (f) des races	Segregation (f), Rassentrennung (f)	segregación (f)

self-

self-government - See under: Three-Self-Movement

1079	self-help	auto-assistance (f)	Selbsthilfe (f)	autoayuda (f)
1080	self-hood	identité (f), "être soi-même"	Eigenständigkeit (f)	identidad (f) propia
1081	(workers') self-management	autogestion (f) (ouvrière)	Arbeiterselbstverwaltung (f)	autogestión (f) (obrera)
1082	self-organization	organisation (f) autonome	Selbstorganisation (f) (der Arbeiterschaft)	organización (f) autónoma

self-propagation - See under: Three-Self-Movement

1083	self-realization	réalisation (f) de soi, épanouissement (m)	Selbstverwirklichung (f)	encontrarse a sí mismo, realización (f) de su propia personalidad
1084	self-reliance	autonomie (f), développement (m)	Eigenständigkeit (f) (=-verantwor-	autonomía (f), desarrollo (m)

	autonome, auto-assistance (f) (capacité d'un peuple à déterminer lui-même ses propres objectifs en matière de développement, et à définir les moyens de les réaliser)	tung /f/, =-initiative /f/), Unabhängigkeit (f), Autonomie (f) (die Möglichkeit eines Volkes, seine Entwicklungsziele und ihre Verwirklichung eigenverantwortlich zu bestimmen)	autónomo (=basado en sus propias fuerzas), desarrollo (m) autogenerado (capacidad de un pueblo para fijarse sus metas en materia de desarrollo, y determinar los medios para alcanzarlas)
1085 Three-Self-Movement: -self-support, -self-government, -self-propagation	mouvement (m) des trois autonomies: -autofinancement (m), -autogestion (f), -mission (f) (témoignage /m/) autonome	Drei-Selbst-Bewegung (f): (Bewegung der dreifachen Autonomie) -Selbsterhaltung (f) -Selbstverwaltung (f) -selbständige Weiterverbreitung (f), Selbstverbreitung (f)	Movimiento (m) de las Tres Autonomías: -autofinanciamiento (m), autosostén (m) -gobierno (m) autónomo -misión (f) autónoma

self-support - See under: Three-Self-Movement

| 1086 seminar | séminaire (m), cycle (m) (=stage /m/) d'études | Seminar (n) | seminario (m) |

sending of the Church - See under: gathering of the Church

| 1087 seniority | ancienneté (f) | Anciennität (f), Dienstalter (n) | antigüedad (f) |

357

service

1088	alternative civilian service	service (m) civil	(Wehr)Ersatzdienst (m), Zivildienst (m)	opción (f) al servicio civil (en lugar del servicio militar)
1089	basic services	infrastructure (f)	Infrastruktur (f)	servicios (mpl) de infraestructura, infraestructura (f)(de servicios)

children's service - See under: children's worship

1090	Christian service in church-sponsored institutions or organizations	diaconie (f) d'institution	Anstaltsdiakonie (f)	diaconía (f) (=servicio cristiano) de la Iglesia a través de sus instituciones
1091	community services	équipements (mpl) collectifs	kommunale Dienstleistungen (fpl)	servicios (mpl) públicos

domiciliary services - See under: home care

1092	organized Christian service of the congregation	diaconie (f) paroissiale	Gemeindediakonie (f)	diaconía (f) (=servicio /m/ cristiano) de la congregación

the Septuagint - See under: biblical studies

1093	session	1. session 2. séance	1. Sitzungsperiode (f), Tagung (f) 2. Sitzung (f)	sesión (f)

358

1094	business session /WCC Assembly/	séance (f) adminis-trative /Assem-blée du COE/	Geschäftssitzung (f) /ÖRK-Vollversamm-lung/	sesión (f) admi-nistrativa /Asamblea del CMI/
1095	deliberative session /WCC Assembly/	séance (f) délibé-rante /Assemblée du COE/	Beratende Sitzung (f) /ÖRK-Vollver-sammlung/	sesión (f) deli-berante /Asamblea del CMI/
1096	general session /WCC Assembly/	séance (f) géné-rale /Assemblée du COE/	Allgemeine Sitzung (f) /ÖRK-Vollver-sammlung/	sesión (f) gene-ral /Asamblea del CMI/

settlements

| 1097 | human settlements | 1. habitat (m) humain 2. agglomérations(fpl) | Habitat (n) des Menschen | 1. asentamientos(mpl) humanos 2. aglomeraciones (fpl) humanas |

sewage

1098	sewage disposal	évacuation (f) des eaux usées (=d'égout)	Abwasserbeseiti-gung (f)	eliminación (f) (=evacuación /f/) de las aguas servidas (=residuales)
1099	sewage system, sewerage	système (m) du tout-à-l'égout	Kanalisation (f)	sistema (m) de alcantarillado
1100	sexism	sexisme (m) (discrimination fondée sur le sexe)	Sexismus (m) (Diskriminierung aufgrund der Ge-schlechtszuge-hörigkeit)	sexismo (m) (discriminación basada en el sexo)
1101	sexist	sexiste	sexistisch	sexista

359

1102 shanties, hovels	baraquements (mpl)	Barackenlager (n)	tugurios (mpl), casuchas (fpl), chabolas (fpl)
shanty town - <u>See under</u>: squatter settlement			
1103 sharing in the Gospel	Partager l'Evangile	Teilhabe(f) am Evangelium	Participar en el Evangelio
1104 sisterhood	sororité (f)	Gemeinschaft (f) der Frauen	hermandad (f)
1105 slum area	quartier (m) de taudis	Elendsviertel (n), Slums (mpl)	barrio (m) de tugurios, barrio (m) de latas, barrio (m) de chabolas /España/, villa (f) miseria /Argentina/, cantègril (m) /Uruguay/, favela (f) /Brasil/, callampa (f) /Bolivia, Chile/
1106 smuggler (of clandestine migrants)	passeur (m)	Mittelsmann (m), Menschenhändler (m)	traficante (m) de mano de obra, pasador (m)
1107 sobornost (Eastern conception of the Church's 'catholicity', its 'collegial' character, the community of	sobornost (f) (conception orientale de la "catholicité" de l'Eglise, son caractère "collégial", communauté de foi et de vie, in-	Sobornost (f) (Orthodoxe Konzeption der "Katholizität" der Kirche, ihres "kollegialen"Charakters, der Gemeinschaft des Glaubens	sobornost (f) (Concepción oriental de la "catolicidad" de la Iglesia, su carácter "colegial", comunidad de fe y de vida, infalible en la integridad

3

60

	English	French	German	Spanish
	its faith and life, unfailingly present in the totality of its body as the people of God united in Christ and manifesting Christ)	faillible dans l'intégrité de son corps en tant que peuple de Dieu réuni en Christ et formant la christophanie)	und Lebens, unfehlbar in der Integrität ihres Leibes, insofern als das Volk Gottes in Christus vereinigt ist und die Christophanie bildet)	de su cuerpo como pueblo de Dios reunido en Cristo y formando la cristofanía)

social

	English	French	German	Spanish
1108	social action	action (f) sociale	soziale Aktion (f)	acción (f) social
1109	social assistance	assistance (f) sociale	Sozialhilfe (f)	asistencia (f) social
1110	social security	sécurité (f) sociale	Sozialversicherung (f)	seguridad (f) social
1111	social service	service (m) social	Sozialdienst (m)	servicio (m) social
1112	social services, social welfare services	services (mpl) sociaux, services (mpl) d'assistance et de protection sociales (comprenant les services publics et les services des institutions privées)	Sozialhilfe (f)(Gesamtheit der durch öffentliche und freie Täger der Wohlfahrtspflege geleisteten Dienste), Sozialwesen (n)	servicios (mpl) sociales, servicios (mpl) de asistencia social (tanto públicos como privados)

social service agency - See under: welfare organization

	English	French	German	Spanish
1113	social therapist	sociothérapeute (m)	Sozialtherapeut (m)	socioterapeuta (m)
1114	social welfare	prévoyance (f) sociale,	Sozialversorgung (f)	previsión (f) social,

	protection (f) sociale, service (m) social; bien-être (m) social		asistencia (f) social, servicio (m) social, bienestar (m) social
1115 social work	travail (m) social	Sozialarbeit (f)	trabajo (m) social
1116 social worker, social welfare worker	travailleur (m) social; assistant (m) social, assistant (m) de service social	Sozialarbeiter (m)	trabajador (m) social; asistente (m) social
1117 medical social worker	assistant (m) social (spécialisé dans le domaine médico-social)	medizinisch ge-schulter Sozial-arbeiter (m)	asistente (m) social médico
1118 psychiatric social worker	assistant (m) social en psychiatrie (=psychiatrique)	psychiatrisch ge-schulter Sozial-arbeiter (m)	asistente (m) social psiquiátrico
society			
1119 affluent society	société (f) d'abondance	Überflussgesell-schaft (f)	sociedad (f) de la abundancia (=de prosperidad cre-ciente)
1120 consumer society	société (f) de consommation	Konsumgesell-schaft (f)	sociedad (f) de consumo
1121 disrupted society	société (f) dis-loquée	gespaltene Gesell-schaft (f)	sociedad (f) desquiciada
1122 multi-racial society	société (f) multi-raciale	gemischtrassige Gesellschaft (f)	sociedad (f) mul-tirracial
1123 permissive society	société (f) per-missive	permissive Gesell-schaft (f)	sociedad (f) per-misiva

1124	responsible society	société (f) consciente de ses responsabilités	verantwortliche Gesellschaft (f)	sociedad (f) responsable
1125	secularized society	société (f) sécularisée	säkularisierte Gesellschaft (f)	sociedad (f) secularizada
1126	sustainable society	société (f) écologiquement responsable	verantwortbare Gesellschaft (f)	sociedad (f) responsable frente a los recursos naturales, sociedad (f) responsable en lo ecológico
1127	Sonship of God	adoption (f) filiale de Dieu	Gotteskindschaft (f)	condición (f) de hijo de Dios
1128	soteriology (doctrine of salvation)	sotériologie (f) (doctrine du salut)	Soteriologie (f) (Lehre vom Heil)	soteriología (f) (Doctrina de la salvación)
1129	South Africa	Afrique (f) du Sud	Südafrika (n)	Sudáfrica (f)
1130	South African Institute of Race Relations	Institut (m) sud-africain des relations raciales	Südafrikanisches Institut (n) für Rassenbeziehungen	Instituto (m) Sudafricano de Relaciones Raciales
1131	Southern Africa	Afrique (f) australe	südliches Afrika (n)	Africa (f) meridional
1132	to sponsor	assumer la responsabilité de; promouvoir; patronner; financer; organiser	verantwortlich zeichnen für; fördern; finanzieren; organisieren	ser responsable; promover, fomentar; patrocinar; financiar; organizar

363

1133 sponsorship	parrainage (m), égide (f), auspices (mpl)	Patenschaft (f), Bürgschaft (f), Verantwortlichkeit (f)	patrocinio (m)

SPROCAS – See under: Study Project on Christianity in Apartheid Society

1134 squatter	1. habitant (m) des bidonvilles 2. squatter (m)	Bewohner (m) eines Barackenviertels	habitante (m) de los tugurios (=de las chabolas /España/ =de villas miseria /Argentina/ =de las callampas /Bolivia, Chile/ = de los cantegriles /Uruguay/= de las favelas/ Brasil/)
1135 squatter settlement, shanty town	bidonville (m)	Spontansiedlung (f), Barackenviertel (n)	tugurios (mpl), barriada (f), favela (f) /Brasil/, chabolas (mpl) /España/, villa miseria (f) /Argentina/, cantegril (m) /Uruguay/, callampa (f) /Bolivia, Chile/
1136 staff	personnel(s) (m), employé(s) (m), effectifs (mpl); collaborateur(s), équipe (f) de collaborateurs; secrétariat (m)	Stab (m), Personal (m), Mitarbeiter (m) (mpl)	personal (m), empleados (mpl), funcionarios (mpl)
1137 junior staff	personnel (m) subalterne	nichtleitende Mitarbeiter (mpl)	personal (m) subalterno

1138	senior staff	cadres (mpl) supé- rieurs, respon- sables (mpl)	leitende Mitar- beiter (mpl)	cuadros (mpl) su- periores, res- ponsables (mpl)
1139	turnover of staff	roulement (m) (=renouvellement /m/) du personnel	Personalschwan- kungen (fpl), Fluktuation (f)	movimiemento (m) de personal
1140	staretz (means an'elder', usually with reference to old and ex- perienced monks /often not in priestly orders/, illuminated by the Holy Spirit and especially gifted in the care of souls)	staretz (m) (signifie "ancien" et désigne de vieux moines / souvent sans prêtrise/ expérimentés, illu- minés par le Saint-Esprit et possédant le charisme de la cure d'âme)	Staretz (m) (russ.: der Alte. Bezeichnet geist- lich erfahrene alte Mönche /häu- fig ohne Priester- weihe/, die vom Heiligen Geist erleuchtet sind und das Charisma der der Seelsorge be- sitzen. Plur.: Starzen)	Staretz (m) (Significa "antiguo" e indica a los mon- jes viejos /a menudo sin haber sido ordenados sacerdotes/ ex- perimentados, ilumi- nados por el Espíritu santo, y que poseen el don de la cura de almas)
	status			
1141	legal status	statut (m) juri- dique	Rechtsstellung (f)	situación (f) legal (=jurídica)
1142	step	échelon (m)	Gehaltsstufe (f)	escalón (m)
1143	steward	1. intendant (m) (des biens confiés par Dieu à l'homme), économe (m) 2. steward (m) /conférences du COE/	1. Haushalter (m) 2. Steward (m) /ÖRK-Konferenzen/	1. mayordomo (m), 2. steward (m) /conferencias del CMI/
1144	stewardship	gestion (f) des	Haushalterschaft (f)	mayordomía (f)

biens confiés par
Dieu à l'homme
(temps, forces,
argent, etc.),
intendance (f)

strike

1145	unofficial strike; wild cat strike	grève (f) sauvage	wilder Streik (m)	huelga (f) no oficial (="salvaje" =espontánea)

structural analysis - See under: biblical studies

Studies - See chapter V, studies

study

1146	study-action process	confrontation (f) permanente du pensé et du vécu	Aktions-Reflexions-Prozess (m)	confrontación (f) permanente de la acción y de la reflexión
1147	Study Project on Christianity in Apartheid Society (SPROCAS)	Projet (m) d'études sur le christianisme dans une société d'apartheid (SPROCAS)	Studienprojekt (n) Christentum in der "Apartheid-Gesellschaft"	Proyecto (m) de Estudios sobre el Cristianismo en una Sociedad de Apartheid (SPROCAS)
1148	comparative studies of creeds and confessions	étude (f) comparée des symboles et confessions de foi	vergleichende Konfessionskunde (f)	estudio (f) comparado de credos y confesiones
1149	ecumenical study	recherche (f) oecuménique	ökumenische Studienarbeit (f)	investigación (f) ecuménica

| 1150 | feasibility study | étude (f) de viabilité | Projektstudie (f), Durchführbar-keitsstudie (f) | estudio (f) de viabilidad |

subscription

| 1151 | combined sub-scription | abonnement (m) combiné (=for-faitaire) | kombiniertes Abonnement (n) | suscripción (f) combinada |
| 1152 | overall sub-scription | abonnement (m) gé-néral (à toutes les publications du COE) | Generalabonnement (n) (auf alle ÖRK-Ver-öffentlichungen) | suscripción (f) general (a todos las publicaciones del CMI) |

subsistence

1153	subsistence farming	agriculture (f) de subsistance	Subsistenzwirt-schaft (f)	agricultura (f) de substistencia
1154	subsistence level, poverty line	minimum (m) vital	Existenzmini-mum (n)	mínimo (m) vital, nivel (m) de subsistencia
1155	substitute	suppléant (m)	Vertreter (m)	suplente (m)

succession

1156	apostolic succession	succession (f) apostolique	apostolische Suk-zession (f)	sucesión (f) apostó-lica
1157	episcopal succession	succession (f) épiscopale	bischöfliche Sukzession (f)	sucesión (f) episcopal
1158	presbyterial succession	succession (f) presbytérale	presbyterale Sukzession (f)	sucesión (f) presbiteral

367

supply

1159	material supplies	ressources (fpl) (=secours /mpl/) matériel(le)s	Hilfsgüter (npl)	suministros (mpl), socorro (m) material
1160	syllabus	programme (m) (d'un cours)	Lehrprogramm (n)	programa (m) (de un curso)
1161	symposium	symposium (m), colloque (m)	Symposium (n)	simposium (m), simposio (m)
1162	synaxis (meeting of Christians for the celebration of the Liturgy)	synaxe (f) (rassemblement des fidèles célébrant la liturgie)	Synaxis (f) (Versammlung der Gläubigen zur Feier der Eucharistie)	Sinaxe (f) (Reunión de los fieles que celebran la liturgia)
1163	synergism (Orthodox understanding of the relationship between grace and liberty)	synergisme (m) (conception orthodoxe des rapports entre la grâce et la liberté)	Synergismus (m) (Zusammenwirken. Orthodoxe Konzeption der Zusammenhänge zwischen Gnade und Freiheit)	Sinergismo (m) (Concepción ortodoxa de las relaciones entre la gracia y la libertad)

synchronic way of reading the Bible - See under: biblical studies

tape

1164	editing of sound tape	montage (m) de bandes magnétiques	Montage (f) von Tonbändern	montaje (m) de cintas magnetofóni-cas
1165	target groups	groupes (mpl) cibles (=priori-taires)	Zielgruppen (fpl)	grupos (mpl) objetivo (=priori-tarios)
1166	task force	groupe (m) d'étude, groupe (m) de travail	Arbeitsgruppe (f), Fachgruppe (f), Sektion (f), Arbeitskreis (m)	grupo (m) (especial) de trabajo
1167	Language Policy Task Force (LPTF) /WCC/	Groupe (m) d'étude "langue et communication"(GELC) /COE/	Fachgruppe (f) "Spra-che und Kommunikation" (LPTF) /ORK/	Grupo (m) Especial de Trabajo "Idioma y Comunicación" (GEIC) /CMI/
1168	regional task force	groupe (m) de travail régional	regionale Ar-beitsgruppe (f)	grupo (m) de trabajo regional
1169	Youth Task Force /Staff Working Group on Renewal/	Groupe (m) de tra-vail "jeunesse" /Groupe de tra-vail "renouveau"/	Arbeitsgruppe (f) "Jugend " /Arbeitsgruppe "Erneuerung"/	Grupo (m)Especial de Trabajo con la Juventud /Grupo de Trabajo "Renovación"/

teacher

| 1170 | remedial teacher, specialist teacher | éducateur (m) spé-cialisé (pédagogie thérapeutique) | Heilpädagoge (m) | educador (m) es-pecializado (enseñanza especial) |
| 1171 | team | équipe (f) | Team (n) | equipo (m) |

1172	team teaching	enseignement (m) en équipe	Team Teaching (m), flexibler Gruppen-unterricht (m)	enseñanza (f) en equipo
1173	social and medical team	équipe (f) médi-co-sociale	sozialmedizinisches Team (n)	equipo (m) médicosocial
1174	Youth Team /Staff Working Group on Renewal/	Equipe (f) "jeu-nesse"/Groupe de travail "renouveau"/	Jugendteam (n) /Arbeitsgruppe "Erneuerung"/	Equipo (m) "Juventud" /Grupo de Trabajo "Renovación"/
1175	technology	1. technologie (f) 2. technique (f)	1. Technologie (f) 2. Technik (f)	tecnología (f)
1176	advanced techno-logy; sophisticated technology	1. technologie (f) de pointe; techniques (fpl) de pointe 2. technologie (f) complexe; techniques (fpl) complexes	hochentwickelte Technologie (f)	tecnología (f) avan-zada; tecnología (f) com-pleja
1177	appropriate technology	1. technologie (f) appropriée (=adaptée) (technologie adaptée à une communauté donnée, à sa situation, à ses besoins, à son contexte culturel spécifique); techniques (fpl) appropriées (=adap-tées) 2. technologie (f) appropriée	bedarfsorientierte (=angepasste) Tech-nologie (f) (eine Technologie, die auf die spe-zifischen sozia-len, wirtschaft-lichen und kultu-rellen Verhält-nisse in einer bestimmten Gemein-schaft zugeschnit-ten ist)	1. tecnología (f) adecuada (tecnología adecuada a una comunidad, a su situación, a sus necesidades, a su contexto cultural específico) 2. tecnología (f) apropiada (tecnología cuyo dominio ha sido total-mente adquirido por

		(technologie qu'une communauté donnée s'est appropriée, a faite sienne); techniques (f) appropriées		una comunidad, que la comunidad se ha apropiado)
1178	intermediate technology	1. technologie (f) intermédiaire 2. techniques (fpl) intermédiaires	intermediäre (=mittlere) Technologie (f)	tecnología (f) intermedia
1179	transfer of technology	transfert (m) des techniques	Technologietransfer (m)	transferencia (f) de tecnología
1180	telos (the final goal, the end in view)	telos (m) (le but final)	Telos (n) (Ende, Ziel, Vollendung)	telos (m) (La meta o el objetivo final)
1181	theandric (denotes the mystery of Christ, its divine-human character; by extension it refers to everything in the Christian life which reflects this mystery; the theandric nature of the Church, of the Scriptures /inspiration/, of every ecclesial act)	théandrique (désigne le mystère du Christ, sa réalité à la fois divine et humaine. Par extension, tout ce qui relève de ce mystère dans la vie chrétienne: la nature théandrique de l'Eglise, des Ecritures/inspiration/, de tout acte ecclésial)	theandrisch (Bezeichnet das Geheimnis Christi, seine gottmenschliche Wirklichkeit. Im weiteren Sinne: alles, was sich im christlichen Leben auf dieses Geheimnis gründet: das theandrische Wesen der Kirche, der Heiligen Schrift /Inspiration/, jedes Aktes der Kirche)	teándrico (Indica el misterio de Cristo, su realidad diviona y humana . Por extensión: todo aquello que es consecuencia de ese misterio en la vida cristiana: la naturaleza teándrica de la Iglesia, de las Ecrituras /inspiración/, de todo acto eclesial)

371

theology

1182	theology of hope	théologie (f) de l'espérance	Theologie (f) der Hoffnung	teología (f) de la esperanza
1183	theology of liberation	théologie (f) de la libération	Theologie (f) der Befreiung	teología (f) de la liberación
1184	theology of mission	théologie (f) de la mission	Missionstheologie (f), Theologie (f) der missionarischen Verkündigung	teología (f) de la misión
1185	theology of revolution	théologie (f) de la révolution	Theologie (f) der Revolution	teología (f) de la revolución
1186	African theology	théologie (f) africaine	afrikanische Theologie (f)	teología (f) africana
1187	biblical theology	théologie (f) biblique	biblische Theologie (f)	teología (f) bíblica
1188	black theology	théologie (f) noire	schwarze Theologie (f)	teología (f) negra
1189	contextual theology	théologie (f) contextuelle	kontextuelle Theologie (f)	teología (f) contextual
1190	dialogical theology	théologie (f) dialogale	dialogische Theologie (f)	teología (f) dialógica
1191	doing theology, practising theology	pratique (f) de la théologie	Betreiben (n) von Theologie, Theologie betreiben	práctica (f) de la teología
1192	ecumenical theology	théologie (f) oecuménique	ökumenische Theologie (f)	teología (f) ecuménica

1193	existential theology	théologie (f) existentielle	existentielle Theologie (f), Theologie (f) der Existenz, existentiale Theologie (R.-K.)	teología (f) existencial
1194	political theology	théologie (f) du politique, théologie (f) politique	politische Theologie (f)	teología (f) política
1195	practical (=pastoral) theology	théologie (f) pratique	praktische Theologie (f)	teología (f) práctica (=pastoral)
1196	theomorphosis (according to the ancient patristic saying: 'God became man in order that man might by grace become divine')	théomorphose (f) (selon l'adage patristique: Dieu devient homme pour que l'homme devienne dieu selon la grâce)	Theomorphose (f) (Gemäss der patristischen Sentenz: Gott wurde Mensch, auf dass der Mensch durch die Gnade göttlich werde)	teomorfosis (f) (Según el adagio patrístico: Dios se hace hombre para que el hombre sea dios según la gracia)
1197	theophany (manifestation of God)	théophanie (f) (phanie: manifestation. Théophanie: manifestation de Dieu)	Theophanie (f) (Phanie: Erscheinung. Theophanie: Erscheinung Gottes)	teofanía (f) (fanía: manifestación; teofanía: manifestación de Dios)
1198	theosis (deification, pneumatization; the penetration of human life and being by	théosis (f) (déification, pneumatisation, pénétration de l'être humain par les énergies	Theosis (f) (Vergottung, Vergeistlichung, Durchdringung des menschlichen Seins durch die gött-	teosis (f) (Deificación, pneumatización, penetración del ser humano por las energías divinas)

the divine energies)	divines)	lichen Kräfte)	
1199 theotokion (liturgical hymn in praise of the Mother of God, having a doctrinal content)	théotokion (m) (chant liturgique en l'honneur de la mère de Dieu, ayant un contenu dogmatique)	Theotokion (n) (Liturgischer Hymnus zu Ehren der Mutter Gottes /mit dogmatischem Inhalt/)	teotokion (m) (Canto litúrgico en honor de la Madre de Dios que tiene un contenido dogmático)
1200 theurgy (the operation of God in the direction indicated by the divine liturgy of heaven)	théurgie (f) (oeuvre de Dieu dans le sens de la liturgie divine céleste)	Theurgie (f) (Werk Gottes im Sinne der himmlischen Liturgie)	teurgia (f) Obra de Dios en el sentido de la divina liturgia celestial)
1201 tokenism	mesure (f) (acte /m/) symbolique (qui sert d'alibi)	symbolische Massnahme (f) (=Handlung /f/) (die Alibifunktion hat)	acto (m) simbólico (que sirve de coartada)
1202 tolerance margin	marge (f) de tolérance	Toleranzgrenze (f)	margen (m) de tolerancia
1203 township /South Africa/	zone (f) d'habitation /Afrique du Sud/ (faubourgs réservés aux Africains sur le pourtour des zones de regroupement blanches)	Township (m), Stadtbezirk (m) /Südafrika/ (rein schwarze Vorstädte in weissen Gebieten)	municipio (m) /Sudafrica/ municipio (m) /Sudafrica/ (suburbios de las zonas blancas, reservados à los africanos)

tradition

1204	history of tra- dition/biblical studies/	histoire (f) de la tradition /études bibliques/	Überlieferungs- geschichte (f) /Bibelstudien/	historia (f) de la tradición /estudios bíblicos/

traditional

1205	traditional healer	guérisseur (m) traditionnel	Heilkundiger (m)	curandero (m)
1206	traditional prac- titioner	praticien (m) traditionnel	Heilpraktiker (m)	curandero (m)
1207	trafficking in migrant labour	trafic (m) de main-d'oeuvre	Handel (m) mit aus- ländischen Arbeits- kräften, Menschenhandel (m)	tráfico (m) de mano de obra
1208	training	formation (f)	Ausbildung (f), (/a/ allgemein- bildend, /b/ berufs- bildend)	formación (f), capacitación (f)
1209	training course	stage (m) (=cours /m/) de formation	Ausbildung(-skurs) (f), Schulung(-skurs) (f)	curso (m) de formación (= de capacitación)
1210	advanced training course	cours (m) de perfectionnement	Fortgeschrittenen- kurs (m)	curso (m) de per- feccionamiento
1211	training school	école (f) profes- sionnelle, centre (m) de formation profession- nelle	Fachschule (f), Berufsfachschule (f)	centro (m) de for- mación profesional

1212	clinical pastoral training (CPT), clinical pastoral education (CPE)	stage (m) de pastorale (=d'aumônerie) dans les hôpitaux	Pastoralklinikum (n), klinische Seelsorgeausbildung (f)	preparación (f) pastoral en los hospitales
1213	field training (in development)	formation (f) sur le terrain (dans les pays en voie de développement)	Durchführung (f) von Praktika (in Entwicklungsländern)	formación (f) (=capacitación /f/) sobre el terreno (en los países en desarrollo)
1214	further training	formation (f) complémentaire, cours (mpl) de perfectionnement	Weiterbildung (pfl), Fortbildung (f),	formación (f) (=capacitación /f/) complementaria, cursos (mpl) de perfeccionamiento
1215	in-plant training	formation (f) dans l'entreprise	innerbetriebliche Fortbildung (f)	formación (f) (=capacitación /f/) en la empresa, formación (f) durante la ejecución del trabajo
1216	in-service training	formation (f) en cours d'emploi, recyclage (m) (formation complémentaire)	Ausbildung (f) (während der Berufstätigkeit), berufliche Weiterbildung (f)	formación (f) (=capacitación /f/) en el empleo
1217	in-service training course	stage (m) de perfectionnement en cours d'emploi, cours (m) de recyclage	Kurs (m) zur beruflichen Weiterbildung	curso (m) de capacitación (=de formación profesional) en el empleo

1218	lay training centre, laity centre, lay academy	centre (m) de formation des laïcs	Laieninstitut (n), (Laien)Akademie (f)	centro (m) de formación de laicos
1219	leadership training	formation (f) des cadres	Heranbildung (f) von Führungs-kräften, Leiterschulung (f)	formación (f) de personal diri-gente
1220	on-the-job training	formation (f) sur le tas (=en emploi)	Ausbildung (f) am Arbeits-platz	aprendizaje (m), formación (f) en el empleo
1221	sensitivity training	sensibilisation (f) aux relations humaines	Sensitivitäts-training (n)	curso (m) de relaciones humanas

special (=remedial) training - See under: special education

| 1222 | teacher training college | 1. école (f) normale d'instituteurs 2. centre (m) (=institut /m/) pédagogique | pädagogische Hochschule (f), Lehrerseminar (n) | 1. instituto (m) (=escuela) normal 2. centro (m) (=insti-tuto /m/) de ciencias de la educación |

theological training - See under: theological education

| 1223 | vocational trai-ning | formation (f) pro-fessionnelle | Berufsausbildung (f) | formación (f) pro-fesional |

transit camp - See under: settlement camp

translation

    dynamic equivalence translation - <u>See</u> <u>under</u>: biblical studies

    formal correspondence translation - <u>See</u> <u>under</u>: biblical studies

1224	travel kit	dossier (m) d'informations COE	ÖRK-Informations-mappe (f)	carpeta (f) con informaciones CMI
	treatment			
1225	equal treatment	égalité (f) de traitement, parité (f)	Gleichstellung (f)	igualdad (f) de trato
	treaty			
1226	Treaty on the Non-Proliferation of Nuclear Weapons	Traité (m) sur la non-prolifération des armes nucléaires (=de non-prolifération des armes nucléaires)	Atomwaffensperr-vertrag (m), Vertrag (m) über die Nichtweiter-verbreitung (=Nicht-weitergabe) von Atom-waffen	Tratado (m) sobre la no Profilifera-ción de las Armas Nucleares
1227	Test-Ban treaty	Traité (m) sur l'interdiction des essais nucléaires (=d'interdiction des essais nucléaires)	Teststop-Abkommen (n)	Tratado (m) de Pro-hibición de los Ensayos Nucleares
1228	tribalism	tribalisme (m)	Tribalismus (m)	tribalismo (m)
1229	triumphalism	triomphalisme (m)	Triumphalismus (m)	triunfalismo (m)

1230	to turn back at the frontier	refouler	zurückweisen	rechazar en la frontera, impedir la entrada
1231	undernourishment, undernutrition	sous-alimentation (f)	Unterernährung (f)	subnutrición (f)
1232	the underprivileged	déshérités (mpl), laissés-pour-compte (mpl), défavorisés (mpl)	Unterprivile-gierte (mpl)	los desheredados (mpl), los olvidados (mpl)
	unemployment			
1233	cyclical unemployment	chômage (m) conjoncturel	konjunkturelle Arbeitslosig-keit (f)	paro(m) (=desempleo/m/) coyuntural
1234	structural unemployment	chômage (m) structurel	strukturelle Arbeitslosigkeit (f)	paro(m) (=desempleo/m/) estructural
	union			
1235	church union	union (f) des Eglises; union (f) d'Eglises	Kirchenunion (f)	unión (f) de las iglesias; unión (f) de iglesias
1236	church union negotiations	négociations (fpl) d'union entre Eglises	Kirchenunionsver-handlungen (fpl)	tratativas (fpl) (=negociaciones /fpl/) de unión entre las iglesias

1237	models of union	modèles (mpl) d'union	Unionsmodelle (npl)	modelos (mpl) de unión
1238	unit	unité (f)	Einheit (f)	unidad (f)
1239	programme unit	unité (f) (de travail)	Programmeinheit (f)	unidad (f) (de trabajo)
1240	sub-unit	section (f)	Untereinheit (f), Arbeitsgruppe (f)	sección (f)

uniting families - See under: reunion of families

unity

1241	the unity we seek	L'unité que nous recherchons	Die Einheit, die wir suchen	La unidad que buscamos
1242	church unity	unité (f) de l'Eglise; unité (f) des Eglises	Einheit (f) der Kirche; Kircheneinheit (f)	unidad (f) de la Iglesia; unidad (f) de las Iglesias
1243	concepts of unity	conceptions (fpl) de l'unité	Einheitskonzeptionen (fpl)	conceptos (mpl) de unidad
1244	corporate unity	unité (f) de corps (=organique)	korporative Einheit (f)	unidad (f) de cuerpo (=orgánica)
1245	organic unity	unité (f) organique (=de corps)	organische Einheit (f)	unidad (f) orgánica (de cuerpo)

381

1246 UNIVERSAL DECLARATION OF HUMAN RIGHTS

Preamble

Whereas recognition of the inherent dignity and of the equal and inalienable rights of all members of the human family is the foundation of freedom, justice and peace in the world,

Whereas disregard and contempt for human rights have resulted in barbarous acts which have outraged the conscience of mankind, and the advent of a world in which human beings shall enjoy freedom of speech and belief and freedom from fear and want has been proclamed as the highest aspiration of the common people,

Whereas it is essential, if man is not to be compelled to have recourse, as a last resort, to rebellion against tyranny and oppression, that human rights should be protected by the rule of law,

Whereas it is essential to promote the development of friendly relations between nations,

Whereas the peoples of the United Nations have in the Charter reaffirmed their faith in fundamental human rights, in the dignity and worth of the human person and in the equal rights of men and women and have determined to promote social progress and

DECLARATION UNIVERSELLE DES DROITS DE L'HOMME

Préambule

Considérant que la reconnaissance de la dignité inhérente à tous les membres de la famille humaine et de leurs droits égaux et inaliénables constitue le fondement de la liberté, de la justice et de la paix dans le monde,

Considérant que la méconnaissance et le mépris des droits de l'homme ont conduit à des actes de barbarie qui révoltent la conscience de l'humanité et que l'avènement d'un monde où les êtres humains seront libres de parler et de croire, libérés de la terreur et de la misère, a été proclamé comme la plus haute aspiration de l'homme,

Considérant qu'il est essentiel que les droits de l'homme soient protégés par un régime de droit pour que l'homme ne soit pas contraint, en suprême recours, à la révolte contre la tyrannie et l'oppression,

Considérant qu'il est essentiel d'encourager le développement de relations amicales entre nations,

Considérant que dans la Charte les peuples des Nations Unies ont proclamé à nouveau leur foi dans les droits fondamentaux de l'homme, dans la dignité et la valeur de la

ALLGEMEINE ERKLÄRUNG DER MENSCHENRECHTE

Präambel

Da die Anerkennung der allen Mitgliedern
der menschlichen Familie innewohnenden
Würde und ihrer gleichen und unveräusser-
lichen Rechte die Grundlage der Freiheit,
der Gerechtigkeit und des Friedens in der
Welt bildet,

da Verkennung und Missachtung der Menschenrechte zu Akten der Barbarei führten, die
das Gewissen der Menschheit tief verletzt
haben, und da die Schaffung einer Welt, in
der den Menschen, frei von Furcht und Not,
Rede- und Glaubensfreiheit zuteil wird, als
das höchste Bestreben der Menschheit verkündet worden ist,

da es wesentlich ist, die Menschenrechte
durch die Herrschaft des Rechtes zu schüt-
zen, damit der Mensch nicht zum Aufstand
gegen Tyrannei und Unterdrückung als letztem
Mittel gezwungen wird,

da es wesentlich ist, die Entwicklung freund-
schaftlicher Beziehungen zwischen den Nationen zu fördern,

da die Völker der Vereinten Nationen in der
Satzung ihren Glauben an die grundlegenden
Menschenrechte, an die Würde und den Wert der
menschlichen Person und an die Gleichberechtigung von Mann und Frau erneut be-

DECLARACION UNIVERSAL DE DERECHOS HUMANOS

Preambulo

Considerando que la libertad, la justicia
y la paz en el mundo tienen por base el
reconocimiento de la dignidad intrínseca
y de los derechos iguales e inalienables de
todos los miembros de la familia humana;

Considerando que el desconocimiento y el
menosprecio de los derechos humanos han
originada actos de barbarie ultrajantes
para la conciencia de la humanidad; y que
se ha proclamado, como la aspiración más
elevada del hombre, el advenimiento de un
mundo en que los seres humanos, liberados
de temor y de la miseria, disfruten de la
libertad de palabra y de la libertad de
creencias;

Considerando esencial que los derechos
humanos sean protegidos por un régimen de
Derecho, a fin de que el hombre no se vea
compelido al supremo recurso de la rebe-
lión contra la tiranía y la opresión;

Considerando también esencial promover el
desarrollo de relaciones amistosas entre las
naciones;

Considerando que los pueblos de las Naciones Unidas han reafirmado en la Carta,
su fe en los derechos fundamentales del
hombre, en la dignidad y el valor de la

383

better standards of life in larger freedom,

Whereas Member States have pledged them-
selves to achieve, in co-operation with
the United Nations, the promotion of universal respect for and observance of human
rights and fundamental freedoms,

Whereas a common understanding of these
rights and freedoms is of the greatest
importance for the full realization of this
pledge,

Now,therefore,

The General Assembly

proclaims

THIS UNIVERSAL DECLARATION OF HUMAN RIGHTS
as a common standard of achievement for all
peoples and all nations, to the end that
every individual and every organ of society,
keeping this Declaration constantly in
mind, shall strive by teaching and education
to promote respect for these rights and
freedoms and by progressive measures, national
and international, to secure their universal
and effective recognition and observance,
both among the peoples of Member States them-
selves and among the peoples of territories
under their jurisdiction.

ARTICLE 1. All human beings are born free
and equal in dignity and rights. They are
endowned with reason and conscience and

personne humaine, dans l'égalité des droits
des hommes et des femmes, et qu'ils se sont
déclarés résolus à favoriser le progrès
social et à instaurer de meilleures conditions de vie dans une liberté plus grande,

Considérant que les Etats Membres se sont
engagés à assurer, en coopération avec
l'Organisation des Nations Unies, le respect
universel et effectif des droits de l'homme
et des libertés fondamentales,

Considérant qu'une conception commune de ces
droits et libertés est de la plus haute importance pour remplir pleinement cet engagement,

L'Assemblée générale

proclame

LA PRESENTE DECLARATION UNIVERSELLE DES
DROITS DE L'HOMME comme l'idéal commun à
atteindre par tous les peuples et toutes
les nations afin que tous les individus
et tous les organes de la société, ayant
cette Déclaration constamment à l'esprit,
s'efforcent , par l'enseignement et
l'éducation, de développer le respect de ces
droits et libertés et d'en assurer, par des
mesures progressives d'ordre national et
international, la reconnaissance et l'appli-
cation universelles et effectives, tant
parmi les populations des Etats Membres
eux-mêmes, que parmi celles des territoires
placés sous leur jurisdiction.

kräftigt und beschlossen haben, den
sozialen Fortschritt und bessere Lebens-
bedingungen bei grösserer Freiheit zu
fördern,

da die Mitgliedsstaaten sich verpflichtet
haben, in Zusammenarbeit mit den Vereinten
Nationen die allgemeine Achtung und Verwirklichung der Menschenrechte und Grundfreiheiten durchzusetzen,

da eine gemeinsame Auffassung über diese
Rechte und Freiheiten von grösster
Wichtigkeit für die volle Erfüllung dieser
Verpflichtung ist,

verkündet

die Generalversammlung

DIE VORLIEGENDE ALLGEMEINE ERKLÄRUNG DER
MENSCHENRECHTE als das von allen Völkern
und Nationen zu erreichende gemeinsame
Ideal, damit jeder einzelne und alle Or-
gane der Gesellschaft sich diese Erklärung
stets gegenwärtig halten und sich bemühen,
durch Unterricht und Erziehung die Achtung
dieser Rechte und Freiheiten zu fördern
und durch fortschreitende Massnahmen im
nationalen und internationalen Bereiche
ihre allgemeine und tatsächliche Anner-
kennung und Verwirklichung bei der Be-
völkerung sowohl der Mitgliedstaaten
wie der ihrer Oberhoheit unterstehenden
Gebiete zu gewährleisten.

ARTIKEL 1. Alle Menschen sind frei und

persona humana y en la igualdad de derechos de hombres y mujeres; y se han decla-
rado resueltos a promover el progreso social
y a elevar el nivel de vida dentro de un
concepto más amplio de la libertad;

Considerando que los Estados Miembros
se han comprometido a asegurar, en cooperación con la Organización de la Naciones
Unidas, el respeto universal y efectivo a
los derechos y libertades fundamentales del
hombre; y

Considerando que una concepción común
de estos derechos y libertades es de la mayor importancia para el pleno cumplimiento
de dicho compromiso;

la Asamblea General

proclama

LA PRESENTE DECLARACION UNIVERSAL DE DERECHOS
HUMANOS como ideal común por el que todos
los pueblos y naciones deben esforzarse, a
fin de que tanto los individuos como las
instituciones, inspirándose constantemente
en ella, promuevan, mediante la enseñanza
y la educación, el respeto a estos derechos
y libertades, y aseguren, por medidas
progresivas de carácter nacional e internacional, su reconocimiento y aplicación
universales y efectivos, tanto entre los
pueblos de los Estados Miembros como entre
los de los territorios colocados bajo su
jurisdicción.

385

should act towards one another in a
spirit of brotherhood.

ARTICEL 2. Everyone is entitled to all
the rights and freedoms set forth in this
Declaration, without distinction of any
kind, such as race, colour, sex, language,
religion, political or other opinion,
national or social   origin, property,
birth or other status.

Furthermore, no distinction shall be
made on the basis of the political, juris-
dictional or international status of the
country or territory to which a person
belongs, whether it be independent,
trust, non-self-governing or under
any other limitation of sovereignty.

ARTICLE 3. Everyone has the right to
life, liberty and security of person.

ARTICLE 4. No one shall be held in
slavery or servitude; slavery and the
slave trade shall be prohibited in all
their forms.

ARTICLE 5. No one shall be subjected
to torture or to cruel, inhuman or
degrading treatment or punishment.

ARTICLE 6. Everyone has the right to
recognition everywhere as a person before the law.

ARTICLE 7. All are equal before the law
and are entitled without any discrimination

ARTICLE PREMIER. Tous les êtres humains
naissent libre
droits. Ils sont doués de raison et de
conscience et doivent agir les uns envers
les autres dans un esprit de fraternité.

ARTICLE 2. Chacun peut se prévaloir de tous
les droits et de toutes les libertés proclamés
dans la présente Déclaration , sans distinction
aucune, notamment de race, de couleur, de
sexe, de langue, de religion, d'opinion
politique ou de toute autre opinion, d'origine
nationale ou sociale, de fortune, de naissance
ou de toute autre situation.

De plus, il ne sera fait aucune distinction
fondée sur le statut politique, juridique ou
international du pays ou du territoire dont
une personne est ressortissante, que ce pays
ou territoire soit indépendant, sous tutelle,
non autonome ou soumis à une limitation
quelconque de souveraineté.

ARTICLE 3. Tout individu a droit à la vie,
à la liberté et à la sûreté de sa personne.

ARTICLE 4. Nul ne sera tenu en esclavage ni
en servitude; l'esclavage et la traite des
esclaves sont interdits sous toutes leurs
formes.

ARTICLE 5. Nul ne sera soumis à la torture,
ni à des peines ou traitements cruels, in-
humains ou dégradants.

ARTICLE 6. Chacun a le droit à la reconnaissance
en tous lieux de sa personnalité juridique.

gleich an Würde und Rechten geboren. Sie
sind mit Vernunft und Gewissen begabt
und sollen einander im Geiste der Brü-
derlichkeit begegnen.

ARTIKEL 2. Jeder Mensch hat Anspruch
auf die in dieser Erklärung verkündeten
Rechte und Freiheiten ohne irgendeine Unterscheidung, wie etwa nach Rasse, Farbe, Ge-
schlecht, Sprache, Religion, politischer oder
sonstiger Überzeugung, nationaler oder
sozialer Herkunft, nach Eigentum, Geburt oder
sonstigen Umständen.

Weiters darf keine Unterscheidung gemacht werden auf Grund der politischen,
rechtlichen oder internationalen Stellung
des Landes oder Gebietes, dem eine Person
angehört, ohne Rücksicht darauf, ob es unabhängig ist, unter Treuhandschaft steht,
keine Selbstregierung besitzt oder irgend-
einer anderen Beschränkung seiner Souve-
ränität unterworfen ist.

ARTIKEL 3. Jeder Mensch hat das Recht auf
Leben, Freiheit und Sicherheit der Person.

ARTIKEL 4. Niemand darf in Sklaverei oder
Leibeigenschaft gehalten werden; Sklaverei
und Sklavenhandel sind in allen ihren Formen verboten.

ARTIKEL 5. Niemand darf der Folter oder
grausamer, unmenschlicher oder erniedrigen-
der Behandlung oder Strafe unterworfen
werden.

ARTICULO 1. Todos los seres humanos nacen
libres e iguales en dignidad y derechos
y, dotados como están de razón y conciencia, deben comportare fraternalmente los
unos con los otros.

ACRTICULO 2. Toda persona tiene todos
los derechos y libertades proclamados en
esta Declaración , sin distinción alguna de
raza, color, sexo, idioma, religión, opinión
política o de cualquier otra índole, origen
nacional o social, posición económica, naci-
miento o cualquier otra condición.

Además, no se hará distinción alguna
fundada en la condición política, jurídica o
internacional del país o territorio de cuya
jurisdicción dependa una persona, tanto si
se trata de un país independiente, como
de un territorio bajo administración fidu-
ciaria, no autónomo o sometido a cualquier
otra limitación de soberanía.

ARTICULO 3. Todo individuo tiene derecho
a la vida, a la libertad y a la seguridad de
su persona.

ARTICULO 4. Nadie estará sometido a esclavitud ni a servidumbre; la esclavitud y
la trata de esclavos están prohibidas en
todas sus formas.

ARTICULO 5. Nadie será sometido a tortu-
ras ni a penas o tratos crueles, inhumanos
o degradantes.

387

to equal protection of the law. All are
entitled to equal protection against any
discrimination in violation of this
Declaration and against any incitement
to such discrimination.

ARTICLE 8. Everyone has the right to an
effective remedy by the competent national
tribunals for acts violating the fundamental rights granted him by the constituion
or by law.

ARTICLE 9. No one shall be subjected to
arbitrary arrest, detention or exile.

ARTICLE 10. Everyone is entitled in full
equality to a fair and public hearing by
an independent and impartial tribunal, in
the determination of his rights and obligations and of any criminal charge against
him.

ARTICLE 11 (1) Everyone charged with
a penal offence has the right to be
presumed innocent until proved guilty
according to law in a public trial at
which he has had all the guarantees
necessary for his defence.

(2) No one shall be held guilty of any
penal offence on account of any act or
omission which did not constitute a penal
offence, under national or international
law, at the time when it was committed.
Nor shall a heavier penalty be imposed
than the one that was applicable at
the time the penal offence was committed.

ARTICLE 7. Tous sont égaux devant la loi et
ont droit sans distinction à une égale protection de la loi. Tous ont droit à une
protection égale contre toute discrimination
qui violerait la présente Déclaration et
contre toute provocation à une telle
discrimination.

ARTICLE 8. Toute personne a droit à un recours
effectif devant les juridictions nationales
compétentes contre les actes violant les droits
fondamentaux qui lui sont reconnu par la
constitution ou par la loi.

ARTICLE 9. Nul ne peut être arbitrairement
arrêté, détenu ou exilé.

ARTICLE 10. Toute personne a droit, en pleine
égalité, à ce que sa cause soit entendue
équitablement et publiquement par un tribunal
indépendant et impartial, qui décidera, soit
de ses droits et obligations, soit du bien-
fondé de toute accusation en matière pénale
dirigée contre elle.

ARTICLE 11. (1) Toute personne accusée d'
un acte délictueux est présumée innocente
jusqu'à ce que sa culpabilité ait été lé-
galement établie au cours d'un procès public
où toutes les garanties nécessaires à sa défense lui auront été assurées.

(2) Nul ne sera condamné pour des actions ou
omissions qui, au moment où elles ont été
commises, ne constituaient pas un acte
délictueux d'après le droit national ou
international. De même, il ne sera infligé

ARTIKEL 6. Jeder Mensch hat überall
Anspruch auf Anerkennung als Rechtsperson.

ARTIKEL 7. Alle Menschen sind vor dem
Gesetze gleich und haben ohne Unterschied
Anspruch auf gleichen Schutz durch das Gesetz. Alle haben Anspruch auf gleichen
Schutz gegen jede unterschiedliche Behandlung, welche die vorliegende Erklärung verletzen würde, und gegen jede Auf-
reizung zu einer derartigen unterschied-
lichen Behandlung.

ARTIKEL 8. Jeder Mensch hat Anspruch auf
wirksamen Rechtsschutz vor den zustän-
digen innerstaatlichen Gerichten gegen alle
Handlungen, die seine ihm nach der Verfassung oder nach dem Gesetz zustehenden
Grundrechte verletzen.

ARTIKEL 9. Niemand darf willkürlich
festgenommen, in Haft gehalten oder des
Landes verwiesen werden.

ARTIKEL 1o. Jeder Mensch hat in voller
Gleichberechtigung Anspruch auf ein der
Billigkeit entsprechendes und öffent-
liches Verfahren vor einem unabhängi-
gen und unparteiischen Gericht, das
über seine Rechte und Verpflichtungen
oder über irgendeine gegen ihn er-
hobene strafrechtliche Beschuldigung
zu entscheiden hat.

ARTIKEL 11. (1) Jeder Mensch, der einer
straf

ARTICULO 6. Todo ser humano tiene derecho, en todas partes, al reconocimiento de
su personalidad jurídica.

ARTICULO 7. Todos son iguales ante la ley
y tienen, sin distinción, derecho a igual
protección de la ley. Todos tienen derecho
a igual protección contra toda discriminación que infrinja esta Declaración y contra
toda provocación a tal discriminación.

ARTICULO 8. Toda persona tiene derecho a
un recurso efectivo, ante los tribunales nacionales competentes, que la ampare contra
actos que violen sus derechos fundamentales
reconocidos por la constitución o por la ley.

ARTICULO 9. Nadie podrá ser arbitrariamente detenido, preso ni desterrado.

ARTICULO 1o. Toda persona tiene derecho,
en condiciones de plena igualdad, a ser oída
públicamente y con justicia por un tribunal
independiente e imparcial, para la determi-
nación de sus derechos y obligaciones o
para el examen de cualquier acusación contra ella en materia penal.

ARTICULO 11. 1. Toda persona acusada de
delito tiene derecho a que se presuma su
inocencia mientras no se pruebe su culpa-
bilidad, conforme a la ley y en juicio público en el que se le hayan asegurado todas las garantías necesarias para sa defensa.

2. Nadie será condenado por actos u omi-

389

ARTICLE 12. No one shall be subjected to
arbitrary interference with his privacy,
family, home or correspondence, nor to
attacks upon his honour and reputation.
Everyone has the right to the protection
of the law against such interference or
attacks.

ARTICLE 13. (1) Everyone has the right
to freedom of movement and residence
within the borders of each state.

(2) Everyone has the right to leave any
country, including his own, and to return
to his country.

ARTICLE 14. (1) Everyone has the right
to seek and to enjoy in other countries
asylum from persecution.

(2) This right may not be invoked in
the case of prosecutions genuinely
arising from non political crimes or
from acts contrary to the purposes
and principles of the United Nations.

ARTICLE 15. (1) Everyone has the right
to a nationality.

(2) No one shall be arbitrarily deprived
of his nationality nor denied the right to
change his nationality.

ARTICLE 16. (1) Men and women of full
age, without any limitation due to race,
nationality or religion, have the right
to marry and to found a family. They are

aucune peine plus forte que celle qui
était applicable au moment où l'acte
délictueux a été commis.

ARTICLE 12. Nul ne sera l'objet d'immixtions
arbitraires dans sa vie privée, sa famille,
son domicile ou sa correspondance, ni
d'atteintes a son honneur et à sa répu-
tation. Toute personne à droit à la protection de la loi contre de telles immixtions
ou de telles atteintes.

ARTICLE 13. (1) Toute personne a le droit
de circuler librement et de choisir sa résidence à l'intérieur d'un Etat.

(2) Toute personne a le droit de quitter
tout pays, y compris le sien, et de revenir
dans son pays.

ARTICLE 14. (1) Devant la persécution, toute
personne a le droit de chercher asile et
de bénéficier de l'asile en d'autres pays.

(2) Ce droit ne peut être invoqué dans le
cas de poursuites réellement fondées sur
un crime de droit commun ou sur des agisse-
ment contraires aux buts et aux principes
des Nations Unies.

ARTICLE 15. (1) Tout individu a droit à
une nationalité.

(2) Nul ne peut être arbitrairement privé de
sa nationalité, ni du droit de changer de
nationalité.

ist so lange als unschuldig anzusehen, bis
seine Schuld in einem öffentlichen Verfahren, in dem alle für seine Verteidigung
nötigen Voraussetzungen gewährleistet
waren, gemäss dem Gesetz nachgewiesen ist.

(2) Niemand kann wegen einer Handlung
oder Unterlassung verurteilt werden, die
im Zeitpunkt, da sie erfolgte, auf Grund
des nationalen oder internationalen Recht
nicht strafbar war. Desgleichen kann keine
schwerere Strafe verhängt werden als die,
welche im Zeitpunkt der Begehung der straf-
baren Handlung anwendbar war.

ARTIKEL 12. Niemand darf willkürlichen
Eingriffen in sein Privatleben, seine
Familie, sein Heim oder seinen Brief-
wechsel noch Angriffen auf seine Ehre
und seinen Ruf ausgesetzt werden. Jeder
Mensch hat Anspruch auf rechtlichen
Schutz gegen derartige Eingriffe oder
Anschläge.

ARTIKEL 13. (1) Jeder Mensch hat das
Recht auf Freizügigkeit und freie
Wahl seines Wohnsitzes innerhalb eines
Staates.

(2) Jeder Mensch hat das Recht, jedes Land,
einschliesslich seines eigenen, zu ver-
lassen sowie in sein Land zurückzu-
kehren.

ARTIKEL 14. (1) Jeder Mensch hat das
Recht, in anderen Ländern vor Verfolgun-
gen Asyl zu suchen und zu geniessen.

siones que en el momento de cometerse no
fueron delictivos según el Derecho nacional
o internacional. Tampoco se impondrá pena
más grave que la aplicable en el momento
de la comisión del delito.

ARTICULO 12. Nadie será objeto de ingerencias arbitrarias en su vida privada, su
familia, su domicilio o su correspondencia,
ni de ataques a su honra o a su reputación.
Toda persona tiene derecho a la protección
de la ley contra tales ingerencias o ataques.

ARTICULO 13. 1. Toda persona tiene derecho
a circular libremente y a elegir su re-
sidencia en el territorio de un Estado.

2. Toda persona tiene derecho a salir de
cualquier país, incluso del propio, y a re-
gresar a su país.

ARTICULO 14. 1. En caso de persecución,
toda persona tiene derecho a buscar asilo,
y a disfrutar de él,en cualquier país.

2. Este derecho no podrá ser invocado contra una acción judicial realmente originada
por delitos communes o por actos opuestos a
los propósitos y principios de las Naciones
Unidas.

ARTICULO 15. 1. Toda persona tiene derecho a una nacionalidad.

2. A nadie se privará arbitrariamente de su
nacionalidad ni del derecho a cambiar de
nacionalidad.

entitled to equal rights as to marriage, during marriage and at its dissolution.

(2) Marriage shall be entered into only with the free and full consent of the intending spouses.

(3) The family is the natural and fundamental group unit of society and is entitled to protection by society and the State.

ARTICLE 17. (1) Everyone has the right to own property alone as well as in association with others.

(2) No one shall be arbitrarily deprived of his property.

ARTICLE 18. Everyone has the right to freedom of thought, conscience and religion; this right includes freedom to change his religion or belief, and freedom, either alone or in community with others and in public or private, to manifest his religion or belief in teaching, practice, worship and observance.

ARTICLE 19. Everyone has the right to freedom of opinion and expression; this right includes freedom to hold opinions without interference and to seek, receive and impart information and ideas through any media and regardless of frontiers.

ARTICLE 16. (1) A partir de l'âge nubile, l'homme et la femme, sans aucune restriction quant à la race, la nationalité ou la religion, ont le droit de se marier et de fonder une famille. Ils ont des droits égaux au regard du mariage, durant le mariage et lors de sa dissolution.

(2) Le mariage ne peut être conclu qu'avec le libre et plein consentement des futurs époux.

(3) La famille est l'élément naturel et fondamental de la société et a droit à la protection de la société et de l'Etat.

ARTICLE 17. (1) Toute personne, aussi bien seule qu'en collectivité, a droit à la propriété.

(2) Nul ne peut être arbitrairement privé de sa propriété.

ARTICLE 18. Toute personne a droit à la liberté de pensée, de conscience et de religion; ce droit implique la liberté de changer de religion ou de conviction ainsi que la liberté de manifester sa religion ou sa conviction seule ou en commun, tant en public qu'en privé, par l'enseignement, les pratiques, le culte et l'accomplissement des rites.

ARTICLE 19. Tout individu a droit à la liberté d'opinion et d'expression, ce qui implique le droit de ne pas être inquiété

(2) Dieses Recht kann jedoch im Falle
einer Verfolgung wegen nichtpolitischer
Verbrechen oder wegen Handlungen, die
gegen die Ziele und Grundsätze der Vereinten Nationen verstossen, nicht in
Anspruch genommen werden.

ARTIKEL 15. (1) Jeder Mensch hat Anspruch auf eine Staatsangehörigkeit.

(2) Niemandem darf seine Staatsangehörigkeit willkürlich entzogen noch
ihm das Recht versagt werden, seine
Staatsangehörigkeit zu wechseln.

ARTIKEL 16. (1) Heiratsfähige Männer
und Frauen haben ohne Beschränkung durch
Rasse, Staatsbürgerschaft oder Religion das Recht, eine Ehe zu schlies-
sen und eine Familie zu gründen. Sie
haben bei der Eheschliessung, während
der Ehe und bei deren Auflösung gleiche
Rechte.

(2) Die Ehe darf nur auf Grund der
freien und vollen Willenseinigung der
zukünftigen Ehegatten geschlossen werden.

(3) Die Familie ist die natürliche und
grundlegende Einheit der Gesellschaft
und hat Anspruch auf Schutz durch Gesellschaft und Staat.

ARTIKEL 17. (1) Jeder Mensch hat allein
oder in Gemeinschaft mit anderen Recht
auf Eigentum.

ARTICULO 16. 1. Los hombres y las mujeres, a partir de la edad núbil, tienen derecho,
sin restricción alguna por motivos de raza,
nacionalidad o religión, a casarse y fundar
una familia; y disfrutarán de iguales derechos en cuanto al matrimonio, durante el
matrimonio y en caso de disolución del
matrimonio.

2. Sólo mediante libre y pleno consenti-
miento de los futuros esposos podrá contra-
erse el matrimonio.

3. La familia es el elemento natural y fundamental de la sociedad y tiene derecho a
la protección de la sociedad y del Estado.

ARTICULO 17. 1. Toda persona tiene derecho a la propiedad, individual y colectiva-
mente.

2. Nadie será privado arbitrariamente de su
propiedad.

ARTICULO 18. Toda persona tiene derecho
a la libertad de pensamiento, de conciencia y de religión; este derecho incluye la
libertad de cambiar de religión o de creencia, así como la libertad de manifestar su
religión o su creencia, individual y colecti-
vamente, tanto en público como en privado,
por la enseñanza, la prática, el culto y la
observancia.

ARTICULO 19. Todo individuo tiene derecho a la libertad de opinión y de expresión;
este derecho incluye el de no ser molestado

ARTICLE 20. (1) Everyone has the right
to freedom of peaceful assembly and association.

(2) No one may be compelled to belong to
an association.

ARTICLE 21. (1) Everyone has the right
to take part in the government of his
country, directly or through freely
chosen representatives.

(2) Everyone has the right to equal access
to public service in his country.

(3) The will of the people shall be the
basis of the authority of government; this
will shall be expressed in periodic and
genuine elections which shall be by universal and equal suffrage and shall be held
by secret vote or by equivalent free
voting procedures.

ARTICLE 22. Everyone, as a member of
society, has the right to social security,
and is entitled to realization, through
national effort and international co-operation and in accordance with the organization and resources of each State, of
the economic, social and cultural rights
indispensable for his dignity and the
free development of his personality.

ARTICLE 23. (1) Everyone has the right
to work, to free choice of employment, to
just and favourable conditions of work and
to protection against unemployment.

pour ses opinions et celui de chercher,
de recevoir et de répandre, sans considérations
de frontières, les informations et les idées
par quelque moyen d'expression que ce soit.

ARTICLE 20. (1) Toute personne a droit à
la liberté de réunion et d'association
pacifiques.

(2) Nul ne peut être obligé de faire partie
d'une association.

ARTICLE 21. (1) Toute personne a le droit de
prendre part à la direction des affaires
publiques de son pays, soit directement,
soit par l'intermédiaire de représentants
librement choisis.

(2) Toute personne a droit à accéder, dans
des conditions d'égalité, aux fonctions
publiques de son pays.

(3) La volonté du peuple est le fondement de
l'autorité des pouvoirs publics; cette
volonté doit s'exprimer par des élections
honnêtes qui doivent avoir lieu périodique-
ment, au suffrage universel égal et au vote
secret ou suivant une procédure équivalente
assurant la liberté du vote.

ARTICLE 22. Toute personne, en tant que
membre de la société, a droit à la sécurité
sociale; elle est fondée à obtenir la
satisfaction des droits économiques, sociaux
et culturels indispensables à sa dignité
et au libre développement de sa personnalité
grâce à l'effort national et à la coopération

(2) Niemand darf willkürlich seines Eigentums beraubt werden.

ARTIKEL 18. Jeder Mensch hat Anspruch auf Gedanken-, Gewissens- und Religionsfreiheit; dieses Recht umfasst die Freiheit, seine Religion oder seine Überzeugung zu wechseln, sowie die Freiheit, seine Religion oder seine Überzeugung allein oder in Gemeinschaft mit anderen, in der Öffentlichkeit oder privat, durch Lehre, Ausübung, Gottesdienst und Vollziehung von Riten zu bekunden.

ARTIKEL 19. Jeder Mensch hat das Recht auf freie Meinungsäusserung; dieses Recht umfasst die Freiheit, Meinungen unangefochten anzuhängen und Informationen und Ideen mit allen Verständigungsmitteln ohne Rücksicht auf Grenzen zu suchen, zu empfangen und zu verbreiten.

ARTIKEL 20. (1) Jeder Mensch hat das Recht auf Versammlungs- und Vereinigungsfreiheit zu friedlichen Zwecken.

(2) Niemand darf gezwungen werden, einer Vereinigung anzugehören.

ARTIKEL 21. (1) Jeder Mensch hat das Recht, an der Leitung der öffentlichen Angelegenheiten seines Landes unmittelbar oder durch frei gewählte Vertreter teilzunehmen.

(2) Jeder Mensch hat unter gleichen Bedingungen das Recht auf Zulassung zu öffentlichen Ämtern in seinem Lande.

a causa de sus opiniones, el de investigar y recibir informaciones y opiniones, y el de difundirlas, sin limitación de fronteras, por cualquier medio de expresión.

ARTICULO 20. 1. Toda persona tiene derecho a la libertad de reunión y de asociación pacíficas.

2. Nadie podrá ser obligado a pertenecer a una asociación.

ARTICULO 21. 1. Toda persona tiene derecho a participar en el gobierno de su país, directamente o por medio de representantes libremente escogidos.

2. Toda persona tiene el derecho de acceso, en condiciones de igualdad, a las funciones públicas de su país.

3. La voluntad del pueblo es la base de la autoridad del poder público; esta voluntad se expresará mediante elecciones auténticas que habrán de celebrarse periódicamente, por sufragio universal e igual y por voto secreto u otro procedimiento equivalente que garantice la libertad del voto.

ARTICULO 22. Toda persona, como miembro de la sociedad, tiene derecho a la seguridad social, y a obtener, mediante el esfuerzo nacional y la cooperación internacional, habida cuenta de la organización y los recursos de cada Estado, la satisfacción de los derechos económicos, sociales y culturales, indispensables a su dignidad y al libre

(2) Everyone, without any discrimination, has the right to equal pay for equal work.

(3) Everyone who works has the right to just and favourable remuneration ensuring for himself and his family an existence worthy of human dignity, and supplemented, if necessary, by other means of social protection.

(4) Everyone has the right to form and to join trade unions for the protection of his interests.

ARTICLE 24. Everyone has the right to rest and leisure, including reasonable limitation of working hours and periodic holidays with pay.

ARTICLE 25. (1) Everyone has the right to a standard of living adequate for the health and well-being of himself and his family, including food, clothing, housing and medical care and necessary social services, and the right to security in the event of unemployment, sickness, disability, widowhood, old age or other lack of livelihood in circumstances beyond his control.

(2) Motherhood and childhood are entitled to special care and assistance. All children, whether born in or out of wedlock, shall enjoy the same social protection.

ARTICLE 26. (1) Everyone has the right

internationale, compte tenu de l'organisation et des ressources de chaque pays.

ARTICLE 23. (1) Toute personne a droit au travail, au libre choix de son travail, à des conditions équitables et satisfaisantes de travail et à la protection contre le chômage.

(2) Tous ont droit, sans aucune discrimination, à un salaire égal pour un travail égal.

(3) Quiconque travaille a droit a une rémunération équitable et satisfaisante lui assurant ainsi qu'à sa famille une existence conforme à la dignité humaine et complétée, s'il y a lieu, par tous autres moyens de protection sociale.

(4) Toute personne a le droit de fonder avec d'autres des syndicats et de s'affilier à des syndicats pour la défense de ses intérêts.

ARTICLE 24. Toute personne a droit au repos et aux loisirs et notamment à une limitation raisonnable de la durée du travail et à des congés payés périodiques.

ARTICLE 25. (1) Toute personne a droit à un niveau de vie suffisant pour assurer sa santé, son bien-être et ceux de sa famille, notamment pour l'alimentation, l'habillement, le logement, les soins médicaux ainsi que pour les services sociaux nécessaires; elle a droit à la sécurité en cas de chômage, de maladie, d'invalidité, de veuvage, de vieillesse ou dans les autres

(3) Der Wille des Volkes bildet die Grundlage für die Autorität der öffentlichen Gewalt; dieser Wille muss durch periodische und unverfälschte Wahlen mit allgemeinem und gleichem Wahlrecht bei geheimer Stimmabgabe oder in einem gleichwertigen freien Wahlverfahren zum Ausdruck kommen.

ARTIKEL 22. Jeder Mensch hat als Mitglied der Gesellschaft Recht auf soziale Sicherheit; er hat Anspruch darauf, durch innerstaatliche Massnahmen und internationale Zusammenarbeit unter Berücksichtigung der Organisation und der Hilfsmittel jedes Staates in den Genuss der für seine Würde und die freie Entwicklung seiner Persönlichkeit unentbehrlichen wirtschaftlichen, sozialen und kulturellen Rechte zu gelangen.

ARTIKEL 23. (1) Jeder Mensch hat das Recht auf Arbeit, auf freie Berufswahl, auf angemessene und befriedigende Arbeitsbedingungen sowie auf Schutz gegen Arbeitslosigkeit.

(2) Alle Menschen haben ohne jede unterschiedliche Behandlung das Recht auf gleichen Lohn für gleiche Arbeit.

(3) Jeder Mensch, der arbeitet, hat das Recht auf angemessene und befriedigende Entlohnung, die ihm und seiner Familie eine der menschlichen Würde entsprechende Existenz sichert und die, wenn nötig, durch andre soziale Schutzmassnahmen zu ergänzen ist.

desarrollo de su personalidad.

ARTICULO 23. 1. Toda persona tiene derecho al trabajo, al la libre elección de su trabajo, a condiciones equitativas y satisfactorias de trabajo y a la protección contra el desempleo.

2. Toda persona tiene derecho, sin discriminación alguna, a igual salario por trabajo igual.

3. Toda persona que trabaja tiene derecho a una remuneración equitativa y satisfactoria, que le asegure, así como a su familia, una existencia conforme a la dignidad humana y que será completada, en caso necesario, por cualesquiera otros medios de protección social.

4. Toda persona tiene derecho a fundar sindicatos y a sindicarse para la defensa de sus intereses.

ARTICULO 24. Toda persona tiene derecho al descanso, al disfrute del tiempo libre, a una limitación razonable de la duración del trabajo y a vacaciones periódicas pagadas.

ARTICULO 25. 1. Toda persona tiene derecho a un nivel de vida adecuado que le asegure, así como a su familia, la salud y el bienestar, y en especial la alimentación, el vestido, la vivienda, la asistencia médica y los servicios sociales necesarios; tiene asimismo derecho a los seguros en caso de desempleo, enfermedad, invalidez, viudez,

to education. Education shall be free,
at least in the elementary and fundamental
stages. Elementary education shall be
compulsory. Technical and professional
education shall be made generally available
and higher education shall be equally
accessible to all on the basis of merit.

(2) Education shall be directed to the
full development of the human personality
and to the strengthening of respect for
human rights and fundamental freedoms.
It shall promote understanding, tolerance
and friendship among all nations, racial or
religious groups, and shall further the
activities of the United Nations for the
maintenance of peace.

(3) Parents have a prior right to choose
the kind of education that shall be given
to their children.

ARTICLE 27. (1) Everyone has the right
freely to participate in the cultural life
of the community, to enjoy the arts and to
share in scientific advancement and its
benefits.

(2) Everyone has the right to the protection of the moral and material interests
resulting from any scientific, literary or
artistic production of which he is the
author.

ARTICLE 28. Everyone is entitled to a social
and international order in which the rights
and freedoms set forth in this Declaration

cas de perte de ses moyens de subsistance
par suite de circonstances indépendantes de
sa volonté.

(2) La maternité et l'enfance ont droit à
une aide et à une assistance spéciales. Tous
les enfants, qu'ils soient nés dans le mariage
ou hors mariage, jouissent de la même protection sociale.

ARTICLE 26. (1) Toute personne a droit à
l'éducation. L'éducation doit être gratuite,
au moins en ce qui concerne l'enseignement
élémentaire et fondamental. L'enseignement
élémentaire est obligatoire. L'enseignement
technique et professionnel doit être géné-
ralisé; l'accès aux études supérieures doit
être ouvert en pleine égalité à tous en
fonction de leur mérite.

(2) L'éducation doit viser au plein épanouisse-
ment de la personnalité humaine et au renforcement du respect des droits de l'homme et des
libertés fondamentales. Elle doit favoriser
la compréhension, la tolérance et l'amitié
entre toutes les nations et tous les groupes
raciaux ou religieux, ainsi que le développement des activités des Nations Unies
pour le maintien de la paix.

(3) Les parents ont, par priorité, le droit
de choisir le genre d'éducation à donner
à leurs enfants.

ARTICLE 27. (1) Toute personne a le droit
de prendre part librement à la vie culturelle
de la communauté, de jouir des arts et de

(4) Jeder Mensch hat das Recht, zum
Schutze seiner Interessen Berufsvereini-
gungen zu bilden und solchen beizutreten.

ARTIKEL 24. Jeder Mensch hat Anspruch auf
Erholung und Freizeit sowie auf eine ver-
nünftige Begrenzung der Arbeitszeit und
auf periodischen, bezahlten Urlaub.

ARTIKEL 25. (1) Jeder Mensch hat Anspruch
auf eine Lebenshaltung, die seine und
seiner Familie Gesundheit und Wohlbefinden,
einschliesslich Nahrung, Kleidung, Wohnung,
ärztlicher Betreuung und der notwendigen
Leistungen der sozialen Fürsorge, gewährleistet; er hat das Recht auf Sicherheit
im Falle von Arbeitslosigkeit, Krankheit,
Invalidität, Verwitwung, Alter oder von
andererweitigem Verlust seiner Unterhalts-
mittel durch unverschuldete Umstände.

(2) Mutter und Kind haben Anspruch auf besondere Hilfe und Unterstützung. Alle
Kinder, eheliche und uneheliche, geniessen
den gleichen sozialen Schutz.

ARTIKEL 26. (1) Jeder Mensch hat das Recht
auf Bildung. Der Unterricht muss wenigstens
in den Elementar- und Grundschulen unent-
geltlich sein. Der Elementarunterricht ist
obligatorisch. Fachlicher und beruflicher
Unterricht soll allgemein zugänglich
sein; die höheren Studien sollen allen
nach Massgabe ihrer Fähigkeiten und
Leistungen in gleicher Weise offen stehen.

(2) Die Ausbildung soll die volle Ent-

vejez u otros casos de pérdida de sus medios
de subsistencia por circunstancias independientes de su voluntad.

2. La maternidad y la infancia tienen derecho a cuidados y asistencia especiales. Todos
los niños, nacidos de matrimonio o fuera
de matrimonio, tienen derecho a igual protección social.

ARTICULO 26. 1. Toda persona tiene derecho a la educación. La educación debe ser
gratuita, al menos en lo concerniente a la
instrucción elemental y fundamental. La
instrucción elemental será obligatoria. La
instrucción técnica y profesional habrá de
ser generalizada; el acceso a los estudios
superiores será igual para todos, en fun-
ción de los méritos respectivos.

2. La educación tendrá por objeto el pleno
desarrollo de la personalidad humana y el
fortalecimiento del respeto a los derechos
humanos y a las libertades fundamentales;
favorecerá la comprensión, la tolerancia y
la amistad entre todas las naciones y todos
los grupos étnicos o religiosos; y promoverá
el desarrollo de las actividades de las
Naciones Unidas para el mantenimiento de
la paz.

3. Los padres tendrán derecho preferente a
escoger el tipo de educación que habrá de
darse a sus hijos.

ARTICULO 27. 1. Toda persona tiene derecho a tomar parte libremente en la vida cul-

399

can be fully realized.

ARTICLE 29. (1) Everyone has duties to the community in which alone the free and full development of his personality is possible.

(2) In the exercise of his rights and freedoms, everyone shall be subject only to such limitations as are determined by law solely for the purpose of securing due recognition and respect for the rights and freedoms of others and of meeting the just requirements of morality , public order and the general welfare in a democratic society.

(3) These rights and freedoms may in no case be exercised contrary to the purposes and principles of the United Nations.

ARTICLE 30. Nothing in this Declaration may be interpreted as implying for any State, group or person any right to engage in any activity or to perform any act aimed at the destruction of any of the rights and freedoms set forth herein.

Declaration adopted by the General Assembly of the United Nations, 10 December, 1948

participer au progrès scientifique et aux bienfaits qui en résultent.

(2) Chacun a droit à la protection des intérêts moraux et matériels découlant de toute production scientifique, littéraire ou artistique dont il est l'auteur.

ARTICLE 28. Toute personne a droit à ce que règne, sur le plan social et sur le plan international, un ordre tel que les droits et libertés énoncés dans la présente Déclaration puissent y trouver plein effet.

ARTICLE 29. (1) L'individu a des devoirs envers la communauté dans laquelle seule le libre et plein développement de sa personnalité est possible.

(2) Dans l'exercice de ses droits et dans la jouissance de ses libertés, chacun n'est soumis qu'aux limitations établies par la loi exclusivement en vue d'assurer la reconnaissance et le respect des droits et libertés d'autrui et afin de satisfaire aux justes exigences de la morale, de l'ordre public et du bien-être général dans une société démocratique.

(3) Ces droits et libertés ne pourront, en aucun cas, s'exercer contrairement aux buts et aux principes des Nations Unies.

ARTICLE 30. Aucune disposition de la présente Déclaration ne peut être interprétée comme impliquant pour un Etat, un

faltung der menschlichen Persönlichkeit
und die Stärkung der Achtung der Menschenrechte und Grundfreiheiten zum Ziele haben.
Sie soll Verständnis, Duldsamkeit und Freund-
schaft zwischen allen Nationen und allen
rassischen oder religiösen Gruppen fördern
und die Tätigkeit der Vereinten Nationen
zur Aufrechterhaltung des Friedens be-
günstigen.

(3) In erster Linie haben die Eltern das
Recht, die Art der ihren Kindern zuteil
werdenden Bildung zu bestimmen.

ARTIKEL 27. (1) Jeder Mensch hat das Recht,
am kulturellen Leben der Gemeinschaft frei
teilzunehmen, sich der Künste zu erfreuen
und am wissenschaftlichen Fortschritt und
dessen Wohltaten teilzuhaben.

(2) Jeder Mensch hat das Recht auf Schutz
der moralischen und materiellen Interessen,
die sich aus jeder wissenschaftlichen,
literarischen oder künstlerischen Pro-
duktion ergeben, deren Urheber er ist.

ARTIKEL 28. Jeder Mensch hat Anspruch auf
eine soziale und internationale Ordnung, in
welcher die in der vorliegenden Erklärung
 angeführten Rechte und Freiheiten voll
verwirklicht werden können.

ARTIKEL 29. (1) Jeder Mensch hat Pflichten
gegenüber der Gemeinschaft, in der allein
die freie und volle Entwicklung seiner
Persönlichkeit möglich ist.

tural de la communidad, a gozar de las artes
y a participar en el progreso científico y
en los beneficios que de él resulten.

2. Toda persona tiene derecho a la protección de los intereses morales y materiales
que le correspondan por razón de las pro-
ducciones científicas, literarias o artísticas
de que sea autora.

ARTICULO 28. Toda persona tiene derecho
a que se establezca un orden social e internacional en el que los derechos y libertades
proclamados en esta Declaración se hagan
plenamente efectivos.

ARTICULO 29. 1. Toda persona tiene debe-
res respecto a la communidad puesto que sólo
en ella puede desarrollar libre y plenamente su personalidad.

2. En el ejercicio de sus derechos y en el
disfrute de sus libertades, toda persona
estará solamente sujeta a las limitaciones
establecidas por la ley con el único fin de
asegurar el reconocimiento y el respeto de
los derechos y libertades de los demás, y
de satisfacer las justas exigencias de la
moral, del orden público y del bienestar
general en una sociedad democrática.

3. Estos derechos y libertades no podrán
en ningún caso, ser ejercidos en oposición
a los propósitos y principios de las Naciones Unidas.

401

groupement ou un individu un droit
quelconque de se livrer à une activité
ou d'accomplir un acte visant à la destruction
des droits et libertés qui y sont énoncés.

Déclaration adoptée le 10 décembre 1948
par l'Assemblée générale des Nations Unies

(2) Jeder Mensch ist in Ausübung seiner
Rechte und Freiheiten nur den Beschrän-
kungen unterworfen, die das Gesetz aus-
schliesslich zu dem Zwecke vorsieht, um
die Anerkennung und Achtung der Rechte und
Freiheiten der anderen zu gewährleisten
und den gerechten Anforderungen der Moral,
der öffentlichen Ordnung und der allgemeinen Wohlfahrt in einer demokratischen
Gesellschaft zu genügen.

(3) Rechte und Freiheiten dürfen in keinem
Fall im Widerspruch zu den Zielen und
Grundsätzen der Vereinten Nationen ausge-
übt werden.

ARTIKEL 30. Keine Bestimmung der vorliegenden Erklärung darf so ausgelegt
werden, dass sich daraus für einen Staat,
eine Gruppe oder eine Person irgendein
Recht ergibt, eine Tätigkeit auszuüben oder
eine Handlung zu setzen, welche auf die
Vernichtung der in dieser Erklärung
angeführten Rechte und Freiheiten ab-
zielen.

Die Erklärung wurde von der Generalversammlung der Vereinten Nationen am
10. Dezember 1948 angenommen

ARTICULO 30. Nada en la presente Declaración podrá interpretarse en el sentido de
que confiere derecho alguno al Estado, a
un grupo o a una persona, para emprender
y desarrollar actividades o realizar actos
tendientes a la supresión de cualquiera de
los derechos y libertades proclamados en
esta Declaración.

Declaración adoptada el 10 de diciembre
de 1948 por la Asamblea General de las
Naciones Unidas

unmarried mother - <u>See</u> <u>under</u>: <u>h</u>ome for unmarried mothers and children

urban

1247 urban area	zone (f) urbaine	Stadtregion (f)	zona (f) urbana
1248 urban development	développement (m) urbain	Stadtentwick-lung (f)	desarrollo (m) urbano
1249 urban growth	croissance (f) urbaine	städtisches Wachstum (n)	crecimiento (m) urbano

urban planning - <u>See</u> <u>under</u>: town <u>p</u>lanning

1250 urban renewal	rénovation (f) urbaine	Stadtsanierung (f)	renovación (f) urbana
1251 urban settlements	agglomérations (fpl) urbaines	städtische Wohnge-biete (npl)	aglomeraciones (fpl) urbanas
1252 urbanization	urbanisation (f)	Urbanisierung (f), Verstädterung (f)	urbanización (f)

video-

| 1253 video-cartridge (=-cassette) | vidéo-cassette (f) | Videokassette (f) | videocassette (f) |
| 1254 video-tape | bande (f) magné-tique vidéo | Videotape (n) | cinta (f) magnetos-cópica |

1255 video-tape recorder	magnétoscope (m)	Videotaperecorder (m)	magnetoscopio (m)
violence			
1256 collective violence	violence (f) collective	kollektive Gewalt (f)	violencia (f) colectiva
1257 counter-violence	contre-violence (f)	Gegengewalt (f)	contraviolencia (f); réplica (f) a la violencia
1258 individual violence	violence (f) individuelle	individuelle Gewalt (f)	violencia (f) individual
1259 institutionalized violence	violence (f) institutionnalisée	institutionelle Gewalt (f)	violencia (f) institucionalizada
1260 psychological violence	violence (f) psychologique	psychologische Gewalt (f)	violencia (f) sicológica
1261 structural violence	violence (f) structurelle	strukturelle Gewalt (f)	violencia (f) estructural
1262 structured violence	violence (f) organisée	organisierte Gewalt (f)	violencia (f) organizada
1263 vitamin deficiency	carence (f) vitaminique	Vitaminmangel (m)	carencia (f) (=deficiencia /f/ =insuficiencia /f/) vitamínica
1264 vocational qualifications; professional qualifications	qualifications (fpl) professionnelles	berufliche Qualifikation (f)	calificaciones (fpl) profesionales

1265 voice quotes	extraits (mpl) d'enregistrement	(Tonband) Mit- schnitte (mpl)	selección (f) de grabaciones

voluntary

voluntary organization - See under: voluntary agency

1266 voluntary service organization	organisation (f) de service volon- taire	Freiwilligen- dienst-Organisa- tion (f)	organización (f) de servicio volun- tario
1267 ecumenical vo- luntary service	service (m) volon- taire oecuménique	ökumenischer Frei- willigendienst (m)	servicio (m) ecuménico voluntario
1268 horizontal approach in vo- luntary service	échange (m) hori- zontal de volon- taires (entre les pays et continents de l'hémisphère sud)	horizontaler Aus- tausch (m) von Freiwilligen (zwischen Ländern und Kontinenten der südlichen Hemisphäre)	intercambio (m) horizontal de voluntarios (entre países y continentes del hemisferio sur)
1269 volunteer	bénévole (m); volontaire (m)	Freiwilliger (m)	voluntario (m)

war

| 1270 war of attrition | guerre (f) d'usure | Zermürbungskrieg (m) | guerra (f) de desgaste |
| 1271 'just war' | "guerre juste" | "gerechter Krieg" | "guerra justa" |

warfare

1272	biological warfare	guerre (f) biologique	biologische Kriegsführung (f)	guerra (f) biológica
1273	chemical warfare	guerre (f) chimique	chemische Kriegsführung (f)	guerra (f) química

water

1274	water supply installations	installations (fpl) d'adduction (=de distribution) d'eau	Wasserversorgungs-anlagen (fpl)	instalaciones (fpl) de agua potable
1275	clean water supply	alimentation (f) en eau potable	Trinkwasserver-sorgung (f)	abastecimiento (m) de agua potable

weapons

1276	weapons of mass destruction	armes (fpl) de destruction massive	Massenvernichtungs-waffen (fpl)	armas (fpl) de destrucción en masa
1277	chemical and bacteriological (biological) weapons	armes (fpl) chimiques et bactériologiques (biologiques)	chemische und bak-teriologische (bio-logische) Waffen (fpl) (=Kampfmittel /npl/)	armas (fpl) químicas y bacteriológicas (biológicas)
1278	conventional weapons	armes (fpl) classiques (=conventionnelles)	konventionelle Waf-fen (fpl)	armas (fpl) de tipo corriente (=convencionales)
1279	defensive weapons	armes (fpl) dé-fensives	Defensivwaffen (fpl)	armas (fpl) defensivas
1280	indiscriminate weapons	armes (fpl) de nature à frapper indistinctement les	Waffen (fpl) zur unterschiedslosen Vernichtung von	armas (fpl) de destrucción total (destinadas tanto

		personnes civiles et les objectifs militaires	Zivilpersonen und militärischen Objekten	a personas como a objetivos militares)
1281	offensive weapons	armes (fpl) offensives	Offensivwaffen (fpl)	armas (fpl) ofensivas
1282	strategic weapons	armes (fpl) stratégiques	strategische Waffen (fpl)	armas (fpl) estratégicas

welfare

| 1283 | welfare organization, welfare agency, social service agency | institution (f) sociale, institution (f) d'action sociale | Wohlfahrtsverband (m) | organización (f) de asistencia social |

social welfare - See under: social

| 1284 | voluntary welfare organization | institution (f) sociale privée | freier Wohlfahrtsverband (m) | organización (f) social privada |

welfare work

1285	prison welfare work	assistance (f) aux détenus	Gefangenenbetreuung (f)	asistencia (f) penitenciaria (= a los reclusos)
1286	white, whites	blanc (m), blancs (mpl)	Weisser (m), Weisse (mpl)	blanco (m), blancos (mpl)
1287	white residence (=area) /South Africa/	zone (f) blanche /Afrique du Sud/	weisses Gebiet (n) /Südafrika/	zona (f) blanca /Sudáfrica/

1288 wholeness	1. santé (f), guérison (f), intégrité (f) physique 2. intégralité (f), indivisibilité (f), cohésion (f) (=solidarité /f/) universelle, unité (f), intégrité (f)	1. Gesundheit (f), Heilung (f), Genesung (f), körperliche Unversehrtheit (f) 2. Ganzheit (f), Unteilbarkeit (f), globaler Zusammenhang (m) (=Solidarität /f/), Einheit (f), Integrität (f)	1. salud (f), integridad (f) física 2. integridad (f), totalidad (f), indivisibilidad (f), cohesión(f)solidaridad /f/)universal, unidad (f)
1289 wholeness of human life	intégralité (f) de la vie humaine	Ganzheit (f) des menschlichen Lebens	integridad (f) de la vida humana
1290 women's liberation movement	mouvement (m) de libération de la femme (MLF)	Frauenbefreiungsbewegung (f)	movimiento (m) de liberación femenina (MLF)
1291 words of institution	paroles (fpl) d'institution	Einsetzungsworte (npl) (= -formel /f/)	palabras (fpl) de institución

work

work force - See under: active population

1292 work at home	travail (m) à domicile	Heimarbeit (f)	trabajo (m) a domicilio
1293 service work	activité (f) (oeuvre /f/) d'entraide	Hilfsdienste (mpl), Hilfstätigkeit (f)	actividad (f) de servicio
1294 shift work	travail (m) par équipe	Schichtarbeit (f)	trabajo (m) por turnos

1295	short-time work	chômage (m) partiel	Kurzarbeit (f)	paro (m) (=desem-pleo /m/) parcial; jornada (f) reducida
1296	worker	travailleur (m); ouvrier (m)	Arbeiter (m); Arbeitnehmer (m)	trabajador (m); trabajador (m) manual, obrero (m), operario (m)

1297	(1)	(1)	(1)	(1)
	unskilled worker manual worker	manoeuvre (m)	ungelernter Arbeiter (m), Hilfsarbeiter (m)	trabajador (m) sin calificación, obrero (m)
	semi-skilled worker	ouvrier (m) spécialisé	angelernter Arbeiter (m), Spezialarbeiter (m)	obrero (m) especializado
	skilled worker, craftsman	ouvrier (m) quali-fié	Facharbeiter (m), gelernter Arbeiter (m)	obrero (m) califi-cado
	(highly skilled worker)	ouvrier (m) hautement qualifié	hochqualifizierter Arbeiter (m), Meister (m), Vorarbeiter (m)	obrero (m) alta-mente calificado

(1) The gradings given here are approximate equivalents not exact trans-lations. They refer to the terms commonly used in Britain,

(1) Il n'existe pas de classification internationale des échelons profession-nels. Les hiérarchies industrielles indi-quées ici corres-pondent respectivement à la Grande-Bretagne,

(1) Eine interna-tionale Standard-klassifikation der Berufsbezeichnungen im Betrieb wurde bisher noch nicht erarbeitet. Die hier genannten Begriffsabgren-

(1) No existe nin-guna clasificación reconocida inter-nacionalmente de las especializa-ciones en el tra-bajo. Las catego-rías que aquí se indican son equi-

	France, West Germany and Spain respectively.	à la France, à la république fédérale d'Allemagne et à l'Espagne.	zungen entsprechen der in Grossbritannien, Frankreich, Spanien und der Bundesrepublik Deutschland heute üblichen Terminologie.	valentes aproximados y no traducciones exactas. Corresponden a los terminos empleados comúnmente en Gran Bretaña, Francia, la República Federal de Alemania y España respectivamente.
1298	agricultural worker	travailleur (m) agricole	Landarbeiter (m)	trabajador (m) agrícola
1299	auxiliary worker	auxiliaire (m)	Helfer (m), Hilfskraft (f); Gehilfe (m); Arzthelfer (m),/CMC/ Heilgehilfe (n), /CMC/	auxiliar (m)
1300	church worker	employé (m) d'Eglise, collaborateur (m) (auprès d'une Eglise); collaborateur (m) paroissial	kirchlicher Mitarbeiter (m)	obrero (m) de la Iglesia
1301	fraternal worker	collaborateur (m) fraternel	kirchlicher Mitarbeiter (m), "Fraternal Worker"	colaborador (m) fraternal
1302	frontier worker	frontalier (m), travailleur frontalier	Grenzarbeitnehmer (m), Grenzgänger (m) /CH/	trabajador (m) fronterizo

1303	indigenous (=national = local) worker	travailleur (m) national (=local)	einheimischer (=inländischer) Arbeitnehmer (m)	trabajador (m) nacional (=local)
1304	manual worker, blue-collar worker	travailleur (m) manuel	Arbeiter (m)	trabajador (m) manual
1305	seasonal worker	saisonnier (m), travailleur saisonnier (m)	Saisonarbeiter (m)	trabajador (m) temporero (=de temporada); trabajador (m) zafral
1306	working age population	population (f) en âge d'être active	Bevölkerung (f) im erwerbsfähigen Alter	población (f) en edad de trabajar
1307	working party	groupe (m) de travail	Arbeitsgruppe (f)	grupo (m) de trabajo
1308	Youth Working Party /Staff Working Group on Renewal/	Groupe (m) d'étude "jeunesse" /Groupe de travail "renouveau"/	Fachgruppe (f) "Jugend" /Arbeitsgruppe "Erneuerung"/	Grupo (m) de Estudio con la Juventud /Grupo de Trabajo "Renovación"/
1309	workshop	séminaire (m), stage (m) de formation pratique; atelier (m) (groupe d'études pratiques)	Seminar (n); Workshop (n), Werkkreis (m)	seminario (m) curso (m) práctico; taller (m)

world

| 1310 | world confessional body | alliance (f) confessionnelle mondiale | konfessioneller Weltbund (m) | alianza (f) confesional mundial |

1311 world confessional families	familles (fpl) confessionnelles mondiales	weltweite Bekenntnis-familien (fpl), Konfessionsfami-lien (fpl)	familias (fpl) confesionales mundiales
1312 world families of churches	familles (fpl) ecclésiales mondiales	weltweite Kirchen-familien (fpl)	familias (fpl) eclesiales mundiales
1313 world view	vision (f) (=conception /f/) du monde, cosmo-gonie (f)	Weltbild (n) (=-verständnis /n/)	concepción (f) del mundo, cosmo-visión (f)

1314 primal world views

World view is chosen in place of 'religion'
because religious systems as such may
decline or vanish altogether while much
of the religious culture with which
they have been associated may con-
tinue. It is the surviving structure of
beliefs and values, the way of life
which may be called a 'primal world
view'.

Primal is used in the sense of 'basic'
or 'fundamental'. The term is chosen
to embrace what has been referred to in
the past by a series of other terms,
each of which is unacceptable today:
e.g. preliterate, primitive, pagan,
animistic, primordial, native, ethnic,
tribal and traditional. Although by
current convention 'traditional' is
often used of indigenous African
forms, it applies equally to all
known religions, and especially to
both Islam and Christianity and is
not distinctive of the religions
of African origin only. (cf. Study
Encounter, Vol. IX, no. 4, 1973)

visions (fpl) premières du monde

Dans cette expression, le mot premier est
utilisé au sens de "fondamental". Il a
été choisi pour recouvrir tout ce que l'on
désignait autrefois par une série d'autres
adjectifs, devenus aujourd'hui inacceptables
dans ce contexte, tels que: non lettré,
primitif, païen, animiste, primordial, in-
digène, tribal, traditionnel.

Si le terme traditionnel s'utilise couram-
ment pour désigner les formes religieuses
africaines, il s'applique en fait également à toutes les religions connues, notamment à l'islam et au christianisme, et
n'est pas exclusivement réservé aux religions d'origine africaine.

Au lieu de "religions", nous avons choisi
d'utiliser l'expression visions du monde:
les systèmes religieux en tant que tels
connaissent en effet parfois le déclin,
allant même jusqu'à disparaître, alors que
la culture religieuse qui y était liée sur-
vit quant à elle dans bien de ses aspects.
Par l'expression visions du monde, nous
désignons l'ensemble des croyances et des
valeurs qui demeurent, ainsi que la manière
de vivre. (En français, on aurait pu aussi
parler d'"archétypes".) (cf. Study Encounter,
Vol. IX, No. 4, 1973)

Ursprüngliche Weltbilder (npl)

Ursprünglich (engl. primal) wird hier im
Sinne von 'grundlegend' oder 'wesentlich'
verwendet. Dieser Begriff soll all das um-
schreiben, was in der Vergangenheit mit
verschiedenen anderen Begriffen bezeichnet
wurde, die in diesem Zusammenhang heute alle
unannehmbar sind, z.B.: ohne schriftliche
Überlieferung, primitiv, heidnisch, ani-
mistisch, primordial, traditionell oder
Zusammensetzungen wie Eingeborenen-,Volks-
oder Stammes-Religionen. 'Traditionell'
wird im allgemeinen Sprachgebrauch zwar
häufig benutzt, um einheimische afrika-
nische Religionsformen zu bezeichnen, doch
trifft das Wort 'traditionell' auf alle be-
kannten Religionen, insbesondere auch auf
Islam und Christentum zu und kennzeichnet
daher nicht nur die Religionen afrikani-
schen Ursprungs.

Weltbild tritt an die Stelle von Religion,
weil Religionssysteme als solche einen
Niedergang durchmachen oder gar völlig
untergehen können,wobei vieles von der
religiösen Tradition, die mit diesen
Systemen verbunden war, fortbestehen
kann. Es ist die Gesamtheit der fortbe-
stehenden Glaubensüberzeugungen und Wert-
vorstellungen, die gesamte Lebensweise,
die man als 'ursprüngliches Weltbild'
bezeichnen kann. (aus: Study Encounter,
Vol. IX, no. 4, 1973)

Concepciones (fpl) primeras del mundo

En esta expresión, la palabra primera es
utilizada en el sentido de 'básico' o
'fundamental'. Corresponde a todo lo que
antes se designaba con una serie de
adjetivos que hoy ya no pueden ser
aceptados, tales como: iletrado, primi-
tivo, pagano, animista, nativo, étnico,
tribal y tradicional.

.cún cuando el término tradicional se
utiliza corrientemente para designar las
formas religiosas africanas, también se
aplica a todas las religiones conocidas,
en particular al islam y al cristianismo
y no es exclusivamente reservado a las
religiones africanas.

En lugar de 'religiones' se ha preferido
el empleo de la expresión concepciones
primeras del mundo: los sistemas religiosos como tales pueden decaer y hasta
desaparecer, mientras que la cultura religiosa a la que estaban asociados sobrevive
en muchos aspectos. La expresión concepción
del mundo, designa el conjunto de creencias
y valores que permanecen así como la
manera de vivir. (cf. Study Encounter,
Vol. IX, No. 4, 1973)

1315 worldliness	profanité (f), mondanité (f)	Weltlichkeit (f)	mundanalidad (f)
1316 worship	culte (m)	Gottesdienst (m)	culto (m)
1317 children's worship (=service)	culte (m) pour enfants	Kindergottesdienst (m)	culto (m) para niños (=infantil)
1318 ways of worship	formes (fpl) de culte, formes (fpl) cultuelles	Gottesdienstformen (fpl)	formas (fpl) cultuales, formas (fpl) de culto

youth

1319 youth centre, youth club	maison (f) des jeunes, club (m) de jeunes	Jugendzentrum (n)	centro (m) (= club /m/) de jóvenes (= juvenil)
1320 youth group	groupe (m) de jeunes	Jugendgruppe (f)	grupo (m) de jóvenes
1321 youth leader	animateur (m) de jeunesse	Jugendleiter (m)	dirigente (m) (=líder /m/) juvenil (=de jóvenes), animador (m) de juventud
1322 youth leadership training	formation (f) d'animateurs de jeunesse	Heranbildung (f) (=Schulung /f/) von Jugendleitern	formación (f) de dirigentes (=líderes) juveniles, formación

			de animadores de juventud
1323 youth movement	mouvement (m) de jeunesse	Jugendbewegung (f)	movimiento (m) juvenil (= de jóvenes)
1324 youth organization	organisation (f) de jeunesse	Jugendorganisation (f)	organización (f) de jóvenes
1325 youth secretary	secrétaire (m) de jeunesse	Jugendsekretär (m)	secretario (m) de juventud
1326 youth work	activité (f) (=travail /m/) de jeunesse	Jugendarbeit (f)	trabajo (m) (=actividad /f/) con la juventud
1327 youth worker	animateur (m) de jeunesse	Jugendleiter (m)	dirigente (m) (=líder /m/) juvenil (=de jóvenes), animador (m) de juventud
1328 ecumenical youth committee	comité (m) oecuménique de jeunesse	ökumenischer Jugendausschuss (m)	comité (m) ecuménico de juventud
1329 ecumenical youth coordination	coordination (f) des activités oecuméniques de jeunesse	Koordinierung (f) der ökumenischen Jugendarbeit	coordinación (f) de las actividades ecuménicas de la juventud
1330 ecumenical youth programme	programme (m) oecuménique de jeunesse	ökumenisches Jugendprogramm (n)	programa (m) ecuménico de juventud (=juvenil)

1331	ecumenical youth secretary	secrétaire (m) oecuménique de jeunesse	ökumenischer Jugendsekretär (m)	secretario (m) ecuménico de juventud
1332	National Ecumenical Youth Council	conseil (m) oecuménique national de jeunesse	nationaler ökumenischer Jugendrat (m)	consejo (m) ecuménico nacional de jóvenes
1333	Pre-Assembly Youth Conference	Conférence (f) de jeunesse préparatoire à la Cinquième Assemblée du COE	Jugendkonferenz (f) vor der Vollversammlung	Conferencia (f) de la Juventud preparatoria de la Quinta Asemblea del CMI
1334	regional youth programme	programme (m) régional de jeunesse	regionales Jugendprogramm (n)	programa (m) regional de juventud (=juvenil)
1335	Regional Youth Secretary	secrétaire (m) régional de jeunesse	regionaler Jugendsekretär (m)	secretario (m) regional de juventud

VIII (1)	VIII (1)
ABBREVIATIONS AND TITLES	**SIGLES ET TITRES**

AACC - All Africa Conference of Churches	Conférence (f) des Eglises de toute l'Afrique (CETA)
ACLD - Agency for Christian Literature Development	Organisation (f) de développement de la littérature chrétienne (ODLC)
Action Apostolique Commune	Action (f) apostolique commune
AFPRO - Action for Food Production	*Action (f) pour la production alimentaire (AFPRO)
AG-KED The Association of the Churches' Development Services	Association (f) des services de l'Eglise pour le développement (AG-KED)
Amnesty International	Amnesty International
Annual Conference of the Secretaries of World Confessional Families (=World Families of Churches)	*Conférence (f) annuelle des secrétaires des familles confessionnelles mondiales (=des familles ecclésiales mondiales)
*ASDEAR - Association for Rural Development	Association (f) pour le développement et l'animation rurale (ASDEAR)
BCC - British Council of Churches	*Conseil (m) britannique des Eglises (BCC)
*BEK - Federation of the Evangelical Churches in the German Democratic Republic	*Fédération (f) des Eglises évangéliques en République démocratique allemande (BEK)
BfdW - Bread for the World	Pain pour le monde (BfdW)

(1) See "Explanatory Note", p. 183

(1) Voir "Notice explicative", p. 183

VIII
ABKÜRZUNGEN UND TITEL (1)

*Gesamtafrikanische Kirchenkonferenz (f) (AACC)

Christlicher Entwicklungsdienst (m) für Literatur (ACLD)

*Gemeinschaftliche Apostolische Aktion (f)

*Aktion (f) für die Nahrungsmittelproduktion (AFPRO)

Arbeitsgemeinschaft (f) Kirchlicher Entwicklungsdienst (AG-KED)

Amnesty International

*Jahreskonferenz der Sekretäre der Weltweiten Bekenntnisfamilien (= der Weltweiten Kirchenfamilien)

*Vereinigung für die ländliche Entwicklung (ASDEAR)

*Britischer Rat (m) der Kirchen (BCC)

Bund (m) der Evangelischen Kirchen in der Deutschen Demokratischen Republik (BEK)

Brot für die Welt (BfdW)

(1) Siehe 'Hinweise für die Benutzung', S. 184

VIII
SIGLAS Y TITULOS (1)

*Conferencia (f) de Iglesias de toda el Africa (AACC)

Organismo (m) para el Desarrollo de la Literatura Cristiana (ODLC)

*Acción (f) Apostólica Común

*Acción (f) para la Producción de Alimentos (AFPRO)

*Asociación (f) de los Servicios de la Iglesia para el Desarrollo (AG-KED)

Amnesty International

*Conferencia (f) Anual de Secretarios de las Familias Confesionales Mundiales (=Familias Eclesiales Mundiales)

*Asociación (f) para el Desarrollo de la Comunidad Rural (ASDEAR)

*Consejo (m) Británico de Iglesias (BCC)

*Federación (f) de Iglesias Evangélicas en la República Democrática Alemana (BEK)

*Pan para el Mundo (BfdW)

(1) Véase "Explicación del uso", pag. 184

421

Brethren   Service

CADEC - Christian Action for Development in the Caribbean

Caribbean Conference of Churches

Caritas Internationalis

CASA - Christian Agency for Social Action, Relief and Development

CCA - Christian Conference of Asia

CCEE - Consilium (n) Conferentiarum Episcopalium Europae /Vatican/

*CCEE - Council of European Bishops' Conferences; CCEE - Council of European Roman Catholic Bishops' Conferences /Vatican/

CCIA - Commission of the Churches on International Affairs

CCJP - Consultation of the Church and the Jewish People

*CCMIE - Catholic Committee for Intra-European Migration of the ICMC

CCPD - Commission on the Churches' Participation in Development

Brethren   Service

*Action (f) chrétienne de développement aux Caraïbes (CADEC)

*Conférence (f) des Eglises des Caraïbes

Caritas Internationalis

*Organisation (f) chrétienne d'action sociale, de secours et de développement (CASA

*Conférence (f) chrétienne d'Asie (CCA)

Conseil (m) des conférences épiscopales européennes (CCEE) /Vatican/

Commission (f) des Eglises pour les affaires internationales (CEAI)

Comité (m) pour l'Eglise et le peuple juif (CEPJ)

Comité (m) catholique pour les migrations intra-européennes de la CICM (CCMIE)

Commission (f) de la participation des Eglises au développement (CPED)

Brethren   Service

*Christian Action for Development in the
Caribbean (CADEC)

*Karibische Konferenz (f) der Kirchen

Caritas Internationalis

*Christliche Organisation (f) für
Sozialwesen, Nothilfe und Entwicklung (CASA)

*Asiatische Christliche Konferenz (f)

*Rat (m) der Europäischen Bischofskonfe-
renzen (CCEE)/Vatikan/

Kommission (f) der Kirchen für Internationale Angelegenheiten (CCIA)

Ausschuss (m) für die Kirche und das Jü-
dische Volk (CCJP)

Katholisches Komitee (n) für Innereuro-
päische Wanderung der ICMC (CCMIE)

Kommission (f) für Kirchlichen Entwicklungsdienst (CCPD)

Brethren Service

*Acción (f) Cristiana para el Desarrollo
del Caribe (CADEC)

*Conferencia (f) de las Iglesias del
Caribe

Caritas Internationalis

Organismo (m) Cristiano para Acción
Social, Socorro y Desarrollo (CASA)

*Conferencia (f) Cristiana de Asia (CCA)

*Consejo (m) de las Conferencias Episcopales
Europeas (CCEE)/Vaticano/

Comisión (f) de las Iglesias para Asuntos
Internacionales (CIAI)

Comité (m) para la Iglesia y el Pueblo
Judío (CIPJ)

*Comité (m) Católico para las Migraciones
 Intraeuropeas de la ICMC (CCMIE)

Comisión (f) sobre la Participación de las
Iglesias en el Desarrollo (CPID)

23

*CCSA – Encounter and Development, Centre for Cooperation and Services in Algeria	Rencontre et développement, Centre de coopération et de service en Algérie (CCSA)
CEC – Conference of European Churches	Conférence (f) des Eglises européennes (KEK)
*CELADEC – Evangelical Latin American Commission on Christian Education	*Commission (f) évangélique de l'éducation chrétienne en Amérique latine (CELADEC)
*CELAM – Latin American Episcopal Conference	*Conférence (f) épiscopale latino-américaine (CELAM)
CEPAL: see under:ECLA	
CETMI – Churches' Committee on Migrant Workers	Comité (m) des Eglises auprès des travailleurs migrants (CETMI)
*CEVAA – Evangelical Community for Apostolic Action	Communauté (f) évangélique d'action apostolique (CEVAA)
CFM – Christian Family Movement	Mouvement (m) chrétien de la famille (MCF)
*CIMADE – Ecumenical Service Agency	Service (m) oecuménique d'entraide (CIMADE)
Christian Aid	Christian Aid
CICARWS – Commission on Inter-Church Aid, Refugee and World Service	Commission (f) d'entraide et de service des Eglises et d'assistance aux réfugiés (CESEAR)
CIDSE – International Cooperation for Socio-Economic Development/Vatican/	Coopération (f) internationale pour le développement socio-économique (CIDSE) /Vatican/

*Begegnung und Entwicklung, Zentrum für Zusammenarbeit und Dienst in Algerien (CCSA)

Konferenz (f) Europäischer Kirchen (KEK)

*Evangelische Kommission (f) für Christliche Erziehung in Lateinamerika (CELADEC)

*Lateinamerikanische Bischofskonferenz (f) (CELAM)

Ausschuss (m) der Kirchen für Fragen ausländischer Arbeitnehmer (CETMI)

*Evangelische Gemeinschaft für Apostolische Aktion (CEVAA)

*Christliche Familienbewegung (f)

*Ökumenisches Hilfswerk (n) (CIMADE)

Christian Aid

Kommission (f) für Zwischenkirchliche Hilfe, Flüchtlings- und Weltdienst (CICARWS)

Internationale Arbeitsgemeinschaft (f) für Sozio-ökonomische Entwicklung (CIDSE) /Vatikan/

*Encuentro y Desarrollo, Centro de Cooperación y de Servicio en Argelia (CCSA)

*Conferencia ( ) de las Iglesias Europeas (KEK)

Comisión (f) Evangélica Latinoamericana de Educación Cristiana (CELADEC)

Colegio (m) Episcopal Latinoamericano (CELAM)

*Comité (m) de las Iglesias para los Trabajadores Migrantes (CETMI)

Comunidad (f) Evangélica de Acción Apostólica (CEVAA)

Movimiento (m) Familiar Cristiano (MFC)

*Servicio (m) Ecuménico de Ayuda Mutua (CIMADE)

Christian Aid

Comisión (f) de Ayuda Intereclesiástica, Servicio Mundial y Refugiados (CAISMR)

*Cooperación (f) Internacional para el Desarrollo Socioeconómico (CIDSE) /Vaticano/

CLD Committee - Christian Literature Development Committee	Comité (m) de développement de la littérature chrétienne (Comité ODLC)
CLD Fund	Fonds (m) ODLC
CMC - Christian Medical Commission	Commission (f) médicale chrétienne (CMC)
*CNBB - Brasilian National Bishops' Conference	*Conférence (f) nationale des évêques brésiliens (CNBB)
COCU - Consultation on Church Union	*Conférence (f) permanente pour l'union des Eglises
Commission of the European Communities	Commission (f) des Communautés européennes
Commission on Faith and Order	Commission (f) de foi et constitution
Commission on Human Rights /UNO/	Commission (f) des droits de l'homme /ONU/
Commission on the Programme to Combat Racism	Commission (f) du Programme de lutte contr le racisme
Commission on the Status of Women /UNO/	Commission (f) de la condition de la femme /ONU/
Committee on "Church Funds for Development Service" (KED)	Comité (m) "fonds de l'Eglise pour le développement" (KED)
*Council of Christian Churches, (GDR)	*Conseil (m) des Eglises chrétiennes en RD.

Ausschuss (m) des Christlichen Entwicklungs-dienstes für Literatur (CLD-Ausschuss)	Comité (m) de Desarrollo de la Literatura Cristiana (Comité ODLC)
CLD - Fonds (m)	Fondo (m) ODLC
Christliche Gesundheitskommission (f) (CMC)	Comisión (f) Médica Cristiana (CMC)
*Nationale Brasilianische Bischofskonferenz (f)	Conferencia (f) Nacional de los Obispos del Brasil (CNBB)
* Konsultation (f) über Kirchenunion in den USA (COCU)	*Comité (m) Permanente sobre la Unión de las Iglesias (COCU)
Kommission (f) der Europäischen Gemein-schaften	*Comisión (f) de las Comunidades Europeas
Kommission (f) für Glauben und Kirchenver-fassung	Comisión (f) de Fe y Constitución
Kommission (f) für Menschenrechte (Menschen-rechtskommission (f))/UNO/	Comisión (f) de Derechos Humanos /ONU/
Kommission (f) für das Programm zur Be-kämpfung des Rassismus	Comisión (f) del Programma de Lucha contra el Racismo
Kommission (f) für die Rechtsstellung der Frau /UNO/	Comisión (f) sobre la Condición Jurídica y Social de la Mujer/ONU/
Ausschuss (m)"Kirchliche Mittel für Ent-wicklungsdienst"	*Comité (m) "Fondos de la Iglesia para el Desarrollo" (KED)
Arbeitsgemeinschaft (f) Christlicher Kirchen in der DDR	*Consejo (m) de Iglesias Christianas en RDA

*Council of Christian Churches in Germany (FRG)

Consilium (n) de Laïcis /Vatican/
*Council on the Laity (of the Roman Catholic Church)/Vatican/

CPC - Christian Peace Conference

CRS - Catholic Relief Services - USCC

CSCE - Conference on Security and Cooperation in Europe

CWME - Commission on World Mission and Evangelism

CWS - Church World Service

DFI - Dialogue with People of Living Faiths and Ideologies

Disarmament Commission /UNO/

DÜ - Service Overseas

DW - Diakonisches Werk

EAGWM - Protestant Liaison Board for World Mission

*Conseil (m) des Eglises chrétiennes en Allemagne (RFA)

*Conseil (m) des laïcs (de l'Eglise catholique romaine)

Conférence (f) chrétienne pour la paix (CCP)

Catholic Relief Services (CRS)

Conférence (f) sur la sécurité et la coopération en Europe (CSCE)

Commission (f) de mission et d'évangé- lisation (CME)

*Service (m) d'entraide des Eglises (Etats-Unis) (CWS)

Dialogue (m) avec les religions et idéologies de notre temps (DRI)

Commission (f) du désarmement /ONU/

Service outre-mer (DÜ)

Diakonisches Werk (DW)

Comité (m) évangélique "mission dans le monde" (EAGWM)

Arbeitsgemeinschaft (f) Christlicher Kirchen in Deutschland	*Consejo (m) de Iglesias Cristianas en Alemania (RFA)
*Laienrat (m) /Vatikan/	*Consejo (m) de los Laicos/ (de la Iglesia Católica Romana)/Vaticano/
Christliche Friedenskonferenz (CPC)	*Conferencia (f) Cristiana por la Paz (CCP)
Catholic Relief Services (CRS)	Catholic Relief Services (CRS)
Konferenz (f) über Sicherheit und Zusammenarbeit in Europa (KSZE)	Conferencia (f) sobre la Seguridad y la Cooperación en Europa (CSCE)
Kommission (f) für Weltmission und Evangelisation (CWME)	Comisión (f) de Misión Mundial y Evangelización (CMME)
*Weltdienst (m) der Kirchen der USA (CWS)	*Servicio (m) de Ayuda Intereclesiástica (Estados Unidos) (CWS)
Dialog (m) mit Menschen verschiedener Religionen und Ideologien (DFI)	Diálogo (m) con las Religiones e Ideologías de Nuestro Tiempo (DRI)
Abrüstungsausschuss (m) /UNO/	Comisión (f) de Desarme /ONU/
Dienste in Übersee (DÜ)	*Servicio de Ultramar (DÜ)
Diakonisches Werk (n)(DW)	Diakonisches Werk (DW)
Evangelische Arbeitsgemeinschaft (f) für Weltmission (EAGWM)	*Junta (f) Evangélica "Misión en el Mundo" (EAGWM)

ECLA - Economic Commission for Latin America /UNO/	Commission (f) économique pour l'Amérique latine (CEPAL) /ONU/
ECLOF - Ecumenical Church Loan Fund	Fondation (f) oecuménique pour l'aide aux Eglises (ECLOF)
ECOSOC - Economic and Social Council/UNO/	Conseil (m) économique et social (ECOSOC)/ONU/
ECSA - Ecumenical Centre Staff Association	Association (f) du personnel du Centre oecuménique (APCO)
Ecumenical Centre	Centre (m) o ecuménique
Ecumenical Development Cooperative Society	Société (f) coopérative oecuménique de développement
Ecumenical Institute, Bossey	Institut (m) oecuménique, Bossey
EEC - European Economic Community	Communauté (f) économique européenne (CEE)
EIRENE - International Christian Service for Peace	Service (m) chrétien international pour la paix (EIRENE)
*EKD, EKiD - Evangelical Church in Germany	*Eglise (f) évangélique en Allemagne (EKD, EKiD)
EKD Commission for Development Affairs	Commission (f) "développement" de l'EKD
EPER - see under:HEKS	
EPS - Ecumenical Press Service	Service (m) oecuménique de presse et d'information (SOEPI)
ER - Ecumenical Review	Ecumenical Review (ER)
ERF - Education Renewal Fund	Fonds (m) pour le renouveau de l'éducation (FRE)

*Wirtschaftskommission (f) für Lateinamerika /UNO/	Comisión (f) Económica para América Latina (CEPAL) /ONU/
Ökumenischer Darlehensfonds (m) (ECLOF)	Fondo (m) Ecuménico de Préstamos a las Iglesias (ECLOF)
Wirtschafts- und Sozialrat (m) (ECOSOC) /UNO/	Consejo (m) Económico y Social (ECOSOC) /ONU/
Mitarbeitervereinigung (f) des Ökumenischen Zentrums (ECSA)	Asociación (f) del Personal del Centro Ecuménico (APCE)
Ökumenisches Zentrum (n)	Centro (m) Ecuménico
Ökumenische Genossenschaft (f) für Entwicklung	Sociedad (f) Cooperativa Ecuménica de Desarrollo
Ökumenisches Institut (n), Bossey	Instituto (m) Ecuménico, Bossey
Europäische Wirtschaftsgemeinschaft (f) (EWG)	*Comunidad (f) Económica Europea (CEE)
Internationaler Christlicher Friedensdienst (m)	Servicio (m) Cristiano Internacional para la Paz (EIRENE)
Evangelische Kirche (f) in Deutschland (EKD, EKiD)	*Iglesia (f) Evangélica en Alemania (EKD, EKiD)
Kammer (f) der EKD für Entwicklungsdienst	*Comisión (f) "Desarrollo" de la EKD
EPS - Ecumenical Press Service	EPS - Ecumenical Press Service
Ecumenical Review (ER)	Ecumenical Review (ER)
Fonds (m) zur Erneuerung der Bildungsarbeit (ERF)	Fondo (m) para la Renovación de la Educación (FRE)

ESP - Ecumenical Sharing of Personnel	Echange (m) oecuménique de personnel (EOP)
European Commission of Human Rights	Commission (f) européenne des droits de l'homme
European Communities	Communautés (fpl) européennes
European Contact Group on Church and Industry	Communauté(f) de travail européenne "Eglise et société industrielle"
European Convention on Human Rights	Convention (f) européenne des droits de l'homme
European Court of Human Rights	Cour (f) européenne des droits de l' homme
EYCE - Ecumenical Youth Council in Europe	Conseil (m) oecuménique de jeunesse en Europe (EYCE)
EYS - Ecumenical Youth Service	Service (m) oecuménique de jeunes (SOJ)
EZE - Protestant Central Agency for Development Aid, Inc.	Office (m) central évangélique d'aide au développement (EZE)
FAO - Food and Agricultural Organization of the United Nations	Organisation (f) des Nations Unies pour l'alimentation et l'agriculture (FAO)
* FEPS - Swiss Protestant Church Federation	Fédération (f) des Eglises protestantes de la Suisse (FEPS)
FFHC - Freedom from Hunger Campaign /FAO/	Campagne (f) mondiale contre la faim (CMCF) /FAO/

Ökumenischer Mitarbeiteraustausch (ESP)	Intercambio (m) Ecuménico de Personal (IEP)
Euro äische Kommission (f) für Menschen-rechte, Europäische Menschenrechtskommission (f)	*Comisión Europea de Derechos Humanos
Europäische Gemeinschaften	*Comunidades (fpl) Europeas
Europäische Arbeitsgemeinschaft (f) "Kirche und Industrie"	*Grupo (m) de Trabajo Europeo "Iglesia e Industria"
Europäische Konvention (f) zum Schutze der Menschenrechte , Europäische Menschenrechtskonvention(f) Europäischer Gerichtshof (m) für Menschenrechte	Convención (f) europea de derechos humanos Tribunal (m) Europeo de los Derechos Humanos
Ökumenischer Jugendrat (m) in Europa (EYCE)	*Consejo (m) Ecuménico de la Juventud en Europa (EYCE)
Ökumenischer Jugenddienst (m) (EYS)	Servicio (m) Ecuménico para el Trabajo con la Juventud (SEJ)
Evangelische Zentralstelle (f) für Entwicklungshilfe e.V. (EZE)	*Oficina (f) Central Evangélica de Ayuda al Desarrollo (EZE)
Ernährungs- und Landwirtschafts-Organisation (f) der Vereinten Nationen (FAO) Schweizerischer Evangelischer Kirchen-bund (m) (FEPS)	Organización (f) de las Naciones Unidas para la Agricultura y la Alimentación (FAO) *Federación (f) de Iglesias Protestantes de Suiza (FEPS)
*Freiheit-vom-Hunger-Kampagne (f) der UN, "Welthungerhilfe" (f) /FAO/	Campaña (f) Mundial contra el Hambre (CMCH) /FAO/

*FPF - French Protestant Federation	Fédération (f) protestante de France (FPF)
FWCC - Friends World Committee for Consultation (Quakers)	*Comité (m) consultatif mondial de la Société des amis (FWCC)
General Conference of Seventh Day Adventists	Conférence (f) générale des adventistes du septième jour
Graduate School of Ecumenical Studies	Centre (m) universitaire d'études oecuméniques
*HEKS, EPER, HEKS-EPER - Swiss Inter-Church Aid	Entraide (f) protestante suisse (EPER)
IARF - International Association for Religious Freedom	Association (f) internationale pour la liberté religieuse (IARF)
IBE - International Bureau of Education /UNESCO/	Bureau (m) international d'éducation (BIE) /UNESCO/
IBRD - International Bank for Reconstruction and Development /ONU/	Banque (f) internationale pour la reconstruction et le développement (BIRD)
ICA - Inter-Church Aid	Entraide (f) des Eglises (ICA)
ICCC - International Conference of Catholic Charities	Conférence (f) internationale des charités catholiques (CICC)
ICCFM - International Confederation of Christian Family Movements	Confédération (f) internationale des mouvements chrétiens de la famille (ICCFM)
ICEM - Intergovernmental Committee for European Migration	Comité (m) intergouvernemental pour les migrations européennes (CIME)
ICJ - International Commission of Jurists	Commission (f) internationale de juristes (CIJ)

*Französischer Evangelischer Kirchenbund(m) (FPF)

*Beratendes Weltkomitee (n) der Freunde (FWCC)

Allgemeine Konferenz (f) der Adventisten des Siebten Tages

Ökumenische Hochschule (f)

Hilfswerk (n) der Evangelischen Kirchen der Schweiz (HEKS)

Weltbund (m) für Religiöse Freiheit (IARF)

*Internationales Erziehungsbüro (f) /UNESCO/

Internationale Bank (f) für Wiederaufbau und Entwicklung , (IBRD)/UNO/

Zwischenkirchliche Hilfe (f) (ICA)

*Internationale Katholische Konferenz (f) Karitativer Verbände

*Weltbund (m) der Christlichen Familienbewegungen (ICCFM)

*Zwischenstaatliches Komitee (n) für Europäische Auswanderung (ICEM)

Internationale Juristenkommission (f) (IJK)

*Federación (f) Protestante de Francia (FPF)

*Comité (m) Consultivo Mundial de la Sociedad de los Amigos (FWCC)

Conferencia (f) General de Adventistas del Séptimo Día

Curso (m) de Estudios Ecuménicos de Postgrado

*Ayuda (f) de las Iglesias Evangélicas Suizas (HEKS, EPER, HEKS - EPER)

*Asociación (f) Internacional por la Libertad Religiosa (IARF)

Oficina (f) Internacional de Educación (OIE) /UNESCO/

Banco (m) Internacional de Reconstrucción y Fomento (BIRF) /ONU/

Ayuda (f) Intereclesiástica (ICA)

Conferencia (f) Internacional Católica de Caridad (CICC)

Confederación (f) Internacional de Movimientos Familiares Cristianos (ICCFM)

Comité (m) Intergubernamental para las Migraciones Europeas (CIME)

Comisión (f) Internacional de Juristas (CIJ)

ICLM - International Christian Leadership Movement	Mouvement (m) international de responsables chrétiens (MIRC)
ICMA - International Christian Maritime Association	Association (f) maritime chrétienne internationale
ICMICA - see under: Pax Romana	
ICMC - International Catholic Migration Commission	Commission (f) internationale catholique des migrations (CICM)
ICRC - International Committee of the Red Cross	Comité (m) international de la Croix-Rouge (CICR)
ICSW - International Council on Social Welfare	Conseil (m) international de l'action sociale (ICSW)
ICVA - International Council of Voluntary Agencies	Conseil (m) international des agences bénévoles (ICVA)
ICW - International Council of Women	Conseil (m) international des femmes (CIF)
ICYE - International Christian Youth Exchange	Echange (m) international chrétien de jeunesse (ICYE)
IDA - International Development Association /IBRD/	Association (f) internationale de développement (AID) /BIRD/
IDOC - International Documentation on the Contemporary Church	Documentation (f) internationale sur l'Eglise contemporaine (IDOC)
IFC - International Finance Corporation /IBRD/	Société (f) financière internationale (SFI) /IBRD/
IFOR - International Fellowship of Reconciliation	Mouvement (m) international de la réconciliation (MIR)

*Internationale Bewegung (f) Christlicher Führungskräfte	*Movimiento (m) Internacional de Dirigentes Cristianos (ICLM)
Internationale Christliche Seemanns-vereinigung(f)	*Asociación (f) Marítima Cristiana Inter-nacional
Internationale Katholische Kommission (f) für Wanderungsfragen (ICMC)	Comisión (f) Católica Internacional de Migración (ICMC)
Internationales Komitee (n) des Roten Kreuzes (IKRK)	Comité (m) Internacional de la Cruz Roja (CICR)
*Internationaler Rat (m) für Sozial-wesen	*Consejo (m) Internacional de Asistencia Social
*Internationaler Rat (m) der freien Wohlfahrtsverbände (ICVA)	Consejo (m) Internacional de Organizaciones Voluntarias (ICVA)
Internationaler Frauenrat (m) (IFR)	Consejo (m) Internacional de Mujeres (CIM)
Internationaler Christlicher Jugend-austausch (m) (ICJA)	Intercambio (m) Cristiano Internacional para la Juventud (ICYE)
*Internationale Vereinigung(f) für Entwicklung (IDA) /IBRD/	Asociación (f) Internacional de Fomento (AIF) /IBRF/
Internationale Dokumentation (f) über die Kirche heute (IDOC)	Documentación (f) Internacional sobre la Iglesia Contemporánea (IDOC)
*Internationale Finanz- Corporation (IFC) /IBRD/	Corporación (f) Financiera Internacional (CFI) /IBRF/
Internationaler Versöhnungsbund (m)	Fraternidad (f) de Reconciliación y Paz

IFOTES - International Federation for
Services of Emergency Telephonic Help

Fédération (f) internationale des services
de secours par téléphone

IMCS - See under: Pax Romana

IMF - International Monetary Fund
/UNO/

Fonds (m) monétaire international (FMI)
/ONU/

IWP - Indicative World Plan for Agricultural Development /FAO/

Plan (m) indicatif mondial pour le
développement de l'agriculture (PIM)/FAO

INODEP - Ecumenical Institute for the
Development of Peoples

Institut (m) oecuménique au service du
développement des peuples (INODEP)

International Conference on Social Welfare

Conférence (f) internationale de l'action
sociale

International Convention on the
Elimination of all Forms of Racial
Discrimination /UNO/

Convention (f) internationale sur
l'élimination de toutes les formes de
discrimination raciale /ONU/

International Covenant on Civil and
Political Rights/UNO/

Pacte (m) international relatif aux
droits civils et politiques /ONU/

International Covenant on Economic,
Social and Cultural Rights /UNO/

Pacte (m) international relatif aux
droits économiques, sociaux et culturels/ONU/

International Covenants on Human Rights
/UNO/

pactes (mpl) internationaux relatifs aux
droits de l'homme/ONU/

International Federation for Inner
Mission and Christian Social Work

Fédération (f) internationale pour la mission
intérieure et le service chrétien

IRFED - International Research and
Training Institute

Institut (m) international de recherche
et de formation (IRFED)

International Institute of Human Rights
(René Cassin Foundation)

Institut (m) international des droits de
l'homme (Fondation René Cassin)

Internationaler Verband (m) für
Telefonseelsorge

*Federación (f) Internacional de Servicios
de Socorro Telefónico

Internationaler Währungsfonds (m)
(IWF) /UNO/

Fondo (m) Monetario Internacional (FMI)
/ONU/

Weltleitplan (m) für die landwirt-
schaftliche Entwicklung /FAO/

Plan (m) Indicativo Mundial para
el Desarrollo Agrícola (PIM)/FAO/

Ökumenisches Institut (n) für die Entwicklung der Völker (INODEP)

Instituto (m) Ecuménico para el
Desarrollo de los Pueblos (INODEP)

*Internationale Konferenz (f) für Sozial-
wesen

*Conferencia (f) Internacional de
Asistencia Social

Internationales Übereinkommen (n) zur
Beseitigung jeder Form von Rassendiskri-
minierung/UNO/

Convención (f) Internacional sobre la
Eliminación de todas las Formas de
Discriminación Racial /ONU/

Internationaler Pakt (m) über bürger-
liche und politische Rechte /UNO/

Pacto (m) Internacional de Derechos
Civiles y Políticos/ONU/

Internationaler Pakt (m) über wirtschaftliche, soziale und kulturelle Rechte
/UNO/
Internationale Pakte über die Menschen-
rechte/UNO/

Pacto (m) Internacional de Derechos
Económicos, Sociales y Culturales /ONU/
Pactos (mpl) Internacionales de Derechos
Humanos/ONU/

Internationaler Verband (m) für Innere
Mission und Diakonie

*Federación (f) Internacional para la
Misión Interna y el Servicio Social
Cristiano

*Internationales Institut (n) für
Forschung und Ausbildung (IRFED)

Instituto (m) Internacional de Investigación
y Formación (IRFED)

*Internationales Institut (n) für
Menschenrechte (René Cassin-Stiftung)(f)

* Instituto (m) Internacional de
Derechos Humanos (Fundación René Cassin)

IPPF - International Planned Parenthood Federation	Fédération (f) internationale du planning familial
IRM - International Review of Mission	International Review of Mission (IRM)
*ISAL - Latin American Commission on Church and Society	*Commission (f) pour l'Eglise et la société en Amérique latine (ISAL), Eglise et société en Amérique latine (ISAL)
ISVS - International Secretariat for Volunteer Service	Secrétariat (m) international du service volontaire (SISV)
IUCW - International Union for Child Welfare	Union (f) internationale de protection de l'enfance (UIPE)
IUFO - International Union of Family Organisations	Union (f) internationale des organismes familiaux (UIOF)
IVS - International Voluntary Service	Service (m) civil international (SCI)
JAM - Joint Action for Mission	Unité (f) d'action missionaire (UAM)
JCA - Joint Church Aid	Joint Church Aid (JCA)
*JESSYC - Interchurch Social and Cultural Service	*Comité (m) évangélique de service social et culturel (JESSYC)
JWG - Joint Working Group (between the Roman Catholic Church and the World Council of Churches)	Groupe (m) mixte de travail (de l'Eglise catholique romaine et du Conseil oecuménique des Eglises, (GMT)
KED - The Churches' Development Service	Service (m) de l'Eglise pour le développement (KED)
KEK - See under: CEC	

Internationale Vereinigung (f) für
Familienplanung

International Review of Mission (IRM)

Lateinamerikanische Arbeitsgemeinschaft
(f) für Kirche und Gesellschaft (ISAL),
  Kirche und Gesellschaft in Lateinamerika (ISAL)

Internationales Sekretariat (n) für
Freiwillige Dienste

Internationale Vereinigung (f) für
Jugendhilfe (IVJH)

Internationale Union (f) der Familien-
verbände

Internationaler Zivildienst (m) (IZD)

Gemeinsames Handeln (n) in der Mission
(JAM)

Joint Church Aid (JCA)

*Evangelischer Ausschuss (m) für Sozial-
und Bildungsarbeit (JESSYC)

Gemeinsame Arbeitsgruppe (f) (der
Römisch-Katholischen Kirche und des
Ökumenischen Rates der Kirchen)

Kirchlicher Entwicklungsdienst (m)(KED)

Federación (f) Internacional de Planificación de la Familia

International Review of Mission (IRM)

Junta (f) Latino americana de Iglesia
y Sociedad (ISAl),
Iglesia y Sociedad en América Latina (ISAL)

Secretaría (f) Internacional para el
Servicio Voluntario (SISV)

Unión (f) Internacional de Protección a
la Infancia (UIPI)

Unión (f) Internacional de Organismos Familiares

Servicio (m) Voluntario Internacional

Acción (f) Misionera Conjunta (AMC)

Joint Church Aid (JCA)

Junta (f) Evangélica de Servicio Social
y Cultural (JESSYC)

Grupo (m) Mixto de Trabajo (de la Iglesia
Católica Romana y el Consejo Mundial de
Iglesias) (GMT)

*Servicio (m) de la Iglesia para el
Desarrollo (KED)

441

LWF - Lutheran World Federation	Fédération (f) luthérienne mondiale (FLM)
LWR - Lutheran World Relief, USA	Lutheran World Relief, Etats-Unis (LWR
Middle East Council of Churches	*Conseil (m) des Eglises du Moyen-Orient
NCC - National Christian Council	Conseil (m) chrétien national (CCN)
NCC - National Council of Churches	Conseil (m) national d'Eglises (CNE)
NCCCUSA - National Council of the Churches of Christ in the USA	*Conseil (m) national des Eglises du Christ aux Etats-Unis d'Amérique (NCCCUSA)
New York Office	Bureau (m) de New York
Nordchurchaid	Nordchurchaid
OAU - Organisation of African Unity	Organisation (f) de l'unité africaine (OUA)
OECD - Organisation for Economic Cooperation and Developpment	Organisation (f) de coopération et de développement économique (OCDE)
Old Catholic International Congresses	Congrès (mpl) vieux-catholiques internationaux
Pax Christi International	Pax Christi International

Lutherischer Weltbund (m) (LWB)	*Federación (f) Luterana Mundial (FLM)
Lutheran World Relief, USA (LWR)	Lutheran World Relief, Estados Unidos (LWR)
*Rat (m) der Kirchen im Mittleren Osten	*Consejo (m) de Iglesias del Oriente Medio
Nationaler Christenrat (m) (NCC)	Consejo (m) Cristiano Nacional (CCN)
Nationaler Kirchenrat (m) (NCC)	Consejo (m) Nacional de Iglesias (CNI)
*Nationalrat (m) der Kirchen Christi in den Vereinigten Staaten von Amerika (NCCCUSA) New Yorker Büro (n)	*Consejo (m) Nacional de las Iglesias de Cristo en los Estados Unidos (NCCCUSA) Oficina (f) de Nueva York
Nordchurchaid	Nordchurchaid
*Organisation (f) für Afrikanische Einheit (OAE)	*Organización (f) de Unidad Africana (OUA)
Organisation (f) für Wirtschaftliche Zusammenarbeit und Entwicklung (OECD)	Organización (f) de Cooperación y Desarrollo Económicos (OCDE)
Internationale Altkatholikenkongresse (mpl)	*Congresos (mpl) Viejos Católicos Internacionales
Pax Christi International	Pax Christi International

(1) Pax Romana, International Catholic Movement for Intellectual and Cultural Affairs (ICMICA)

Pax Romana, Mouvement (m) international des intellectuels catholiques (MIIC)

(2) Pax Romana, International Movement of Catholic Students (IMCS)

Pax Romana, Mouvement (m) international des étudiants catholiques (MIEC)

PCC - Pacific Conference of Churches

*Conférence (f) des Eglises du Pacifique (CEP)

Pontifical Commission Justice and Peace
Pontificia Commissio (f) Justitia et Pax

Commission (f) pontificale, Justitia et Pax
Commission (f) pontificale justice et paix

PCR - Programme to Combat Racism

Programme (m) de lutte contre le racisme (PLR)

RCC - Roman Catholic Church

Eglise (f) catholique romaine (ECR)

Risk

Risk

Rural Agricultural Mission

Mission (f) en milieu rural

Sacred Congregation for the Doctrine of the Faith /Vatican/

Sacrée Congrégation (f) pour la doctrine de la foi /Vatican/

Sacred Congregation for the Evangelisation of the Peoples (=for the Propagation of Faith)/Vatican/

Sacrée Congrégation (f) pour l'évangélisation du monde /Vatican/

SALT - Strategic Arms Limitations Talks

Pourparlers (mpl) sur la limitation des armes stratégiques (SALT)

SCM - Student Christian Movement

Association (f) chrétienne d'étudiants, Mouvement (m) chrétien d'étudiants

(1) Pax Romana, Internationale Bewegung (f) der Katholischen Akademiker

Pax Romana, Movimiento (m) Internacional de Intelectuales Católicos (MIIC)

(2) Pax Romana, Internationale Katholische Studenten-Bewegung (f)

Pax Romana, Movimiento (m) Internacional de Estudiantes Católicos

*Pazifische Konferenz (f) der Kirchen

*Conferencia (f) de las Iglesias del Pacífico

Päpstliche Studienkommission (f) Justitia et Pax

Comisión (f) Pontificia Justitia et Pax

Programm (n) zur Bekämpfung des Rassismus (PCR)

Programa (m) de Lucha contra el Racismo (PLR)

Römisch-Katholische Kirche (f)(RKK)

Iglesia (f) Católica Romana (ICR)

Risk

Risk

Kirchlicher Dienst (m) in ländlichen Gebieten

Misión (f) Rural

Kongregation (f) für die Glaubenslehre /Vatikan/

Sagrada Congregación (f) para la Doctrina de la Fe/Vaticano/

Kongregation (f) für die Verkündigung des Evangeliums unter den Völkern (oder für die Glaubensverbreitung)/Vatikan/

Sagrada Congregación (f) para la Evangelización de los Pueblos/Vaticano/

Gespräche (npl) über die Begrenzung der strategischen Rüstung (SALT)

Conversaciones (fpl) sobre la limitación de las armas estratégicas (SALT)

Christliche Studentenbewegung (f)

Movimiento (m) Estudiantil Cristiano (MEC)

Secretariat for Migration	Secrétariat (m) des migrations
Secretariat for Non-Believers /Vatican/	Secrétariat (m) pour les non-croyants /Vatican/
Secretariat for Non-Christians /Vatican/	Secrétariat (m) pour les non-chrétiens /Vatican/
Secretariat for Promoting Christian Unity /Vatican/	Secrétariat (m) pour l'unité des chrétiens /Vatican/
SEG - Staff Executive Group	Groupe (m) exécutif du personnel (SEG)
SIPRI - Stockholm International Peace Research Institute	Institut (m) international de recherches sur la paix de Stockholm (SIPRI)
SODEPAX - Committee on Society, Development and Peace	Commission (f) pour la société, le développement et la paix (SODEPAX)
Special Fund to Combat Racism	Fonds (m) spécial de lutte contre le racisme
SRG - Staff Representative Group	Groupe (m) représentatif du personnel (GRP)
Standard Minimum Rules for the Treatment of Prisoners /UNO/	Ensemble (m) de règles minima pour le traitement des détenus /ONU
Study Encounter	Study Encounter
Syndesmos - World Fellowship of Orthodox Youth Organisations	*Syndesmos Association (f) mondiale des organisations de la jeunesse orthodoxe
TEF - Theological Education Fund	Fonds (m) pour l'enseignement théologique (FET)

Sekretariat (n) für Migration	Secretaría (f) de Migraciones
Sekretariat (n) für die Nichtglauben-den/Vatikan/	Secretariado (m) para los no Creyentes /Vaticano/
Sekretariat (n) für die Nichtchristen /Vatikan/	Secretariado (m) para los no Cristianos /Vaticano/
Sekretariat (n) zur Förderung der Einheit der Christen /Vatikan/	Secretariado (m) para la Promoción de la Unidad de los Cristianos/Vaticano/
Gruppe (f) leitender Mitarbeiter (SEG)	Grupo (m) Ejecutivo de Personal (SEG)
Internationales Institut (n) für Friedensforschung Stockholm (SIPRI)	*Instituto (m) Internacional de Investiga-ciones sobre la Paz de Estocolmo (SIPRI)
Ausschuss (m) für Gesellschaft, Ent-wicklung und Frieden (SODEPAX)	Comisión (f) para la Sociedad, el Desarrollo y la Paz (SODEPAX)
Sonderfonds (m) zur Bekämpfung des Rassismus	Fondo (m) Especial de Lucha contra el Racismo
Mitarbeitervertretung (f) (SRG)	Grupo (m) Representativo del Personal (SRG)
Mindestgrundsätze (mpl) für die Be-handlung der Gefangenen /UNO/	Reglas (fpl) mínimas para el tratamiento de los reclusos /ONU/
Study Encounter	Study Encounter
*Syndesmos, Weltbund (m) Orthodoxer Jugendorganisationen	* Syndesmos, Asociación (f) Mundial de las Organizaciones de Juventud Ortodoxa
Theologischer Ausbildungsfonds (m) (TEF)	Fondo (m) de Educación Teológica (FET)

UBS - United Bible Societies	Alliance (f) biblique universelle (ABU)
UCC, USA - United Church of Christ, USA	*Eglise (f) unie du Christ, Etats-Unis d'Amérique (UCC,USA)
UIM - Urban Industrial Mission	Mission (f) en milieu urbain et industriel (MUI)
*ULAJE - Union of Latin American Ecumenical Youth	*Union (f) de la jeunesse oecuménique en Amérique latine (ULAJE)
UNAPAC - International Christian Union of Business Executives	Union (f) internationale chrétienne des dirigeants d'entreprise (UNAPAC)
UNCTAD - United Nations Conference on Trade and Development	Conférence (f) des Nations Unies sur le commerce et le développement (CNUCED)
UNPD - United Nations Development Programme	Programme (f) des Nations Unies pour le développement (PNUD)
UNDRO - Office of the Disaster Relief Coordinator/UNO/	Bureau (m) du coordonnateur des secours en cas de catastrophe (UNDRO) /ONU/
*UNELAM - Evangelical Commission for Latin American Unity	*Mouvement (m) pour l'unité évangélique en Amérique latine (UNELAM)
UNHCR - Office of the United Nations High Commissioner for Refugees	Haut Commissariat (m) des Nations Unies pour les réfugiés (UNHCR)
UNIDO - United Nations Industrial Development Organization	Organisation (f) des Nations Unies pour le développement industriel (ONUDI)
United States Conference for the World Council of Churches	*Conférence (f) des Eglises américaines membres du Conseil oecuménique des Eglises

Weltbund (m) der Bibelgesellschaften (UBS)

Sociedades (fpl) Bíblicas Unidas (SBU)

*Vereinigte Kirche (f) Christi, Vereinigte Staaten von Amerika (UCC,USA)

*Iglesia (f) Unida de Cristo, Estados Unidos de América (UCC,USA)

Kirchlicher Dienst (m) in der urbanen und industriellen Gesellschaft (UIM)

Misión (f) Urbana e Industrial (MUI)

*Union (f) der Ökumenischen Jugend in Lateinamerika (ULAJE)

Unión (f) Latinoamericana de Juventudes Ecuménicas (ULAJE)

Internationale Union (f) Christlicher Unternehmervereinigungen (UNAPAC)

Unión (f) Internacional Cristiana de Dirigentes de Empresa (UNAPAC)

Konferenz (f) der Vereinten Nationen für Handel und Entwicklung - Welthandelskonferenz (UNCTAD)

Conferencia (f) de las Naciones Unidas sobre Comercio y Desarrollo (UNCTAD)

Entwicklungsprogramm (n) der Vereinten Nationen (UNDP), UN-Entwicklungsprogramm (n)

Programa (m) de las Naciones Unidas para el Desarrollo (PNUD)

*Amt (n) des Koordinators für Katastrophenhilfe/UNO/

Oficina (f) del Coordinador del Socorro para Casos de Desastre /ONU/

*Bewegung (f) für Evangelische Einheit in Lateinamerika (UNILAM)

Movimiento (m) pro Unidad Evangélica Latinoamericana (UNELAM)

Amt (n) des Hohen Kommissars der Vereinten Nationen für Flüchtlinge (UNHCR)

Oficina (f) del Alto Comisionado de las Naciones Unidas para los Refugiados (UNHCR)

Organisation (f) der Vereinten Nationen für Industrielle Entwicklung (UNIDO)

Organización (f) de las Naciones Unidas para el Desarrollo Industrial (ONUDI)

*Konferenz (f) Amerikanischer Kirchen für den Ökumenischen Rat der Kirchen

*Conferencia (f) de las Iglesias Americanas Miembros del Consejo Mundial de Iglesias

449

UNRWA - United Nations Relief and Works
Agency for Palestine Refugees in the
Near East

Office (m) de secours et de travaux des
Nations Unies pour les réfugiés de Palestine
dans le Proche-Orient

UPCUSA, UPUSA - United Presbyterian Church
in the USA

*Eglise (f) presbytérienne unie aux Etats-
Unis d'Amérique (UPCUSA, UPUSA)

WACC - World Association for Christian
Communication

Association (f) mondiale pour la communication chrétienne (AMCC)

WARC - World Alliance of Reformed Churches

Alliance (f) réformée mondiale (ARM)

WCC - World Council of Churches

Conseil (m) oecuménique des Eglises (COE)

WCF - World Confessional Families

familles (fpl) confessionelles mondiales

WCF - World Congress of Faiths

Congrès (m) mondial des religions (WCF)

WCL - World Confederation of Labour

Confédération (f) mondiale du travail (CMT)

Week of Prayer for Christian Unity

Semaine (f) de prière pour l'unité des
chrétiens

WELG - Women's Ecumenical Liaison Group

Groupe (m) féminin de liaison oecuménique
(WELG)

WFP - World Food Programme

Programme (m) alimentaire mondial (PAM)

World Alliance of YMCAs,
World Alliance of Young Men's Christian
Associations

Alliance (f) universelle des UCJG,
Alliance (f) universelle des Unions
chrétiennes de jeunes gens

Hilfswerk (n) der Vereinten Nationen für Palästinaflüchtlinge im Nahen Osten (UNRWA)	Organismo (m) de Obras Públicas y Socorro de las Naciones Unidas para los Refugiados de Palestina en el Cercano Oriente (OOPS)
*Vereinigte Presbyterianische Kirche (f) in den USA (UPCUSA, UPUSA)	Iglesia (f) Presbiteriana Unida en los Estados Unidos de América (UPCUSA, UPUSA)
Weltbund (m) für Christliche Kommunikation (WACC)	*Asociación (f) mundial para Comunicación Cristiana (WACC)
Reformierter Weltbund (m) (RWB)	Alianza (f) Reformada Mundial (ARM)
Ökumenischer Rat (m) der Kirchen (ÖRK)	Consejo (m) Mundial de Iglesias (CMI)
Weltweite Bekenntnisfamilien (fpl), Konfessionsfamilien (fpl)	Familias (fpl) C onfesionales Mundiales
Welt-Religions-Kongress (m)(WCF)	Congreso (m) Mundial de Religiones (WCF)
Weltverband (m) der Arbeitnehmer (WVA)	Confederación (f) Mundial del Trabajo (CMT)
Gebetswoche (f) für die Einheit der Christen	Semana (f) de Oración por la Unidad Cristiana
Ökumenischer Verbindungsausschuss (m) für Frauenarbeit (WELG)	Grupo (m) Femenino de Enlace Ecuménico (WELG)
Welternährungsprogramm (n)	Programa (m) Mundial de Alimentos (PMA)
Weltbund (m) der CVJM Weltbund (m) der Christlichen Vereine Junger Männer	Alianza (f) Mundial de ACJ Alianza (f) Mundial de Asociaciones Cristianas de Jóvenes

World Bank	Banque (f) mondiale
World Confessional Bodies	alliances (fpl) confessionnelles mondiales
World Convention of Churches of Christ	*Convention (f) mondiale des Eglises du Christ
WMC - World Methodist Council	*Conseil (m) méthodiste mondial (WMC)
World Families of Churches	familles (fpl) ecclésiales mondiales
WSCF - World Student Christian Federation	Fédération (f) universelle des associations chrétiennes d'étudiants (FUACE)
World YWCA World Young Women's Christian Association	Alliance (f) mondiale des UCF, Alliance (f) mondiale des Unions chrétiennes féminines
WYP - World Youth Project	Projets (mpl) d'entraide mondiale de jeunesse (PEMJ)
YMCA - Young Men's Christian Association	Unions (fpl) chrétiennes de jeunes gens (UCJG)
YWCA - Young Women's Christian Association	Unions (fpl) chrétiennes féminines (UCF)

Weltbank (f)	Banco (m) Mundial
Konfessionelle Weltbünde (mpl)	Alianzas (fpl) confesionales mundiales
*Internationaler Konvent (m) Christ-licher Kirchen (Jünger Christi)	*Convención (f) Mundial de Iglesias de Cristo
*Weltrat Methodistischer Kirchen (WMC)	*Consejo (m) Metodista Mundial (WMC)
* Weltweite Kirchenfamilien (fpl)	Familias (fpl) Eclesiales Mundiales
Christlicher Studentenweltbund (m)	Federación (f) Universal de Movimientos Estudiantiles Cristianos (FUMEC)
Weltbund (m) der CVJF Weltbund (m) Christlicher Verbände Junger Frauen	Asociación (f) Cristiana Femenina Mundial
Weltjugendprojekte (npl) (WYP)	Proyectos (mpl) para la Juventud Mundial (PJM)
Christliche Vereine (mpl) Junger Männer (CVJM)	Asociaciones (fpl) Cristianas de Jóvenes (ACJ)
Christliche Verbände (mpl) Junger Frauen (CVJF)	Asociaciones (fpl) Cristianas Femeninas Mundiales

IX

<u>INDEX ALPHABETIQUE</u>

<u>FRANÇAIS</u>

Groupe exécutif du personnel
(SEG) p. 445
Voir aussi sous: 584
Groupe exécutif restreint
du personnel 583
groupe d'experts 875
Groupe féminin de liaison
oecuménique (WELG) p. 449
groupe informel 579
groupe de jeunes 1320
groupes marginalisés 581
groupes marginaux 580
groupes prioritaires 1165
Groupe régional de liaison 582
Groupe restreint 577
groupe sauvage 579
groupe de travail 590, 1166,
1307
Groupe de travail "jeu-
nesse" 1169
groupe de travail régional 1168
GRP - Groupe représentatif
du personnel p. 445
guérison 1288
guérisseur traditionnel 1205
guerre biologique 1272
guerre chimique 1273
"guerre juste" 1271
guerre d'usure 1270

habitat humain 597,1097
habitat rural 1035
hagiophanie 598
halte-garderie 635
handicapés mentaux 599
handicapés physiques 600
Haut Commissariat des Nations
Unies pour les réfugiés
(UNHCR) p. 447
HEKS, EPER, HEKS-EPER p. 433
herboriste 629
héréditaires (carac-
tères) 552
héréditaire (patri-
moine) 552
herméneutique
Voir sous: recherche
biblique 78
hésychasme 630
Hispano-américains 631
home pour enfants 634
home pour personnes
âgées 637
homologue (groupe) 296
homologue (organisme) 296
homologue (personnel de
l'organisme) 297
hôpital central 640
humain (l') et son
accomplissement 643
humains (l'être et le
devenir) 643
humanité (l') et sa
réalisation 643
hygiène du milieu 438
hygiène (d') 605

IARF p. 433
ICA p. 433
ICCFM p. 433
ICMA p. 435
ICSW p. 435
ICVA p. 435
ICYE p. 435
identité 1080
IDOC p. 435
IFOTES p. 437
illuminés 433
immigration (législation
sur l') 647
immigrée (femme) 749
immixtion (=ingérence) dans
la vie privée 954
imposition des mains 693
impuissance 942
indemnité 568
indemnités et avantages
divers 515
indigénisation 653
indivisibilité 1288
infirmière auxiliaire 837
infirmière des collectivités
838

473

infirmière de la santé
  publique 840
informateur 217
information en retour 472
infrastructure 1089
INODEP - Institut oecuménique
  au service du développement des peuples p. 437
insoumis 1019
Institut international des
  droits de l'homme
  (Fondation René Cassin) p.437
Institut international de
  recherches sur la paix de
  Stockholm (SIPRI) p. 445
Institut oecuménique,
  Bossey p. 429
institut pédagogique 1222
Institut sud-africain des
  relations raciales 1130
institution 96
institution d'action
  sociale 1283
institution bénévole 29
institution collectrice
  de fonds 25
institutions d'entraide
  (ecclésiastiques) 27
institutions d'entraide
  en relation avec la
  CESEAR 26
institution de financement 24
institutions parrainées 28
institution sociale 1283

institution sociale privée
  1284
instruction 401
instruction scolaire 1045
intégralité 1288
intégralité de la vie
  humaine 1289
intégrité (physique) 1288
intendance 1144
intendant (des biens con-
  fiés par Dieu à l'homme)
  1143
intercélébration
  Voir sous: communion 218
intercommunion
  Voir sous: communion 218
interdits (placer sous l'effet
  d') 69
intérêt 238
interpellation 128
interpeller 129
interruption de grossesse 2,
  943
interruption de grossesse sur
  indications eugéniques/
  médicales/sociales/morales 4
interruption de grossesse
  (information sur 1') 3
inventaire général des
  besoins 235
IPPF p. 439
IRFED - Institut international
  de recherche et de for-
  mation p. 437
IRM - International Review of
  Mission p. 439

ISAL p. 439

jardin d'enfants 672
jardin Robinson 16
JCA - Joint Church Aid p. 439
JESSYC p. 439
"Jesus people" 658
jeu de rôles 1029
jeûne sacramentel 1037
jeunesse (activité, tra-
  vail de) 1326
jeunesse (coordination des
  activités oecuméniques
  de) 1329

kairos 669
KED p. 425 , p. 439
KEK p. 423
kénotique 670
kerygma, kérygme 671
koinonia 218

IX

<u>ALPHABETISCHES REGISTER</u>

<u>DEUTSCH</u>

499

511

515

NOTES

NOTES

NOTES

IX

<u>INDICE ALFABETICO</u>

<u>ESPAÑOL</u>

AACC pag. 420
abandono escolar (porcentaje
   de) 386
aborígenes 1
aborto 2
aborto provocado 5
academia evangélica 6
Acción Apostólica Común pag.420
acción complementaria 496
Acción Cristiana para el
   Desarrollo del Caribe
   (CADEC) pag. 422
Acción para la Producción
   de Alimentos (AFPRO)
   pag. 420
acción social 1108
acedia 7
ACJ - Asociaciones
   Cristianas de Jóvenes
   pag. 452
actividad consecutiva 496
actividades interdiscipli-
   narias 521
actividades recreativas 699
actividad de servicio 1293
actividad sobre el terreno
   484
actividad de vanguardia 521
acuerdo doctrinal 384
Acuerdo de Leuenberg 700
aculturación 12
adivino 381
administración 720
administración local 562
administración de per-
   sonal 723

administrador 725
administrador de hospital 639
admisión limitada/ general/
   recíproca
   Véase: Comunión 218
afiliación 745
AFPRO pag. 420
Africa meridional 1131
africaans 19
africander 20
afroamericanos 21
ágape 23
AG-KED pag. 420
aglomeraciones humanas 1097
aglomeraciones rurales 1035
aglomeraciones urbanas 1251
agricultura de subsistencia
   1153
agua potable (abastecimiento
   de) 1275
agua potable (instalaciones
   de) 1274
AIF - Asociación Internacional
   de Fomento pag. 436
alcantarillado (sistema de)
   1099
alfabetización 702
alfabetización funcional
   (programa de) 703
Alianzas Confesionales
   Mundiales pag. 452
   Véase también: 1310
Alianza Mundial de ACJ pag.450
Alianza Mundial de Aso-
   ciaciones Cristianas
   de Jóvenes pag. 450

alimentación 473, 844
alimentación complemen-
   taria 474
alimentación (higiene de
   la) 503
alimentario (aditivo) 499
alimentaria (ayuda) 500
alimentaria (carencia) 718
alimentario (déficit) 540
alimentaria (educación) 845
alimentaria (estadística) 506
alimentarias (necesidades)
   504
alimentario (programa) 846
alimentaria (situación -
   mundial) 509
alimentaria (tecnología) 508
alimenticio (producto) 498
alimento 498
alimento complementario 474
alimentos (demanda de) 502
alimentos (escasez de) 505
alimentos (suministro de)
   507
alojamiento provisional 105
"Al servicio de la causa de
   la comunidad" 184
alteridad 872
AMC - Acción Misionera Conjunta pag. 440
   Véase también: 792
Amnesty International pag.420
anáfora 41
analfabetismo 644
analfabetos 645
análisis estructuralista
   método del) Véase: in-
   vestigación bíblica 78

536

537

iglesias reformadas 161
iglesia regional 162
iglesias responsables de
    (de los) proyecto(s) 978
iglesias del silencio 164
iglesia subterránea 166
Iglesia Unida de Cristo,
    Estados Unidos de América,
    (UCC, USA) pag. 448
Iglesia Universal 167
Iglesia (autoridades de la) 141
Iglesia (cánones de la) 140
Iglesia (constitución de
    la) 139
Iglesia (disciplina de la) 143
Iglesia (normas de la) 140
Iglesia (obrero de la) 1300
Iglesia (responsable de) 142
Igualdad de oportunidades
    (=de posibilidades) 863
igualdad de trato 1225
iluminados 433
IMCS
    Véase: Pax Romana (2) pag.444
impedidos mentales 599
impedimentos físicos (personas
    con) 600
impedimentos mentales
    (personas con) 599
imposición de manos 696
impotencia 942
incapacitados mentales 599
indigenización 653
información de prensa 101
información (curso de) 56
informante 217

infraestructura 1089
infraestructura (servicios de)
    1089
injerencia (=intromisión) en
    la vida privada 954
inmigración (corriente de) 655
inmigración (legislación
    sobre) 647
inmigración (leyes de) 647
inmigrante 747
inmigrantes (contingente de)
    655
inmigrantes (entradas de)
    655
inmigrante (mujer) 749
INODEP pag. 438
instituciones de ayuda
    mutua en relación con la
    CAISMR 26
institución de financiación 24
instituciones patrocinadas 28
institución (privada) de tra-
    bajo voluntario 29
instituciones de servicio
    (eclesiásticas) 27
instituto de ciencias de la
    educación 1222
Instituto Ecuménico, Bossey
    pag. 430
Instituto Ecuménico para el
    Desarrollo de los
    Pueblos (INODEP) pag. 438
Instituto Internacional de
    Derechos Humanos (Funda-
    ción René Cassin) pag.438

Instituto Internacional de
    Investigación y For-
    mación (IRFED) pag. 438
Instituto Internacional de
    Investigaciones sobre la
    Paz de Estocolmo (SIPRI)
    pag. 446
instituto normal 1222
Instituto Sudafricano de
    Relaciones Raciales 1130
instrucción 401
instrucción escolar 1045
insuficiencia vitamínica 1263
integridad 1288
integridad física 1288
integridad de la vida humana
    1289
Intercambio Cristiano Inter-
    nacional para la
    Juventud (ICYE) pag. 436
intercelebración
    Véase: Comunión 218
intercomunión
    Véase: Comunión 218
interpelar 129
interrupción del embara-
    zo 2, 943
interrupción del embarazo
    por indicaciones eugénicas/
    médicas/sociales/morales 4
interrupción del embarazo
    (asesoramiento sobre la) 3
inventario general de
    necesidades 235
investigación bíblica 78
investigación ecuménica 1149

IPPF pag. 440
IRFED pag. 438
IRM - International Review of
    Mission pag. 440
ISAL - Iglesia y Sociedad en
    América Latina pag. 440
IUFO pag. 440
IVS pag. 440

jardín de infantes 672
JCA - Joint Church Aid pag.440
jefe 695, 855
Jefe de Información 859
Jefe de la sección Tesorería 602
Jefe del Servicio Lingüístico
    1056
JESSYC - Junta Evangélica de
    Servicio Social y Cultural
    pag. 440
"Jesus people" 658
jornada reducida 1295
juicio oral 628
junta 88
junta directiva 88
Junta Evangélica "Misión en
    el Mundo" (EAGWM) pag. 428
Junta Latinoamericana de
    Iglesia y Sociedad (ISAL)
    pag. 440

juventud (actividad con la)
    1326
juventud ecuménica (coordi-
    nación de las activi-
    dades de la) 1329
juventud (trabajo con la) 1326

kairos 669
KED pag. 428, pag.440
KEK pag. 424
kenótico 670
kerygma 671
kindergarten 672
koinonía
    Véase: Comunión 218

latas (barrio de) 1105
lectura diacrónica
    Véase: investigación
    bíblica 78
lectura literaria e
    histórica de la Biblia
    Véase: investigación
    bíblica 78

lectura litúrgica de la
    Biblia
    Véase: investigación
    bíblica 78
lectura sincrónica de la
    Biblia
    Véase: investigación
    bíblica 78
leyes de pases 889
ley de tenencia de tierras
    688
ley sobre las zonas homogéneas
    reservadas a los distintos
    grupos raciales 573
ley (imperio de la) 692
libertad condicional con régi-
    men de prueba 955
libertad vigilada (régimen
    de) 955
libreta de referencia 888
Libro de Concordia 241
líder 695
líder de estudios bíblicos
    Véase: investigación
    bíblica 78
líder de jóvenes(=juvenil)
    1321, 1327
líder de programas de
    desarrollo 345
líder de trabajo en comuni-
    dades 348
liderazgo 696
Lista de proyectos 970
Lista de proyectos (solici-
    tud de inscripción en
    la) 965
literatura apocalíptica
    Véase: investigación
    bíblica 78

BILINGUAL AND PLURILINGUAL DICTIONARIES
DICTIONNAIRES BILINGUES ET MULTILINGUES
ZWEI- UND MEHRSPRACHIGE LEXIKA
DICCIONARIOS BILINGÜES Y MULTILINGÜES

Cuyás, Arturo. Appleton's New Cuyás English-Spanish and Spanish-English Dictionary. Nuevo Diccionario Cuyás Inglés-Español, Español-Inglés de Appleton. New York, Appleton-Century-Crofts, 1972.

Dictionnaire moderne français-espagnol, espagnol-français. Ramón García-Pelayo y Gross et Jean Testas. Paris, Librairie Larousse, 1967.

Harrap's New Standard French and English Dictionary. Part one, French-English. J.E. Mansion. Revised and edited by R.P.L. Ledésert and Margaret Ledésert. Paris/London, Bordas, in association with Harrap, London, 1972. 2 vol.

Harrap's Standard French and English Dictionary. Part two, English-French, with supplement (1962). Edited by J.E. Mansion, Bordas, in association with George G. Harrap and Company Ltd.,London, 1971.

Harrap's Standard German and English Dictionary. Ed. Trevor Jones. London, Harrap & Co.Ltd., 1963-1974 (A-R, volumes S-Z to follow).

Langenscheidts Enzyklopädisches Wörterbuch der englischen und deutschen Sprache, Teil I Englisch-Deutsch. Hrsg. von Dr. Otto Springer. Berlin und München, Langenscheidt, 1969.

Langenscheidts Handwörterbuch, Teil II, Deutsch-Englisch. Hrsg. von Heinz Messinger. Berlin und München, Langenscheidt, 1969.

Slaby-Grossmann. Wörterbuch der spanischen und deutschen Sprache, Deutsch-Spanisch, Spanisch-Deutsch. Wiesbaden, Brandstetter Verlag, 1970.

Weis-Mattutat. Wörterbuch der französischen und deutschen SPrache, Teil I Französisch-Deutsch. Hrsg. von Erich Weis unter Mitwirkung von Heinrich Mattutat. Stuttgart, Ernst Klett Verlag, 1967.

555

Weis-Mattutat. Wörterbuch der französischen und
deutschen Sprache, Teil II Deutsch-Französisch.
Bearbeitet von Heinrich Mattutat. Stuttgart,
Ernst Klett Verlag, 1967.

*

* *

Conference Terminology. A manual for conference-
members and interpreters, in English, French
Spanish, Russian, Italian, German. Edited by
Jean Herbert. New York, Elsevier Publishing
Company, 1962.

Deak, Etienne et Simone. Grand dictionnaire
d'américanismes. Paris, Dauphin, 1966.

Diccionario politécnico de las lenguas española e inglesa. Madrid, Castilla, 1965.
2 vol.

Doucet, Michel. Dictionnaire juridique et
économique, tome I français-allemand. Paris,
Librairies techniques, 1966.

Doucet, Michel. Wörterbuch der deutschen und
französischen Rechtssprache. Teil II Deutsch-
Französisch. Munchen und Berlin, C.H. Beck'
sche Verlagsbuchhandlung, 1966.

Glosario Inglés-Español, para uso de los traductores del GATT. Acuerdo General sobre
Aranceles Aduaneros y Comercio. Ginebra, GATT,
1974.

Glossaire anglais-français à l'usage des traducteurs du GATT. Accord général sur les tarifs
douaniers et le commerce. Genève, GATT, 1971.

Glossaire de termes financiers et monétaires,
français-italien-anglais-allemand-néerlandais,
PE 31.017. Parlement européen, Division de la
traduction, Bureau de terminologie. Luxembourg,
Parlement européen, 1972.

Ginguay, Michel. Dictionnaire d'informatique
anglais-français. Paris, Masson et Cie. 1970.

Haensch, Günther. Wörterbuch der internationalen Beziehungen und der Politik, Deutsch-Eng-
lisch-Französisch-Spanisch. München, Max Hueber
Verlag, 1965.

Haensch, Günther; Renner, Rüdiger.Terminologie allemand-français. Deutsch-Französische Wirtschaftssprache. München, Max Hueber Verlag, 1965.

Hoof, Henri van. Economic Terminology English-French. Terminologie économique anglais-français. München, Max Hueber Verlag, 1967.

INITIALS, Abkürzungen von Namen internationaler Organisationen. Zusammengestellt von Fritz Ruppert. Essen, Vulkan-Verlag, Dr.W. Classen, 1966.

Macrothesaurus. A basic list of economic and social development terms, vol. I, English edition. Paris, Organisation for Economic Co-operation and Development, 1972.

Macrothesaurus. Liste des principaux descripteurs relatifs au développement économique et social, tome II, édition française. Paris, Organisation de coopération et de développement économiques, 1972.

Macrothesaurus. Verzeichnis der Grundbegriffe wirtschaftlicher und sozialer Entwicklungsterminologie, III Deutsche Ausgabe. Hrsg. von der OECD in Zusammenarbeit mit der Deutschen Stiftung für Entwicklungsländer. Paris, Organisation für Wirtschaftliche Zusammenarbeit und Entwicklung, 1973.

Multilingual Demographic Dictionary, English Section. Prepared by the Demographic Dictionary Section of the International Union for the Scientific Study of Population. New York, United Nations, Department of Economic and Social Affairs, 1958.
Dictionnaire démographique multilingue, volume français. Préparé par la Commission du dictionnaire démographique de l'Union internationale pour l'étude scientifique de la population. New York, Nations Unies, Département des affaires économiques et sociales, 1958.

Multilingual Systematic Glossary of Environmental Terms, English Text, unche/72/misc.1. Prepared by Dr.I. Paenson. Geneva, United Nations, 1971.
Glossaire multilingue systématique de termes se rapportant à l'environnement, texte français, unche/72/misc.1. Préparé par Isaac Paenson. Genève, Nations Unies, 1972.
Glosario multilingüe sistemático de términos relacionados con el medio, texto español, unche/72/misc. 1. GE.72-2349. Preparado por el Dr.I. Paenson. Ginebra, Naciones Unidas, 1971.

Nobel, Albert; Veillon, E. Medizinisches Wörterbuch. Dictionnaire médical. Medical Dictionary. Bern, Medizinischer Verlag Hans Huber, 1969.

Renner, Rüdiger; Sachs, Rudolf. Deutsch-Englische Wirtschaftssprache. German-English Economic Terminology. München, Max Hueber Verlag, 1970.

Robb, Louis. Engineers' Spanish-English, English-Spanish Dictionary. New York, J. Wiley, 1955.

Robb, Louis. Spanish-English, English-Spanish Dictionary of Legal Terms. New York, J. Wiley, 1955.

Vocabularium bibliothecarii, English-French-German-Spanish-Russian. Compiler: Anthony Thompson. Paris, UNESCO, 1962.

Werner, Heinz; König, Ingeborg. Glossare zur Arbeitsmarkt- und Berufsforschung, Englisch-Deutsch, Deutsch-Englisch, GlossAB Englisch 7/1974. Stuttgart, W. Kohlhammer GmbH, 1974.

Werner, Heinz; König, Ingeborg. Glossare zur Arbeitsmarkt- und Berufsforschung, Französisch-Deutsch, Deutsch-Französisch,GlossAB Französisch 12/1972. Stuttgart, W. Kohlhammer GmbH, 1972.

Yearbook of International Organizations, 14th (1972-73) edition. Bruxelles, Union of International Associations, 1972.

ENGLISH REFERENCE BOOKS

Collins, F. Howard. Authors' and Printers' Dictionary. A guide for authors, editors, printers, correctors of the press, compositors and typists. 10th edition revised. London, Oxford University Press, 1967.

The Concise Oxford Dictionary of Current English. eds. H.W. Fowler and F.G. Fowler. Based on the Oxford Dictionary. 5th edition, revised by E. McIntosh. Oxford, Clarendon Press, 1974.

Fowler, H.W. A Dictionary of Modern English Usage. 2nd edition revised by Sir Ernest Gowers. Oxford, Clarendon Press, 1965.

Hart's Rules for Compositors and Readers at the University Press, Oxford. 37th edition completely revised. London, Oxford University Press, 1967.

Nicholson, Margaret. A Dictionary of American English Usage. Based on Fowler's Modern English Usage. New York, Oxford University Press, 1967.

Roget's Thesaurus of English Words and Phrases. New edition completely revised and modernized by Robert A. Dutch. London, Longmans, 1967.

The Shorter Oxford English Dictionary on Historical Principles. prepared by William Little, H.W. Fowler, J. Coulson. revised and edited by C.T. Onions. Third edition, revised with addenda. Oxford, Clarendon Press, 1959.

Webster's New Dictionary of Synonyms. Springfield, Massachusetts, G & C Merriam Co., 1968.

Webster's Seventh New Collegiate Dictionary. Based on Webster's Third New International Dictionary. Springfield, Massachusetts, G & C Merriam Co., 1969.

Webster's Third New International Dictionary of the English Language. ed. Philip Babcock Gove. Springfield, Massachusetts, G & C Merriam Co., 1969.

*

*   *

Bauer, Johannes B. Encyclopaedia of Biblical Theology. Originally published as 'Bibeltheologisches Wörterbuch', Verlag Styria, Graz-Vienna-Cologne, 1959. Translation made from the third enlarged and revised edition of 1967. London and Sydney, Sheed and Ward, 1970. 3 vols.

A Concise Dictionary of the Bible. ed. James Hastings. revised edition Frederick C. Grant and H.H. Rowley. New York, Charles Scribner's Sons, 1963.

Concise Dictionary of the Christian World Mission. eds. Stephen Neill, Gerald H. Anderson, John Goodwin. United Society for Christian Literature, London, Lutterworth Press, 1970.

A Dictionary of the Social Sciences. eds. Julius Gould and William L. Kolb. compiled under the auspices of UNESCO. New York, The Free Press, 1969.

A Documentary History of the Faith and Order Movement. ed. Lukas Vischer. St. Louis, Miss., The Bethany Press, 1963.

Fey, Harold E. The Ecumenical Advance. A History of the Ecumenical Movement. Vol. 2 1948-1968. London, S.P.C.K., 1970.

Nelson's Complete Concordance of the Revised Standard Version. Compiled unter the supervision of John W. Ellison. New York, Thomas Nelson & Sons, 1957.

The New International Dictionary of the Christian Church, ed. J.D. Douglas. Exeter, The Paternoster Press (British edition), 1974.

The New Westminster Dictionary of the Bible. ed. Henry Snyder Gehmann. Philadelphia, The Westminster Press, 1970.

The Oxford Dictionary of the Christian Church. ed. F.L.Cross and E.A. Livingstone. 2nd edition. London, Oxford University Press, 1974.

Penguin Reference Books. Dictionaries of Biology, Computers, Politics, Psychology, Science etc. London, Penguin Books.

Rouse, Ruth; Neill, Stephen Charles. A History of the Ecumenical Movement 1517-1948. 2nd edition with revised and expanded bibliography. London, S.P.C.K., 1967.

OUVRAGES DE REFERENCE FRANÇAIS

Foulquié, Paul; Saint-Jean, Raymond. Diction-naire de la langue philosophique. Paris, Pres-ses Universitaires de France, 1969.

Grévisse, Maurice. Le bon usage, grammaire française avec des remarques sur la langue fran-çaise d'aujourd'hui. Gembloux/Paris. Duculot/Hatier, 1969.

Petit Larousse illustré. Paris, Librairie Larousse, 1975.

Le petit Robert. Dictionnaire alphabétique et analogique de la langue française. Paul Robert. Paris, Société du Nouveau Littré, 1968.

Le Petit Robert 2. Dictionnaire universel des noms propres alphabétique et analogique. Paul Robert. Paris, SEPRET, 1974.

*

* *

Ancien Testament. Traduction oecuménique de la Bible, A.T. TOB. Edité par les sociétés bibli-ques. Paris, Société biblique, 1975.

Nouveau Testament. Traduction oecuménique de la Bible. N.T. TOB. Edité par les sociétés bibli-ques. Paris, Société biblique, 1972.

La Bible française avec commentaires Scofield. Texte Segond révisé. Genève, Société biblique, 1975.

Bonnes nouvelles aujourd'hui. Le nouveau Testa-ment traduit en français courant d'après le texte grec. Edité par les sociétés bibliques. Paris, Société biblique française, 1971.

Concordance de la Bible, Nouveau Testament. Texte français: Bible de Jérusalem. M. Bardy, O. Odelain, P. Sandevoir, R. Séguineau. Paris, Cerf, 1970.

Concordance des Saintes Ecritures, d'après les versions Segond et synodale. Lausanne, Société biblique auxiliaire du canton de Vaud, 1965.

Dheilly, J.. Dictionnaire biblique. Tournai, Desclée, 1964.

Encyclopédie de la foi. Sous la direction de H. Fries. Paris, Cerf, 1967. 4 vol. (Edition originale parue en allemand au Kösel Verlag, Munich, sous le titre: Handbuch theologischer Grundbegriffe).

Vocabulaire biblique. Publié sous la direction de Jean-Jacques von Allmen. Neuchâtel, Delachaux et Niestlé S.A., 1956.

561

Vocabulaire de théologie biblique. Publié sous
la direction de Xavier Léon-Dufour. Paris,
Cerf, 1971.

*

*   *

Birou, Alain. Vocabulaire pratique des sciences
sociales. Paris, Editions économie et humanisme,
Les éditions ouvrières , 1968.

Dictionnaire de science économique. Par une
équipe sous la direction de Alain Cotta. Tours,
Mame, 1968.

Lexique de termes juridiques. Sous la direction
de Raymond Guillien et Jean Vincent. Paris,
Dalloz, 1972.

Le travail dans l'entreprise ét la société
moderne. Collection "Les dictionnaires du savoir
moderne". Direction générale: Pierre Morin.
Paris, Bibliothèque du CEPL, 1974.

DEUTSCHE NACHSCHLAGEWERKE

Der Grosse Duden (Rechtschreibung, Grammatik, Fremdwörterbuch, Vergleichendes Synonymwörterbuch). Mannheim/Zürich, Bibliographisches Institut.

Entwicklungspolitik - Handbuch und Lexikon. Hrsg. von H. Besters und E. Boesch. Stuttgart/Berlin, Kreuz-Verlag. Mainz, Matthias-Grünewald-Verlag, 1966.

Fey, Harold E. Geschichte der ökumenischen Bewegung - 1948-1968. Göttingen, Vandenhoeck & Ruprecht, 1974.

Fischer-Lexikon Christliche Religion. Hrsg. von O. Simmel und R. Stählin. Frankfurt, Fischer Bücherei, 1957.

Fischer-Lexikon Soziologie. Hrsg. von R. König. Frankfurt, Fischer Bücherei, 1967.

Hartfiel, Günter. Wörterbuch der Soziologie. Stuttgart, Alfred Kröner Verlag, 1972.

Praktisches Bibellexikon. Hrsg. von Anton Grabner-Haider. Freiburg/Basel/Wien. Verlag Herder, 1969.

Rechtswörterbuch. Hrsg. von Dr. Carl Creifelds. München, C.H. Beck'sche Verlagsbuchhandlung, 1973.

Die Religion in Geschichte und Gegenwart (RGG). Hrsg. von Kurt Galling. Tübingen, J.C. Mohr (Paul Siebeck), 1965.

Taschenlexikon Religion und Theologie. Hrsg. von Erwin Fahlbusch. Göttingen, Vandenhoeck & Ruprecht, 1971.

Wahrig, Gerhard. Deutsches Wörterbuch. Gütersloh, Bertelsmann Lexikon-Verlag, 1968.

Wehrle-Eggers. Deutscher Wortschatz. Ein Wegweiser zum treffenden Ausdruck. Frankfurt, Fischer Bücherei, 1961.

Zürcher Bibel-Konkordanz. Bearb. von Karl Huber und Hans Heinrich Schmid. Zürich, Theologischer Verlag, 1973.

OBRAS DE REFERENCIA EN ESPAÑOL

Coraminas, Juan. Diccionario crítico etimoló
gico de la lengua castellana. Madrid, Gredos,
1974.

Diccionario de la lengua española. Real Áca-
demia Española. Madrid, Espasa-Calpe, S.A.,
1970.

Enciclopedia Universal Herder. Barcelona,
Herder, 1972.

Esbozo de una gramática de la lengua española.
Real Academia Española. Madrid, Espasa-Calpe,
1973.

Moliner, María. Diccionario del uso del español.
Madrid, Gredos, 1971. 2 vol.

Sainz de Robles, Federico C.. Ensayo de un
diccionario español de sinónimos y antónimos.
Madrid, Aguilar, 1973.

Seco, Manuel. Diccionario de dudas y dificultades del idioma. Madrid, Aguilar, 1970.

Allmen, Jean-Jacques von. Vocabulario bíblico.
Madrid, Morava, 1968. (Original francés:
Vocabulaire biblique. Neuchâtel, Delachaux
et Niestlé S.A., 1954.)

Bauer, Johannes B.. Diccionario de Teología.
Barcelona, Herder, 1967. (Original alemán,
publicado por Ediciones Herder, 1959.)

Denyer, C.P.. Concordancia de la Sagradas
Escrituras. Miami, Editorial Caribe, 1969.

Díez Macho, Alejandro; Bartina, Sebastián.
Enciclopedia de la Biblia. Barcelona., Garriga,
1963.

Nelson, Wilton. Diccionario ilustrado de la
Biblia. Miami, Caribe, 1974.

La Santa Biblia. Versión de Reina (1569) -
Valera (1602), revisada. México. Sociedades
Bíblicas en América Latina, 1960.

*

* *

*

* *

Casares, Julio. Diccionario ideológico de la
 lengua española. Barcelona, Gustavo Gili,
 1966.

Terceiro, José. Diccionario de economía.
Algorta-Vizcaya, Zero, 1973.

NOTES

NOTES

NOTES